Dec. 1992

Fat:

What a talented guy
you are. Even better, you're
a great person with a
wonderful spirit. I'm looking
forward to working with you
for a long time ... hopefully
in San Diego a few times!
Thanks ...

God bless,
Chris Mortenson

PLAYING
FOR
KEEPS

How One Man Kept the Mob
from Sinking Its Hooks
into Pro Football

Chris Mortensen

SIMON & SCHUSTER

New York   London   Toronto   Sydney   Tokyo   Singapore

SIMON & SCHUSTER
Simon & Schuster Building
Rockefeller Center
1230 Avenue of the Americas
New York, New York 10020

Designed by Irving Perkins Associates
Manufactured in the United States of America

1   3   5   7   9   10   8   6   4   2

Library of Congress Cataloging in Publication Data

Mortensen, Chris.
Playing for keeps : how one man kept the mob from sinking its
hooks into pro football / Chris Mortensen.
p.   cm.
Includes index.
1. Football—United States—Corrupt practices.   2. Sports agents—
United States.   3. Organized crime—United States.   I. Title.
GV959.M67   1991
796.332′63′0973—dc20   91-34928
CIP
ISBN: 0-671-72937-3

Photo Credits
AP/Wide World Photos, 20, 21, 23, 24; *The Atlanta Journal-Constitution,* 3, 4, 5, 16;
Bill Smith/*Sports Illustrated,* 1; © Alex Webb/Magnum Photos, 22

To my late father,
for whom my heart and soul still ache.
Peace and salvation.

This book was compiled from personal interviews with more than two hundred participants and research from more than three thousand pages of documents and transcripts over a four-year span. It was recreated in part by splicing documents with interviews. Where there was a conflict of versions, the author noted the conflict or chose the more credible version.

1

IT WAS a typically cold and windy morning in Chicago, with winter pounding spring into submission. Kathy Clements, bundled against the cold, fumbled with the key to her office in her gloved hands as she tried to slide it into the lock on the door. Why did she always have to be first at the office, she wondered.

Once inside, she cranked up the thermostat and waited a few minutes before she slipped off her coat and gloves. She got the coffee maker going, poured herself a cup, added some cream and sugar, and took a seat behind her desk. It was nine o'clock on Monday, March 16, 1987.

Her attention was drawn to the newspaper lying on her desk. It was the March 12, 1987, issue of the *Atlanta Constitution*. It had been sent to her Federal Express by the reporter the previous Friday. Its headline read: AGENT ADMITS GIVING CASH TO COLLEGE PLAYERS. Then, in smaller type: *Threats Reported . . . Mafia Link Denied.*

Clements grew uneasy as she read the story about New York sports agents Norby Walters and Lloyd Bloom. Just a few days ago she had speculated aloud to the reporter that "this could be the tip of an iceberg."

Clements was a thirty-two-year-old sports agent, one of the few women in the field. Her husband was Tom Clements, a former Notre Dame quarterback. The year before, she had negotiated his contract with the Canadian Football League and discovered that the give-and-take battle of negotiations, even on a small scale, was very alluring. Later she approached Chicago sports agent Steve Zucker about joining his agency in nearby Skokie, Illinois.

It wasn't long before Clements realized that being a sports agent was a cutthroat business. She recruited some of college football's best, only

9

to learn that many of them had already signed with an agent before their college eligibility had expired. Yet she had charm and smarts, and being a shapely brunette with olive skin and big brown eyes didn't hurt her cause.

Two of the first players she helped Zucker recruit were Washington defensive end Reggie Rogers and Nebraska tailback Doug Dubose. Both, she and Zucker learned, had already signed with Walters and Bloom. Both wanted out. She saw no reason why these smooth talkers from New York deserved to cash in on the players just because they had bought them early.

The same thing had happened in 1986 when Tennessee wide receiver Tim McGee left Walters and Bloom to join Zucker, before Clements had joined the agency.

McGee, Rogers, and Dubose were all mentioned in the newspaper article. So were several other star players: The story recounted Walters's cocky confession that, yes, he was ignoring NCAA (National Collegiate Athletic Association) rules and signing players early but that, no, he had not threatened anyone as the story alleged. Clements believed otherwise.

Moments later she felt a stiff breeze from outside blow through the building. In a short time she heard something . . . somebody. She called out.

"Who's there?"

Kathy knew it couldn't be Zucker. He was in Palm Springs for a well-deserved rest. Besides, Steve never came to work this early. She figured it was Jami Zimberoff, their secretary and receptionist. It was not. Zimberoff was sitting in a dentist's chair a few miles away.

Clements felt a nervous chill run through her body as she glanced up from her desk and saw a male figure in a dark ski mask, gloves, blue jean jacket buttoned to the top, and dark pants. He glanced into the other office that belonged to Zucker and then turned back in her direction. He lurched toward her without speaking a word.

Instinctively, Clements rose from her desk to confront the menacing intruder. The man struck her in the face with a gloved fist. Then another. He slapped her. Clements stumbled sideways.

This can't be happening, she thought. Then her thoughts became muddled as she went into shock.

The intruder pulled something shiny out of his jacket, reached out, and slashed at Clements, drawing blood from her arm.

Bleeding and dazed, Clements limped desperately toward the bathroom, with the masked, silent intruder following. Gasping for air, she opened the door, thinking she could lock herself inside. But it was too late—the assailant's hand grabbed her shoulder, spun her around, and set her up for a final blow.

The full thrust of the powerful fist struck Clements in the abdomen, and she slumped to the floor and blacked out.

After five or ten minutes passed, Clements opened her eyes and found an empty hallway. She got slowly to her feet and made her way woozily to the telephone, praying that her attacker had vanished. She dialed 911.

When Jami Zimberoff arrived shortly before 10 A.M., she noticed an ambulance and police cars in front of the office building. She parked her car, turned off the engine, and walked slowly toward the scene. Then she saw Clements tightly bundled on a stretcher. Kathy's eyes were glassy; she looked dazed and bewildered. Her face had clearly been beaten.

"My God," said Jami. "What happened?"

FBI SPECIAL Agent George Randolph walked stiffly from his car, craving another cup of coffee. He didn't know whether his bones were still chilled from the freeze that morning or whether he just hadn't gotten enough sleep the night before. Whatever it was, his head, which was no longer fully protected by his thinning light-brown hair, was cold as he walked into the office, rubbing frost from his neatly trimmed mustache.

Barely settled at his office desk, he heard the minute hand on the wall clock tick and looked up. Only 7:15 in the morning. Damn, he thought. More coffee. Black. He didn't want to have to pick up the phone until he got his motor running. He headed for the snack room.

Randolph was actually waiting for a call this morning from a key underworld informant. George was a point man on Chicago's Organized Crime Task Force. With twelve years of experience, much of it dealing with white-collar crime and mob activity, he knew how to work the streets and develop leads. Word was out that there would be a mob hit any day now. Only the Task Force didn't know who was going to get whacked. George suspected it would be someone with a "juice debt," somebody who had turned to the mob loan sharks for cash and couldn't pay the exorbitant interest. Those guys ended up either dead or beaten. It happened a lot in his town. George knew a mob job when he saw one.

Randolph got his cup filled and walked back to his desk. He began to flip through a copy of the *Chicago Sun-Times*. It was St. Patrick's Day, and Randolph's green necktie reflected his family's Irish blood line. He smiled, knowing the Chicago River already had been dyed green overnight. Maybe he would head downtown to the pub where his FBI gang hung out after work. The holiday season didn't end in Chicago until it blew out St. Patty's Day.

It was only 7:25 in the morning, though. Too early to be thinking about sharing a laugh and war stories with his pals. As George continued with his morning routine, he paused, like most law enforcement officials in Chicago, to read "Petacque's Beat." Art Petacque, a Pulitzer Prize–winning columnist, who is recognized as the dean of police-beat reporters in Chicago, writes daily for the *Sun-Times*.

PRO GRIDDER'S WIFE BEATEN IN SKOKIE OFFICE OF AGENT, the headline read.

Petacque's story began, "A hulking masked intruder beat the wife of Canadian Football League player Tom Clements into unconsciousness on Monday in the Skokie office where she works for attorney and pro sports agent Steve Zucker.

"Clements recently received a threatening phone call from a man purporting to be a business rival of Zucker," Petacque wrote. "Skokie detectives also found a clipping, which they believed came from a New York City newspaper, about the rivalry between Zucker and an agent located there."

The phone rang, interrupting his reading of the article. He hesitated, then picked up the receiver: "Randolph."

It was Bob Walsh, Assistant FBI Special Agent in Charge, calling from the Organized Crime Task Force command center in downtown Chicago. Walsh wondered if Randolph had gotten anything from his source.

"Not yet," George said. "I'm still waiting to hear from the jag-off."

"Jag-off" was Randolph's pet name for the undesirables he dealt with. It dated him to the 1960s, when a teenager would call a dopey pal a "jack-off," but if anybody's parents got within earshot, the slang became "jag-off."

Twelve years with the bureau, and it seemed there were more and more jag-offs to deal with. Randolph was trying to think of another angle when his boss extended an invitation that Tuesday morning.

"Some gal got beat up on the north side," Walsh told him. "She works with that sports agent Zucker, the guy who represents Jim McMahon."

Randolph glanced down at the newspaper in front of him. "Yeah, I was just reading about it," he said. Everyone knew McMahon, the cocky Chicago Bears quarterback who had become a national celebrity after leading the team to the Super Bowl a couple of years before.

"Anyway, we got a call and there might be some O.C. here," said Walsh, using the FBI slang for organized crime. "Couple of New York guys maybe. Want to go sneak around the crime scene and talk to Zucker?"

Randolph got the address of Zucker's office in Skokie, which was about twenty minutes east from his office in Arlington Heights, a northern suburb, where he had been assigned five months earlier.

Driving toward Skokie and Lake Michigan, Randolph couldn't help but daydream about the summer. In just a few months, he would be sailing his thirty-foot slip, drinking cold beer, and listening to Harry Caray from Wrigley Field. That, along with his son's high school and American Legion ballgames, would keep his weekends pretty full.

He pulled into the parking lot of a condominium office complex at 5225 Old Orchard Road, the address that Walsh had given him. Randolph drove his Oldsmobile slowly through the maze of dark-brown brick buildings, looking for Suite 26B. The sign, ZUCKER AND ASSOCIATES, told him he had the right place.

He opened the door to the building and was shoved inside by the wind at his back. Two men were there to greet him. One was Skokie Police Detective Dennis Dagelman. The other was Steve Zucker, a man in his forties, with a short crop of brown wavy hair. He looked weary, like Randolph had felt earlier. Dark circles were under his eyes. Zucker told them he had just hurried back from Palm Springs, where he was supposed to be on vacation. Kathy Clements was like a kid sister to him, he explained, though their business relationship was less than a year old.

There wasn't much of a crime scene. Zucker had been planning to move to a larger office, and the incident had shaken him. He asked the movers to get his stuff out that morning. The place had been vacated, with Dagelman's approval. Randolph was a little annoyed about it, but he bit his tongue.

All of them sat on the floor because there was no furniture. Dagelman went over the report that Skokie Police Sergeant Charles Olshock had filled out after talking with Clements, who had been treated and released from Skokie Valley Community Hospital.

Clements had described her attacker as a white male who wore a ski mask and gloves. He struck her in the face and stomach. Cut her arm. Stalked her. Smacked her in the gut. She lost consciousness. When she awoke, she called for help but also noticed that Zucker's office had been ransacked. Zucker, though, found nothing missing.

No rape attempt. No money missing from her pocketbook.

Zucker asked if Clements could have been a victim of mistaken identity.

"The way this place is set up, the way the buildings zigzag, I don't think so," said Randolph. "Looked like somebody knew exactly where he was going."

They had some small talk. Zucker seemed reserved, still shaken. Dagelman asked about the newspaper article that was found on Clements's desk. It was a story from the *Atlanta Constitution* focusing on the activities of a New York sports agent, Norby Walters.

Walters had admitted in the article to giving cash to lure college football players into his fold before their eligibility had expired. That was the dirty side of the business, Zucker explained to Dagelman, but he claimed that his hands were clean. The *Constitution* also reported a more sensational element, that Walters had threatened to "break legs" of players who were backing out of the contracts they had signed with him. The fifty-five-year-old Walters, who was a leading booking agent in the music industry, had a young partner named Lloyd Bloom.

Randolph suggested that they check out Walters and Bloom. Zucker downplayed the idea at first. Then as the three of them got up and Randolph began to follow Dagelman into Clements's office, he felt a hand tugging at his suit. As he turned to look, Zucker cocked his head back. Randolph got the message.

"Steve, why don't you show me the rest of the complex?" George said.

Randolph sent his own body language to the police detective. Dagelman told them he had to make a few phone calls. Randolph and Zucker went for a stroll outside, out of sight. Zucker stopped.

"I think this is a job for you guys," he told Randolph.

He spoke in low tones. He didn't want Dagelman to slip outside and hear him. He didn't want city police working on the case.

They started walking again. Zucker told Randolph about threats that Walters and Bloom had been making to him and Clements. Three college football players with promising National Football League careers had walked away from Walters and Bloom and signed with Zucker and Clements. One was Tim McGee, who had been a first-round pick of the Cincinnati Bengals the year before. The other two were University of Washington defensive end Reggie Rogers, a certain top-ten pick in the NFL draft next month, and Nebraska tailback Doug Dubose, whose Heisman Trophy run had been derailed by a knee injury. Clements had been very active in recruiting Dubose, which seemed to have touched a nerve with Walters, Zucker explained.

"Why'd they leave?" Randolph asked.

"They figured out that Walters and Bloom were a joke," said Zucker. "They bought them off early. Nobody had ever heard of these guys until last year, and all of a sudden they're everywhere, handing out cash like it was candy. But they were going to take ten percent off the top. That's against the rules in our business."

Randolph wanted to know what an NFL first-rounder made. It varied, but McGee had signed a four-year $1.35 million deal with the Bengals. Randolph was no math whiz, but he figured that would have paid Walters and Bloom $135,000 up front.

"How many players do these guys have?" the FBI agent asked.

"Nobody knows," said Zucker. "There are a lot of rumors. Some say thirty, some say sixty."

"All in the past year?" Randolph asked, raising his eyebrows.

"Maybe two years, no longer than that," said Zucker. "But nobody's ever seen anything like it."

Zucker suggested that Randolph read the lengthy story which appeared five days earlier in the *Atlanta Constitution.* Randolph asked about the New York clipping that Petacque had referred to in his column, but Zucker said the reporter must have been referring to the *Constitution* article.

"This Walters guy says he's big-time in the music biz," Zucker told Randolph. "He talks big anyway. He wines and dines all these players, gets them limos, introduces them to all these entertainers. It's a hard sell. There have been some Mafia rumors. I don't know."

Actually, Zucker did know about crime. He had once been an assistant district attorney and had assisted in the prosecution of Yippie leader Abbie Hoffman and the Chicago Seven. He later went into criminal defense, but wound up despising some of the clients he represented, particularly drug dealers and rapists.

Zucker explained to Randolph that he was "burned out" as a lawyer when an acquaintance introduced him to McMahon two years earlier. Zucker and the quarterback hit it off. McMahon had been represented by Jerry Argovitz and had by then formed his own opinion about agents.

"Jim told me, 'All agents are crooks,'" Zucker explained to the FBI agent. "I'm beginning to see why he felt that way."

McMahon asked Zucker to represent him, and Zucker thought the work might be fun and potentially lucrative. Then McMahon became a sensation by leading the Bears to the Super Bowl. Suddenly Zucker was negotiating deals with book publishers, Pepsi-Cola, Taco Bell—you name it.

Representing McMahon had become a full-time job in itself, so he welcomed the opportunity to add an associate like Clements.

"She's one sharp lady," Zucker told Randolph.

The lawyer-turned-sports-agent had also gotten a call from an insurance broker in the spring of 1986, asking him if he would like to represent Tim McGee. Zucker went to visit the Tennessee receiver at his home in Cleveland.

On the morning of the NFL draft the previous April, McGee called and hired Zucker. Then, after he was selected twenty-first overall in the first round by the Bengals, he gave Zucker some distressing news.

"He told me he had signed a contract earlier with somebody called Uncle Norby," Zucker explained. "He had signed before his senior season at Tennessee."

Zucker said that Walters had called him shortly after the draft and introduced himself as McGee's agent. At that time Walters was cordial and had only wanted the money he had advanced McGee. It was about $10,000, an amount McGee had told Zucker he would repay Uncle Norby.

"There was no battle, no fight, no nothing."

Then things heated up. McGee did not repay Walters, so he now wanted in addition a percentage of the contract he had signed with the Bengals. That was unworkable. Walters threatened to sue McGee, and Zucker challenged him on it. No lawsuit materialized.

Zucker and Clements, his new associate, had their first full-fledged recruiting period after the 1986 college football season. Zucker arranged to meet Rogers, then one of the highest-ranking seniors eligible for the draft, at the Indianapolis Scouting Combine where the NFL had invited 350 players for extensive testing and workouts.

Zucker and Clements drove to Indianapolis and picked up Rogers and Dubose at the Holiday Inn, where the NFL had reserved rooms for the players. Zucker bought dinner for them at St. Elmo's, one of the city's finest steak houses. One week later, on February 9, Rogers signed a contract with Zucker and Clements. A few days after that, Dubose also signed. That was only a month ago, Zucker reminded Randolph.

Zucker discovered soon after that Rogers and Dubose also had been bought early by Walters and Bloom.

"Seems like every player I talked to had a story about those guys," Zucker said.

Zucker was flustered by the state of the business. He called the NFL Players Association to complain about Walters and Bloom but was told, "Unless an agent and a player are willing to take them on, there's nothing we can do."

Zucker dug in but was exhausted by the middle of March and decided to take off for a week's vacation in Palm Springs. He had just settled in when he was informed that Kathy Clements had been beaten.

As he packed his bags to head back to Chicago, the phone rang again in his condo.

"Steve, Art Petacque here," said a gruff voice on the other end of the phone.

"I don't have much time, Art," Zucker said to the reporter.

"I guess you know what happened," said Petacque. "Awful. Have you talked to the gal? Who coulda done this?"

Zucker had not spoken with Kathy, and he was in a hurry to get back home to see her. He told Petacque that their conversation had to be off the record, and he painted a broad picture for the reporter. He also knew that Petacque had strong ties to every level of Chicago law enforcement.

"Can you make a couple of calls for me?" Zucker said. "Maybe the FBI, the U. S. Attorney?"

"You got it," replied Petacque. The reporter made the calls, and the story ended up on Bob Walsh's desk in the O.C. command center.

"Do you have that newspaper story?" Randolph asked Zucker.

It was at home, but Dagelman had a copy, Zucker told him. About that time they saw the Skokie detective heading their way. The FBI agent shook hands with Zucker and then bid farewell. They would be in touch, he said. Dagelman followed them out and expressed frustration.

"He [Zucker] isn't cooperating that much," Dagelman told the agents. "I wonder if he's hiding something."

The detective then mentioned Sergeant Olshock's first reaction: "Looks like a message beating."

Randolph nodded. "Yeah, there could be something to that," he said. It looked to him like a mob job.

Dagelman got into his car and drove away. Randolph had already arranged to meet Zucker and Clements the next day at Zucker's home.

Randolph looked at his watch. It was almost four o'clock. He got in his car and went to meet his buddies at the pub. After all, it was St. Patrick's Day.

.   .   .

RANDOLPH DROVE into a wealthy subdivision in Winnetka and parked in front of Zucker's house. He was feeling "about half" after last night. He reached over and closed his briefcase, which he had opened to look for an aspirin bottle on the way over. He grabbed the briefcase and soon rang the doorbell. Zucker greeted him.

"Come in," he told the FBI agent, who welcomed the warmth of the sprawling bilevel house.

A woman with dark hair started to rise from the white sofa, but Randolph, figuring it was Clements, told her, "Don't get up." She stood anyway, and when Zucker introduced them, she extended her hand.

Randolph knew immediately that this woman had been traumatized. The left side of her face was swollen, reddish, almost purple. Her left eye was bloodshot. She looked nervous—no, scared. He already felt as if he wanted to protect her.

"Sorry about what happened," Randolph said to her. He could tell she appreciated the gentleness in his voice.

Randolph reopened his briefcase and pulled out a pen, a legal notepad, and a manila folder. From the folder he removed the Skokie police report dated March 16.

"I know you've done this at least once, but I'd like to go over it with you," said Randolph. Clements nodded.

There was very little Clements said that deviated from Sergeant Olshock's report. The only thing she seemed fuzzy on was how her upper right arm had been cut. She was pretty sure the attacker had taken a stab at her, but she wasn't certain if it was a knife or a letter opener. No weapon had been found at the crime scene by the police.

It all happened so fast, she said. She was terrified. Randolph thought that the cut might have even happened when she fell; perhaps she had sliced her arm on the corner of a desk. But he had no doubt that she was reliving the fright of the incident.

Randolph looked at the police report. Among the questions about the suspect's description, a *W* appeared under race.

"How'd you know he was white?" Randolph asked.

"I could tell through the eye holes on the mask."

Randolph saw that the attacker was about six feet tall. Under weight, the word "slim" appeared.

The evidence technician who arrived at the scene with Sergeant Olshock did not find any significant physical evidence. The incident was listed as an aggravated battery.

"Did the guy say anything, anything at all?"

"No. Nothing."

Clements, sitting on a white sofa, took a sip of hot tea. There had been no St. Patrick's Day celebration for her the night before. She had slept well because the doctors had prescribed a sedative. But now, looking at the *Atlanta Constitution* on the glass coffee table, she was reliving the horror of March 16.

Randolph wanted to know if her senses could tell him anything else that wasn't on the report.

Wait. Yes, there was. The suspect had an odor—dirt, grease, oil, something like that.

On the report Sergeant Olshock had asked Clements if there had been "any threatening or suspicious phone calls" recently. Clements told the policeman that there had not been any.

Randolph then looked at Zucker.

"What about Walters and Bloom?" he asked, looking back at Clements.

She shook her head.

"I just can't believe they would do this, as much as I hate them," she said.

But there had been threats, Zucker said.

"What kind of threats?" asked Randolph. "Why?"

In the past two weeks Walters had been calling them constantly, Zucker explained. Walters was threatening to sue, which, of course, is no threat in America.

There had to be more than that, Randolph suggested.

"You wouldn't believe his foul mouth," Zucker said. "He told me that I didn't know what he was messing with."

Randolph sat up while scribbling away on his yellow legal pad.

"Did you ask him what he meant by that?" the FBI agent probed.

Zucker had not pressed the issue. Clements then spoke.

"He was accusing me of some pretty nasty things," she told Randolph. "I mean, he all but suggested . . . he did suggest that I . . . well . . . to get these players."

Walters had used almost every obscenity imaginable, she said, and had degraded her by calling her a "gutter broad," a "whore," and a "cunt." He specifically accused her of hopping in the backseat of a car with Dubose to get his name on a contract. All lies, she said. Filthy lies.

Walters wanted the money back that he had lent the players, which totaled about $50,000, and he wanted a percentage of their NFL deals. The calls had also gotten nastier in the past ten days because Walters had accused her and Zucker of "planting rumors" with the Atlanta reporter who was doing an investigative piece.

But there was something else, she remembered.

Two months earlier, in Mobile, Alabama, where she was attending the Senior Bowl All-Star Game workouts in late January, Walters and Bloom had been a sideshow all to themselves. The Senior Bowl was significant because it was the one postseason game that NFL scouts controlled. One night at the Stouffer's Riverview Plaza, the Senior Bowl headquarters, as Clements sat at the second-floor bar while coaches and personnel directors mingled, Bloom slid onto a stool next to her. They had some small talk. Bloom, she said, was always dressed in designer warmups with a huge gold chain around his neck. He was friendly enough, but then he mentioned the money McGee owed the agents.

"What happened?" interrupted Randolph.

Clements said that Bloom smiled. Then he told her, "You know, Kathy, where we come from, people who don't pay their bills get their hands broken."

Randolph stopped writing. He knew that he wanted this case badly now.

"I didn't think much of it," Clements told him. "I thought he was joking."

Randolph made sure that Clements's address and phone number were the same as on the police report. She and her husband and two children lived in Glencoe, another Chicago suburb. Randolph told her that he would ask his bosses for permission to put her house under surveillance. He wanted her phone tapped, and she would have to call a special number and inform the FBI wherever she went.

"I don't mean to scare you," Randolph said, "but it really is better for us to take these precautions."

He closed his briefcase. Zucker handed him the copy of the *Atlanta Constitution,* and Randolph carried it to the car. Before he turned on the ignition, he looked at the story. On the front page, surrounded by the article, was a picture of Norby Walters: whitish hair, thin-rimmed glasses, a show-biz smile, and his right hand propped under his chin. Definitely a publicity shot.

Definitely a jag-off, Randolph said to himself.

2

GEORGE RANDOLPH sank his two-hundred-pound frame into his La-Z-Boy for the night and reclined into a comfortable position. With the *Atlanta Constitution* in his lap and his legal notepad on the table to his right, he switched on his reading lamp.

"Cathy, get me a Coke," he said with a wave of the hand.

His wife just glared back at him. Teenage sweethearts from rival high schools in southern Illinois, they had been married for sixteen years now. He had been the captain of his Steeleville basketball team, and she had been the head cheerleader for Trico. They both graduated in 1968. They were small-town Midwesterners, and she had been there as her husband rose from an FBI clerk to special agent status, tackling organized crime in the city where Al Capone became a legend.

Cathy Randolph knew her husband was tainted with chauvinism, but she could hold her own in a fight, and George knew it. But this was no time to pick a fight; Cathy got the Coke.

George held the sports section of the Atlanta paper, which felt strange. He was used to the *Sun-Times* and the *Chicago Tribune*. George loved sports. He loved the Chicago Bears, especially their macho coach. Mike Ditka was his kind of guy. He followed the Cubs, mostly because he liked Harry Caray; he had grown up listening to him when he was an avid St. Louis Cardinals fan.

Sports was now showing him a new face, and he didn't like it. That picture on the cover of the Atlanta paper bugged him. Norby Walters had con man written all over him.

"Let's find out more about this jag-off," he said, unfolding the newspaper. Cathy had heard that before.

Right off the top, Randolph read how Norby Walters had admitted he

21

was paying college football players to sign representation agreements with him. Walters defended his style, and he was quoted: "If I were a businessman making an investment, I would think nothing of putting down $500,000 to build a McDonald's on the corner block."

What a bunch of shit, Randolph thought.

Then came the part that intrigued him most. The paper said, quoting sources from the NFL Players Association, that two unidentified players complained recently that Walters had threatened to "break their legs."

"Their stories were almost identical," the NFLPA source was quoted as saying. "He said he'd have somebody come down from Vegas and break their legs."

The hair on the back of Randolph's neck began to rise. Las Vegas was a notorious haven for mobsters. He scribbled on his pad: *Call the NFL Players Association.*

Walters denied in the story that he had made the threats. "It makes me want to puke," he said.

Then Walters also denied that he was linked to the Mafia and accused rival agents of planting rumors that he was a "pimp, a Mafioso, cocaine dealer, and that the FBI was investigating me, none of which is true."

Randolph smiled. We are now, jag-off, he thought to himself.

The story mentioned Auburn running back Brent Fullwood, who was identified as one of the players Walters had paid prior to his senior season.

Two other big names jumped out as being under NCAA investigation for links with the agent: Ohio State wide receiver Cris Carter and Michigan State running back Lorenzo White. Randolph knew that both were prominent in Big Ten Conference football and both had one season left of eligibility.

Call the Big Ten, Randolph scribbled, and he jotted down the names and schools of Fullwood, Carter, and White.

He read on. The newspaper had gotten hold of a lawsuit filed in New York by Walters against Iowa running back Ronnie Harmon, who had been the number-one draft pick of the Buffalo Bills last year. Walters was suing Harmon for $500,000 for breach of contract. The contract and a promissory note were attached as exhibits to the lawsuit, the paper said. It showed that Harmon signed with Walters on March 9, 1985, the spring before his senior season at Iowa.

The lawsuit claimed that Harmon was given $54,924.42 in cash, gifts, and a car—$32,000 as a down payment for a lease on a Mercedes, according to the story.

Randolph stopped reading to write down Harmon's name, another Big Ten guy. He wrote down $55,000 and underlined it twice. A lot of dough, he thought.

Walters boasted that he was out to prove "contract law." The fact that Walters was making his unethical behavior public by filing the lawsuit didn't bother Randolph. A lot of criminal leads have developed from lawsuits.

The story named other players linked with Walters and Bloom, including Reggie Rogers, Doug Dubose, Tim McGee, Harmon, Carter, White, and Fullwood. There was also Tony Woods of Pittsburgh, Tommy Powell of Auburn, Kenny Flowers and Terrence Flagler of Clemson, Ron Morris and Terance Mann of SMU, Edwin Simmons of Texas, John Clay of Missouri, Paul Palmer of Temple, Devon Mitchell of Iowa, Garland Rivers of Michigan, Mark Ingram of Michigan State, and Rod Woodson of Purdue.

Randolph wrote down all the names. Beautiful, he thought. Plenty of leads.

The name of Walters's New York–based company was World Sports and Entertainment, Inc. The story mentioned that he had been a long-time music agent, and Walters said that he represented such entertainers as Peabo Bryson, Kool and the Gang, Luther Vandross, and Patti La-Belle.

Randolph had heard of Kool and the Gang but had no idea who the others were. He read the names again, jotted them down, and recalled the conversation he had had with his FBI buddies on St. Patrick's night when he told them about the Clements beating. The entertainment business had a reputation for using thugs to enforce contracts. They theorized that perhaps Walters was applying the same practices to the sports field.

The Atlanta story went on to quote Walters as he argued about the hypocrisy of college sports, speaking specifically about the recent scandal at SMU and noting that the governor of Texas, Bill Clements, had sanctioned secret payoffs to SMU players.

It's a point, Randolph thought. But it can't be that way everywhere. Randolph figured that the majority of major universities ran clean programs, and the fact that the NCAA cracked down on the cheaters meant that the system worked. At least he'd get to see how well the system worked if the case went anywhere.

The story ended with Walters vowing to fight the system, claiming, "Nobody in this world can intimidate me but God."

Randolph looked again at the picture of Walters: Okay, jag-off, let's see just how big you are, he thought.

Randolph was anxious to dig into this case. He was convinced from the beginning that the beating of Kathy Clements was a mob action, and he was no stranger to moblike messages. Clements and Zucker seemed to be telling the truth about the threats from Walters and Bloom, and the way the office complex was laid out left a strong impression.

"A masked man just didn't show up with nothing to do and start beating her up. He knew exactly what he was doing," Randolph had told Zucker. It was something he repeated to himself again and again.

THE ALARM clock went off at five o'clock on Thursday morning. Randolph rose and peeked outside, knowing there had been another night of frost. It was still dark, but he decided to jog his usual two miles because he was trying to trim the spare tire around his waist. The run also gave him time to organize his day. He slipped on his gray sweats and pulled a navy blue Stag Beer stocking cap over his head.

As his feet hit the pavement, his breath steaming away, Randolph's thoughts raced through the past two days: the sight of Kathy Clements's battered face, her scared look, the stories Zucker and Clements had told him, the story he had read the night before, the Norby Walters mug shot. His adrenaline was pumping.

Randolph had filed his report with Bob Walsh, strongly suggesting that clues linked the case to organized crime, and he received clearance from Walsh to explore all the leads he had compiled. Although Walsh had handpicked Randolph to head his Organized Crime Task Force, he decided to let the agent explore this case.

"George's instincts about O.C. are always dead-on," said Walsh. "He told me right off the bat that he thought it was O.C."

Randolph dropped what he was doing at the time and began to dictate teletypes requesting specific field work from other FBI offices across the country. After dictating the teletypes into a recorder, he gave the tape to one of the stenographers, who would then transmit it. He also had to choose from one of three codes for the teletypes: routine, immediate, or priority.

"Immediate," he dictated, which meant he could expect some results fairly soon.

His instructions listed the name of the player, the university, and the nature of information he was seeking. There had been a beating, and two sports agents, Norby Walters and Lloyd Bloom, were suspects. Possible organized crime links. Possible extortion. Interstate activity. Possible fraud. He wanted to know what every player had to say about his dealings with Walters and Bloom. Ask the players if they know the names of other players connected to them. Find out if any of the players were threatened.

Randolph also decided to instruct the agents to ask if either Walters or Bloom had supplied the players with cocaine or other drugs, since Walters himself had brought up the rumors in print.

Randolph called Steve Zucker and Kathy Clements and made certain that the security arrangement they had discussed had been acted upon. Clements's phone was now equipped with a special recording device designed to activate as soon as the receiver was picked up. Randolph had requested through the telephone company a detailed record of phone calls that had been made to Zucker's office.

Randolph had gotten a tip that the NFLPA had names of more players associated with Walters and Bloom. Furthermore, he had been told that the NFLPA had some letters from players complaining about some underhanded tactics and threats these sports agents had made. He called the Chicago Bears, identified himself, and wanted to know how he could contact the NFL Players Association. He jotted down the number: (202) 463-2200. From the area code Randolph knew that the NFLPA had to be in Washington, D.C., where he had done his Marine Corps Reserve duty, worked as an FBI clerk, and gotten his degree from American Union College.

Randolph had written down the name of Michael Duberstein, the NFLPA's chief researcher, who was mentioned in the Atlanta story as being critical of the contracts Walters and Bloom had signed with the players. He asked for Duberstein when a secretary answered the phone.

Duberstein was willing to help with other names he had heard. He also gave Randolph the impression that many of the players were potentially high draft choices for next month's draft.

Randolph then asked about the threats and the complaint letters players had sent.

"I think you should speak to somebody in our legal department," Duberstein told him.

"Fine."

Randolph next spoke with Mark Murphy, the former Washington

Redskins defensive back. After Randolph explained the nature of his call, Murphy said, "You'll have to subpoena that information."

Randolph took the phone away from his ear for a second. He took a deep breath and exhaled. He decided he had better overstate the case.

"Look, I've got a woman sports agent who's already been beat up, players are being threatened, and we could be dealing with the Mafia," Randolph told Murphy. "Fine, if some players get beat up tonight or they wind up dead, I'm gonna make sure I tell everyone that the NFL Players Association told me to get a subpoena first to find out who these victims could be."

"I'll call you back in a minute," Murphy said.

Randolph got the sense that Murphy was "a first-year law student acting like a Supreme Court Justice." It turned out he was right about Murphy being a law student.

While waiting for a return call, Randolph added the names he had gotten from the NFLPA to his teletype. Walters and Bloom had been very busy in Texas: Jeff Atkins and Jerry Ball, also of SMU, and Everett Gay and William Harris of Texas.

It wasn't long before Murphy called back. There had been four players complaining about threats. One was Ron Morris, an SMU wide receiver. Another was his teammate Jerry Ball. Texas's Edwin Simmons, a running back, may have some information. And Brent Fullwood had been told that his new agent could get "knocked off."

A few seconds of eerie silence elapsed before Randolph said, "Thanks. I'll be in touch."

THAT NIGHT Randolph heard news reports about denials from various players and colleges that the newspapers had linked to Walters and Bloom. He could tell the story was hot, but he wasn't quite ready for Friday morning's headline in "Petacque's Beat" in the *Chicago Sun-Times*: U.S. PROBES MOB LINK IN SPORTS AGENT CASE.

> An unsolved beating of a professional football player's wife has set off a federal investigation of a possible crime-syndicate type of racketeering in the sports agent business.
>
> Federal investigators, we've learned, are looking into the mysterious beating of Kathy Clements, 32, wife of Canadian Football League player Tom Clements. The government agents say the case might lead them to evidence of a syndicate type of intimidation and extortion—"muscling in"—that could violate federal laws.

Randolph paused and thought, Who the hell is talking to this guy?

Actually, a fairly high-ranking FBI official was suspected of feeding Petacque, who was a veteran at this stuff. Petacque specialized in painting an underworld picture of law-versus-mob with his reporter's brush.

> The federal sleuths . . . plan initially to look into the business in Chicago and New York City.

Petacque quoted a Skokie police sergeant named Phillip O'Keefe as noting that

> Clements's assailant administered a professional type of beating. The man said nothing, wore a ski mask, stole nothing, made no attempt at sexual assault—merely did the job with dispatch and vanished, like a syndicate thug.
>
> O'Keefe, Zucker, and a well-placed U.S. Justice Department source told us the Clements beating could be a message to agents in the business to coerce them into sharing fees from what is now a big business.

Petacque then quoted that source.

> This has happened before to managers of boxers and entertainers, and we hope this isn't an effort to repeat this because of the big bucks involved now in salaries paid superstars and their managers.

Randolph sighed, knowing that even if the case hadn't had organized crime clues, Petacque still would have put a mob spin on it. His stories never lacked flair. Still, Randolph wasn't pleased.

That aside, the FBI special agent put a call in to Big Ten Conference headquarters in nearby Schaumburg. He spoke directly with Wayne Duke, the husky-voiced commissioner. He explained what he was doing and asked if he could come over and talk about the conference and NCAA policy concerning agents and athletes.

"I can tell you right now it's against the rules," Duke said.

"Don't the athletes have to sign some papers?" Randolph asked, remembering that even as a college student himself he was always signing forms.

"Yes," Duke told him. It was a fairly extensive procedure. There were student-athlete affidavits, Big Ten eligibility forms, NCAA eligibility forms, financial aid forms.

"I'd like to look at those forms," Randolph told the commissioner. He also asked Wayne Duke if there had been an NCAA investigation underway about the agents' dealings.

"Only after the newspaper called," Duke told him.

Randolph made a note to send a teletype to Atlanta to have the FBI question the reporter who wrote the story.

A half hour later he was face-to-face with Wayne Duke, who handed the FBI agent some papers and said, "I think this is what you're looking for."

He first examined the Big Ten Conference statement of eligibility. There were blanks for the student-athlete's personal information and then there were twelve questions. Randolph looked at number 7 and circled it with a red-ink pen: "Have you ever signed a professional athletic contract in your sport or been represented by an agent?"

At the end of the twelve questions was the following statement: "I certify, upon penalty of ineligibility for intercollegiate athletics, that the above statements are complete and accurate."

Then came the Big Ten Conference statement of financial support. Again he circled in red the first paragraph:

> I understand that under Conference Rule 7 I will be ineligible for intercollegiate athletics if I accept financial aid other than (a) from my family, (b) from the university under a tender, (c) in the form of a grant-in-aid scholarship having nothing to do whatsoever with my athletic interests, (d) work other than provided in a tender at which I actually earn the going rate of pay; or bona fide loans.

At the bottom there was a further affirmation that the foregoing was a "complete and accurate statement."

Randolph next studied the two-page NCAA student-athlete statement. Statements 5, 6, and 7 were of particular interest:

> 5. I am not aware of any NCAA violations involving me and my institution;
> 6. I have revealed any involvement on my part in organized crime activities, both past and present, concerning intercollegiate athletics competition, including solicitation made to me in this regard;
> 7. I understand under the provisions of Constitution 3-6-(a) and 3-9-(d) I may jeopardize my eligibility to participate in intercollegiate athletics competition by falsely or erroneously signing this certification statement.

Finally he looked at the student-athlete affidavit regarding financial aid:

"I (name of student-athlete), after first being duly sworn on my oath, truthfully and fully answer the following questions relating to my continuing eligibility for participation in intercollegiate athletics."

Six questions followed, basically to determine if the student-athlete was receiving any outside benefits that would make him ineligible for financial aid from the university.

The student-athlete was then asked to sign the statement, sworn and subscribed to by a notary public.

Sworn affidavits, oaths, notarized, financial aid—Randolph was guided by a fairly basic principle in law: When you sign a statement falsely to receive a benefit, it's fraud.

Pure and simple fraud, Randolph said to himself. Doesn't matter if you're Joe Athlete or Joe Blow.

The FBI special agent filled in Duke on some of the details surrounding Walters and Bloom. Duke seemed anxious to assist and also gave Randolph the name of the Big Ten attorney, Byron Gregory, whose office was in downtown Chicago.

By now Randolph wanted to make contact with the U. S. Attorney in Chicago, Anton R. Valukas, or "Tony," as he was known. He wanted a legal opinion on his fraud theory. Valukas wasn't in. Randolph left a message with Valukas's secretary to call him as soon as possible, then spoke with Deputy Chief U. S. Attorney Ira Raphelson of the criminal division. Raphelson told him he appeared to be on solid ground.

That weekend at home Randolph received a call from Tony Valukas and told him about his week, starting with the Clements beating.

"Come see me first thing Monday morning," Valukas told him.

DRIVING DOWNTOWN on March 23, Randolph tried to find the best way to sell Valukas on the case. He figured that just the mention of "organized crime" would excite the U. S. Attorney. The beating itself was also a serious unsolved crime. Randolph also would hammer home the point that two New York agents—one of them involved in the entertainment world—were hustling football stars, many of them from the Big Ten Conference. That would appeal to any Chicago prosecutor.

Randolph also planned to point out that Iowa's Ronnie Harmon walked off with $55,000. He would explain to Valukas that it appeared the athletes had lied on their college financial forms and that the FBI agent had already gotten a legal opinion from one of Valukas's top assistants, Ira Raphelson, that this could indeed be a viable fraud case.

If Randolph could sell Valukas, the U. S. Attorney would notify the FBI that he wanted Randolph to continue to work on the case. That would give Randolph a little breathing room to work on his own without his superiors interfering.

He had tremendous respect for Valukas, who had been in office for two years, succeeding the very popular Dan Webb. Valukas didn't have Webb's flair or perhaps even his balls, but he had become very powerful and quite effective in the position.

Randolph also knew Valukas liked him. In the past he had both worked for him and against him, and he had succeeded both ways.

Webb and Valukas were close friends, going back to the days when they were both Assistant U. S. Attorneys under future Illinois governor Jim Armstrong. Once, when Webb was U. S. Attorney and Valukas was in private practice, they were opposing each other on a huge case. Still, Webb and Valukas decided to take time out for their annual fishing trip together. Valukas also decided to use Webb's absence as an opportunity to hide his wealthy client in Amsterdam.

Randolph followed the client across the Atlantic, with his primary informant in tow. Then, as Webb and Valukas were chumming around the lakes and rivers of America, Randolph wired his informant, an acquaintance of Valukas's client, and sent him aboard the yacht where the suspect was hiding. Before it was over, the informant came back with the incriminating tape Webb had been looking for.

Valukas was livid when he found out about it. Webb won the case.

There was a payback, though, when Valukas moved into office. One day he summoned Randolph to his office.

"Yes, sir," the FBI agent said as he reported.

"I have a very sensitive case, a major kidnapping," Valukas told him. "I want you on it."

Randolph begged off. He was up to his neck in work, and he didn't need another major case.

"George, I need you," Valukas said. "You're an asshole, and that's what I want on this case."

Randolph argued and basically told Valukas to find himself another FBI agent. He excused himself. He had barely gotten out of the elevator when his beeper went off. It was his boss, so he got to a phone right away.

"Get your ass up to see Valukas—now!"

Randolph made a U-turn for the elevator. When he walked back into Valukas's office, Valukas was grinning from ear to ear. Once it was clear that neither one of them was willing to put up with the other one's shit, they got along just fine.

By the time Randolph arrived at the Dirksen Federal Building, he was ready to discuss the case with Valukas. Still, when he met with the U. S. Attorney, he was once again struck by his appearance. Valukas always seemed rigid and precise. He had short brown hair and a sharp, angular face with a thin, grim-looking mouth. Behind his round wire-rimmed glasses Valukas looked like he could be a gestapo officer.

"Tell me what you've got," Valukas said.

"Tony," Randolph said, "it's premature, but this is what I suspect. . . ."

Randolph proceeded to lay out all the elements he had discovered—a beating, threats, possible extortion, Big Ten football, possible fraud—and then he mentioned the magic letters: "It smells with O.C.," he told Valukas.

The U. S. Attorney arched an eyebrow and spoke his own magic words: "Run with it."

Valukas asked Randolph which AUSA he wanted. The U. S. Attorney might not ask this of an FBI agent, but Randolph was a veteran with a rather blunt approach, and Valukas wanted to make certain they were in sync. The FBI agent thought about it. Most of the Assistant U. S. Attorneys he had worked with had recently left for private practice. He would have preferred Scott Turow, with whom he had worked closely on several cases before, but Turow had left office for private practice and to pursue his writing passions.

"How about Howard Pearl?" Randolph asked.

Valukas nodded. That was exactly the person he had in mind as well. Randolph had just worked a mail fraud case with Pearl, and they had gotten a conviction. Pearl's work had impressed Randolph, particularly his understanding and application of the powerful mail fraud laws.

Pearl was a few years younger than Randolph. The two were sort of an odd couple, but that had also been the case with Turow. Despite his thinning light-brown hair, Randolph looked solid. At five feet eleven inches and two hundred pounds, he looked like a typical Midwesterner with big hips and thighs. Pearl had a full head of dark curly hair—some thought it was permed. He was six feet two inches and had a slender build. Randolph was street tough and street smart. Pearl, a bespectacled Harvard grad, was street innocent and book smart. But he had a tenacity that the FBI agent appreciated, and it had recently worked to his advantage in a major victory.

Later that day Randolph laid out the case for Pearl. He could tell the AUSA was fired up.

"Let's go to town with it," Pearl said.

Now that the FBI agent knew he had Valukas's blessing, he had time to work the way he liked to work a case.

"Look, Howard," Randolph warned, "this is going to be a mess. It has to be full speed ahead. I can't have you off running to some trial in the middle of it. It's day and night on this one, I can tell."

Pearl was an avid jogger, so Randolph figured he would have the stamina for the case.

"What are we waiting for?" Pearl asked.

The first thing Randolph wanted from Pearl was a subpoena for all of Walters's records. They would ask for anything and everything in terms of records relating to World Sports and Entertainment from January 1, 1985, their best estimate of how long the sports agents had been in business. Contracts, travel records, wire transfers, cash disbursement journals, canceled checks, all financial ledgers, promissory notes, credit card receipts, phone bills—you name it, Pearl and Randolph asked for it.

Pearl checked over the subpoena and smiled. "Think that'll do?"

Randolph smiled back. "Yeah, for now."

Within a few days Randolph began getting scattered feedback from his teletypes. Many of the players who had been contacted were confirming their relationships with Norby Walters and Lloyd Bloom. Some of the information appeared promising, some of it would need some digging. He would need to see the actual written reports by the agents who interviewed the players. Some of the players were impossible to reach.

The phone rang. FBI Special Agent Joe Masterson was calling from Dallas.

"I got something for you, and I think it's what you're looking for," Masterson told Randolph.

The Dallas FBI agent had just met with Ron Morris, the SMU wide receiver. Morris told him about threats Bloom had made the previous October while trying to get him to sign a second representation contract to reaffirm their commitment. Morris had refused and was trying to jump to another agent.

"What'd Bloom say?" Randolph asked.

"He told Morris that the money came from people in Los Angeles who don't play around, people who don't care what they would do to him and his family," Masterson said.

"Are you shittin' me?"

There was more. The next month Morris told the FBI that Bloom called again and told Morris that he would have "someone from Vegas break your legs" and that he'd never play football again. He reminded the SMU star that the money he received did not belong to Norby Walters but came from "bigger backers" from Los Angeles "who don't care what they do."

Randolph couldn't believe what he was hearing.

"Not only that," Masterson said, "but Bloom told him that these backers would blow up his new agent's house."

Joe Masterson told Randolph something else that got his heart pumping: Morris had six tape recordings of telephone conversations with Bloom and Walters. The early threats are not on the tapes, but Special Agent Masterson said they were "fairly powerful."

"You got the tapes?" Randolph asked.

"All six of them."

"Send 'em."

Randolph asked Masterson what he thought of the picture they had in front of them.

"O.C.," Masterson replied without hesitation.

The next day Masterson called back with more chilling news. He had something to tell about Jeff Atkins, the SMU running back also linked to Walters and Bloom.

"Look, this might be more serious than you thought," Masterson told Randolph. "I can't find Atkins, but somebody driving his car two weekends ago was just gunned down. Homicide."

Randolph almost didn't say good-bye. When he hung up the phone, he called Pearl and told him the news. Pearl quietly replied, "Oh, shit."

Randolph headed straight for the tape recorder to send out a new teletype regarding his case.

"Priority . . . act with urgency."

3

WHEN THE package arrived on March 26, George Randolph already knew its contents. Still, he opened it carefully. Inside were six cassette tapes marked by date. Also inside was Joe Masterson's FD 302, the FBI standard report the special agent had completed based on his interview with Ron Morris.

Morris explained that he had signed a contract with Walters and Bloom in November 1985, late in his junior season. By October 1986 he also had gotten involved with Sherwood Blount, an SMU booster, Masterson noted, who had previously gotten the school in hot water with the NCAA.

When Morris tried to break things off with Bloom and Walters, Bloom traveled to Dallas to have a serious discussion about their future. He wanted to lay it on the line, and he did.

According to Morris on the FD 302, Bloom told the player that the money given to him had come from "people in Los Angeles who don't play around, people who don't care what they do to you and your family."

In early November 1986, Bloom called Morris and said that Norby Walters would "have someone from Vegas break your legs. . . . You'll never play again."

Then came the reminder that Walters and Bloom had "bigger backers" from Los Angeles. These backers wouldn't be afraid to blow up his new agent's house, Bloom allegedly told Morris.

Randolph read on, but he was eager to listen to the tapes. He set up a machine on his desk, plugged in some headphones, and grabbed the tape dated November 17, 1986.

Right off he heard a phone ringing and a female answering the phone.

"Lloyd Bloom, please."

"Who's calling?"

"Ron Morris."

"Ronald!"

That had to be Bloom. They had some small talk, and then the conversation took off.

MORRIS: I don't think I'm going to be able to make it, man, tomorrow, because you know Kandi's pregnant and we have those, ah, night classes for the baby . . .

BLOOM: Okay.

MORRIS: And, uh, I won't be able to have the money or anything anytime soon.

BLOOM: Uh huh.

MORRIS: So maybe they can give you a little more time on it or something . . .

Randolph pressed the pause button, wrote *They* and underlined it, then started the tape again.

MORRIS: But I won't be able to make it tomorrow, is what I'm saying.

BLOOM: I understand that. I don't have a problem with that. I mean, what are we going to do here, Ronald? Norby doesn't want to let you out of the contract.

MORRIS: Yeah, why? I mean, ya know when I first signed, you know, y'all told me if maybe if I wanted to go somewhere else, it would be cool . . . just as long as I paid.

Randolph thought Morris sounded nervous. Bloom sounded as if he was from Brooklyn.

BLOOM: Norby doesn't want to let you out of the contract, you know. He's willing to bring the whole SMU program down. They're on probation now.

MORRIS: Do what now?

BLOOM: You know, SMU's in trouble now with this kid, David Stanley.

MORRIS: Uh huh.

BLOOM: Norby said . . .

Suddenly the tape cut out. There was no sound. Then some static and some inaudible words.

"Shit," Randolph said, pounding his fist on the desk. The sound picked up.

MORRIS: What do you plan on doing?

BLOOM: Even though you sign a contract, even if after you graduate and you're out of school . . . if the NCAA knows you signed early . . . We have a copy of your contract . . . The program still goes down.

MORRIS: So you will turn my contract in?

BLOOM: Norby'll turn the contract in if we do not negotiate your contract. . . . Just giving you Norby's word.

MORRIS: Where's . . . where's Norby at now?

BLOOM: Norby's at home. He's sick today. . . . Even if once you get drafted, if Norby turns that contract in, then the SMU program will have the death penalty. They can't play for two years. And I don't think you would want to make the whole program go down, do you?

Randolph stopped the tape, taking notes about the contract, SMU, and the death penalty. He was thinking that Walters and Bloom "were real assholes," and Bloom was already walking a fine line of extortion. The FBI agent resumed playing the tape.

MORRIS: Nah. This stuff has got me mind-boggled. I can't even think straight on this stuff.

BLOOM: Norby's exact words. He says besides whatever else he would do . . .

Pause button. Randolph again took note: *Besides whatever else he would do* . . . He rewound and started again.

BLOOM: He says besides whatever else he would do, he would go to the NCAA with your contract, and even once you're drafted, you'll be playing pro football, but for SMU, the whole program will be out of business and it will be because of your contract. . . . You know that's the deal. SMU program goes down, but I don't think you'd want to . . . where your name is the one that brought the SMU program down.

MORRIS: Of course not.

BLOOM: And Norby said he's dead serious.

MORRIS: Yeah, I felt that way when you told me the last time I mentioned it to you.

Randolph turned up the volume.

BLOOM: Excuse me . . .

MORRIS: Yeah, never mind.

BLOOM: Norby's not fucking around. Norby's definitely not fucking around—know what I'm talking about? What has happened, he doesn't give a shit about Sherwood Blount, Burnham, or anybody. He said nobody can help. He said the NCAA really wants to fuck up SMU right now.

MORRIS: Man, what did you tell . . . Norby this for me . . . ah, the statement . . . did, did, did he really say that? . . . I mean, you know, what I'm talking about. About the L.A. people?

Randolph sat up. His back muscles tightened.

BLOOM: I'm not going over anything.

MORRIS: Okay, I'm just saying . . . did he really say it?

BLOOM: You can talk to Norb.

MORRIS: Okay, I want to talk to him. 'Cause I mean Kandi, I mean this . . . you got her pretty worried, and I know I'm worried about it, but what I'm saying, I think you all just—

BLOOM: Ron, Ron, Ron. I'm not going to say anything. I'm not going to go over anything with you.

Morris sounds scared, Randolph scribbled on his notepad.

MORRIS: Okay, so Norby will.

BLOOM: I don't think Norby will go over it with you, but Norby told me to relay what ya know the deal is, all right? And that's the deal. . . . Another thing is the whole SMU program. I don't give a shit . . . now you might say, I don't give a shit about the SMU program.

MORRIS: But I do.

BLOOM: That's right.

MORRIS: I do.

BLOOM: And I can promise you that will happen. As I sit here talking to you right now, that will definitely happen if we don't negotiate your contract. The whole SMU program . . . and I don't give a shit because I represent Patti LaBelle, the superstar, so I can be out of business tomorrow and still be rich.

Morris then asked Bloom how he could talk to Norby. Bloom gave him Norby's home number, which Randolph also jotted down. The conversation got back on track.

BLOOM: The whole SMU program will go down. . . . Ron Meyer and Sherwood Blount will go down.

Randolph stopped the tape again. Joe Masterson's FD 302 mentioned that Sherwood Blount and Ron Meyer were the new agents that had signed Morris, also prematurely, in violation of NCAA rules. Meyer had been the SMU coach. Randolph scratched his head, wondering, What is this shit? He returned to the tape.

MORRIS: Well, why, I can't just pay the money—

BLOOM: You made a contract!

MORRIS: Huh!

BLOOM: Ronald, I'm not in the business just to get my money back. I'm not in the business just to lend money and get my money back.

MORRIS: Yeah, but what you told me . . . you said, 'Hey, Ronald, me and you cool.' Me and you ain't never had any problems, nothing like that, and now here you are—

BLOOM: I've got partners, and Norby doesn't want to run that way. . . .

Randolph stopped the tape. Bloom didn't say "partner," he said "partners." Back to the tape.

MORRIS: Okay, so I'm not threatened anymore then, right?

BLOOM: Huh?

MORRIS: I'm not threatened anymore then, right?

BLOOM: I'm not talking about nothing . . .

Come on, you SOB, Randolph was thinking.

MORRIS: Okay, so I'm cool.

BLOOM: I discuss nothing over the phone.

There has been a threat, Randolph said to himself. Bloom is onto Morris.

BLOOM: Ron, we'll go with whatever we have to, but I'm not threatening you. . . . I'm just telling you the real deal. . . . We're gonna screw the whole SMU program and . . . death penalty.

MORRIS: Well, you have threatened me, that's what I'm saying. That's what I'm worried about. Because I worry about my family, and I worry about myself, and . . . and I don't want Kandi worrying about anything.

BLOOM: Ronald, all I told you on the phone right now—

MORRIS: Well, you know what I'm talking about. I mean . . . discussed it before. You ain't 'bout to say it. . . . I don't care. I'm not asking you to say anything. But I'm just worried about my well-being and Kandi's well-being . . . and of course I'm worried about SMU. . . . I'm worried about all of this . . . because I think you guys are playing dirty.

BLOOM: SMU is going down the drain, I'm telling you right now . . . (inaudible) . . . and tape it.

MORRIS: Well, I wish I did have a tape. I wish I did have a tape.

Okay. Well, when we going to meet, man? 'Cause I don't have the money now, and I know I'm not going to have it tomorrow.

BLOOM: Ron, I don't want the money back. We want to negotiate your contract.

MORRIS: What did you tell me last week?

BLOOM: You can have another party at the negotiations . . . to see that everything is fair. We would never do anything wrong.

Morris let out a laugh. Randolph was laughing, too.

MORRIS: You would never do what?

BLOOM: We would never do anything bad with your contract. But you signed with us, which lets us negotiate your contract. Now if you want to have somebody there . . . just to see that everything's on the up and up . . . but we will be paid our commission.

MORRIS: Even, even if, even if you don't do my negotiation, you still want your commission?

BLOOM: That's correct.

MORRIS: But you never did anything, so that's stealing.

BLOOM: That's not stealing. You signed a contract.

MORRIS: For me it is.

BLOOM: The state of New York, the law . . . once you sign a contract . . .

MORRIS: But, Lloyd, what I'm saying is, you hadn't did anything for me, and now . . .

BLOOM: We supported you, we gave you money at times of need. That's enough. Ronald, we gave you money when you needed money. Now all of a sudden you found somebody else. You want somebody else to do your contract.

MORRIS: I want to talk to Norby.

BLOOM: Look, Norb's gonna tell you the same thing.

MORRIS: Okay, I believe you, but I still want to hear it from him.

The conversation wound down with Bloom mentioning the SMU situation again. Randolph shut off the tape and went over his notes. Several things had made an impression.

First and foremost, Morris sounded nervous and scared. Bloom sounded like a Brooklyn jerk, aggressive, obnoxious, a punk, a wise guy, but not the boss. Norby ran the show. But who were "they" and "partners" that Bloom alluded to? When Morris tried to press Bloom about the L.A. people and the previous threats, Bloom was wise to him, saying, "I'm not going over anything" and "I discuss nothing over the phone." Bloom suspected the conversation might be taped. There was some cryptic talk to reaffirm that something had been said before. Bloom had said of Norby, "Besides whatever else he would do" and that Norby was "dead serious" and "not fucking around."

Randolph listened to the next two tapes, marked November 19, 1986,

and November 20, 1986. They were brief conversations between Morris
and Bloom attempting to arrange a meeting between Morris and Walters. The only thing that was remotely interesting was Bloom's repeated
urgings that Morris understand "honesty is the best policy . . . it would
be best for everybody."

Then came a tape marked November 21, 1986—Norby. Ah, Randolph
thought, now it was time to meet the jag-off. He inserted the tape into
the machine, adjusted the huge headphones resting on his head, and
listened. Initially there were some exchanges between a secretary for
World Sports and Entertainment and Morris. Finally came a new voice:
"Uncle Norby here." There it was. Uncle Norby.

MORRIS: What's happening?

WALTERS: What up?

Randolph shook his head. Did this fifty-five-year-old man really just
ask, "What up?"

MORRIS: Hey, nothing. What's going on?

WALTERS: Hello, man—I'm, I, I, I'm trying to reach you, and get
   you, and this and that. I don't know. You're the busiest guy in
   town.

Morris laughed. Already he seemed more at ease than he did with
Bloom.

WALTERS: You're the busiest guy in town.

MORRIS: Oh, man.

WALTERS: Tell me what up?

There he goes again, doing that black act, Randolph thought.

MORRIS: Man, I don't know what's happening, man. I'm just chillin',
   just trying to get this season over with.

WALTERS: Here's what I think we should do.

MORRIS: What's that?

WALTERS: Here's what I think we should do.

MORRIS: Okay.

WALTERS: I think that after the first of the year . . . let all this shit chill
   out. . . . Okay, let all this shit chill out, let the season finish, go to any
   . . . Are you going to any of the bowl games?

MORRIS: Yeah, I'm gonna play in the Senior Bowl.

WALTERS: Very good. I wanna be there, you understand? But that's after
   the first of the year. What I think we should do is, one of two things
   . . . either, either you come to New York with Kandi, or I come to
   Dallas alone. And let's do it whenever is a convenient time for the two
   of us, okay?

MORRIS: All right.

WALTERS: Eyeball to eyeball, one on one. Let us see if we have a problem, if we don't have a problem. . . . If we do have a problem, let's resolve it.

MORRIS: Okay, that's great.

WALTERS: Lloyd is on line two. Lloyd just came on.

MORRIS: Okay.

Randolph could tell Morris was disappointed.

BLOOM: How you doing, Ronald? Hold on one second.

MORRIS: Okay.

WALTERS: I mean, we never had any major problem. If there seems to be a problem, then let's resolve whatever has to be resolved, in whatever fashion we think is the best way.

MORRIS: That's cool with me.

WALTERS: Because you and I . . . have no problems, and, and, and, and, and . . . I'm doing too good in my life, and I'm making too much money, and I'm having too much fun, and I'm doing too much wonderful things, you know—

MORRIS: I know that's right, yeah.

WALTERS: To let it be dampened by any nonsense, okay?

MORRIS: Okay.

WALTERS: The Senior Bowl is on.

MORRIS: I'm going to play also in the East-West Shrine Bowl.

WALTERS: January seventeenth is the Senior Bowl. There's so many fuckin' bowls, I can't keep up with all the bowls, you know what I mean? I think just one is enough—either the East-West game or the Senior Bowl. I'll put it to you this way, I think the Senior Bowl is the way to go.

MORRIS: Because that's the pro scouts' bowl, right?

WALTERS: That's the real deal. We're advising everybody in the family to go there.

Randolph didn't miss it: "family."

Walters and Morris talked more about the bowl games. Norby was making Morris laugh. Then he started rolling.

WALTERS: Okay, I'm going away on holiday Tuesday for Thanksgiving. I'm going to Saint Marten . . . you know, in the Caribbean.

MORRIS: Uh huh!

WALTERS: Where the rich folk go.

MORRIS: Where rich folk . . . Okay, I can dig that.

WALTERS: (Laughing) There's nothing wrong with that, is there?

MORRIS: No, ain't nothing wrong with that.

Randolph rolled his eyes as Walters jumped tracks.

WALTERS: Yesterday I sat with Luther Vandross and almost put to bed, uh, we're very close now with a two-and-a-half-million-dollar deal. Yesterday I'm negotiating a two-and-a-half-million-dollar deal for Luther Vandross for Pepsi-Cola . . .

MORRIS: Okay.

WALTERS: Three weeks ago I negotiated a four-million-dollar deal . . . cut a check for six hundred and five dollars. . . . Uh, I'll give you the details later. Uh, uh, just recently I cut a . . . listen . . . listen to . . . Are you sitting down?

MORRIS: Uh, no . . . I'm at a pay phone.

Good thinking, Morris.

WALTERS: Okay, you're on a pay phone. You ought to sit down for this number . . . four million dollars. I just made a deal for Run DMC.

MORRIS: Oooooooh.

WALTERS: For a thing called Adidas. You know, the sneakers?

MORRIS: Yeah.

WALTERS: Four million. Now, you didn't see it in the papers. But when Herschel Walker got a million-dollar deal—Herschel Walker won the Heisman Trophy four years ago, is that correct?

MORRIS: That's right.

WALTERS: Now in these four years Herschel Walker never got a fuckin' commercial, an endorsement, sponsorship, or anything, correct? You know, you never saw anything, right?

MORRIS: Right.

WALTERS: Okay. Finally, finally, finally, now because they made a deal with the Dallas, uh, Cowboys, finally he lucked out, and he made a fabulous deal, and I won't knock it. . . . He got a million dollars, and it made all the papers.

MORRIS: Exactly.

WALTERS: Now check this out. Now I made a deal for four million dollars, and it didn't, it didn't make the paper.

MORRIS: Um hum.

WALTERS: You don't want to bring out—you following what I'm trying to bring up here? I make so many fuckin' deals, and things are like so fuckin' great! Now really I'm just saying this to you so you'll understand. . . . I'm so fuckin' busy.

MORRIS: Right.

WALTERS: Doing so many wonderful fuckin' things.

MORRIS: Uh huh.

WALTERS: Doing so incredible for my clients, doing such shit that I don't want to go through changes with Ron Morris . . . you know what I mean?

MORRIS: Right. That's why I want to get it worked out definitely.

WALTERS: Hey, I just, I just want to get it worked out because as far as I'm concerned, I'm the best MOTHERFUCKING SALESMAN IN THIS FUCK-ING COUNTRY!

Norby's voice jumped up several decibels. Randolph lowered the volume.

WALTERS: The best salesman in the . . . You know what an agent is called? He's a salesman. You know an insurance salesman is called an insurance agent, is that correct?

MORRIS: That's correct.

WALTERS: A real estate salesman is called a real estate agent.

MORRIS: Agent, mmm hmmm.

WALTERS: People are called agents, but the real name of the game is still salesman.

MORRIS: Okay.

WALTERS: Okay!

MORRIS: Okay.

WALTERS: Norby Walters, hands down, without a fuckin' doubt, is the best seller of black talent today in the United States of America.

Randolph punched the machine and made it stop. Who is this jag-off? he asked himself.

MORRIS: I can dig that.

WALTERS: You can dig it, right?

MORRIS: I can dig it.

WALTERS: That's the bottom line. Now I know we've had some shit, but you and I are going to come down there, we're going to work out every shit that we have to work out, but I just want to be the foremost and absolute thing on your mind. All the fuckin' attorneys and all the accountants and all the everybodies in the world can't, aren't capable of bringing the dollars to the table. . . . You here on the line?

MORRIS: Mm hmmm.

WALTERS: Having the sophisticated hipness to understand how to bring the bucks to the table is the bottom line of the business. Since you and I have spoken in the past couple of months, Mr. Jermaine Jackson has joined this family. You know the name?

MORRIS: Uh huh.

WALTERS: Mr. Lou Rawls has joined this family.

MORRIS: I know the name.

WALTERS: You know that name, okay. Miss Chaka Khan has joined the family.... That's just a few. I would give you mo ... Oh, Mr. Frankie Beverly and Maze . . . has joined this family. Now you grew up listening to Frankie Beverly and Maze, didn't you?

Randolph shakes his head. Who the hell is he talking about?

MORRIS: Oh, yeah.

WALTERS: One of your heroes of rock and roll?

MORRIS: That's my man.

WALTERS: Check it out, man.... I made for this year for Frankie Beverly more fucking money than he's ever made in his fucking life without a smash album. I have grossed him more fuckin' dollars. He said to me two weeks ago, "Norby Walters, I cannot understand why I didn't come to you years ago." I said, "Frankie, I've been romancing you for years. You're the jerk. I was the one who was trying. You were the one who was shucking and jiving." He said, "Why didn't you beat me up, why didn't you shake me," and . . . you understand the point I'm bringing to you?

MORRIS: I understand.

WALTERS: The name of the game is—

MORRIS: Uh, uh, no. Let me talk to you for a minute.

WALTERS: Please.

MORRIS: Okay, I've got to go, but let me, just let me leave you with this thought. . . . Okay, you know, me and you always shot straight—

WALTERS: Please!

MORRIS: And me and Lloyd, you know we have always shot straight. . . . Okay, the last time he was down here—now I just want you to think about this, and we'll talk about it when you get here, so we won't talk about it now.

WALTERS: Yeah.

MORRIS: You know.

The player sighed. Randolph figured Morris was trying to get a message to Walters in case Bloom was still listening. Morris was thinking about the threats.

MORRIS: You know.

WALTERS: I know.

MORRIS: Okay.

WALTERS: Excuse me, I do know.

MORRIS: You know.

WALTERS: I know some strange shit.

MORRIS: Very strange.

WALTERS: Excuse me, I know.

MORRIS: Very strange.

WALTERS: But Norby Walters is Norby Walters. I'm the guy who's been in business now for almost thirty years.

MORRIS: Yeah.

WALTERS: Listen, 'cause here's the thing I want to bring out to you, man. Listen to this. Norby Walters came to Texas. You joined Norby Walters. Lloyd Bloom is my young sidekick.

MORRIS: All right.

WALTERS: Okay. Norby Walters is the star maker. Norby Walters is the man who made Luther Vandross. I'm the man who remade Kool and the Gang. I'm the man who remade Patti LaBelle. I'm the man who discovered the New Edition, okay? Not Lloyd Bloom.

MORRIS: Okay.

WALTERS: Be very— Let's understand that very much now. . . . I am the man that you see all the write-ups. I am the man that you see on television. I'm the fuckin' guy that was on Carson's show. I'm the fuckin' guy that had a Kirshner NBC special. I'm the guy, man, that's looked at as the man. . . . I got a young partner.

MORRIS: Okay.

WALTERS: You know what I'm saying?

MORRIS: Yeah.

WALTERS: I got a very young partner . . . sometimes a little overram, overly rambunctious, sometimes a little overly rambunctious. But Norby Walters is your man. I am the man. The buck stops here. I'm the fuckin' man who makes the megamillion-dollar deals. I'm the man that all these clients are assigned to.

MORRIS: But do you understand what I'm talking about?

WALTERS: Sure, I understand what you're talking about.

MORRIS: Okay, 'cause I'm just saying . . . Okay.

WALTERS: I understand, I understand perfectly. That's why I want to—

MORRIS: Can you at least apologize to my wife, because she's worried about it. . . . That's what I wanted you to know.

WALTERS: Let me tell you something. If you want your lady, if you want your wife to sit there with me, you and I—I said I just wanted it to be just you and I . . . but, but, it's cool. . . . If you honestly feel that you want to have her there, then that's cool.

MORRIS: Right.

WALTERS: I want to tell you something right now: I have seven major Fortune 500 companies lined up now that are ready to come with me and my football clients. And first round I have . . . Okay, I have seven right now that are ready to roll with me, to deal, to talk about endorsements, merchandise, sponsorships.

Randolph rubbed his hand through his scalp. For the next three minutes he listened to Walters again talk about how he was going to make "fabulous fuckin' deals" for everyone. And that was supposed to impress Morris's wife, Kandi.

WALTERS: I want Kandi to know me, to feel the vibration. After two, three hours, she's going to hug and kiss me. I know she's going to say, "Uncle Norby Walters," 'cause, hey, I'll pick up the fuckin' phone and have her speak to Luther, and let Luther tell her. I mean I'll have Kool from Kool and the Gang, I'll have Frankie Beverly, I mean I'll have people she's grown up listening to, people who do ten million dollars a year. . . . I take care of their life.

MORRIS: Right.

WALTERS: You know, I ain't no young snot-nosed shit. I'm not talking about my young partner, I'm talking about Norby Walters. You're talking to the chief.

Randolph didn't know how much more he could stand. He's smothering the kid, he said to himself.

WALTERS: I'm gone for Thanksgiving, and when I come back, I really got a lot of shit. I'm cohosting a big party for Dave Winfield . . . you know, for the Yankees? Putting on an incredible party, and I've invited a lot of my stars. He's asked me to help him out for the Winfield Foundation for the kids and stuff, so I promised him I'd help out. I'm delivering about eight or ten stars to the party, you know. It will be a huge party at Radio City and, uh, I'm sort of a cohost for this big party, you know.

MORRIS: Okay.

WALTERS: So next week, when I sit there with Kandi, she . . . feel the vibration . . . like I say, man, shit, I'll, I'll, I'll call up goddamn Andrew Young, the mayor of goddamn Atlanta. I'll take it to the distance, you know what I mean?

MORRIS: Okay.

WALTERS: Motherfuckers that will say to Kandi, "Kandi, Norby Walters is the hardest working white man in America on behalf of black America."

Gimme a break, jag-off.

WALTERS: I'm the cat that's raising all the money for Jesse for the 1988 presidential campaign. They forced me to raise money. I'm going to put on a series of concerts for them, one a month to raise the money for the voter registration campaign for 1988 for black America.

MORRIS: All right.

WALTERS: How heavy can you get?

MORRIS: Not too much heavier than that.

WALTERS: Yeah. (Laughing) I mean, I'm taking it the distance. I mean the fuckin' motherfucker man is gonna run for the President of the United States, and they've asked me to raise money to go into black communities, to knock on doors. You know what? It's as if they're hiring your wife, Kandi Morris, to go in and say, "Are you registered?" Well, somebody's got to get three hundred dollars a week to do that, you know what I mean?

MORRIS: Right.

WALTERS: You can't get any heavier than that, right? We ain't talking about bullshit, making some deal with a bullshit football club now. We're talking about the world, we're talking about life, we're talking about Ronald Morris's life after football . . . which can end in a day.

Randolph was so dizzy now, he didn't know if Walters was sending a hidden message to Morris. Either way, he was not sure Morris could have deciphered one through all the bullshit. But Walters had just laid out some heavy names. The conversation was winding down.

WALTERS: Check this line.

MORRIS: Okay.

WALTERS: Check this line. . . . As always . . .

MORRIS: As always . . .

WALTERS: I love you madly.

MORRIS: All right, man.

WALTERS: You know that.

MORRIS: Okay. Tell Lloyd, tell Lloyd to be cool.

WALTERS: Can I tell you something, man?

MORRIS: Okay.

WALTERS: I fight with him every day to be cool.

MORRIS: Okay, I know that. I saw that when I was up there. I saw that.

WALTERS: You saw that, didn't you?

MORRIS: I saw that.

WALTERS: You see, I gotta, I gotta fight with him every day to be cool.

They exchanged more jive pleasantries and ended the conversation.

Randolph got up from his desk and walked around his office, saying to himself, I don't know if I've ever heard so much bullshit in my life. And there were two more tapes. Randolph opened a desk drawer and found some aspirin. His head had a dull pounding, like a rubber mallet tapping away on his skull. He looked back at the desk. Damn, two more tapes. The first one opened some more doors.

WALTERS: I'm going to give you three cats. You tell me if you think they're first-rounders or not.

MORRIS: Okay.

WALTERS: John Clay of Missouri.

MORRIS: Okay.

WALTERS: You know he's going to be a first-rounder.

MORRIS: Uh huh.

WALTERS: He is.

MORRIS: Okay.

WALTERS: Rod Woodson from Purdue.

MORRIS: Okay.

WALTERS: First round.

MORRIS: Okay.

WALTERS: And Paul Palmer from Temple. He's this number-two kid that took the Heisman Trophy. He broke the NCAA record, man, for rushing and all-purpose yardage. This year, just broke Tony Dorsett's record. He's going to be the second person with the highest votes behind Vinny Testaverde.

MORRIS: Uh huh.

WALTERS: I just gave you those three, just now. . . . They're pure first-rounders.

MORRIS: Okay.

WALTERS: And I just want to tell you this: There are five other pure first-rounders, but they're still going to bowl games, so I can't say their name.

MORRIS: Oh, really?

Randolph was alert again.

WALTERS: Uncle Norby's going to control the first round this year.

Randolph stopped the tape. He wrote down Uncle Norby's words.

WALTERS: (Laughing) I'm the guy that's going to force an extra two hundred to two hundred and fifty thousand dollars for every one of them motherfuckers, man. Everyone in my family . . .

MORRIS: That's kicking.

WALTERS: Hey, you know I'm a kicking—I just gave you three monsters. There are five more . . . can't say their names 'cause they're going to bowl games.

MORRIS: That's cool.

They had more talk about the first-rounders. Walters told Morris, "You're going to go late first round, unless it gets fucked up." They talked about the money Morris might make.

WALTERS: We're talking about a million, about a million six.

MORRIS: What about sign?

WALTERS: I'd say about seven hundred and fifty to eight.

MORRIS: Okay, I can dig that. I can dig that.

The two had some laughs. Randolph could see that Walters had Morris eating out of his hands because he was talking money. Then he repeated his boast about how he would dominate the 1987 NFL draft.

WALTERS: Because I'm going to hold out the whole fucking first round.

MORRIS: Right, 'cause you said you got control of that.

The two men talked about "Jeff," who Randolph figured was Atkins. That's right: the fatal shooting.

Randolph scrambled through the papers Joe Masterson had sent him from Dallas. There was a newspaper clipping from the *Dallas Morning News:* NO ARREST IN MAN SLAIN IN CAR. *Auto Registered to Ex-SMU Player Atkins.*

The story read:

> Police reported no arrests or new developments Sunday in the death of an apartment complex maintenance man to former Southern Methodist University football player Jeff Atkins, officials said.
>
> David Simpson, 31, was shot several times by one or more assailants about 8:50 P.M. Friday as he sat in Atkins's 1984 Datsun 300ZX, which was parked at an apartment complex in the 4700 block of Denton Drive in Dallas.

The story said that homicide police had not yet talked to Atkins about the shooting. It said that Atkins was a former high school All-America at Fort Worth Eastern Hills and "last year became the Southwest Conference's ninth-leading career rusher."

Another clipping was attached, a story that said Atkins finally had been found by police. Atkins told police that he did not know the victim but had lent the car to another man. No arrests had been made.

Atkins was also identified in the story as one of thirteen SMU players

who were paid to play during the 1988 season, leading to SMU's receiving the "harshest penalty in NCAA history" on February 25. Randolph
remembered the story. It was only a month ago.

Something else grabbed his attention. The newspaper reported that
Atkins said he had "completed a four-week treatment program for cocaine and alcohol addiction." The clipping also said that police did not
suspect Atkins was a target. But a third clipping quoted a Dallas police
investigator as saying: "We don't know if Atkins may have been the
target and it was a case of mistaken identity. If that is true, he (Atkins)
needs to get in touch with us as soon as possible."

That clipping was older than the other. Still, Randolph wondered if
Masterson had found Atkins.

Randolph wanted to finish the tapes. He picked up with Walters
bragging again about how much money he was making for his entertainers. He was dropping their names and the names of companies, such as
Coca-Cola.

WALTERS: Who else in this business has the juice to pick up and call all
    these Fortune 500 companies, man? Nobody but Norby Walters,
    'cause I'm the guy that represents all the major black artists of this
    country and knows which companies are willing to put a black face as
    their spokesman. 'Cause most companies are racist motherfuckers,
    man, 'cause they figure they might offend all them redneck mother-
    fuckers.

MORRIS: (Laughs) I'm following you.

WALTERS: You know it took me years to figure out which companies—
    and check this last line—which cat on the inside of that company, the
    one who's got the power to make the deal, who will take the kickback
    from me. You got that line.

Randolph stopped the tape. He got the line. "Kickback" was a red
flag.

WALTERS: Which cat will give me a four-hundred-thousand-dollar deal
    or a five-hundred-thousand-dollar deal and know that I'm picking up
    my forty or fifty and say, "Eeh, eeh, eeh, uhm (Clears throat), Norb,
    can we, ah, eeeh, uhm, get straight?" (Laughs).

Morris laughed. Randolph was back in tune now.

WALTERS: You know, you know, I'm going to kick over half the scratch
    that I'm making . . . you dig what I mean?

Randolph thought, I dig what you mean, jag-off. Norby knew the
lingo. Kickback. Juice. Scratch. Those were the street words for the big
American dollars.

WALTERS: Hey, like I said, our wire may have gotten crossed . . . you know I'm talking the right shit. (Laughs) . . . But the important thing is that you're talking about a long-term situation in a short-term business. You know, you fuck up your leg tomorrow, you're out of the business.

What did he mean by that? Randolph wondered. Was it another message or just the guy talking about the realities and risks of being a football player?

Walters then tried to talk Morris into coming to New York rather than having him go to Dallas.

WALTERS: You are going to fall down when you see our new operation . . . moved to an incredible building, took over half a floor. You're going to fall down when you see this now.

Then Walters said something that genuinely caught Randolph off guard.

WALTERS: Good luck with your finals, 'cause that's important also. Keep working on that, man. Get as best as you can there, 'cause it's really very important. There's plenty of tomorrows, and you need that.

Randolph heard them exchange good-byes. By now he thought that Norby Walters was one of the strangest, most captivating con men he had ever run across.

On the last tape Walters and Morris were trying to pin down a date for a New York visit. Meanwhile, Walters informed Morris that his old SMU coach and new agent, Ron Meyer, had just been named head coach of the Indianapolis Colts.

WALTERS: Here's a guy that's talking to you and a couple of other cats about what he's going to do for them, and meanwhile he's quickly looking for a job for himself. . . . So what the whole thing comes down to is all bullshit.

RANDOLPH WAS done. His head wasn't just throbbing now, it was spinning. He called Pearl.

"I'm coming down with these Morris tapes," he told the prosecutor. "I think Tony will find them interesting. I mean, you won't believe these guys."

Randolph met later that day with Valukas and Pearl. They all listened to the tapes—stop, rewind, play again and again. Some three hours later they were done and stood looking at one another, shaking their heads in disbelief.

Before long Tony Valukas began smiling, grinning as big as Randolph had ever seen him, almost like the day he was summoned back to the U. S. Attorney's office. They all started grinning.

Lloyd Bloom and Norby Walters had just given them the pep talk of their life.

The phone rang. Pearl picked it up.

"It's for you, George."

It was Kathy Clements. She had just received an anonymous call. "A man said he knew where my kids went to school," she said, sounding on the verge of tears.

"I'll be right there," Randolph said.

4

HER FACE was no longer swollen and bruised, but her eyes darted with anxiety and her feet were fidgety. Kathy Clements clasped her hands and told George Randolph about the anonymous caller. She was visibly shaken, and the FBI agent understood why.

Clements had been at the new office Zucker had opened in Northbrook when she was told there was a telephone call on hold for her. She picked up.

"Your kids have been in an accident at school. . . . You better go home," a male voice told her.

Clements ran out of the office, jumped into her Corvette, and broke all the speed limits racing to her home in Glencoe. Almost as soon as she walked in the door, the phone was ringing.

"We just wanted to show you we knew where your kids went to school."

The coarse male voice abruptly went silent and the phone was hung up.

Clements called the school and learned that there had been no accident involving her children. It had been an ordinary day.

George Randolph was disappointed that the telephone call had not been recorded by the device connected to Clements's telephone. While talking to her sister the night before, Clements had used the privacy button and had forgotten to reactivate it when she left for work that morning.

The FBI agent tried to reassure her: "Your name's been in the paper, and this type of thing happens because there are a lot of sick people out there. We'll check some things out."

Randolph told her that the house would remain under spot surveil-

lance and that her children's school would be observed, too. He went
back to the Dirksen Federal Building and told Pearl what happened.

"It's a blatant act of intimidation," Pearl said.

Randolph prepared some forms that would allow the FBI to access
telephone records. It was a hassle because the expense of tracing such a
call would cost the bureau about $700. Randolph had to run a gauntlet
of bureau officials, repeatedly explaining the necessity of the expense.
Finally it was approved.

The telephone records showed that the calls which coincided with the
time of the calls to Clements came from a pay phone at the nearby
Olympia Country Club. Randolph visited the club to see if anyone saw
a man using the phone around that time, but nobody could help.

"Weird," Randolph said.

Randolph filed away the records and the incident, but he could not
dismiss the notion that it was a prank. It seemed that the message of
intimidation already had been delivered in the form of the beating. Police
surveillance remained for security reasons, but Randolph hoped that
Norby Walters or Lloyd Bloom would dare to call her. They never did
after the beating.

More than anything, at this stage, Randolph wanted Norby Walters's
records. The next day he was going to press hard to ensure that the FBI
office in New York proceeded quickly with the subpoena.

On March 27 Randolph received a call from Richard Tofani, Jr., a
fellow FBI special agent in New York. The subpoena had been served on
Norby Walters at his World Sports and Entertainment offices at 1700
Broadway in Manhattan. The documents were to be delivered no later
than April 6 for presentation to the grand jury.

"So what was this jag-off like?" Randolph asked Tofani.

Norby was a smoothie but a fast-talking operator, Tofani explained.
He had the look, the talk, the act of a New York agent. The walls of the
office were decorated with gold records. When they had delivered the
subpoena, Walters had tried to impress Tofani and his partner with the
people he represented. Walters had dropped names in rapid-fire fashion—entertainers such as Marvin Gaye, Dionne Warwick, Kool and the
Gang, and the Jacksons. So many names Tofani couldn't keep track.

Randolph could imagine the scene, having heard Norby Walters on
the Morris tapes.

"What did he think of our subpoena?" Randolph asked.

Walters was agitated initially by the FBI intruding into his palace,
then he started playing "What, me?" Norby explained that he had done

nothing wrong, that everybody in the business was doing it, and that his pursuit of college athletes was no different from somebody investing money in McDonald's. That same old line. Randolph had read it in the *Atlanta Constitution.*

There was something about Norby Walters that rang a bell with Tofani.

"I know the name sounds familiar," Tofani said.

Randolph leaned forward, anxious to hear more. Please, he asked, please tell me more about Norby Walters. Tofani said he would dig deeper and get back to him.

ESCORTED BY his agent, Steve Zucker, Tim McGee took a seat in the office of the U. S. Attorney and shook hands with Tony Valukas, Howard Pearl, and George Randolph. Right from their first meeting Randolph had expressed an interest in meeting with McGee, Doug Dubose, and Reggie Rogers—the three clients now represented by Zucker and Clements. Zucker thought that Tim McGee was the most capable of telling the feds about Norby Walters and Lloyd Bloom. There was no deal struck. The government team at this point was ready to meet the players, but this was a fairly informal session.

It could have been an intimidating moment, but McGee seemed more humble than scared, which was okay with everyone. He was the first football player they were meeting face-to-face, and everything about McGee seemed so normal. There was no jive talk, and he was well groomed. He was the smallest man in the room at five feet ten inches and 175 pounds. Better yet, McGee had been one of Walters's and Bloom's early first-round draft picks and was coming off his rookie season with the Cincinnati Bengals.

McGee explained that he wasn't surprised when he originally received a telephone call from Norby Walters and Lloyd Bloom. Tennessee coach Johnny Majors was calling McGee the best receiver he had ever coached, including Willie Gault. McGee had been named to the 1985 *Playboy* magazine All-America team, and many agents had sought him out. McGee still had the magazine, which pictured him wearing his Tennessee uniform, number 88. He and Bo Jackson, then a hotshot running back for Auburn, sandwiched Brigham Young University quarterback Robbie Bosco.

McGee said he would never forget the day Bloom called. It was their introduction—Bloom had called them the "agents to the stars."

Bloom told McGee that the "agents to the stars" wanted to fly him to New York to "check out the operation." They would have a limousine waiting for him, Bloom promised. He might even meet some of those stars. Come on, have a good time. It can't hurt. That was the pitch. It was the best invitation yet from an agent. McGee accepted and was told there would be a prepaid airline ticket waiting for him at Hopkins Airport in Cleveland, McGee's hometown, where he was spending the summer. The trip alone constituted an NCAA violation because McGee did not pay for it himself.

When McGee arrived at LaGuardia Airport, there was a man holding a card with the name "McGee" scribbled on it. Before McGee could open his mouth, another fairly young man, about twenty-five, in a suit, stepped forward. He had a puffy face and brushed-back brown hair. He grabbed McGee's hand and somewhat enthusiastically introduced himself as Lloyd Bloom. They hopped into a limo waiting outside and drove into Manhattan. Bloom never stopped talking and told McGee that he was going to love "Uncle Norby."

Valukas, Pearl, and Randolph all grinned at the mention of Uncle Norby.

McGee proceeded to tell the prosecution team that after he arrived in Manhattan, his meeting with Norby Walters was unforgettable. Norby was slick and a sharp dresser. His hair was almost silver, with only a trace of black. Norby took over the show, saying he was the "agent to the stars," clearly keeping Lloyd in the background. Walters kept bragging that Bloom, his "young partner," was one of the most knowledgeable football agents in the business. McGee had never heard of either man.

But McGee was impressed with Walters, who fascinated him. There were gold records on the wall and autographed pictures of artists such as Kool and the Gang, Luther Vandross, Patti LaBelle, Gloria Gaynor, and the New Edition. Walters handed him an issue of *Billboard* magazine. Inside was a fifteen-page article on Norby Walters, including pictures of him with Marvin Gaye, Lionel Richie, Rick James, Jimmy Cliff, Rodney Dangerfield!

McGee also had a good time with Lloyd Bloom. Bloom was a happy-go-lucky guy who worked hard at impressing McGee, bragging that he had once worked at Studio 54. When he and Bloom went out nightclubbing, Bloom would slip the doormen cash to get them inside. He also claimed he was married to the costar on the "Mike Hammer" television series. The prosecution team looked at one another. That was the first they had heard of that. Bloom, married to a Hollywood actress?

Before McGee went home that weekend, Walters made a hard, tempting sales pitch to him about signing a representation agreement for his NFL career. Norby Walters claimed that the agents were operating their sports business like the entertainment business, that they were only going after the elite football stars, and that nobody, but nobody, could make money for him like Norby Walters could in the endorsement field.

McGee explained that with one season left in college it was against the rules, but Walters pooh-poohed the thought. McGee knew that others before him and around him were ignoring the rules as well. Walters opened a briefcase and laid out a bunch of $20 bills, maybe a hundred of them.

"I bet your eyes got big," Pearl interrupted with a warm grin.

"Oh, yeah," McGee said, returning the smile. "Real big."

It would be a little advance, $2,500 up front and $250 a month. McGee didn't want too much cash in his pocket, Norby explained, or he would draw suspicion around the Tennessee campus. If he needed more money, all he had to do was call and the agents would wire him some cash. It was all so easy. And then Walters put a promissory note and a contract in front of McGee. It was the first time that McGee felt really uncomfortable. What did he really know about Norby Walters and Lloyd Bloom? Could they keep a secret?

"Nobody's gonna find out," Walters assured him.

Walters told him the contract and note would be put in the company vault and that virtually nobody but the agent himself had access to the vault. To make things even less suspicious, Walters said he would post-date the contract to January 2, 1986, after the last possible bowl game would be played and McGee's eligibility at Tennessee expired. The agents would then negotiate McGee's contract when he was drafted. They would take their commission off the top, and a beautiful business relationship would have begun, Walters explained.

"Just sign here . . . and here."

McGee took the pen and signed. Walters handed him the cash. Bloom broke into a big grin and vigorously grabbed McGee's hand, telling him it was the best decision the player would ever make. McGee thanked "Mr. Walters." The agent would have none of that now.

"Just call me Uncle Norby," Walters told him. "You're part of the family now."

Randolph raised his eyebrows. "The family." Norby Walters and his family.

Valukas, Pearl, and Randolph wanted to know if Walters and Bloom had ever approached McGee about drugs or girls. There was nothing about drugs. As for girls, Uncle Norby was always surrounded with beautiful women at the parties and concerts that McGee attended, at the agent's expense, on follow-up trips to New York. The best trip without a doubt was to the Grammys, the biggest awards night in the music industry. He went as Uncle Norby's personal guest and sat next to Prince. He met Luther Vandross and was introduced to Whitney Houston, and suddenly his crush on the pop star seemed a little more real. Uncle Norby gave him an elbow and a wink and told him that he might be able to "set something up" between Whitney Houston, beautiful singer, and Tim McGee, star football player.

During the summer of 1986 and through the football season, Norby Walters kept his word and wired money to McGee—usually $250, minus the transfer fee. But there were times when McGee would ask for more to help his mother, whose rented house in Cleveland constantly needed plumbing, heating, and roofing repairs. Sometimes she needed help with the rent. Uncle Norby never turned him down.

Despite the feeling of obligation and even warmheartedness McGee felt toward Walters and Bloom, when his season ended at Tennessee, he started learning more about the agent business. It became clear to him that he would be a first-round draft pick in April. Agents were calling him like crazy. He was named first-team All-American and a unanimous All–Southeastern Conference selection. Tennessee went to the prestigious Sugar Bowl, and McGee caught seven passes for ninety-four yards and scored one touchdown in the game. McGee also played in a couple of postseason college all-star games, the Senior Bowl and the Hula Bowl.

Walters and Bloom also went to those games. It was there that he began to feel somewhat uncomfortable, as if they owned him, as if he was their property. Instead of advice he occasionally received orders.

Valukas wanted to know what kind of orders. McGee said it was like, "Don't do this . . . don't listen to that guy . . . don't sign that . . . don't go there." It wasn't anything serious, but the attitude had changed. They wanted more control. And Norby Walters and Lloyd Bloom were never inconspicuous at these places. They were flashier than the rest, talked loud, and bragged about who they were. Yet it seemed that nobody in football had ever heard of them. It bothered McGee, and he began to wonder whether the agents would know how to handle his contract because, in fact, Norby Walters and Lloyd Bloom had never represented a first-round NFL draft choice. He was also starting to hear things about Norby Walters from people who worked for him in New York.

"What kind of things?" Valukas quizzed.

A friendly secretary in the office used to try to flirt with him occasionally, McGee said. She told him things—that Norby wasn't always an upbeat hipster. Uncle Norby had a dark side, she said. The entertainment world often got ugly. Uncle Norby could be Uncle Nasty. You didn't want to get on Uncle Norby's bad side, she warned McGee.

"Does she still work there?"

"I think so. Well, I don't know. She was talking about quitting," McGee said.

Valukas, Pearl, and Randolph knew they had to get to this woman.

"What else bothered you?" asked Valukas.

Even though the United States Football League was making a pitch for him in 1986—the Memphis Showboats had acquired his rights— McGee was nervous because the USFL was in the throes of a major lawsuit that would determine its future. Then, as the NFL draft approached, McGee began having serious doubts about whether he wanted Walters and Bloom negotiating his contract. He had met a few other agents, including Zucker, with whom he felt comfortable. He liked the idea that Zucker was an attorney. On draft day he telephoned Zucker and asked him to represent him. When the Bengals called him to tell him he was the twenty-first pick of the first round, he informed the NFL club that his agent was Steve Zucker.

Meanwhile, Norby Walters was calling the Bengals to tell the club, somewhat jubilantly, that he would be representing Tim McGee. The club delivered the news to Walters that the player had already named Zucker as the agent of record. McGee knew right away that Walters had discovered his switch because of the phone calls he was getting from Uncle Norby. McGee was scared. He had never been afraid to sacrifice his body for the sake of a catch on a football field, but now he was afraid to speak with Norby Walters.

McGee continued to ignore the calls and asked Zucker to deal with the problem. Uncle Norby also called McGee's mother, Athree, and occasionally appealed to the player's sisters, who thought their brother had done Uncle Norby wrong. McGee admitted he did feel bad at times, but he stuck to his decision and eventually sent word to Walters that he would repay him the money the agent had lent him. Yet McGee reneged on his promise to repay Walters, despite receiving a $350,000 signing bonus from Cincinnati.

Tony Valukas wanted to know why the player hadn't repaid his debt of more than $10,000. McGee hinted that it may have been an act of defiance because Norby Walters had frequently called his mother, threatening to sue the player and expose his early dealings. Then there was Lloyd Bloom's remark to Kathy Clements three months ago at the Senior Bowl, after McGee had already finished his rookie season in the National Football League. The threat about possibly breaking his hands did not bolster his enthusiasm to meet his obligation. Besides, how could Lloyd Bloom break his hands?

Howard Pearl also asked McGee about the NCAA eligibility procedure at Tennessee. Had he signed all the necessary forms to play his senior season? Yes. Did he lie on the forms? Yes. Did he receive his scholarship benefits and any financial aid after that? Yes. Were Norby Walters and Lloyd Bloom aware that McGee was concealing his arrangement with the agents? Of course.

"Did you know you were committing a fraud in violation of federal laws?" Tony Valukas asked Tim McGee.

The room got quiet.

"I didn't really think of it like that," the player responded. "I knew it was wrong."

The meeting between McGee and the government men broke up. If McGee did anything, he gave them a fairly vivid picture of Walters's and Bloom's tactics.

Before he left, Randolph asked McGee if he had that copy of *Billboard* magazine, and McGee said he believed he had one somewhere at his mother's home in Cleveland. He would get them a copy as soon as possible. He also would search for anything else that the government might consider evidence.

Randolph was hoping that all the players would be as cooperative as McGee. They might catch a break.

GEORGE RANDOLPH and Howard Pearl received the records from World Sports and Entertainment on April 9. A list of players under contract to WSE was provided and broken down by draft years—1985, 1986, and 1987. It was obvious that the operation was growing quickly because in 1985 there were three players listed, in 1986 there were twelve, and in 1987 there were thirty-five.

The 1985 players were Tracy Henderson (Iowa State), Vincent Hall (Middle Tennessee State), and Byron Linwood (TCU).

The 1986 players were Egypt Allen (TCU), Anthony Beverly (SMU), Raven Caldwell (Arkansas), Maurice Douglass (Kentucky), Kenny Davis (TCU), Ronnie Harmon (Iowa), Carl Hilton (Houston), Devon Mitchell (Iowa), Tim McGee (Tennessee), Craig Swoope (Illinois), Lester Williams (Iowa State), and Brad Sellers (Ohio State). Sellers was the only basketball player among the group.

The 1987 players were Jeff Atkins and Jerry Ball (SMU), Robert Banks (Notre Dame), John Clay (Missouri), Doug Dubose (Nebraska), Brent Fullwood (Auburn), Charles Faucette (Maryland), Terrence Flagler, Terrance Roulhac, and Kenny Flowers (Clemson), Everett Gay and William Harris (Texas), Mark Ingram (Michigan State), Keith Johnson (Georgia), Roderick Jones (Washington), Marc Logan (Kentucky), Terance Mann (SMU), Alvin Miller (Notre Dame), Ron Morris (SMU), Andrew Mott (Southern Mississippi), Frankie Neal (Fort Hays State, Florida), Bob Perryman (Michigan), Paul Palmer (Temple), Tim Peoples (Washington), Tom Powell (Auburn), Garland Rivers (Michigan), Reggie Rogers (Washington), Edwin Simmons (Texas), Timmy Smith (Texas Tech), George Swarn (Miami, Ohio), Raymond Tate (Houston), Rod Woodson (Purdue), James Williams (Fresno State), Tony Woods (Pittsburgh), and Adrian White (Florida).

Norby Walters and Lloyd Bloom had gotten around. From California to Florida to Nebraska to Washington to Texas to Ohio. Walters and Bloom had touched down everywhere, it seemed. Their access seemed to have no limits, from SMU to Notre Dame.

But something was wrong here. Randolph went back over the list. He saw no names of college underclassmen. No Cris Carter of Ohio State. Randolph started thumbing through the actual contracts to see what was in them, but he could barely read the names.

"These aren't the originals," he said to Pearl. "Fucking copies! Horseshit copies."

Randolph checked everything again just to make certain. Things didn't match the information he had already gathered.

"Something's fucked up here," he said. "One thing my daddy always taught me is that numbers don't lie."

Pearl looked at the FBI agent and asked, "What?"

"He's absolutely holding out on us," Randolph said. "This is bullshit. Absolute bullshit. I want that son of a bitch here. Throw his ass in front of the grand jury now and get him under oath saying he's complied with the subpoena. This is bullshit."

George Randolph could feel the top of his head starting to burn red. He looked at the bespectacled prosecutor. Howard Pearl had never seen Randolph in a street fight, but that's what it looked like he was getting ready for.

"This is some serious shit," Randolph told the AUSA. "We gotta go after this son of a bitch right this minute. You gotta back me up. We gotta have the original documents for a lab analysis. We gotta get his ass in front of the grand jury. Now!"

Pearl didn't hesitate but furiously punched in the telephone number of Michael Feldberg, Norby Walters's attorney.

Moments later he was on the phone with the attorney, almost screaming that the government believed Norby Walters had withheld the contracts of several undergraduates. The contracts were poor photocopies, not originals, the prosecutor complained.

"Somebody's in big trouble," Pearl warned Feldberg. "You tell your client he's got a date next week with the grand jury."

Pearl even suggested that Feldberg himself might have to go before the grand jury. That ignited a spark. The two men argued. Feldberg told Pearl that the "fraud theory" the government was "drumming up" was a nuisance to his client and was a publicity gimmick. By now Pearl was screaming into the telephone.

"It's no theory!" Pearl yelled. "It's a fraud!"

Finally Feldberg told Pearl he would get back to him as soon as he could talk with Walters. The two men didn't exchange good-byes. Randolph felt reassured by the prosecutor's offensive.

Later that day Feldberg got back to Howard Pearl. Yes, the list was incomplete. There were seven or eight more names. Six of them were undergraduates. Walters was very sensitive about their names and did not want the players to lose their eligibility.

"I want everything tomorrow," Pearl said. "I want all the names, and I want the original contracts. And I want Norby Walters or a custodian of those records in that office to be here next Tuesday to tell the grand jury that there has been full compliance. And while he's at it, he can explain how six contracts were withheld."

The next day the records arrived. No longer broken down by "drafts," it was just a list of players, fifty-eight in all. That was seven more than the previous list, though nothing sounded familiar about the first name,

Stefon Adams, who was simply listed as being with the L. A. Raiders, with no college identified.

Then a name jumped out: Cris Carter of Ohio State. A wide receiver, Carter was already receiving publicity as a Heisman Trophy candidate for the 1987 college football season, though opening kickoff was still five months away.

The other new names were Teryl Austin and Charles Gladman of Pittsburgh, Terry Coner and Derrick McKey of Alabama, and James Lott of Texas—six underclassmen in all. But nowhere did it list Michigan State's Lorenzo White, who was perhaps the leading Heisman Trophy candidate for the next football season.

Randolph wondered how many other players had been recruited by the agents and how many were being recruited that spring. Nevertheless, he had to start the meticulous process of going through each player's contract. Meanwhile, Howard Pearl, using the list of players and schools, began issuing subpoenas for the players' eligibility documents. It would be no easy task. Besides the addresses and phone numbers of the thirty-two colleges, Pearl needed current addresses for fifty-one of the players, many of whom had already left school. He hoped Walters's records were still accurate.

Randolph began by looking at a contract that belonged to Pittsburgh's Tony Woods, an All-American linebacker who had already met with the FBI. The contract read: "World Sports and Entertainment, Inc. . . . Uniform Football Representation Agreement."

Initially there were blanks in the first paragraph for the date, year, player's name, and player's residence. Then there was a handwritten notation that the agreement was made on the "2nd day of January, 1987" by and between "Tony Woods" residing at "69 Stengel Ave., Newark, N.J. 07112." The contract was five pages long and covered an extensive amount of representation rights assigned to WSE, including the negotiation of Woods's football contract and all "endorsement, promotional opportunities, and outside business activities."

One clause particularly caught Randolph's attention. By signing the agreement Woods would allow Walters to "endorse Player's name upon and cash checks . . . and retain therefrom all sums owing to WSE." Under "Compensation," the contract stated that Walters would receive six percent—not ten percent as he had understood—of the player's professional football contract. There were other items that jumped out, thanks to what Randolph had read in the newspapers and had discussed with the NFL Players Association. The contract stated that Walters would be paid his percentage based "upon the total value of the contract" and "payable within three days" of signing the contract.

"Total value of the contract shall mean the total of all salaries, signing and other bonuses, and all other cash or cash equivalent compensation to which Player could receive under such contract or series of contracts," the contract read.

What alarmed the NFL Players Association the most was the clause that allowed Norby Walters to collect up front on the "total value" as well as on all bonuses, though only three percent of all NFL contracts were guaranteed. That technically meant that Walters could get his fee right away on an incentive bonus clause (for instance, $25,000 for Pro Bowl selection) even though the player might never achieve that bonus. Not only that, the player also had signed over power of attorney, which would allow Walters to handle and sign all the player's checks. Thus, the player would have no control over how and when the fee was paid. As a kicker, Walters would receive ten percent of all endorsement money.

No wonder the NFLPA had told the newspapers and Randolph that the contracts Walters and Bloom had used for players were "the worst we've ever seen."

On page five of the agreement there were two signatures, those of Norby Walters and Tony Woods. Interestingly, there was another blank line that read, "Parent or guardian if player is under 21 years of age."

Also attached was a two-page promissory note, though the address at the top was different (200 West 51st Street) than the office that Norby Walters now used (1700 Broadway). The left side of the promissory note read: "Amount $2,500." On the right side was a handwritten date: February 10, 1985.

Randolph looked at the representation contract, which was dated January 2, 1986. That was an eleven-month difference between the two dates, just as Tim McGee had told the prosecution team.

On the second page of the promissory note, which also assigned negotiating rights to the agents, was the signature of Tony Woods. Below it, in huge scribbling handwritten letters, were the words, "If Tony Woods does not play professional football, this debt is null and void. Norby Walters."

Randolph started thumbing through the rest of the agreements. All of the contracts were dated January 2 or 3, depending on the year.

"These guys must be supermen," Randolph cracked. "They got everybody signed up on the same day."

He knew better, of course. He knew better because all of the promissory notes had the genuine dates that the players had committed to the agents. Almost all of them were dated the previous spring or summer, with the amounts varying from $2,500 to $5,000. Based on information the FBI had gathered and the *Atlanta Constitution* report, that did not include the monthly payments Walters made to the players.

Some contracts had to be set apart. Three were basketball representation agreements, belonging to Ohio State's Brad Sellers and Alabama's Terry Coner and Derrick McKey. The Alabama players had been signed recently, in January 1987.

"Looks like they were just getting started in the basketball business," Randolph said to Pearl.

ON SUNDAY, April 28, 1987, for the first time ever, George Randolph had a reason to watch the National Football League's annual draft.

Randolph again eased into his La-Z-Boy chair, switched on the television, and grabbed his remote control. As ESPN's broadcast began, Randolph grabbed his roster, the list of thirty-six players who had signed contracts with Norby Walters and Lloyd Bloom. You can't tell the players without a scorecard, Randolph mused to himself. By the numbers alone, this was supposed to have been the biggest draft yet for Walters and Bloom.

Chris Berman, ESPN's host, began by reminding viewers that the Tampa Bay Buccaneers had signed University of Miami quarterback Vinny Testaverde as the draft's number-one pick overall, and NFL Commissioner Pete Rozelle stepped to the microphone to make it official.

"Next up, the Indianapolis Colts," Rozelle told the audience.

A few minutes passed, and then, to nobody's surprise, Alabama linebacker Cornelius Bennett was chosen.

Randolph checked the list. He wondered whether Walters and Bloom had taken a shot at Bennett. He fit the profile of the player they had sought, or at least part of it—he was black, and as far as the government could tell, the agents had not tried to recruit any white player.

"Next up, the Houston Oilers," Rozelle announced.

Testaverde's teammate, Miami fullback Alonzo Highsmith, was the choice of the Oilers. Again, Highsmith was black, but he did not make the Norby Walters honor roll.

Bet they tried, Randolph said to himself.

The Green Bay Packers chose next. A few minutes passed before Rozelle stepped to the microphone.

"The Green Bay Packers select . . . Brent Fullwood, running back, Auburn," the commissioner announced.

Bingo. Randolph knew without even looking that Fullwood had signed with Walters and Bloom. He looked down at his roster, and there was Fullwood, listed number six on the government's copy of the agents' 1987 draft list. Randolph grabbed a pencil and put a check mark by Fullwood's name and scribbled in, *Green Bay Packers, 1st round.*

After a few more picks, Rozelle announced, "The Detroit Lions select . . . Reggie Rogers, defensive end, University of Washington."

Bingo. Rogers was one of the Zucker-Clements clients, and Zucker had told Randolph that Rogers should be one of the top ten picks in the draft.

Before the first round was over, Randolph had quite a few check marks on his list.

Brent Fullwood (number 4, Green Bay Packers), Reggie Rogers (number 7, Detroit Lions), Rod Woodson (number 10, Pittsburgh Steelers), John Clay (number 15, Los Angeles Raiders), Tony Woods (number 18, Seattle Seahawks), Paul Palmer (number 19, Kansas City Chiefs), Terrence Flagler (number 25, San Francisco 49ers), and Mark Ingram (number 28, New York Giants).

That ended the first round. Randolph tallied up his sheet and smiled. Of the twenty-eight players chosen, eight of them had dealt with Walters and Bloom. The NFLPA had explained that most agents considered themselves lucky to get one first-round player, and it's a great day if you have two. By those standards, Walters and Bloom were superstars.

The second round threw out a few more Walters-Bloom names, starting with Atlanta's selection of Terrence Flagler's backfield mate at Clemson, Kenny Flowers.

The ESPN airtime was winding down when Randolph's attention was suddenly pulled back to the screen.

"The Chicago Bears select . . . Ronald Morris, wide receiver, SMU."

The FBI agent almost jumped out of his chair. Of all things, his hometown team had selected Ron Morris, who was now one of the main characters in the Walters-Bloom case. Randolph's mind started spinning. Morris had already been named in the *New York Times* and in the *Atlanta Constitution* as one of the players who had been threatened, though the reports had varied as to whether Walters and Bloom had threatened to break Morris's legs or hands.

Randolph decided it was good that the Bears had chosen Morris. That would make it logistically easier to communicate with him since he figured to be a primary witness. But wait. Randolph started thinking about the publicity again. Most football players had big egos, and he worried that Morris, if questioned about Walters and Bloom, would boast that nobody could scare him. That kind of public comment could be damaging to an extortion charge. Still, Morris sounded scared on the tape, and a jury would detect that.

But, just to be safe, Randolph got on the telephone to the Bears. He asked the switchboard operator who was in charge of player personnel. Either that, or he needed to speak with Mike Ditka. The operator asked Randolph what he wanted, and he finally identified himself as an FBI special agent. She explained that Bill Tobin was in charge of player personnel and the team's draft. A few minutes passed as Randolph was put on hold. Finally a male voice answered: Bill Tobin. The FBI agent explained to Tobin that there was a "sensitive" case and that Morris had been one of the players threatened with bodily harm. But the thoughts of Tim McGee, a smallish receiver, saying that he didn't take Lloyd Bloom seriously struck Randolph.

"The last thing I need is this big, tough football player yapping to the press about how he wasn't scared of nobody," said Randolph. "So can you tell him to keep his mouth shut about this?"

Tobin agreed and explained that the club probably would be flying Morris into town that night or the next day.

The second round of the draft ended with the Giants again selecting from the Walters-Bloom list: Florida defensive back Adrian White. That made it eleven players, to the best of Randolph's knowledge, in the first two rounds. He would check the newspapers in a day or so to get the full tally.

Other players, in fact, were sprinkled throughout the draft. Jerry Ball, the SMU nose tackle, was selected high in the third round by the Detroit Lions. But a few players were shut out, particularly Doug Dubose, whose major knee injury in the 1986 preseason had buried Nebraska's Heisman Trophy campaign for the tailback.

By the government's count, about thirty of the thirty-six players landed on NFL clubs that spring of 1987.

On Monday night, April 29, Randolph was watching the local television news when the announcer plugged the upcoming sports segment before the commercial break: "Meet the Bears' top draft picks, right after this message."

Randolph's heart beat a little faster. He moved his La-Z-Boy forward and sat on the edge of the cushion. When the commercial ended, the sportscaster began by talking about the Bears' first draft pick, Michigan quarterback Jim Harbaugh. It had stirred up a controversy in town because everybody assumed that Jim McMahon was going to be the man for a long time. Then it was mentioned that the Bears also had gotten a receiver to catch passes for McMahon and Harbaugh. Suddenly there was footage of Ron Morris catching a touchdown pass for SMU, and then there was Morris surrounded by microphones at the Bears camp earlier that day. Sure enough, the subject came up.

"Can you tell us about these threats you reportedly received?" somebody asked the SMU player.

Randolph held his breath as Morris opened his mouth.

"No comment."

Randolph exhaled and clenched his fist. Tobin and Morris had come through.

RANDOLPH FLIPPED through the Western Union telegraphic money orders. Norby Walters had major accounts with two such sources, Western Union and U. S. Funds Express. And if it wasn't Norby Walters on the "activity list" as the sender of wire transfers, it was Irene Walters. Must be his wife, the FBI agent figured, taking note.

Randolph soon began studying the Western Union money orders made out to Ronnie Harmon, the former Iowa running back and a first-round draft choice of the Buffalo Bills in 1986.

There was $250 on April 8, 1985, almost one month after the Iowa running back had signed a contract with Walters. On May 3, a $200 money order. Eleven days later Harmon received another $600. Then came $500 on June 24, followed by another $500 the very next day.

"The guy was burning the cash pretty fast," Randolph said. "As fast as Uncle Norby could send it."

There was no record of a July payment, but on August 3, Walters wired Harmon $250. One month later, another $250. Then $250 more on October 2, November 4, December 2, December 6, and December 16.

In addition to the $2,500 Harmon received when he signed a deal with Walters on March 9, Randolph accounted for a little more than $6,000 in wire transfers. If the government could prove its fraud case, it seemed to Randolph that wire fraud was a slam-dunk for the government.

There were other expenses attached to Harmon: several trips to New York, three, four, five trips to Los Angeles, a total of $12,157 in travel expenses, a $2,000 cash advance, another $1,500 for an unexplained purpose. Concert tickets were marked on the account. There was $350 spent on a "Kevin Harmon." Most of the expenses came during the summer of 1985 and during Ronnie Harmon's senior season at Iowa, in which the Buckeyes won the 1985 Big Ten championship.

Howard Pearl had a succinct reaction to the money dropped on Harmon.

"Pigs, that's what they are," the Assistant U. S. Attorney said.

"Unfuckingbelievable," muttered Randolph.

They didn't know who they were more disgusted with, Norby Walters or Ronnie Harmon.

Randolph moved on to scanning the invoices from the travel agency that serviced Norby Walters Associates and World Sports and Entertainment, Inc. He couldn't believe the activity. Dallas; Seattle; Atlanta; Los Angeles; Columbia, South Carolina; Miami; Orlando; Ann Arbor; Columbus; Houston; Louisville; Washington, D.C.; Pittsburgh; Nashville; Memphis; Omaha; South Bend; St. Louis; Lafayette, Indiana; San Francisco; Sacramento; New Orleans . . . over and over and over again. Randolph estimated that Walters and Bloom must have traveled more than three hundred times during the past two years. The travel expenses alone, including plane rides, car rentals, hotel bills, entertainment, and meals, had to be staggering.

Randolph knew these records were valuable clues, but he was overwhelmed by the prospect of sorting everything out. He needed help. He called his boss, Bob Walsh, explained his dilemma, and asked if he could get Diane Benson—a young, sharp FBI agent—assigned to the Walters-Bloom case. Walsh didn't hesitate to approve.

Randolph called Benson and briefly explained the case. She would meet him at the federal building. Meanwhile, Randolph went back to examining the travel records. Something caught his eye, then leaped at him. He checked the travel agency's invoice again to make sure.

On March 17, one day after Kathy Clements was beaten by the masked intruder, Norby Walters had taken a late-night flight out of New York to Chicago. His return flight to New York was early the next morning, which meant Walters spent twelve hours in Chicago. Twelve hours for what? Randolph's mind started working: What if Norby Walters made a cash-and-carry visit for services rendered? Randolph called

Tony Valukas and Howard Pearl to tell them of his discovery and suspicion. They agreed that it would be a critical piece of evidence if Randolph could ever find the man responsible for the beating.

As the hair began to rise on the back of Randolph's neck, the telephone rang. It was Joe Masterson, the FBI special agent from Dallas.

"Right now it looks as if the Jeff Atkins shooting was a drug deal," Masterson told Randolph. "No connection right now." Still, it was drugs. Randolph wondered how many of the Walters-Bloom clients had a problem with cocaine.

The phone rang again. It was another special agent, Richard Tofani, calling from New York. He explained that all the FBI agents in New York worked in units assigned to monitor the five crime families. Randolph gripped the telephone a little tighter.

"Norby Walters," Tofani explained, "has a pretty heavy connection to the Colombo family."

Two names in particular stuck to Walters: Sonny and Michael Franzese, Randolph was told.

"Big-timers."

"How big?"

"Well, both guys are in jail," said Tofani. "But both are capos."

Randolph knew that meant the Franzeses were Mafia captains, one bullet away from Godfather status. His adrenaline started pumping furiously.

Sonny Franzese was Michael's father, Tofani explained. A very vicious man, Sonny would have been the boss of the Colombo family if he hadn't gotten nailed for conspiracy. Michael was young, about thirty-five or thirty-six, but he was the brightest of the new wave of La Cosa Nostra.

"Michael was a big moneymaker for the mob," said Tofani. Michael Franzese had just begun a prison term for racketeering.

Randolph hung up the phone and almost sprinted down the hall to Valukas's office.

5

Tony Valukas's eyes grew wide behind his wire-rimmed glasses as George Randolph told him that their boy, Norby Walters, had a connection to Sonny and Michael Franzese of the Colombo crime family in New York.

"How much of a connection?" Valukas asked.

"This agent in New York says it could be pretty heavy," said Randolph. "Hell, with the entertainment stuff, Walters had to be dirty. I'm telling you, it's O.C."

Both men were pacing the room. Their minds raced, then they remembered to call Howard Pearl to break the news to him.

"This case is absolutely a major priority," Valukas told the men. "Let's proceed. No turning back now."

First things first. Where were Sonny and Michael Franzese imprisoned? It took one phone call to find out that John "Sonny" Franzese was locked up at the federal penitentiary in Petersburg, Virginia, and Michael Franzese had recently settled into the federal prison at Terminal Island in Los Angeles. Valukas would make calls to his connections in the U. S. Justice Department, which Randolph knew were pretty powerful. Pearl would begin getting the evidence ready for the federal grand jury. If the case's sense of urgency had slipped temporarily because of the lack of a connection between Walters and the Jeff Atkins shooting, it had now risen to a new level.

The picture that was emerging was quite dramatic. Norby Walters, the "agent to the stars" in the world of black entertainment, was connected to a pair of Mafia captains. Now he was crossing over to sports. In just two years he and his young punk partner, Lloyd Bloom, had infiltrated universities across the country and signed football players at an incred-

71

ible rate. There was cash. Always cash. They had paid a lot of money to these players.

And there were threats. Randolph suddenly remembered that Ron Morris had told Dallas FBI Special Agent Joe Masterson that Bloom had said the money was coming from "bigger backers from Los Angeles." Michael Franzese was in Los Angeles now. It didn't matter that he was in prison. Mafia bosses often ran their business from behind bars. Broken legs, broken hands, those are all Mafia methods of intimidation, if a bit primitive by 1987 standards. Still, Lloyd Bloom was primitive, based on the tapes Randolph had heard.

Randolph had to learn more about the beating. He had to find the man who did it. He had already sent out feelers to his underground sources, people who had been arrested by the FBI. When a source had something, he'd get a phone call to his beeper with a secret code letting him know who was calling. Then he would meet the source in a place that was safe for both the source and himself. It might be a bar, a restaurant, a hotel, or a parking lot.

The problem was that there was so much paperwork to be done. The government still thought its best chance to solve the Clements beating was to dig deeper into the Walters operation, starting with the athletes.

Randolph worked all day and night, munching on sandwiches delivered in the afternoon. He sent priority teletypes to the FBI offices in Virginia and Los Angeles, asking the bureau to question Sonny and Michael Franzese about anything and everything regarding their association with a New York agent named Norby Walters. Randolph wanted to go himself, but the FBI had its red tape. It would be a day or two before anybody would get back to him. There were also no guarantees that either Franzese would be willing to talk about Walters.

Early the next afternoon word came back from Los Angeles. They could forget about talking to Michael Franzese. No explanation, just forget it. Randolph and Pearl called the Los Angeles bureau wanting to know if any attempt would be made to talk with Michael Franzese. No, forget it. It's a wasted lead, they were told. Both the FBI agent and the prosecutor were deflated. And Randolph was angry that nobody would even try.

With Sonny Franzese, it was the same. At least the bureau had made contact with Sonny, but he had no interest in talking to anybody. There was nothing to compel either Franzese to cooperate. A dead end was a dead end.

But Randolph still wanted to know more about the men. He called

New York and asked if somebody would help him out with Sonny and Michael Franzese. Again he was told that was impossible. He called Los Angeles and got the same answer. Nobody in the bureau wanted to step forward. Finally Randolph called an acquaintance in Los Angeles, an agent named John O'Neill, and asked if he would check into Michael Franzese for him. O'Neill was working a case but told Randolph he'd give it a shot.

There was plenty of other work piling up, thanks to dozens of leads coming in from players who were finally being rounded up in different parts of the country. Pearl was working on subpoenas for players to come to Chicago to meet with the prosecution team and perhaps to go in front of the grand jury. First they needed to meet with each player individually, review their interviews with the FBI, and organize files for each one of them, based on the records they had received from Norby Walters and the records they would receive from the universities.

Then word came from Pittsburgh. Tony Woods, the Pitt All-American linebacker, had made his own tape recording of a "threatening" telephone conversation he had with Walters and Bloom and another man named Terry Bolar. Clearly the players had been suspicious of Walters and Bloom.

Randolph couldn't believe his luck. People don't make tapes unless they feel they have a cause, he had learned in other criminal cases. Ron Morris obviously had a reason. Now Tony Woods had felt compelled. According to the FBI report, this ninety-minute-or-so tape was made in the office of Woods's insurance agent, Eric Metz, after Woods had informed Walters and Bloom that he was leaving them for Arizona sports agent Bruce Allen, son of the legendary football coach George Allen. The day before the conversation was taped, Bloom allegedly had threatened Woods that they would expose the player for being on the take while playing at Pitt. Woods had been drafted in the first round the previous week by the Seattle Seahawks. Their conversation did not have a specific date attached, but it apparently had taken place in February or March.

Once again Randolph put on a pair of headphones and pushed the play button on the tape machine. From the very start Randolph could sense that Bloom was very angry at Woods. He was going right to the player's heart, threatening to expose his younger brother, Darryl Woods, a sophomore at the University of Pittsburgh.

BLOOM: Norby says I have to do what I have to do now.

Randolph could feel himself getting angry.

BLOOM: Now Norby's talking about . . . because he got a plane ticket that your brother once came in with you. And your brother's name, he wants to give that to the NCAA so your brother can't play football for the next three years. So I think you better talk to Norby and, ya know, just go over things with him because he don't kid.

To Randolph, Bloom sounded serious and threatening. As Bloom spoke, Randolph wrote on his notepad that Norby *don't kid.*

BLOOM: Okay, he does not care, 'cause he wants to bring down the Pitt program on probation because . . . you took money all year . . . 'cause the NCAA has nothing to do with us.

Bloom turned the telephone over to Terry Bolar, who had been hired by Norby Walters to "put out fires." Bolar was black and attempted to use his race to convince players to stay with Uncle Norby.

BOLAR: What's happening, Tony?

WOODS: What's up?

BOLAR: Hey, how's everything?

WOODS: All right.

BOLAR: Don't be down there being nervous, dude.

WOODS: Huh?

BOLAR: Don't be down there, being nervous shit.

WOODS: No, I'm not.

BOLAR: I'm telling the honest-to-God truth, and I'm always gonna shoot straight with you, man.

WOODS: Mm hmm.

BOLAR: Ya know, I'm a brother just like you are.

WOODS: Mm hmm.

BOLAR: Ya know, but the thing, what I'm trying to tell you is, man, I don't want to see no brother get fucked.

WOODS: Uh huh.

BOLAR: Ya know, because, hey, we already had to struggle too long and too hard as it is.

WOODS: Uh huh.

BOLAR: Ya know . . . and then there goes your career flashing right in your eyes, and then you're gonna have it turned around, and pay more than one agent at the end . . . and also look bad as an individual for signing early with an agent . . . accepting money . . . helping your family.

WOODS: Mm hmm.

BOLAR: True enough, Bruce Allen has told you all these things. He knows all these different players, general managers. He got this kinda pull, he got this kinda pull. . . . Bruce Allen can't do a goddamn thing for you. . . . Ya know, I'm just shooting straight with you, man, 'cause I'm real. And, ah, another thing about Bruce is, Bruce is gonna tell you everything you wanna hear up until the time for him to negotiate your contract and get his money.

WOODS: Mm hmm.

BOLAR: Ya know, and being you just another nigger to him. . . . I understand a lot of agents probably called you at the time they found out you had signed with Norby.

WOODS: Mm hmm.

BOLAR: Start dogging the man up. . . . "Norby's in the Mafia, Norby sells cocaine."

Randolph slammed the stop button and rewound the tape. He listened again to Bolar's throwing out the rumors about the Mafia and cocaine. He marked down the number on the tape machine button in case he wanted to fast-forward to it at another time. He started thinking about Sonny and Michael Franzese. How heavy are these guys? Who are these guys? He wanted to know now.

BOLAR: . . . "Norby's in the Mafia."

WOODS: Oh yeah.

Wait. Woods responded differently. He didn't say "Mm hmm" or "Uh huh." After Bolar mentioned the Mafia, Woods said, "Oh yeah." So Woods must have heard something. The FBI agent made a note.

BOLAR: "You go with Norby Walters, you won't be drafted as high" . . . because, ah, NFL people think that you, being associated with him, might be tied up with some of the things that he's doing.

Very interesting, Randolph thought.

BOLAR: I'm not here trying to tell you nothing wrong, man. I'm shooting straight with you 'cause I'm your brother. . . . Ya know, I don't want to see you get fucked around because you don't deserve to get fucked around. But Norby, at the same time, ain't gonna let hisself get fucked around.

WOODS: Mm hmm.

BOLAR: Because this man is a businessman, and it ain't the fact that he's threatening you or nothin', it's just the fact that he's hurt for the thing that he felt like he done for you. I feel like if I would've been with Norby at the time he signed you, you'd still be here. Because all of this negative shit, I would've been able to help you overcome that shit, because being what it was . . .

WOODS: Mm hmm.

BOLAR: Regardless, brother to brother, or whatever color, I'm just shooting straight with ya. . . . Like I say, you and Norby, that decision was made between you and Norby. You know you can talk to him about what's happening.

Norby Walters was soon on the telephone.

WALTERS: Hey, smiling man from BLS country.

Stop. Randolph still had trouble with this jive act. What the hell was a "smiling man from BLS country"? Randolph broke for a cup of coffee. He knew there was more jive than he could take. Back to the tape machine, the coffee smelling strong but real, the FBI agent continued reviewing the tape of Tony Woods and Norby Walters.

Woods was laughing. One thing about it, Norby Walters could always make these guys laugh. He had appeal. He had an act.

WALTERS: Home boy.

WOODS: Uh huh.

WALTERS: Home boy.

WOODS: What's up?

WALTERS: Rick James been asking about you.

WOODS: Who's . . . oh, yeah.

WALTERS: Yeah.

Randolph thought about the name, Rick James. Oh, yeah, he was one of Walters's entertainers. A singer. Tony Woods must have met Rick James.

If Tony Woods was starting to relax, Walters snapped him back to reality.

WALTERS: I have to take a very hard look at my situation.

WOODS: Mm hmm.

WALTERS: And then . . . what happened is that a couple of the cats in the family, like yourself . . . and a few others . . . made that kind of choice to leave me. Okay?

WOODS: Mm hmm.

WALTERS: I have to say that you were the first one. And I think that it created a trigger effect on a number of other minds that if Tony Woods, a New York cat, could leave Norby Walters . . . ya know what I mean?

WOODS: Mm hmm.

WALTERS: All the others fell for the same type of okeydoke.

WOODS: Mm hmm.

Then Norby Walters had a proposal for Tony Woods if he would stay on as a client.

WALTERS: I will take zero commission. I will take zero commission, and I will give you one hundred thousand dollars. I will make an agreement that if you get drafted lower than the first round, I will take zero commission and give you one hundred thousand dollars.

WOODS: Hmmm.

WALTERS: How do you like that?

WOODS: Huh . . .

WALTERS: You're going in the first round, my bro—

Woods laughed. Randolph was shaking his head in disgust.

WALTERS: Am I ballsy when I say that?

WOODS: Yeah.

WALTERS: That's a big set of New York balls, right?

WOODS: Yeah.

A big set of New York balls. A Chicago jury is gonna love that.

WALTERS: The point of it is, man, is that why should I be penalized? I'm a guy who did the right thing every step of the way.

WOODS: Mm hmm.

Walters went on reasoning with Woods and talking about himself, claiming he did $50 million to $100 million annually in business.

WALTERS: You don't hear any shit about him fuckin' anybody. The man is the biggest in fuckin' show business. He represents the superstars. . . . Now I'm coming into the football world.

Yes, he has crossed over to sports. Randolph kept thinking about Sonny and Michael Franzese.

WALTERS: You say, "Damn, if he can do for me in football what the fuck he's done for them other motherfuckers, man" . . . well, that's the reason that you gave me the job to begin with. . . . Listen, that was my pitch, wasn't it?

WOODS: Mm hmm.

WALTERS: So what am I supposed to do, Tony? What I gotta do is protect my ass to the highest level.

WOODS: Mm hmm.

WALTERS: Now, ya know, I don't wanna, I don't wanna be . . . I don't wanna be a rat. I don't want to create problems with Pittsburgh. I don't want to create problems with the Woods family. I don't want to.

WOODS: Mm hmm.

WALTERS: But . . . ah, the point is, what am I supposed to do? Am I gonna sit there like I'm a jerkoff? The last thing I am, Tony Woods, is a fifty-five-year-old jerkoff?

(Silence.)

WALTERS: Ya know, I've been working too hard, too long. . . . I've made too much money. I have too big of a reputation in this world for me to allow myself . . . having done the right thing.

WOODS: Uh huh.

WALTERS: Every step of the way with you, to be put in the position of where I'll have to walk away. . . .

There was bitter anger in the agent's voice.

WALTERS: So what I believe is, what we should do is allow me to represent you and tell Mr. Bruce Allen, "Bruce, I think I've redecided. Let me go represent Norby because I'm gonna have such headaches, Bruce." Say, "Bruce, you're a friend of mine, you were guiding me right. . . . What I don't need right now is to go into a major legal law battle with Norby Walters. This guy is gonna spend money 'cause he's got the bucks, and he's gonna go for it. I'm gonna wind up in a major lawsuit while I'm trying to think about playing football. This guy's gonna have me doing interrogations, or bringing me to New York every other week. He's gonna fuck with my mind, and it's gonna be a drag. I can get so fucked up. He's gonna wind up bringing the school into it. . . . He's gonna wind up bringing my brother into it. . . . He's gonna wind up bringing my family into it."

The intimidation Walters was laying on Woods appeared to Randolph to be malicious. There was a raspy, ominous tone to the words coming out of Norby Walters's mouth. This was Uncle Nasty. This is how mob guys really leverage people. They don't go around threatening to break legs every day. The punks do that. The federal laws addressed a certain kind of extortion—economic harm. In Randolph's mind this could be an extortionate act. He continued to listen to the agent deliver this would-be speech for Woods, who was silent now.

WALTERS: "It's gonna be so goddamn embarrassing for me, Bruce Allen, for me and my family, and my school, and it just doesn't make sense . . . since I don't think Norby Walters is a fuck-up businessman to begin with. The only reason I left was because I thought maybe I won't get high on the draft. But now I know I'm going in the first round. There's no question."

WOODS: Mm hmm.

WALTERS: So what I'm saying to you is that I feel that . . . that you have to do right now . . . you have no allegiance to Bruce Allen. . . . Hey, I don't disrespect him, by the way.

WOODS: Mm hmm.

WALTERS: But you have no allegiance to him. . . . This is your life on the line.

Randolph brought the tape to a slamming halt. He rewound it briefly.

WALTERS: . . . This is your life on the line.

The FBI agent wanted to hear it again, that bitter, raspy voice: "This is your life on the line." Walters sounded deadly serious. Was it a death threat? No. The agent wanted to make it clear to Tony Woods that his life would be ruined unless he folded. This was dirty business, and Randolph kept thinking about Sonny and Michael Franzese. Who are these guys? How powerful are they? He restarted the machine.

WALTERS: This is your reputation, this is your family, this is your school, this is everything that you've done for all these years on the line right now. Bruce Allen is gonna jeopardize that for you by keeping you in that frame of mind. . . . You know something? The stakes are too high here.

WOODS: Mm hmm.

WALTERS: "I can't afford to have Norby Walters walk into court and keep bringing me back into court, and stand up and show documents that, in fact, I signed early with him."

WOODS: Hm mmm.

WALTERS: "Because if he does that, he's gonna fuck up my whole school. I won't be able to go back to Pittsburgh. I'm gonna be like I'm a shit. My family's gonna be shit, my brother will be thrown out of school. . . . Everything is gonna get fucked up. . . . Bruce, I showed you that I wanted to be with you, but the stakes for my life are too high."

WOODS: Mm hmm.

WALTERS: I'm talking about Tony Woods. I'm talking about you. I'm talking about your reputation. I'm talking about having to spend all these dollars, man, to battle me. Because I have to brag to you . . . you know I've been making it for a long time.

WOODS: Mm hmm.

WALTERS: So I don't have to brag to you. I don't have to say, "Hey, man, I got all this fuckin' money." Let's just say I'm a businessman who's gonna spend whatever dollars it takes over the next year or two, okay? And I will, ya know what I mean? Just, just, just rake it up hard, man, because I must protect my position. Because I'll tell you why. Because if Tony Woods can leave me without honoring a bona fide contract. And by the way . . . we discussed this now with a lot of different heavy litigators here, right in New York. My son is a lawyer with the biggest corporate law firm in New York.

WOODS: Mm hmm.

WALTERS: Two of his litigators came down and sat with four of our litigators over at Shea and Gould and unanimously said this is contract law. There is no way, absolutely zero way they can win. We have to win. Shea and Gould, Lonny Trost, is my first cousin. He's a major partner over there. Everybody has said there's no way. So what's gonna happen is that we're gonna go to a lawsuit. You'll spend fifteen or twenty or twenty-five thousand dollars in fees. In the final analysis you'll lose. You'll have to pay me my fees, my six percent commission. And remember, I'm suing you for half a million dollars, too.

WOODS: Mm hmm.

WALTERS: And I don't know what the judge will award me but, baby, you'll never know what the judge will do. Maybe they'll give me one dollar, maybe he gives me half a million. 'Cause if I can prove in court that since you left me, six other players left me, and I'm gonna lay it at the doorstep, and I'm gonna put the blame at the foot of Tony Woods.

WOODS: Mm hmm.

WALTERS: Because I have to do that because I'm trying to prove my case very hard, and I'm saying I'm suing you for half a million dollars' worth of damages because of the commissions which I could lose on other people. So I'm playing very hardball here.

By now that should have been clear to Woods. But Randolph didn't believe this was just a conversation about a lawsuit. This was a man hammering hard, walking the dangerous edge with a sledgehammer, a man wanting to regain control. Norby Walters was no longer a man jive-shucking. He was, in his own words, playing hardball.

WALTERS: This is my life on the line. . . . Now it is your life.

The voice was hard and raspy, sizzling over the tape, burning Randolph's ears. He had to hear it again just as Norby Walters felt he had to say it again.

WALTERS: This is my life on the line. . . . Now it is your life. To me, I say you have to examine it because it is your life, your reputation, your business, your family, your brother, your school. . . . Everything is gonna be tainted and tainted bad. It's gonna be terrible for you.

WOODS: Mm hmm.

WALTERS: The point is, man, Norby Walters and Lloyd Bloom are businessmen who have done the right thing . . . to bring shame and all kinds of terrible shit because as we go into court, this stuff's gonna come out and your brother, too. I mean, it was like Lloyd said . . . I mean, bro, I have to say everything, man, okay? That your brother took trips to New York. . . . He's gonna lose his eligibility, your school is going to go on probation, Mom and Dad are gonna be brought into it . . . because I have checks made out to them.

Randolph scribbled away on his legal pad. Clearly Walters worked hard on parents. It was a clever hook. Certainly most of the players they recruited came from low-income households where money would be too tempting. There was no way a son could turn that down, to help his parents. It was a perfect hook. Randolph wanted to find the checks to Woods's parents that Walters was talking about.

WALTERS: They were in full knowledge and knowing everything. So it isn't that they could claim unknowledge.

Unknowledge? Unknowledge? Randolph almost gagged on his coffee. This jag-off has his own language.

WALTERS: They accepted money. I sent money to them, so they can never get up in court and say, no, I didn't. No, no, they accepted money . . . three thousand dollars on one time, three thousand dollars on another time, and, and, and all this shit's gonna come out in court. Now what are you gonna win by this? Nothing.

WOODS: Look, Norb, right now I have to leave. I have to work out, but—

WALTERS: All right, babe.

WOODS: I'll get back.

WALTERS: Call me later.

WOODS: Okay.

WALTERS: I'll be here.

WOODS: All right.

WALTERS: Okay, man.

WOODS: Bye-bye.

The dial tone played in Randolph's headphones before he realized the ninety-minute conversation was over. The FBI agent was stunned. There were no physical threats on this tape, but Norby Walters had just laid a heavy trip on Tony Woods's head. The pressure on Woods seemed unbearable. Woods must have lost some sleep over this. Otherwise, he wasn't human.

"This is my life on the line. . . . Now it's your life on the line." Randolph would never forget those words. He had to learn more about Norby Walters, about any connections to Sonny Franzese, Michael Franzese, and the Colombo family.

6

STAYING ON top of the mounting paperwork remained a priority. FBI agent Diane Benson spent much of her time organizing files. She meticulously charted each player's participation in the Walters-Bloom scheme. Starting with the date he signed, she traced the dates of the wire transfers, entertainment trips, and the total debt each player had accrued.

It was a job Randolph had started, and he continued to help with it since he was getting no other help from the bureau. He and he alone had to pursue more than three hundred leads, a number that seemed to multiply each week. He would arrive at the office, usually by 7 A.M., prioritize his leads, and initiate the necessary paperwork.

For every player there must have been six leads to pursue. Some players provided a dozen or more leads, such as Tim McGee's statement about the female employee who had warned him of Uncle Norby's dark side. Every lead demanded that Randolph pursue it himself by telephone or that he send out teletypes specifying his needs, and going through the merciless process of waiting for somebody in the bureau to get back to him. Then he'd see that a player in Texas said something about a teammate, but that teammate already had been questioned by the FBI. So out went more phone calls, more teletypes, more waiting, more prodding, more leads. It was a vicious cycle.

Once in a while he couldn't figure out what his fellow agents in the field were doing. One day Randolph received a report saying that Magic Johnson had been questioned about Norby Walters because an FBI agent in Los Angeles had been told that one of Walters's players may have been Magic's guest at a Lakers game.

When the phone stopped ringing for the day, Randolph spent two or three hours every night, from about seven to ten, typing up the questions that remained unanswered and slipping those questions into each player's file. The files were constantly being updated.

There were loose ends and dead ends. William Harris, the former All-American tight end who had taken more than $30,000 from Walters and Bloom, was kicked out of school at Texas and enrolled at Bishop College in Dallas. Bishop College ended its football program after the 1986 season, and school officials had either destroyed or lost the eligibility forms Harris had signed. It seemed that some players had disappeared, so Randolph had to track down the NFL camp each player had gone to, and the chase was on.

That work drove Randolph nuts, but it had to be done since the players were the government's path to the organized crime connection. Finding that connection rested on Randolph's ability to uncover the exact relationship between Norby Walters and Sonny and Michael Franzese, and trying to find a break, if any, on the Kathy Clements beating.

"We absolutely knew that for us to get to the Clements beating and all the other stuff, it was going to take some time, and the players were going to give us that time and eventually the hook," Howard Pearl recalls.

Nevertheless, Randolph believed that the evidence of extortion and the promise of the Franzese connection could keep Valukas's support, and he was right.

Valukas had confidence in Randolph's and Pearl's ability to put together a case. Even if the mail fraud theory with the colleges as victims was a little shaky, Valukas stressed to Pearl and Randolph that it was an essential hook if the Chicago office was going to get a chance to expose a legitimate case of organized crime.

Every case has its own legal strategy, and it was essential now to establish that the Northern District of Illinois had jurisdiction to prosecute the case. Because the Kathy Clements beating might remain unsolved, the government needed to establish its mail fraud theory within the Big Ten Conference. Tony Valukas and Howard Pearl reasoned that if they established jurisdiction, the racketeering laws would allow them to include other selected colleges as well as the suspected extortion activity, and anything else Randolph's organized crime work uncovered.

Valukas and Pearl knew the federal mail fraud statute well; it outlawed the use of United States mails in furtherance of a fraudulent scheme. A young Chicago prosecutor, Matthias Lydon, had almost single-handedly broadened the use of the mail fraud statute back in the early 1970s when he successfully tried a case that brought a conviction based on an "intangible rights" theory. That theory ensured a basic legal right to honesty in dealings between individuals and corporations, regardless of whether a person or company was defrauded of actual money or property. There was no such thing as "no harm, no foul." If there was a foul, you were going to pay for it. The subsequent court rulings that upheld the conviction eventually resulted in numerous mail fraud convictions across the nation.

Randolph didn't care about the "intangibility" of the mail fraud statute. As far as he was concerned, this was a real fraud, and conversations, with Big Ten officials at least, led him to believe that many more athletic programs were clean than dirty. To get Norby Walters, the Franzeses, and the Colombo family, they needed to establish jurisdiction. They needed the mail fraud counts. They needed the Big Ten Conference.

But Valukas and Pearl had a general understanding that college athletics was riddled with corruption. They would have to be precise and careful in presenting this fraud case. They decided to use Ronnie Harmon's records as a test case. Pearl retrieved the records supplied by the University of Iowa via the subpoena. There was an NCAA student-athlete statement that Harmon had signed as well as a financial aid affidavit, a Big Ten statement of eligibility, a Big Ten statement of financial report, and the university's certified eligibility list for the 1985 football season. There was also an NCAA Championship certification of eligibility list submitted for Harmon's participation in the Rose Bowl.

Then Valukas, Pearl, and Randolph got Harmon's contracts, promissory notes, and other records of financial favors received from Norby Walters.

Harmon's promissory note for the initial $2,500 was signed on March 10, 1985, the spring of his junior year at Iowa. Thereafter he received monthly payments.

Harmon's student-athlete statement was dated August 25, 1985. On that statement Harmon certified that he "was not aware of any violations" involving himself. On that statement alone, Harmon had fraudulently stated he was eligible when in fact he knew he was not.

There was no way Harmon could claim "unknowledge," as Walters might put it, because on his Big Ten statement of eligibility he specifically wrote "No" in response to the following question: "Have you ever signed a professional athletic contract, or been represented by an agent?"

Harmon also falsely stated on his financial aid applications that he had not received any money or loans from outside sources. The financial aid statement was notarized, and Harmon had sworn in an oath that his statements were true.

Harmon made similar false statements for his Rose Bowl participation.

In all instances every member of the Iowa athletic department signed the certification forms, which were then approved by a faculty representative. The University of Iowa subsequently mailed the certification forms to the Big Ten Conference, which reviewed the papers and then mailed them to the NCAA. They used the United States mails.

Harmon's scholarship that year was worth $6,242.41. He also received $900 in a Pell Grant stipend, which was government money used for needy students. That was real money, real property, the government reasoned. Harmon committed a fraud. He not only defrauded the university, he caused every member of the athletic department to participate in the fraud.

How did that involve Norby Walters and Lloyd Bloom? Clearly, the agents knew that the players should have been ineligible to play and accept their scholarship benefits. They would have thereby induced the fraudulent act. Norby Walters would have been in the clear if they had announced to the world that "Ronnie Harmon just signed a contract with me." But Norby Walters went to extremes to conceal the arrangement, hiding the contracts in the company vault. Withholding from the government the contracts of the underclassmen was an acknowledgment by Walters that he knew this arrangement had to remain a secret. And thanks to the Western Union transfers as well as the telephone conversations, Walters may have also committed wire fraud, the government reasoned.

"So we can prosecute Walters and Bloom for the fraud," said Randolph.

In theory, at least.

"The players, too," Valukas replied. "The players have to be held accountable, or else it won't work. They're culpable, too."

Pearl sided more with Randolph than Valukas.

"We have to have victims," the FBI agent said. "You just can't make the school the victim. I mean, these jag-offs targeted all these black players. Most of their families don't have a penny to their name. They were victims, too."

"If we're going through with this," Valukas said, "we're going to prosecute them as coconspirators."

Pearl did point out that many of the players were "pigs" with the money. Ronnie Harmon and his $54,000. John Clay, $32,000. Paul Palmer, $30,000. Rod Woodson, $21,000. FBI agent Diane Benson was still compiling the figures, but a conservative estimate was that Walters and Bloom had dropped about $800,000 on the fifty-eight players over the two-year span. That didn't count travel expenses.

"We'll definitely prosecute the players on the biggest take," said Valukas.

"Then how are we going to get witnesses?" asked Randolph. "I mean, these guys are going to get lawyers. Their lawyers aren't going to let them cooperate if we're prosecuting all of them."

"It's no different than any other kind of plea bargaining that goes on in criminal cases," said Valukas. "If the players want to cut a deal, they're going to have to cooperate and testify. Otherwise, they're going to jail, and they can forget their football careers and all the money they think they're going to make. Don't you think that will get their attention?"

Randolph and Pearl laughed. "Oh yeah," they said almost in unison.

"Besides," said Valukas, "how many of these players do you think actually reported their earnings from Uncle Norby to Uncle Sam?"

The government was prepared to introduce the case to a federal grand jury. In May 1987 a special grand jury consisting of twenty-four men and women was convened; it would meet every Tuesday to hear the evidence for this case. A foreman was selected, and at least nineteen of the twenty-four jurors needed to be present to hear the testimony and weigh the evidence.

Howard Pearl directed the entire grand jury investigation while reporting to Valukas.

Federal grand jury proceedings are secret by law, and any breach of this secrecy—testimony, in particular—was subject to criminal prosecution. This included prosecutors, FBI agents, lawyers, anybody.

The grand jury procedure is less formal than a federal trial. The jurors themselves are allowed to question witnesses. Though generally the grand jury ultimately hands down an indictment when the U. S. Attorney asks for it, there have been occasions when a grand jury has refused. When a grand jury does vote to indict, the foreman and the U. S. Attorney must each sign the indictment.

The subpoena powers of a federal grand jury provide the government with broad access. Consequently, federal cases involving organized crime seldom hand down indictments quickly, because those subpoena powers are narrowed after the indictment.

Valukas carefully considered his strategy regarding the grand jury because the Walters-Bloom case was generating a lot of publicity. This was not usually a good sign for a grand jury investigation because of the potential for leaks, especially with the large number of witnesses that would be brought to Chicago. Consequently, Valukas preferred a fairly swift investigation, despite knowing that Randolph needed time to pursue the organized crime aspects as well as the Clements beating. Howard Pearl never thought it would be a swift probe.

Only the prosecutors are allowed inside the grand jury room. In other words, Randolph would not be allowed access unless he testified, which generally happens during the course of an investigation. Defense lawyers are entitled to counsel their clients only outside the grand jury room; a witness, though, can ask to be excused at any time to seek such advice.

At this stage the government wanted to bring some of the fundamental elements of the Walters-Bloom investigation to the grand jury. There were the threats, the possible obstruction of justice by Walters in withholding the contracts of the underclassmen, and the necessary step of explaining the process in which the players falsely signed papers to obtain their scholarship benefits. This all went hand in hand with indoctrinating the grand jury with the federal criminal statutes that were being applied in this case. All of these responsibilities fell on Pearl.

IN EARLY May, Pearl and Randolph were waiting for Michael Feldberg, Walters's attorney, to arrive with somebody to take responsibility as "custodian of the records" at World Sports and Entertainment, Inc. When the receptionist on the fifteenth floor of the U. S. Attorney's office buzzed Pearl to announce that Mr. Feldberg had arrived, Randolph walked down the hall to greet him.

In the reception area Randolph saw a nice-looking man in a dark-blue suit with dark, wavy hair and glasses. He identified himself as Michael Feldberg. A smile was exchanged, and Randolph laughed to himself because he had already found out through an acquaintance that Feldberg, like Howard Pearl, was a Harvard graduate.

There was a petite woman with brownish-tinted hair standing behind Feldberg. She could have passed for the lawyer's Jewish mother or aunt, but Feldberg introduced her as Irene Walters. It was Norby's wife! Randolph led them to Pearl's small office, and Pearl was visibly disturbed that Feldberg had brought this woman as the custodian he was about to take in front of the grand jury to verify that the subpoena for

Norby Walters's records had been met with full compliance. Irene Walters appeared understandably scared and confused as Pearl led her and Feldberg to the elevators and up to the sixteenth floor where the grand jury was convening in room 1625.

Only Pearl and Irene Walters were allowed inside the grand jury room. Feldberg and Randolph waited outside and started to chat about their acquaintance, a fellow named Tom Price, who was now an Assistant U. S. Attorney in Kansas City. It wasn't long before the door flew open and Pearl pointed at Feldberg and said, "We have a big problem here. Let's go!" Irene Walters looked more scared than ever now, as the four of them returned to the fifteenth floor. Pearl asked Mrs. Walters to remain in the reception area, saying she should ask the receptionist if she needed anything.

Pearl stomped back to his office, trailed by Feldberg and Randolph. All three men were barely inside when Pearl pivoted and screamed at Feldberg, "This is bullshit! Fucking bullshit! You've just wasted my time, the government's time, and the government's money."

Feldberg snapped back, "What the hell are you talking about?"

"That old lady doesn't know shit," Pearl screamed. "She's never even seen the subpoena until now! You really fucked this up."

Feldberg was turning beet red. He said that Irene Walters did a lot of the bookkeeping for her husband and should have met the government's simple needs.

"Maybe I'll just throw your ass in front of the grand jury," Pearl threatened.

"Who the hell do you think you are?" Feldberg snapped again, and this time he stepped toward Pearl.

The two men were now nose to nose, and Randolph decided it was getting out of hand. He tried to step between them but was jostled. They were screaming, spit flying from their lips, veins bulging in their necks, and there was no way either man could have understood what the other was saying. Randolph forced his way between them, then grabbed both men by their neckties.

"Cool it!" the FBI agent yelled. "If one of you assholes pops me, I'm gonna kick both your asses."

Both men backed off, and Randolph let go of their ties. Feldberg grabbed his briefcase and said he was departing. Pearl wanted to argue more.

"Let him go," Randolph said.

As Feldberg was about to leave Pearl's office, the prosecutor warned,

"This thing isn't over. Your client already has an obstruction charge coming his way." Feldberg started to renew the argument, but Randolph urged him to leave.

When he was alone with Pearl, Randolph said, "Damn, Howard, you went nuclear on the guy." Then the FBI agent smiled. He was proud of the prosecutor. He knew now that Howard Pearl was definitely capable of a street fight.

VALUKAS HAD instructed Pearl and Randolph to arrange for Harmon and a few other players to come to Chicago "for a little heart to heart" and maybe an appearance before the grand jury. Randolph went back to Pearl's office and got the name of Harmon's agent and lawyer, Martin Rauch, who had an office in Buffalo, where Harmon was now playing in the National Football League. Pearl made the call, and his conversation was going smoothly until the prosecutor informed Rauch that Harmon was also the target of the investigation on mail fraud and income tax evasion charges.

"Then Ronnie isn't coming in without immunity," said Rauch. "You know, this kid can help you guys. He's got a tape recording of Walters making his big sales pitch on the day he signed with them. You should listen to it. I never heard anything like it. You want to talk about income tax evasion—Walters actually tells the kid and his father that it's okay to cheat on taxes."

"What?" Pearl asked, a shrillness rising in his voice. Then he put his hand over the phone.

"Harmon's got a tape, too," the prosecutor excitedly told Randolph. "Made it on the day he signed."

The FBI agent's jaw dropped. "Are you shitting me?" he asked. "What the hell is going on?"

Pearl went back to the phone. "We can't talk any deal until we see what he has to offer. Right now he's in a lot of trouble, and this isn't a game, understand? He needs to understand that. It's your job to make him understand that. Got it?"

Rauch still wasn't buying it. He told Pearl he would formally request a grant of immunity in a letter.

"It's not going to work that way!" Pearl yelled. "Understand? We're not fucking around here, okay?"

Pearl slammed down the phone. "Oh, man, if I have to go through fifty-eight of these, I don't know what I'll do," he said.

Randolph jumped up, saying, "We gotta get that tape. We gotta get that tape. Did he say where he had it? I mean, the last thing we need is for some tape to get lost or erased. We gotta get it."

"You try," Pearl said.

Randolph called Rauch.

"Listen, asshole," Randolph warned. "I have the United States Attorney of Chicago wanting to throw your guy's ass in jail. He doesn't care if Ronnie Harmon is Mr. Joe Great Football Player. So get the tape here."

Rauch politely refused and said, "I don't understand you guys. What's the criminal intent here on the part of Ronnie Harmon?"

"It's a fraud!" Randolph yelled. "The guy took money. He lied to the school. It's a fraud."

Randolph hung up the telephone.

"Gotta get that tape," he said.

The FBI special agent called Big Ten Conference headquarters and asked for Wayne Duke, the commissioner.

"What's the story on Ronnie Harmon?" Randolph asked Duke. "What kind of guy was he supposed to be?"

"All I know," Duke said, "is the guy was a pretty good football player who played the worst game in the history of the Rose Bowl, as far as I'm concerned."

"What?"

"The guy fumbled four times and dropped a touchdown pass," said Duke. "Hadn't been for him, Iowa would have beat UCLA. People up in Iowa were real mad about it. Shoot, I think his teammates were upset about it. There was an altercation in the locker room between the players. And ever since this story came out about all the money the kid took from the agent, people up there have been wondering if something funny was going on."

There was silence now on Randolph's end, and all Randolph could think about was Sonny and Michael Franzese, the Colombo family, the $54,000 bill that Harmon ran up, the $32,000 down payment on the Mercedes. Was it a post–Rose Bowl gift?

"George?" Duke called out over the phone.

"I'll have to get back to you," said Randolph. "Thanks."

Back down the hall he went to see Tony Valukas. Randolph told the U. S. Attorney about his conversation with the Big Ten commissioner.

Valukas said, "Let's be very careful here."

Valukas made Randolph think about it. It was important not to get

carried away. Besides, why would the guy blow the Rose Bowl deliberately when he had a bright NFL future? Harmon was the sixteenth
player chosen in the first round by the Buffalo Bills in the 1986 draft.
Players fumble. It could have been nerves. A bad game. And if a player
did fix a game, the only way to find out was a confession by the player
or the one who made the bribe. There wasn't much chance of that. Not
yet anyway. Randolph had enough hard leads to pursue without a
sensational wild-goose chase. He went back to work.

THE PROSECUTION team had to stay on top of many developments. In
Tuscaloosa, Alabama, an FBI agent wanted to notify the school of
Derrick McKey's involvement with Norby Walters and Lloyd Bloom.
McKey, a six-foot-nine center, had been the Southeastern Conference
Player of the Year in basketball and was a junior with one year of
eligibility remaining. The school could get in trouble, the agent told
Randolph, and McKey himself had to make a decision in a few weeks to
declare himself eligible for the NBA draft; otherwise, he would be out in
the cold for a full year.

Randolph understood the concern, but he told the agent that he would
have to get it approved through the U. S. Attorney. This would be his
first major disagreement with Pearl, who told Randolph that he didn't
care what happened to the university or McKey. Things were too sensitive right now, and he was already taking heat from Michael Feldberg
about the publicity that was generated. Since the grand jury was now
sitting on this case, federal laws were strict about any disclosure. There
was no telling how long this case would go on, and for all Pearl knew,
McKey would again falsely certify himself in the fall to renew his scholarship if he didn't voluntarily come forward. It was the kid's responsibility to blow the whistle on himself, Pearl reminded Randolph.

Randolph got back to the FBI agent in Tuscaloosa and explained the
circumstances to him. Pearl had been adamant about not saying anything to the University of Alabama.

But not a week had passed before they saw the headlines: ALABAMA
STAR DECLARED INELIGIBLE FOR DEALING WITH AGENT.

"How the hell did the school find out?" Pearl demanded.

"I have no idea," said Randolph. "But what's done is done."

Pearl "went nuclear" when he found out that the university discovered
McKey's involvement with Norby Walters and Lloyd Bloom through
the FBI investigation that was underway in Tuscaloosa, according to the

newspapers. Pearl wanted to "nail" the FBI agent working the case down there.

Meanwhile, as Pearl expected, Michael Feldberg was on the telephone from New York, accusing the prosecutor of leaking the information not only to the school but to the media. Feldberg claimed he would file government misconduct charges. The two men blew their fuses again, and the next day was just as bad.

There was a follow-up letter on May 15 to Pearl from Feldberg:

> As we discussed on the telephone last Thursday and Friday, the government has disclosed grand jury matters absent a court order.
>
> In particular, our client World Sports and Entertainment ("WS&E") has produced, pursuant to a grand jury subpoena, voluminous documents, including contracts of players with remaining collegiate eligibility. In response to the subpoena, we discussed with you the delicacy of the players' situations in light of the "intangible rights" mail fraud theory you are pursuing. According to your theory, various schools, conferences, and the NCAA were defrauded by the players, who accepted scholarship money based, you tell us, upon their representations that they had not signed a contract with an agent. We have pointed out that WS&E, of course, had no relationship with the schools, conferences, or the NCAA, and therefore made no representations or omissions of any kind that could be deemed opposite to such a theory, and that any representations made by the players to the school preceded any contract between the players and WS&E.

Pearl boiled over the letter, which went on to reiterate the charges about grand jury disclosures. The prosecutor particularly seethed about the part that "any representations made by the players to the school preceded any contract between the players and WS&E." Feldberg obviously didn't understand that the certification process was done annually in August. The attorney must have assumed that the players certified only once, at the start of their freshman year. Clearly, the players signed early with Walters and Bloom and then went back and lied to the schools about their eligibility. Pearl accused Feldberg of not doing a thorough study.

Randolph also reviewed the FBI report from Tuscaloosa regarding Derrick McKey and Terry Coner, a starting guard on the team who had just finished his eligibility. Both players said they were recruited by Terry Bolar, that Lloyd Bloom had come into Tuscaloosa, and that in a hotel room across from the university they sealed the deal with $3,000 in cash. They had never met Norby Walters, but Bolar was again directly connected to the scheme. Randolph had to find out more about this guy.

Some of the information on Terry Bolar he was looking for was provided by the newspaper reports. The *Atlanta Constitution* and *New York Newsday,* which had also been working on the story, reported that Bolar and former Detroit Lions star Ron Jessie had been hired by Walters not only as recruiters but as buffers to "put out fires."

There were also other newspaper reports on the activities of Walters. Following an earlier report, the *Chicago Tribune* on May 16 carried the headline: FEDERAL GRAND JURY TO INVESTIGATE AGENT. The story reported that Ohio State athletic director Richard Bay and Pittsburgh athletic director Ed Bozik had confirmed that they had been subpoenaed to appear before the grand jury for the coming Tuesday, May 19. Ronnie Harmon had also been subpoenaed, the newspaper reported, but quoted Martin Rauch as saying, "He's subpoenaed, but he won't be there next week. There's no necessity for him to be there next week."

These were the kinds of leaks that Valukas had worried about, and he feared that there would be more as time passed. The pressure of protecting the grand jury and the government's schedule could impact the case. Already the government could see that some of the defense lawyers weren't taking the Chicago investigation seriously. They were going to have to play hardball.

7

I<small>F</small> T<small>ONY</small> Valukas and Howard Pearl were disgusted with players on the take from Norby Walters and Lloyd Bloom, it was sparked by selected piggish behavior. They could excuse a Tim McGee, who used Walters and Bloom to pay bills for his mother. They could not excuse a Ronnie Harmon, who milked the Norby Walters cow until his hands were sore.

Unfortunately, the legal twist on the case prevented Valukas and Pearl from putting the screws to the likes of SMU's Jerry Ball and Texas–Bishop College's William Harris, two players who ran up the bill to over $30,000 and seemed to wallow in it. There was no way SMU could be a victim of fraud, and Harris's lost records at Bishop left the government without any proof that he had lied on his scholarship forms.

Pearl actually saw more players who were inclined to do right by their folks than not.

Regardless of how he felt, Pearl had been charged by his boss to take an ironfisted approach with the players. Valukas clearly wanted the players to be accountable for their actions. Their hands were out, most of them lied on the forms, they knew the rules.

Pearl was to prosecute the players as coconspirators, and three months into the investigation he was offering players a deal if they agreed to plead guilty to one count of mail fraud. The implication was that the players would have a felony record and potential federal prison time as they started their National Football League careers.

If the players seemed shocked by this incredible development—no matter how the government tried to explain it, the players thought they had only broken NCAA rules—Valukas and Pearl had even worse news for them: Some of them were racketeers, and all of them were income tax evaders.

94

The players tagged as racketeers were the ones who recruited teammates for Walters and Bloom and received fees for their work. As for the no-interest "loans" from Norby Walters and Lloyd Bloom, the government told the players they were nothing but inducements and payoffs and should have been reported to the IRS. The players all participated in this criminal conspiracy.

George Randolph thought of the payoffs more as bribes than anything else. He saw the players as unsophisticated, no matter how streetwise or cool they appeared.

Randolph, a hard ass by nature, thought the government should go relatively easy on the players. To him they were the victims, the targets of two flesh-hungry sports agents who wanted nothing more than to get their mitts on the money the players would earn in the NFL.

Randolph also believed that the players were the targets of a larger scheme. He hadn't quite focused on it, but the beating of Kathy Clements, the threats to the players, and the cash-and-carry sales pitch had organized crime written all over them.

On May 19 three players were scheduled to meet with the prosecution team for the little "heart to heart" Valukas had promised. They were Doug Dubose, the running back from Nebraska; Terance Mann, the defensive tackle from SMU; and Edwin Simmons, the running back from Texas.

All three were sitting in a room outside Valukas's office when Randolph introduced himself. The FBI agent was cordial. He did not want to come across as intimidating because he wanted the players to relax and tell the truth. Having compared Walters's records with some of the FBI reports that had come in from across the country, Randolph knew that some of the players had a little problem with the whole truth, nothing but the truth. Of course, they weren't under oath.

"Here are the rules of the game," Randolph told the players. "Don't lie, don't b.s. anybody. If you remember that, you'll probably have no problems here."

Still, just by looking at Valukas's face, Randolph could tell that the players were in for a rough day. Pearl had warned the players that they needed lawyers. He would not deal with a player until he had legal representation.

Simmons went in first, and Valukas pulled out the player's file, complete with the contract, promissory note, and copies of the Western Union money orders that had been wired to Austin, Texas.

Simmons seemed extremely big for a running back, about six feet four inches and 220 pounds. He had not been drafted, apparently due to a knee injury, but the FBI report dated April 27 noted that Simmons had been one of the greatest high school running backs in Texas history. He was well mannered and well dressed, but scared. He verified some of the facts. In March 1986 he received a telephone call in his dormitory from Norby Walters, who bragged about being the "agent to the stars," having represented such entertainers as Patti LaBelle and Luther Vandross. Walters, along with his associate, a guy named Lloyd Bloom, wanted to pay a visit to the player.

The following Sunday, Simmons remembered, Walters and Bloom met him at the Marriott Hotel at Highway 290 and Interstate 35 in Austin. They showed Simmons a *Billboard* magazine article. Randolph looked at Valukas and Pearl and shook his head. Norby Walters laid out a "promotional pitch" and a contract. Out came $2,500 in cash and a promise from Walters that they would postdate the contract to January 2, 1987, "so nobody will suspect anything."

All so familiar. But Simmons did not sign for $2,500. He signed for $4,000 and a promise of $250 monthly payments. He admitted to Valukas that he negotiated a better deal.

"I didn't think twenty-five hundred dollars was enough for me to take a chance of being caught," Simmons explained.

Valukas moved on, asking Simmons whether he received his $250 monthly payments. Simmons answered affirmatively. But what about the regular monthly $477 money orders? Valukas was staring at the player now. Simmons said they were for his car payments.

"Anything else?" Valukas asked.

Simmons said he couldn't remember. Valukas then pulled out a money order for $1,200.

"What was this for?" he asked Simmons, who again said he couldn't remember.

There was one trip to Los Angeles and two trips to New York. Another $605. In fact, during the next ten months Simmons received $11,000.

"Did you report this money when you filed your income tax return?" Valukas asked.

Simmons's eyes darted around the room, looking for help. He didn't remember, he said.

"Get yourself a lawyer," Valukas snapped at him. "You're going to need one because you could end up in jail, young man."

Valukas rattled off information about the federal mail fraud statutes and income tax evasion. He mentioned something about obstruction of justice.

Valukas also asked Simmons, who had been the nation's most touted high school running back when he was recruited, about NCAA rules that may have been violated by school officials.

Simmons wasn't going to mess around with Valukas anymore. Yes, he replied. He received some cash once from a coach, and he was also lined up with a car by a booster.

Tears welled up in Simmons's eyes before he was dismissed from the room.

Dubose and Mann had better memories than Simmons. When the day was finished, though, they also understood that their affair with Norby Walters and Lloyd Bloom was no longer a little con game. Tony Valukas had literally laid down the law, perhaps hoping the message would get back to the other players.

Randolph felt some sympathy for the players. Even with a warning they must have felt blindsided. He tried to make them more relaxed and offered to give all three a ride to O'Hare Airport. Taking the elevator down to the parking garage, he unlocked the doors to his hand-me-down bureau car, an Oldsmobile Century. Dubose got in the front seat while Mann, who must have weighed three hundred pounds, sat in the back, along with Simmons.

As soon as Randolph backed out of his parking spot, he could tell the car dipped badly in the rear. The tires rolled slowly as he drove the Oldsmobile toward the ramp, the rear bumper scraping along the cement. There was some laughter, cutting the tension, as he pulled out of the basement of the federal building and into the fading daylight. Then Dubose spotted some handcuffs on the front seat next to him.

"What are those for?" Dubose asked, smiling.

"In case one of you assholes pulls anything," Randolph replied.

"Oh, I knew we were going to jail," cracked Dubose.

Mann wanted to know what time it was because he thought he might miss his flight to Dallas.

"Don't worry," Randolph said, reaching underneath the dashboard and pulling out his red light. "If we're late, we'll make it."

"Turn it on, turn it on," Dubose begged like a little kid. "Turn on the siren. Special privileges."

Randolph laughed. There would be no special privileges for these football players. Those days are over, he joked. One of them didn't laugh.

In the rearview mirror, Edwin Simmons still looked like a very shaken young man.

SHORTLY AFTER May 19, more players started arriving in Chicago. This itself was a massive headache. For every eight players that were scheduled, about four showed up. This sent Randolph on a telephone hunt, tracking down players who were no-shows to explain that if they were absent again, the grand jury could find them in contempt, and their problems would multiply. Randolph began to wonder why he wanted to be soft on these guys.

It became a game of tag with some players, and Randolph tried just about everything to drag them to Chicago. One of these players was Adrian White of the New York Giants. He wouldn't return phone calls, so Randolph finally dialed the Giants training facility and asked for somebody who could get White's attention.

"Coach Parcells, please."

"May I ask who is calling?"

"FBI Special Agent George Randolph."

Bill Parcells was on the phone shortly. Randolph apologized for bothering the coach, but there was the matter of Adrian White, his young defensive back, who had failed to appear in Chicago. Randolph didn't have to talk long before Parcells got the picture.

"Do me a favor," Parcells said. "Maybe you guys can straighten him out." Then he joked, "Why don't you just tap him on the helmet at the fifty-yard line and have an agent hand him the subpoena? Maybe that'll get his attention."

They had a laugh. Adrian White was in Chicago the next week.

Along with him were some of the greediest players to take handouts from Norby Walters and Lloyd Bloom. One thing the thirty-four-year-old Pearl was going to find out from each player was how he spent his money. He wanted them all to account for every penny. He knew it was impossible, but he was going to demand this information.

"I think I even told him that I spent a nickel on a piece of bubble gum," said Brent Fullwood.

For Pearl it was time to act on Valukas's order to lay it on the line, though he made certain each player was represented by an attorney. That's what he was thinking as he studied the file on John Clay, the offensive lineman from the University of Missouri, a recent number-one draft pick of the Los Angeles Raiders. Clay had been a "pig" with the money, taking in more than $30,000. Not only that, several players had fingered Clay as an active recruiter of other college stars.

The prosecution team had confirmed that several players received "finder's fees" from Walters and Bloom for recruiting their teammates. These fees ran from about $1,000 to $1,500.

Pearl, who had already jogged his six miles that morning, was getting pumped up for his meetings with John Clay and Paul Palmer. They were the only two first-round draft picks who had not defected from "the family," even after it had been widely reported that a federal grand jury was investigating the agents. Why did they stay? Like Clay, Palmer had obtained from Norby Walters a little more than $30,000. Were they in too deep? Did they succumb to the pattern of threats that Walters and Bloom would "expose" their early dealings?

John Clay had been a reluctant witness partly because Norby Walters had been sending money to his parents in St. Louis and had allegedly reminded the player's father, a U. S. Postal Service employee, that bad publicity could bring shame upon the family. The prosecution team didn't know this at the time, and Pearl was determined to lay down the law with him and Palmer.

"I'm gonna tell that SOB that every morning he wakes up, he's gonna have to ask himself, 'Is this the day I'm gonna be indicted?' " Pearl told George Randolph.

Randolph cracked a little smile and sipped his coffee. He looked at this nice Harvard boy and laughed.

"You haven't got the balls to tell that to his face," the FBI agent playfully challenged the prosecutor.

"Watch," said Pearl.

A few hours later a very big man introduced himself to Howard Pearl and George Randolph as John Clay. He looked about six feet four inches, 320 pounds. His face was rounder than the picture in the Missouri media guide, which devoted more than a page to the All-American tackle.

The Raiders had lined Clay up with a Los Angeles attorney named Paul Flynn, a former Assistant U. S. Attorney and a law professor at Pepperdine University. Pearl had already warned Flynn that Clay was in "deep trouble," but Flynn couldn't understand why.

"These guys are the victims," Flynn told him.

"Bullshit," Pearl said, doing his best to play the part, even though he might have agreed with the lawyer.

Clay and Flynn were now on the fifteenth floor of the Dirksen Federal

Building in Chicago. Randolph knew he was going to enjoy this meeting, but he felt certain that Pearl would back off a little—well, almost certain. Pearl seemed to be psyching himself up for the day, and soon he was lecturing Flynn and Clay on what could have been perceived as false statements to a federal officer about the totality of his involvement with Norby Walters and Lloyd Bloom.

Racketeering, mail fraud, wire fraud, perjury, income tax evasion—Pearl started rattling off the potential charges that Clay faced.

"I doubt if you'll even have a football career by the time you get out of prison," Pearl said.

Clay seemed somewhat aloof, and that lit a bigger fire in Pearl. Clay might have been a big man, but Howard Pearl was sticking out his chest now.

"Let me tell you something," Pearl started again. "From here on out, you're gonna have to wake up every morning and ask yourself, 'Is this the day I'm gonna be indicted?' "

Randolph looked at Pearl in astonishment. He had said it. And John Clay looked like a man—a very big man—staggered by a left hook.

Paul Palmer received the same treatment. He was smaller, about five feet ten inches, 175 pounds, and was equally silent, perhaps in a state of shock, when the prosecutor told him that his career could be interrupted by a possible jail term.

It was especially disturbing to the government that Palmer continued to defend Walters in newspaper articles, including one that appeared on May 20, 1987, in the *Chicago Tribune,* reprinted from a story written by Randy Covitz of the *Kansas City Star-Times:* CHIEFS' TOP PICK PALMER STANDS BY AGENT WALTERS.

"My reason for staying with them is I feel good about them, and they haven't done anything to me that would not make me trust them," Palmer was quoted as saying. Palmer also said he did not receive any money from Walters during his senior year at Temple University, where he had led the nation in rushing in 1986.

    I talked to them at the start of my senior year, and I talked to them at the end of my senior year. I told them when I first talked to them that I'd appreciate it if they left me alone because I really wanted to concentrate on working out and getting myself ready and having a productive season. . . . They respected that fact and left me alone.
    There were no inducements. A lot was written. It turned out to be a case of poor journalism.

"Paul was not one [who received money]," Walters was quoted as saying. "He signed after his eligibility."

Paul Palmer felt compelled to cover himself every step of the way. He also lied to the FBI agents in Philadelphia who had initially questioned the Temple star. It was not unusual for subjects not to tell the truth in their initial meetings with FBI agents gathering facts, but it did classify as a violation—lying to a federal officer.

Palmer and Walters had further perpetrated the deception against Temple by their actions after the *Atlanta Constitution* had named Palmer as being involved with the New York agent. The article had left the relationship between the player and agent looking suspicious. The following day Temple athletic director Charles Theokas announced he would conduct an immediate investigation into the allegations, which had been somewhat distorted in an Associated Press report.

Pearl and Randolph had a copy of Temple's investigative report, dated March 18, 1987, which was only six days after the story originally broke in Atlanta. It showed that Theokas had a face-to-face meeting with Palmer and a telephone conversation with Norby Walters, who agreed to forward a copy of the player's contract to the school. The contract Walters sent was dated January 2, 1987, which was after Palmer's final game. A note attached to the contract said, "Charlie . . . So as not to further confuse the issue, as to the contents on the percentages of the contract, I have just given you the cover and last page. That's the date and signature part. Regards, Norby Walters."

Temple had a press conference at 3 P.M. on March 18 and absolved Palmer. Theokas reported to Temple vice president H. P. Swygert: "As a result of these findings, I feel comfortable that Paul, in fact, did nothing improper."

To show how government minds think, Pearl and Randolph at first were disappointed to learn that Walters forwarded Palmer's contract via Federal Express instead of the United States mails, but they were delighted to learn that Theokas mailed his report to the NCAA, which gave more support to the government's mail fraud allegations and showed that Walters and Palmer knowingly and willfully deceived the school.

"Funny, but Uncle Norby seemed to omit this," Pearl said, holding up a promissory note that Palmer had signed on June 17, 1986, for $4,000. Then the prosecutor started thumbing through a handful of Western Union and U. S. Funds Express money orders from Norby Walters to Paul Palmer, a series of $250 payments mixed in with payments of $450,

$100, $200, $350, $493.50, and $500. There were trips to New York, a bunch of entertainment expenses, a clothing run.

Pearl then showed Palmer the NCAA eligibility, certification, and affidavit forms he had signed in August 1986, stating he had not been involved in any violations. Thus, he remained eligible and continued to receive his scholarship benefits.

"This is fraud," Pearl charged.

Two of the more pathetic football players the government encountered were Washington defensive end Reggie Rogers and Auburn running back Brent Fullwood. Ironically, of Norby Walters's class of 1987, they were the two highest first-round draft picks, Fullwood going number four to the Green Bay Packers and Rogers going number seven to the Detroit Lions. By the time the government sized them up as witnesses, there was no way it could let them take the stand.

Rogers was an emotional mess, no doubt staggered the previous summer when his older brother Don died of a cocaine overdose in the early morning hours of his bachelor party. Don Rogers, a safety for the Browns, had played earlier that season in the Pro Bowl.

During the summer of 1987, Reggie Rogers had brought the government an interesting Polaroid snapshot he said was taken immediately after Norby Walters and Lloyd Bloom had made their high-powered sales pitch. The photo showed Rogers with a huge grin, holding the $5,000 fantailed in his hands like a peacock. The picture was worth five thousand words.

But Rogers had corrupted himself in other areas, having double-dealt with another agent, Patrick Healy of Tacoma, Washington. He had also signed with Walters after he signed his eligibility certification papers with Washington. Thus, where it concerned Walters, Rogers wasn't lying when he stated he had not jeopardized his eligibility.

He further frustrated Pearl and Randolph with his attention span. Trying to get a lucid statement out of Rogers gave them splitting headaches. Randolph had the responsibility of taking Rogers to lunch. When they left the Dirksen Federal Building and reached Jackson Street, they walked past a shoeshine stand. Rogers wanted to stop.

"Later," Randolph told him. "Catch it on the way back."

They walked around the block to a sandwich shop. When they were finished, the FBI agent decided to take the six-foot-seven defensive end on a slightly different route to the federal building, thinking they could get on an elevator before Rogers remembered the shoeshine stand. They were almost to the swinging glass door when Rogers bolted across the street.

So Randolph stood there and waited as Rogers got his shoes shined. When the job was done, Rogers took a wad of cash out of his pocket. Randolph figured he had just gotten his signing bonus with the Lions. Rogers peeled off a $10 bill, handed it to the shoeshine man, and started to walk away. Randolph fetched the $10 bill out of the shoeshine man's hand and called Rogers back.

"It's two bucks," Randolph told him.

"Hey, man, that's all right," Rogers said. "Let him keep it."

Randolph asked the shoeshine man for $7 in change. The man reluctantly obliged. Randolph gave the $7 to Rogers, who looked at the FBI agent as if he was definitely unhip.

Later that day Randolph was ready for a drink or several aspirin when he escorted Rogers to the U. S. Marshal's office to arrange a return flight for him to Seattle. Rogers wanted to fly first class. Randolph laughed. Then Rogers freaked when he realized he was not booked on a direct flight but would have to change planes in Minneapolis.

"I can't do this! I can't do this!" Rogers screamed, throwing himself off-balance and almost facedown on the floor. "I gotta get a straight flight."

Randolph explained that the government got the cheapest rates, and this was the route Rogers would have to take. The player was almost crying now.

"I'll never get home," Rogers said.

Randolph figured Rogers was scared of changing planes.

"Okay," Randolph reasoned. "I'll write out everything for you on these three-by-five index cards. Just follow the directions, and it'll be a piece of cake."

"No, no," Rogers said in a panic. "It's got to be a direct flight, or I'll never get home."

Enough was enough.

"Here's the ticket," snapped Randolph. "If you want to fly direct, pay your own way."

On the drive home that night, Randolph began to wonder about the education Rogers had received.

That SOB probably can't read, the FBI agent thought.

Pearl had another theory. "It was shocking how incredibly sheltered the players had been through high school and college. Everything had

always been taken care of for them. Reggie Rogers probably never had
to change planes on his own."

BRENT FULLWOOD raised the same suspicions. The Auburn running back
could have been a critical witness, but after a couple of meetings with the
government, they knew it would be impossible to pull off. Fullwood had
a fairly powerful story to tell, no matter how he fractured the English
language.

The man who succeeded Bo Jackson at Auburn had decided to switch
agents from Norby Walters and Lloyd Bloom to a local agent and
lawyer, George Kickliter. This infuriated Walters and Bloom because
they knew they had locked up the elite running back in the draft, and
they had done so fairly cheaply. Fullwood's bill was $8,042, dating back
to August 10, 1986, prior to Fullwood's senior season.

According to Fullwood—who was consistent in accounts to the government, his criminal defense lawyer, his new agent, a university investigative group, and a reporter—Bloom threatened to "knock off" Kickliter. Another time, Bloom changed that to "bump off."

Fullwood relayed the information to Kickliter, who in his best country
drawl asked the running back, "Brent, what do y'all think old Lloyd
Bloom meant by that?"

"Mr. Kickliter," Fullwood said, "I think it means they're gonna kill
you."

Kickliter himself had telephone encounters with Walters and Bloom
that were threatening. The agent told the FBI that Bloom hinted he and
Walters were linked with organized crime.

"He told me that they had to answer to their own boss from Las
Vegas," Kickliter said, "and that their boss didn't mess around."

Kickliter told the FBI that he "fortified" himself at that point. In other
words, he explained, he purchased a handgun.

But the government could not get Kickliter on the witness stand
without using Fullwood, who once looked outside a window in the
federal building, pointed his finger at Lake Michigan, and asked, "What
ocean is that?"

Other players involved in the Walters-Bloom case could not resist
picking on Fullwood. They observed Howard Pearl's and George Randolph's aggravation when Fullwood told them he would be unable to
read his statement to the grand jury because he had forgotten his glasses.
They had never seen Fullwood wearing glasses.

A group of players were waiting outside the grand jury room one day when Texas wide receiver Everett Gay started making fun of Fullwood.

"You ought to be pissed off," Gay told Fullwood.

"What do you mean?" the Auburn player replied.

"You have to pay back your school and can't even read," Gay said.

"At least I can pay mine back," Fullwood cracked. "I just got six hundred thousand dollars (from the Green Bay Packers) for signing my name to a contract."

Fullwood may have had a bankful of money, but a couple of instances further undercut his usefulness to the government.

He once insisted that he get his witness fee check cashed before he left Chicago. One of the members of the prosecution team directed him to a bank two blocks away that would cash the check, but when the government man started giving directions about street signs, Fullwood panicked. Instead, the directions had to be given by landmarks.

"See that large building over there," the government man said. "You turn left . . ."

Where Fullwood really messed up with the government came on July 15, 1987, the day after he was in Chicago.

The *Atlanta Constitution,* the newspaper that had been dogging the story from the start, sent a reporter to intercept Fullwood at O'Hare Airport before and after his grand jury testimony. The headlines screamed EX-AUBURN STAR: AGENT GOT DEATH THREAT.

The story's lead: "Former Auburn University running back Brent Fullwood said he testified before a federal grand jury here Tuesday that agent Lloyd Bloom threatened to 'bump off' his current agent, George Kickliter."

Fullwood laid out his story for the reporter. He also told how Walters and Bloom had offered him $8,000 for turning the agents onto linebacker Cornelius Bennett, an acquaintance from rival Alabama, who eventually became the NFL's number-two pick in the draft that spring. Fullwood said he ignored the $8,000 inducement to hook Bennett.

The Atlanta story was picked up nationally and also ran on the front page of the *Chicago Tribune* sports section.

It infuriated Howard Pearl, who wanted an explanation from Fullwood's lawyer, Matthias Lydon, the former prosecutor who had successfully tried the landmark "intangible rights" mail fraud case out of the same office a decade earlier. Lydon had sensed something was amiss the day before when Fullwood told him that he had gotten a ride into town with a "very nice man" who had greeted him when he stepped off a

United Airlines flight from Orlando. Fullwood forgot to tell Lydon that the nice man had identified himself as a reporter and carried a notepad and tape recorder, and that the reporter met him again that night.

Federal criminal laws prohibit the disclosure of grand jury information. Fullwood's action had further cemented his elimination as a witness.

Publicity was becoming a thorny issue. Valukas, Pearl, and Randolph wanted information sealed off because of earlier allegations from Walters's attorney, Michael Feldberg, about government misconduct. But the *Atlanta Constitution* had broken the barriers about a number of issues and had even acquired the list of athletes who were being subpoenaed by the government. And there seemed to be no stopping various defense lawyers and player agents from revealing what their clients were telling the government, not to mention what the players themselves were revealing to reporters.

One of the wildest stories the prosecution team heard, which was never reported by the press, came out of their meetings with Clemson stars Terrence Flagler and Terrance Roulhac. Both players told George Randolph that there had been an incident the night they signed with Norby Walters and Lloyd Bloom in June 1986 which had ended up in the Clemson police station.

Walters and Bloom had been confronted by a stranger that night at a local hotel. There was a commotion in the hall, and the last time Flagler and Roulhac looked over their shoulders, Walters and Bloom had grabbed the man. The players left immediately, only to be called down to the Clemson police station later that night for questioning.

Armed with the contracts the players had signed on that date, Randolph routinely called the Clemson police station and asked for a copy of the report. He got the runaround. No report could be found. Incident? What incident? A half-dozen telephone calls were fruitless, and the FBI agent knew exactly what was going on.

"If I don't get a police report on what happened that night, I'm cutting a subpoena for your chief to come up here and tell a federal grand jury what happened to it," Randolph explained.

The police report miraculously surfaced and found its way to Chicago. FBI agents in Atlanta were summoned to question the stranger. His name was Gary Defauw, a twenty-eight-year-old high-tech electronics salesman.

Defauw had driven from his business in Atlanta to Clemson and checked into the local Holiday Inn when he heard some loud voices in the next room that evening. Defauw leaned a little closer to the wall and

soon realized that Flagler and Roulhac were getting hustled by somebody who was relentlessly obnoxious.

It was Norby Walters.

Defauw understood what was happening. His room had a door ad-
joining the room where Uncle Norby closed the deal. He opened his side
and listened intently. He grabbed a notepad by his bed and scribbled
notes as fast as he could.

"This guy kept telling the players how he represented all the great
entertainers in the country and how he was the number-one agent in the
world, and that from now on they would be part of his family and to call
him Uncle Norby," Defauw said. "He went on and on and on. He told
them they could come to New York whenever they wanted, that he'd
have all the girls they needed. He told one of them that he thought the
New York Giants would take him in the first round. He also told them
that he was connected to George Steinbrenner and that Steinbrenner
personally wanted both Flagler and Roulhac."

(If Walters had any connection to Steinbrenner, it was through his law
firm, Shea & Gould, where his cousin, Lon Trost, represented the New
York Yankees.)

Defauw said he knew the names of the players because Walters kept
identifying them, such as "Terrence Flagler, let me tell you what I'm
gonna do for you."

"I knew what was happening, and I knew it was wrong," said Defauw.
"I mean, I never heard anything like it. You could even hear him flop
down the cash on the table, and Walters was telling them that he would
postdate the contracts and hide them in his office vault."

A little more time passed—filled with the sounds of a joyous occasion—before Defauw heard the two players agree to take the money and
sign some papers.

Then Defauw heard the door open. His curiosity was boundless now.
He had to see these characters, so he quietly opened his door and stepped
out to peek.

Norby Walters and Lloyd Bloom were still standing in front of their
door and wheeled to see the man next to them. Their mouths dropped
open.

Defauw doesn't know why, but he blurted out, "I heard everything."

When Norby Walters and Lloyd Bloom grabbed Gary Defauw by the
arms, Flagler and Roulhac took off.

"Come on, we're gonna go have a talk," Walters told Defauw, who
was escorted to the coffee shop.

They moved to a section of the coffee shop that was closed and sat down at a table.

Defauw will never forget the two men. Norby Walters looked very slick and was wearing some very expensive threads. In Defauw's own words, "Bloom looked like a hit man. At least he was playing the part."

Norby Walters twisted his neck around to see if anybody else was eavesdropping, then he pointed his finger at Defauw.

"You ought to call your daddy and tell him you're happy to be alive," Walters told him.

Defauw reiterated that he heard the sales pitch, the entire transaction, and that he thought it was wrong.

"If you say anything to anybody about this, you're . . ." said Walters.

"It was wrong," Defauw replied, not even pausing to think what Norby Walters had just told him.

Walters took a deep breath.

"What's it gonna take to keep you quiet?" the agent asked.

Defauw said he wasn't looking for money.

"You don't know who the fuck you're messing around with," snapped Walters. "You are messing with the wrong people. Definitely messing with the wrong people."

Defauw's heart was pounding, and now he was scared. Both Walters and Bloom looked dead serious.

Defauw decided to excuse himself, but not before Walters reminded him that he was "messing with the wrong people."

When Defauw got up, he saw Walters whisper something to Bloom and thought he heard something like "Follow him . . . find out where he's from."

Defauw could feel Bloom's presence behind him, but as he turned down the hall, he saw Bloom head for the front desk, where he inquired about him. At that point Defauw hustled to his room, called the local police, and explained what had just happened. The Clemson police told him to wait there until they arrived.

They responded fairly quickly, and Defauw remembers the shocked faces of Norby Walters and Lloyd Bloom when the police told all of them they were going to the station for questioning. Walters protested, claiming he had a plane waiting for him. It didn't matter—they were all going to the police station.

When they arrived, a local detective was there to listen to the story.

The detective then called Sergeant Greg Masceri and said, "We've got a fucking mess on our hands. You better get down here."

Masceri took Defauw, Walters, and Bloom upstairs and activated a tape recorder to get the story. Masceri wanted to know why Defauw was in town and whether he was a Clemson booster or anything like that. No, Defauw told him; he got his degree from Michigan State. He was a high-tech electronics salesman from Atlanta, and he overheard Norby Walters pitching to Terrence Flagler and Terrance Roulhac.

When Sergeant Masceri heard Defauw tell what happened again, Masceri got up and said, "I'm gonna leave the room. You need to hash this out between each other."

Defauw looked at Sergeant Masceri incredulously.

"I want to talk to the coach or the athletic director," said Defauw, who knew that Danny Ford was the Clemson coach. "They need to know about this."

Alone again with Walters and Bloom, Walters tried a new angle with Defauw but one that was familiar to others: "You know, I represent Patti LaBelle and some of the biggest stars in the music industry. . . . If you ever need anything . . ."

Outside the room, Defauw believed he heard the police call the Clemson athletic director, who at that time was Bobby Robinson. He also heard somebody say, "Go get Flagler and Roulhac."

It was getting late when Sergeant Masceri and other police officers told Walters and Bloom to leave the room. Then the police sat down with Defauw and started asking him about the night's events.

"What were you doing eavesdropping like that?" one policeman asked.

The question was offensive. Defauw explained that Norby Walters had been very loud and that it was impossible not to hear what was happening.

"Why'd you confront them?" the officer asked. "Were you looking for money?"

Defauw couldn't believe his ears. "No, but they offered," he replied.

Another policeman spoke up: "You might've gotten yourself in a little mess here. Why don't you just get out of town real quick like?"

Defauw said, "I think Coach Ford has a right to know something."

He was told that somebody representing Clemson was downstairs in the police station. Defauw insisted on talking to whoever was there from Clemson, but the police grew agitated by his demands.

Defauw said they threatened to charge him with crimes such as solici-
tation of a bribe and something called "eavesdropping." Now he was no
longer as scared of Norby Walters and Lloyd Bloom as he was of the
Clemson police. He was sent back into the room alone. It was well after
midnight now, and he looked at the table and saw the tape recorder. He
glanced over his shoulder and saw nobody. He opened the recorder,
removed the tape, and slid it into his pocket. He thought he was crazy.
It was like a bad dream.

Thirty minutes later officers brought him a paper with a statement
saying that he would not pursue the allegations he had made about
Norby Walters and the Clemson football players. Defauw was dumb-
founded.

"You ain't leaving until you sign it," he was told.

One last time he asked to speak with Coach Ford or the Clemson
athletic director. They told him it was his last chance to sign the paper
and get out of town without further hassle. Defauw signed the statement.
When he went downstairs, he thought he saw Flagler and Roulhac in a
room. Two policemen hustled him out a rear door and into a squad car.
They drove him to the hotel and instructed him to check out, get in his
car, and drive out of town. After packing his bags, Defauw got into his
car and headed for Atlanta on Interstate 85. The Clemson police were his
escorts. Defauw nervously watched them in his rearview mirror.

Defauw was in a state of shock by the time he got home around 5 A.M.
He had the tape, a theft that may have been the only crime he committed
that night. The next day he called his lawyer and told him about the
threats from Norby Walters and the Clemson police. The lawyer wanted
him to call the local newspaper, but Defauw rejected the idea.

He never saw anything in the newspaper that fall about any Clemson
players signing with an agent. There was no announcement by the
school. The Clemson police department had kept mum. Terrence Flagler
and Terrance Roulhac played with no hint that they may have been
ineligible for that 1986 football season.

Defauw was tempted to come forward when his newspaper, the Atlanta Constitution, started breaking news stories the following spring
about Norby Walters, but he was still scared. He stayed silent.

Gary Defauw finally had somebody to whom he could tell his story.
His notes and tapes were then safely secured by the FBI in Atlanta, and
along with a comprehensive FD 302 report, the government had a terri-
fying tale of just how deep corruption in college football had sunk—so
deep, it was a story they didn't dare bring to a jury.

On July 14, Ohio State star wide receiver Cris Carter told his story to the grand jury.

Two days later, following a report in the *Atlanta Constitution* that Ohio State was now aware of Carter's involvement with Walters and Bloom, Cris Carter was declared ineligible for his senior season in 1987, igniting a major controversy between college football coaches and the NFL, which had reluctantly admitted Carter to the supplemental draft. Nevertheless, Carter lost a lot of money in contract negotiations because his leverage was gone. Carter would be a vital witness for the government because of these reasons and because he was a Big Ten Conference player.

Carter was only a sophomore when Norby Walters and Lloyd Bloom reached out to him, which the government saw as the beginning of a new pattern. No player was too young to recruit if the talent was rated high enough. Ironically, the agents' initial contact was quite aboveboard. They sent him a letter, via the Ohio State athletic department, introducing themselves. That was perfectly okay according to the NCAA rules. The athletic department delivered the letter to his locker.

Carter didn't respond to the letter, but he soon received a phone call from Lloyd Bloom, who had acquired the telephone number from Ohio State basketball star Brad Sellers. Sellers had joined the family during the NIT tournament in 1986 when the Buckeyes played at Madison Square Garden.

The agents to the stars invited Cris Carter to New York to check out the operation. Cris said he didn't have time. He was in the middle of spring football. He was already being touted on numerous preseason All-America teams after his sophomore season. In a week he was going to fly to Miami to be honored as a member of the *Playboy* magazine All-America team.

Cris Carter suggested that one of his brothers, George, check out World Sports and Entertainment. George Carter, one of seven children, had just been released from state prison after a sixteen-month stay for burglary and forgery. Though Cris's oldest brother, Butch, a former Indiana basketball player who was in the NBA, despised George, Cris felt differently.

George Carter, then twenty-six, called Lloyd Bloom and accepted the invitation to fly to New York. The agents sent him an airline ticket via Federal Express, and George went. George was impressed with the Norby Walters show, the operation, the gold records on the wall, and all the entertainers that Uncle Norby represented.

George Carter also met the Reverend Al Sharpton, who was in Norby
Walters's office that Friday. Norby and Al both acted like very close
friends, George told Cris. Reverend Sharpton put in a good word for
Norby.

Eventually Norby Walters made his sales pitch to George Carter.
They wanted to represent Cris. They asked how much his brother needed
to "make life comfortable." Cris would have to sign an agreement, which
the agents promised would be sealed in a vault.

George Carter actually balked when he was told that Cris would have
to sign something, but Norby Walters told George to return to the Hotel
Novatel, call Cris, and think about it.

George called his brother and told him how impressed he was with
Norby Walters. Cris wanted to know more.

"If they're big enough to represent Patti LaBelle and Rick James,
they're big enough to represent you," George told his younger brother.
"If those people trust Norby . . ."

Cris Carter wanted to know about money. George explained, "You
can get as much as you want, but this ain't no free money. It's interest-
free, but you gotta pay it back." And he had to sign a contract. The two
brothers said that $5,000 up front and $300 monthly and maybe a car
would be tempting.

George Carter told Lloyd Bloom what it would take. Bloom talked to
Walters, who said, "No problem."

George Carter went back to Norby's office, where Norby reached in
a pocket and pulled out $300—for George. That weekend George had a
good time with Lloyd Bloom.

A few days later Cris Carter received a telephone call from Norby
Walters, who whispered raspily on the phone, "Lloyd's on the way with
the scratch."

Scratch, another slang expression for cash.

George and Cris picked up Bloom at the Columbus airport. George
drove his tiny Mercury Lynx, Lloyd sat in the passenger seat, and Cris
was in the back. They pulled over when it was convenient. Bloom handed
Cris Carter a Louis Vuitton pouch and said, "Five grand." He also
handed Cris a contract. Cris signed and handed it back. Bloom looked
at George and handed him the contract, too.

"You gotta sign, too, because Cris ain't twenty-one, and that's New
York law," the agent said.

George Carter said, "You didn't tell me anything about that."

Suddenly Cris spoke up: "Sign it, George. It ain't nothing."

Lloyd Bloom told George that when Cris turned twenty-one they would tear up this contract and sign a new one. George signed.

Cris Carter received star treatment from then on, and George went along for the ride. The trips to New York were frequent. Lloyd Bloom played Mr. Big Shot. One time he picked them up in a Mercedes 1000 and boasted that he and Jermaine Jackson had the only models in the United States.

The Carters thought Lloyd Bloom must have been one of the richest young men in the country, but they also started to notice that Norby Walters pushed Bloom around. Sometimes Norby's temper turned hot, and Norby would ask them to leave the office. They started to wonder about Norby Walters. Then one day when George was in town alone, he was allowed to listen to Norby Walters and Lloyd Bloom talk tough with "one of the players down in Texas" about Jeff Atkins, and they mentioned that Atkins might never play football again if he didn't stop ignoring the agents. Soon afterward Atkins called them back.

George Carter later said, "Norby told me, 'That's how you take care of problems.' "

George Carter told his brother Cris what had happened.

"Norby talks like he's got some muscle behind him," George said.

Cris Carter had a splendid junior season, setting school records for receptions (69), yards (1,127), and touchdown catches (11).

Two of the touchdowns came against Purdue's star defensive back Rod Woodson. Before that game, Lloyd Bloom told Cris Carter he'd pay him $250 a touchdown against any other member of "the family." He received $500 for his two scores against Purdue. Later, Cris Carter was also kicked out of the game because he fired the ball at Woodson after he was pushed out of bounds following a catch.

Bloom also paid Cris Carter $250 for scoring once against Iowa's Devon Mitchell.

This was the first and only sign that the sports agents were investing in player performances. Maybe it was on the upside, but the downside was obvious.

The spring of 1987 was the beginning of the end of Cris Carter's abbreviated career at Ohio State. First came the *Atlanta Constitution* story that connected him with Norby Walters. Initially Carter was livid, believing the agents had leaked his name. That was not what happened, however.

Ohio State football coach Earle Bruce was very tight with Carter. He looked the player square in the eye and asked if there was anything to the stories that he was hooked up with Norby Walters. Carter looked him in the eye and said, "No."

Earle Bruce defended Carter internally and to the media.

But Cris Carter began to arouse even more suspicion among his teammates, who had noticed that the star receiver was driving a 300 ZX, had upgraded his wardrobe, and was picking up dinner and drink tabs with some regularity. Some players were envious.

Then Carter compounded his problem after an NFL draft party for Ohio State teammate Pepper Johnson, a linebacker who had been chosen by the New York Giants earlier in the day. There was cocaine in people's pockets at the party. Cris Carter took a few hits.

The next day, to his shock, Cris received a call in his dorm room from an assistant coach and was told to get over to the football office. Cris thought the coach sounded serious. When he got there, he was asked to provide a urine sample.

Cris Carter suspected he had been the victim of a team snitch, which was ironic. Several years earlier his brother Butch had turned in several teammates for smoking marijuana to Indiana basketball coach Bobby Knight, and the players were suspended.

The next day Cris Carter was suspended, though the announcement said "violation of team rules." An Ohio newspaper eventually linked the suspension to drug use but never named the drug. Speculation arose that it was because of his brother George's relationship with Norby Walters.

George Carter had indeed been put on Norby Walters's payroll, but it turned out to be just for effect, to put George on good terms with the Ohio Parole Board.

Cris Carter was reinstated, but then more bad news hit. The U. S. Attorney in Chicago subpoenaed his school records. Soon the FBI was knocking on his door. He knew his time as a Buckeye was drawing to a close.

He cried the day he confessed to Earle Bruce that he had lied to him previously.

Another Big Ten star, Purdue's Rod Woodson, made headlines on Friday, May 22, when he was banned by commissioner Wayne Duke from participating in the Big Ten track and field championships for "failing to disclose that he had signed with a professional sports agent and received money from an agent."

Woodson, who was hailed as the best athlete in the 1987 NFL draft, was an accomplished track star and the Big Ten favorite to win the 110-meter hurdles. He had also been scheduled to compete in the 100-

and 200-meter dashes, as well as the 400-meter relay. Technically, the NCAA rules would have allowed Woodson to be a professional in one sport but not in another. But, as Duke noted, his failure to disclose his relationship with Walters had tainted his eligibility. Woodson reluctantly admitted his violation only after Walters filed a $500,000 lawsuit against him, attaching the contract and promissory note, and documenting approximately $21,000 in cash and benefits that the player had received. Walters had also cosigned a loan with the Irving Trust Company in New York for the purchase of a Ford Mercury, which was registered in Woodson's grandmother's name. Woodson had explained to his coaches and the athletic department officials that the car was a gift from his grandmother for the start of his senior year.

Woodson was prominent on the government's "hit list" because he was high profile. He had taken a considerable amount of money, and he had not been totally truthful with FBI agents who came knocking on his door the month before. But there was still some question about Tony Valukas's determination to prosecute the athletes as coconspirators. For one thing, it had become clearer that there were going to be a lot more "dirty" schools than "clean" schools. Many players readily told the prosecutors about money and benefits they received.

Later, after Valukas left office for private practice, he conceded that "there was a certain naivete at the beginning of the investigation where we may have thought SMU was the exception rather than the rule, believing that most college athletic programs operated aboveboard. It didn't take long to realize most college programs had problems. And that was very troublesome."

As Valukas had instructed, Howard Pearl told Rod Woodson that the easiest way out of this mess was to plead guilty to mail fraud, which by law carried a maximum penalty of five years in prison and a $250,000 fine. The government would recommend a lesser sentence, perhaps even a suspended sentence, if the player cooperated. It was a confusing, scary time for Woodson and the other players. Taking money from an agent had become a federal crime.

Still, Pearl and Randolph believed the players were victims, targeted by Walters and Bloom as unsophisticated athletes, and they again wondered who the government would use as witnesses if they prosecuted everyone.

The solution was offered in part by Eugene Parker, Woodson's attorney from Fort Wayne, Indiana. Parker laid out the realities of life for many of these players, such as Rod Woodson. The lawyer's argument was so compelling that Pearl and Randolph urged him to meet with Valukas.

Parker was able to show Valukas, Pearl, and Randolph that Woodson received perhaps only half of the $21,000 that Walters had sent. The rest of it went to Woodson's mother, who was in dire need of money and couldn't stop asking Uncle Norby for cash on a regular basis. At one time the boiler or heater had broken down, and the only way they could get it fixed was to ask the agent for money. Uncle Norby obliged. He always obliged.

The other aspect Eugene Parker laid out for the prosecution team was how unfair the NCAA had made life for college athletes. Yes, players received room, board, and a scholarship, but that was about it. College athletes received no other stipends, no laundry money, nothing. They weren't even allowed to get jobs during their season, and the demands were rather substantial out of season. Players in financial need could apply for federal Pell Grant stipends of up to $2,100 a year, but the NCAA had then restricted the maximum for an athlete to $900. A regular student could get $2,100 annually, but a so-called student-athlete could receive only $900. The rest went to the same university that was bringing in millions of dollars in the business of big-time college athletics.

Star players could not capitalize locally or nationally on their celebrity. There were no endorsements or commercials for college football players. Track and field athletes made thousands of dollars—Carl Lewis made more than a million dollars—and retained their amateur status for the Olympics. So what was an amateur athlete?

And if a college football player was struggling financially and losing interest in school, he had no viable alternative. The National Football League barred underclassmen from entering its annual draft. This left college players vulnerable to a sports agent like Norby Walters offering Faustian deals.

Parker suggested a solution, not only for Rod Woodson but for most of the fifty-eight players who had dealt with Norby Walters and Lloyd Bloom. He proposed that Woodson pay back Purdue University for the senior season in which he should have been ineligible. That was around $6,000.

It made perfect sense to Tony Valukas, Howard Pearl, and George Randolph. The prosecution had already talked about establishing a Pre-Trial Diversion Program for many of the players; they could avoid prosecution by agreeing to cooperate, testify, and perform community service under the supervision of the United States Probation Department. Restitution to the schools was a nice twist because it would show a judge and subsequently a jury that the schools had been defrauded of real money. It also held the players somewhat culpable. After all, they were the ones who falsely signed their certification papers. They lied to the schools about their relationship with Walters and Bloom. They couldn't walk away unscathed, or it would be considered just another con job.

Woodson was an ideal candidate for this program because the government needed Big Ten Conference athletes to establish jurisdiction for the Northern District of Illinois. It would also create the pool of necessary witnesses to take the stand against Walters and Bloom.

There wouldn't be the headache of trying the players separately for mail fraud, and it would no longer look as if the government was going after athletes, who some critics claimed were already being mistreated by college football's "plantation" mentality.

The restitution program could solve a lot of thorny issues. Even though the Supreme Court had handed down its landmark McNally decision, dismissing mail fraud prosecution related to "intangible" rights, the fact that the players were repaying money to the colleges would show a judge and jury that there was something tangible in this case.

Still, there was skepticism about the mail fraud theory in the U. S. Attorney's office. Tony Valukas called together his top eight assistants, and they went through the case as it stood. Strip away the possible extortion and the potential to uncover organized crime, Valukas told them. The U. S. Attorney asked his top legal minds whether they would prosecute this case against Norby Walters and Lloyd Bloom on the mail fraud charges, portraying the colleges as victims.

The scorecard was 7–1. That was seven "no" votes, and one "aye."

"Everybody thought we couldn't prove mail fraud without defending the sanctity of college athletics. We thought we could," Pearl said.

8

ONE OF the seemingly endless projects that George Randolph took on was running computer background checks on every athlete who had put a signature on a contract offered by Norby Walters and Lloyd Bloom. Many of the players had had little run-ins with the law. That meant tracking down various police reports and inserting them into the player files. Randolph's skepticism about the players was growing every day.

By contrast, the background checks on Norby Walters and Lloyd Bloom were almost too clean. Randolph needed to know more about both men. He had already learned quite a bit about how each of them operated from the tapes and from the testimony of the players. Randolph knew from the tapes that Walters claimed to have a $50 million to $100 million business in the entertainment world. Randolph followed up on his claims, even calling Coca-Cola headquarters in Atlanta to find out if Walters had truly made the million-dollar endorsement deals he boasted about with the players. Coca-Cola officials said that Walters had done only a small amount of business with the company.

Randolph also knew that the silver-haired Walters had a "dark side." It had come through clearly on the Tony Woods tape. He had also followed through on his threats to file lawsuits against a half-dozen players. Randolph, Pearl, and Valukas saw the suits as part of Uncle Norby's larger plan to expose players who had jilted him. Using the public lawsuits and his subsequent interview with the *Atlanta Constitution,* Walters had succeeded in dragging the players through a series of personally embarrassing headlines and university investigations.

Although they were clearly damaging to his business, Walters didn't think of the suits as suicide. He still had John Clay and Paul Palmer as clients, and another five highly valued underclassmen signed to con-tracts. He was protecting himself from future defections, and he knew he could count on his ability as a salesman and the temptation of money to override any negative publicity.

Randolph didn't get to see the full picture until he met the agent for the first time. On August 18, 1987, Walters made the first of three subpoenaed appearances before the grand jury. While Walters's new team of criminal lawyers—led by Robert Gold of New York—argued with Tony Valukas and Howard Pearl about the mail fraud case, Norby tried to make friendly conversation with Randolph. The FBI agent could see that Norby had a gift for gab, a real salesman's touch and, yes, charm and charisma. Norby Walters even tried to pitch concert tickets for his acts.

"Norby, shut up," Gold said.

Every once in a while Robert Gold had to remind his client with whom they were dealing.

Even if the FBI didn't find much on the computer background checks, Walters and Bloom were always eager to talk with the press. And when they spoke, Randolph listened. One of those pieces was the *Billboard* magazine "article" the athletes had mentioned. The article had a two-tier headline that read:

WITH A RARE BLEND OF HEART, SOUL & SENSE
NOBODY BOOKS IT BETTER THAN NORBY WALTERS

There were other smaller headlines embedded in the story such as, *Black Music's Leading Booking Agent.* Norby Walters was celebrating his fifteenth anniversary in the business. Randolph looked for the date of the article. It was December 17, 1983, which meant Walters had been in business since 1968. Something seemed strange about this piece, which ran fifteen pages. Randolph looked more closely at the fine print that ran parallel to the story. This was no regular article, it was a *Billboard* ad-vertising supplement. Norby Walters must have paid for this publicity.

Randolph thumbed through the pages before he read them. There was a picture of Norby Walters with two apparent partners in his business: Sal Michaels and Jerry Ade. "We Have the Stars . . . and Have for 15 Years!" Pictures of the stars were pasted all over the page, and there were many other photos throughout the supplement. There were pictures of Norby Walters with Rodney Dangerfield, with Marvin Gaye, with Rob-ert "Kool" Bell. Norby, Ade, and Michaels with Lionel Richie. Another with Ashford and Simpson, one with Rick James, one with Jimmy Cliff. Just as Tim McGee had remembered.

There were little captioned salutes to Norby Walters. Reverend Al Sharpton, identified as the president of the National Youth Movement, was quoted, "I think Norby Walters is symbolic of the man who helps bring others toward their dream. He has represented for black artists a bridge over the uncertain waters of show business. He guides them to the shore of commercial success."

Randolph wondered if Sharpton was getting a take of the business; Sharpton had already been seen in Norby's offices by George Carter. Randolph continued with the *Billboard* supplement and noticed that one salute came from Rick James, the singer mentioned on the Tony Woods tape. "He's special, and he's the greatest agent of all time," James said. "He's Uncle Norby. . . . When I'm down, he picks me up."

Randolph was curious about what Walters did in the business. The article said he was the "booking agent" for all these entertainers, which meant he booked the acts into various clubs and arenas across the country. But didn't he also say he represented these artists in their commercial endorsements? Is he an agent or a booking agent? Or both? Randolph made a note to find out.

Randolph noticed that there was a question-and-answer interview between *Village Voice* music critic Nelson George and Norby Walters. Nelson George asked the questions, and Norby Walters responded by describing how he had gotten into the entertainment business.

Walters explained that his father was a Jewish immigrant from Poland who became known as Soldier Meyer when he was an army lightweight champ. After the army Soldier Meyer became a concessionaire on Coney Island, and Norby Meyer helped his father work "freak shows" and "girlie shows."

"Wouldn't you know it," Randolph muttered.

Norby told Nelson George, "My friends were home with marbles and baseball tickets, and I was working girlie shows."

Anyway, Norby Meyer, as he was known then, went to Brooklyn College while his father opened Soldier Meyer's Jazz Club in 1949 where, according to Walters, artists such as Thelonious Monk, Miles Davis, Stan Getz, Lester Young, Charlie Parker, Sarah Vaughan, Billy Eckstine, and somebody called Symphony Sid all got a boost in their careers.

Walters himself claimed he grew up in a "poor Jewish neighborhood" in Brownsville that eventually became integrated with New York black kids.

"So I was dealing with a black presence most of my life," Walters said.

Norby Meyer, along with his brother Walter, bought the nightclub from their father in 1952 and decided to rename it Norby & Walter's Bell Air Night Club. It opened next door to the famous Copacabana. Opening night was memorable, Norby told the interviewer, because when the neon sign was hung above the club, the ampersand was inadvertently omitted, so it read Norby Walter's Bell Air Night Club. Norby and his brother Walter were at the door greeting guests on the club's premiere night. People were asking, "Which one is Norby Walters?" His brother was angry over the confusion and never forgave him for it.

"After four or five guests, I became Norby Walters," he said, adding that he had changed his name legally from Norby Meyer.

The club eventually closed, and Walters got into the agent business in 1968, at first booking lounge acts. Nelson George then mentioned to Walters, "It seems like from 1978 on you started getting superstars."

Walters explained,

That was the turning point because at that time we signed Marvin Gaye, who was our first star of such a magnitude. Marvin was already a legendary character. Having taken Marvin on a twenty-four-city tour, including Hawaii and Japan, where he never missed a date, many different artists were looking at us differently. They realized that if we could take Marvin Gaye and tour him in twenty-four cities that we had the capability to represent anyone. In 1978 Gloria Gaynor made another smash hit, "I Will Survive," which was a worldwide smash hit.

Walters bragged about the other artists that came on board and said, "From 1980 to 1983 everyone we had signed seems to have gone to number one." He dropped the names again, including a group called the New Edition with a hot young singer named Bobby Brown. The group, Walters said, was "the 1983 answer to the Jacksons."

Interestingly, Nelson George did ask Walters, "How do you feel about the criticism of this white booking agent with all of these black acts?"

Walters replied,

I've heard a lot of criticism from people who don't know any better. I think I'm extremely qualified to sell entertainment. I've been involved with selling entertainment since I was eight years old. That makes it forty-three years. I've sold every type of show, from girlie shows to belly dancers to comics to Latin bands, from every phase of contemporary music, but most importantly my true roots have gone back over some thirty years in black music. I gave Thelonious Monk one of his earliest chances. Miles Davis had his first band in my club, and JJ Johnson had his first band in this club. I don't have to prove my credentials of how long I've been involved with black music when most of the critics who are criticizing me didn't pay any dues and didn't do anything to help black music.

The supplement closed with a full-page ad that had a picture of Norby Walters, Jerry Ade, and Sal Michaels. There was no hint of a partner or associate named Lloyd Bloom. At the top of the page were big bold letters, that read, THANKS TO ALL OUR FRIENDS FOR ALL YOUR HELP. Underneath were thirty-two lines of these "friends," many with a familiar ring: "Anheuser-Busch, the Commodores, Clive Davis, Aretha Franklin, Gloria Gaynor, Grandmaster Flash, Marvin Gaye, Rick James, the Jacksons, Chaka Khan, Kool & the Gang, Don King . . ."

Don King! The boxing promoter? Randolph scribbled the name on his legal pad and continued to read the list. Why would he thank Don King . . . and what about Al Sharpton?

"Don Kirshner, Chaka Khan, Patti LaBelle, Midnight Star, Teena Marie, New Edition, O'Jays, Quentin Perry, Reverend Al Sharpton, Peter Tosh, Luther Vandross, Dionne Warwick, Bobby Womack. . . ."

Randolph figured there must have been four hundred names on the list. The bottom of the ad listed telephone numbers for the East Coast office and a West Coast office in Los Angeles. Maybe that would help in getting the L.A. FBI office to cooperate. This was a handy advertising supplement. Norby Walters had provided a long list of potential contacts.

Randolph found it fascinating, regardless of how slanted it was or the fact that Walters had probably footed the bill for the publicity. It seemed clear that Norby Walters was indeed a force in the entertainment world.

Randolph thought if he were a young athlete reading this *Billboard* magazine "article" about Norby Walters, agent to the stars, he'd be impressed. He could also understand why the athletes might initially be impressed by Lloyd Bloom. He was a good-looking guy. He was married to a young model-actress, Donna Denton (Palmiotto was her maiden name), who had once been called "The Face" after she appeared on the cover of several magazines. She had also been a costar on the "Mike Hammer" series and was now living in Hollywood pursuing a film career.

Randolph's background check showed that Denton had divorced Bloom in 1986, but the two had reconciled in Sherman Oaks, California, by the summer of 1987. Despite his strengths, though, it was clear to the government that Bloom was a bungler and might have single-handedly blown the Walters operation with his loudmouthed personality and blatant threats.

His tongue definitely got him in trouble. Even after it was publicized that a federal grand jury had convened to investigate the agents' activities, Bloom still couldn't keep his mouth shut. His interviews with the *Washington Post* and the *Atlanta Constitution* during the summer of 1987 stupefied Randolph and the government, but provided even more background about the agents to the stars. Bloom talked somewhat freely of the operation and, in essence, told his life story, as if he were jealous of the publicity Norby Walters was getting.

Randolph found that Bloom consistently told the same story of how he got hooked up with Norby Walters. Bloom had been a New York boy, born in Brooklyn on April 7, 1959, and was raised in Westchester County. He was the oldest of four children of Stuart and Myrna Bloom, who owned a highly successful credit and collection agency. Randolph thought this was funny since the background check on Bloom revealed he had filed for bankruptcy in New York in 1987. He had almost $200,000 in debts and a little more than $1,000 in assets. His Mercedes had been repossessed. Apparently his parents' business hadn't made an impression on him.

Bloom played football at Irvington High in New York and said he weighed about 225 pounds as a linebacker and tight end. He had been disappointed that no major college recruited him, though he did give the game another try at a local junior college.

Norby Walters didn't remember, but the first time he met Lloyd Bloom was at one of the concerts he booked for the Village People and Gloria Gaynor in 1978. Gloria Gaynor's hit "I Will Survive" was Lloyd Bloom's favorite song. Bloom had hustled to get backstage, where he not only met Gaynor but also shook hands with Norby Walters.

Bloom wanted to live in the limelight and establish himself in Manhattan. He started as a bouncer at Studio 54, the hottest nightclub in New York, and then got ambitious by organizing parties for private groups and corporations.

Watching TV one night, Lloyd Bloom jumped off his couch when he saw "Don Kirshner's Rock Concert" doing a salute and special on Norby Walters, who was celebrating his fifteenth year in the business, now established as the biggest booking agent of black entertainers in the country. That was the same Norby Walters he had shaken hands with five years earlier at the Gloria Gaynor concert. Lloyd Bloom got an idea. He called Norby Walters and told him he wanted to throw a lavish party, all at his expense, honoring the booking agent. Norby thought it was a splendid idea. The party was held in early 1984, and both Walters and Bloom conceded it was a major smash. Bloom kept in contact, occasionally getting concert tickets from Walters. One day in late summer or fall of 1984, the twenty-five-year-old Bloom approached the fifty-four-year-old Walters and made a proposal.

The way both men explained it, Bloom told Norby, "You're number one in the music industry, and I have great knowledge about sports, especially football. I played the game. Why not expand into sports? It's another form of entertainment. You can become number one in sports, too. I'll do the legwork, you fund the operation."

Norby Walters looked at the ambitious young man and saw a bit of himself. Bloom told Walters that the initial costs would be between $100,000 and $200,000. Norby Walters shook hands on the deal and soon formed a new division of Norby Walters Associates and named it World Sports and Entertainment, Inc.

The first player Bloom and Walters signed was an All–Big Ten Conference wide receiver, Tracy Henderson of Iowa State, who had lost his eligibility in the middle of his 1984 season for breaking a number of team rules.

When Walters and Bloom went to their first postseason game, the Senior Bowl in January 1985, they were having trouble signing college football's biggest stars. It didn't take them long to figure out that most players had signed early with an agent, despite the NCAA rules.

As Bloom told the *Washington Post,* "Norby said, 'Ah ha! That's the game! If they've all signed early, then the only way to join them is to beat them doubly at their own game.' "

Ronnie Harmon, an Iowa junior raised in New York, was signed two months later. It was no coincidence that, like Henderson, Harmon was black.

"We stick to blacks," Bloom conceded to the *Washington Post.* "We're plugged into the black market."

Howard Pearl and George Randolph already understood that the agents targeted only black players. They figured that the socioeconomic climate made black players more susceptible to hustlers like Norby Walters and Lloyd Bloom.

Randolph also knew Bloom had a nasty temper. Most of the threats of bodily harm had been made by him, according to the tapes and player interviews. But the government believed Walters was aware of the threats and had supervised them. Whether Norby Walters was actually a member of the Mafia or not, the pattern of threats was certainly imitating life in the mob.

Even if Lloyd Bloom had gone a bit overboard with the mobster routine, he still must have been quite persuasive. Some of the players took him very seriously. The government found out that the players at SMU made a pact to protect one another after Bloom's threats to Ron Morris and Jeff Atkins.

Jerry Ball, a three-hundred-pound All-America defensive tackle and future star for the Detroit Lions, told the FBI and eventually the Chicago prosecution team a fascinating story of how he once took matters into his own hands on a weekend when Lloyd Bloom traveled to Dallas.

Bloom made contact with Ball from an airport hotel, and Ball told the agent that he would pick him up in his van later that evening. When Bloom got into the van, Ball started driving in an obscure direction.

"Where are we going?" Bloom asked him.

Shortly afterward, where there was no sign of human life, Jerry Ball pulled over and reached under his seat. He pulled out a .357 Magnum and pointed it at Bloom.

"Quit fucking around with my brothers," Ball told him.

Bloom's eyes grew as wide as Texas.

"Come on, Jerry, put the gun away," he said. "Stop joking around."

"I ain't joking," Ball said.

"Hey, everything's cool," said Bloom. "Nobody's threatened."

Ball then drove Bloom back to the hotel. Bloom later confirmed to the government and a reporter that the incident happened.

Nevertheless, Bloom stupidly continued to expose himself and Walters to potentially explosive situations by making more threats.

As both Edwin Simmons, the Texas running back, and Everett Gay recalled for the government, Lloyd Bloom telephoned Simmons in his dormitory room in mid-November 1986 and wanted to know why Gay wasn't picking up his money. Bloom told Simmons he had heard rumors that Gay was thinking about leaving the agents.

"No one does Norby like that," Bloom told Simmons.

Bloom stressed to Simmons that if he was Gay's buddy, then he should do his friend a favor—or else.

"If he leaves, we make a phone call to Las Vegas. Then somebody's gonna come down and make sure that Everett Gay doesn't play football again," Bloom told Simmons. "He might break his legs."

That weekend, before Texas played a game, Simmons passed along the message to Gay. By then many of the Texas players thought Bloom and his Brooklynese act were almost comical. They laughed about the threats on the team bus. They joked about broken kneecaps, and Simmons told him he had better not go up for any passes because he might not come down or might come down with broken legs.

But after the game, and through the rest of the weekend, Everett Gay was not very amused about the message that had been delivered. As Gay later testified, Bloom did not back down from the message sent through Simmons.

"Bloom told me that they had a situation with Tim McGee once, and they had to send some people to his parents' house to collect some money," Gay recalled. "He said, 'That's why we have friends in California, to make sure we don't get messed over.' "

No one had shown up at McGee's house, of course, but Bloom knew how to intimidate people. Bloom also had an unsettling effect on other players he threatened. Ron Morris had been genuinely scared. Bloom had also done some of his best work on Chicago Bears defensive back Maurice "Mo" Douglass, a former Kentucky star.

When Randolph met with Douglass in the Chicago Bears cafeteria at Lake Forest, he knew he was a young man who had not let the macho side of being a football player get the best of him. Douglass told Randolph that Bloom threatened to have "somebody break your legs."

Douglass was one of the few players who actually waited until after his eligibility had expired before signing with the agents on December 27, 1985. The problem was, Douglass told Bloom, he had already signed with St. Louis agent Jim Steiner on November 27, which was also after the Kentucky season.

"Why'd you sign with Walters and Bloom then?" Randolph asked.

"Bloom said that it was no problem, that it would be taken care of."

Douglass had been razzle-dazzled. After Bloom told him about all the entertainers the agents represented, he immediately accepted an invitation to travel to New York to "check out the operation." Bloom met him at the airport in a shiny black Mercedes-Benz. They drove into Manhattan, where Douglass met Walters at his office. He got the treatment—"the agent to the stars." He was impressed, signed the deal, and walked out with $2,500 in cash.

Pretty soon Bloom approached him about his former Kentucky teammate, star running back Marc Logan, who still had a season remaining. Bloom offered Douglass $1,500 to arrange a meeting with Logan in Lexington. Another done deal.

During the next couple of months Douglass received more money, including a down payment for a car. His tab was up to $8,712.45 as the NFL draft approached in April 1986.

Jim Steiner convinced Douglass that he should honor their original deal. Besides, as Steiner pointed out, Walters and Bloom had never done an NFL contract. It made sense to Douglass. He notified Walters and Bloom that he was sticking with Steiner.

Lloyd Bloom started calling Douglass at his mom's home in Cincinnati.

"He told me that if I didn't return the money and the car, he'd have somebody rough me up," Douglass told Randolph. "He said I might not make it to the draft, that he may have somebody break my legs."

Randolph wanted to know how Douglass responded.

"I paid him back," the player said.

The FBI agent's heart beat faster. Douglass explained that he paid back half the money, and then Bloom made another threatening phone call during his rookie season in the NFL in 1986. Bloom wanted the rest of the money.

"So I gave it to him," said Douglass.

The payments were made by checks through his new agency, Douglass believed. They would be essential.

"I take it you were scared," Randolph asked Douglass.

"Well, yeah, not so much of Bloom, but I had seen their operation. I knew they had a lot of money, and I didn't know what they could have done to me," the Bears defensive back said. "I was scared, actually. Really scared."

"Anything else you did about it?"

Douglass thought about Randolph's question. Yes, there was something: "I told my mother that if anything ever happened to me, to notify the police and tell them that Lloyd Bloom had threatened me."

Douglass's story later made an impression on Howard Pearl, who said, "Here was a guy who had absolutely no reason to give up Walters and Bloom. He wasn't under threat of prosecution because he didn't take money until after his eligibility. Those threats were very unsettling to him, trust me."

Lloyd Bloom was really building a case for the government.

Then something extraordinary happened. On August 26, 1987, the NCAA did something it had never done before. It restored the eligibility of Pitt defensive back Teryl Austin, one of the underclassmen who had signed with Norby Walters and Lloyd Bloom.

It was something Howard Pearl and George Randolph had never expected. A player who signed early with an agent could never be eligible to play sports, the NCAA had assured the government. Now it was doing a complete reversal, and the government wanted to know why. The reinstatement of Teryl Austin could sabotage the government's investigation and case.

The NCAA explained, through assistant executive director Steve Morgan, that by reinstating Austin it was initiating something of an "amnesty program" for college athletes who may have gotten involved with a sports agent. Austin would have to pay a penalty— a two-game suspension plus documentation that he had repaid any money taken from Walters and Bloom and that he had severed his agreement with the agents—but he could resume playing if he met the criteria. Morgan said the NCAA was inviting other athletes to come forward, hoping to get a handle on the sports agent problem in college athletics. No one came forward. The government wasn't surprised.

When the NCAA reinstated Pitt defensive back Teryl Austin, Ohio State coach Earle Bruce started screaming for the reinstatement of Cris Carter. It didn't happen, but it was another bitter pill for the government as it tried to build its case.

Tony Valukas might have shut down the entire investigation at that time, were it not for his faith in George Randolph and Howard Pearl, and some extraordinary reporting by *Sports Illustrated*'s Bruce Selcraig, who had previously been an investigator for the U. S. Senate. He had decided back in January to check out Norby Walters and Lloyd Bloom but was frustrated when he saw the *Atlanta Constitution* break its string of sensational stories on the agents.

But Selcraig's contacts in Washington were vast. He had been tipped that Norby Walters had an association with Sonny and Michael Franzese, two reputed captains in the Colombo crime family of New York. Selcraig did not nail down a direct business relationship between Walters and organized crime, but he came as close as one could get. And much to the government's dismay, he got Michael Franzese to agree to an interview. Seven months of digging by Selcraig produced a fascinating account of Norby Walters and Lloyd Bloom in the August 3, 1987, issue. Selcraig did his best to shoot holes in Uncle Norby's claims of having nothing to do with the mob after Walters was quoted as saying,

"I don't even know what the word Mafia is. I've never met anybody like that."

Selcraig used no less a source than Norby's brother Walter, who told *Sports Illustrated* about the people who visited Norby & Walter's Night Club, another joint opened by the agent. "All five (New York Mafia) families were well represented. We were friends with all of them. They were good customers. . . . He (Norby) could bull—with anybody. He could talk with a Mafia captain. He could talk with a hooker off the street. He knew how to handle everybody. Best up-front man in the business, maybe in the whole United States."

Selcraig also obtained a New York State Liquor Authority report that showed that Norby & Walter's Night Club, which had opened in 1966, lost its liquor license because the nightspot had a "highly adverse police and license history for assaults and prostitution activities."

On March 22, 1968, the establishment closed when two mobsters, Oresto Joseph Bruni and Rosario "Sonny" Parisi, were gunned down in the club.

Walter Walters also recalled that two men killed at Norby's nightclub were underlings of a reputed major Mafia figure, Carmine Lombardozzi. After the gunfire ended, Walter Walters told Selcraig that his brother Norby hustled Lombardozzi out through a passageway that led to the Copacabana.

Apparently Walter Walters saw nothing damning in his quotes to the *Sports Illustrated* reporter. Norby Walters knew differently and was furious with his brother. It didn't help that William Harris, the tight end who was booted out of Texas for accepting trips to New York to visit Walters and Bloom, was also quoted about the Mafia.

"They've got friends in Las Vegas," Harris told *Sports Illustrated.* "Tough friends. They told me about their Mafia people. I heard Lloyd talk about one of them. We were at the Beverly Hills Hotel, in the lobby. He pointed to a guy and said, 'That dude's in the Mafia. He owns a casino in Las Vegas.' Lloyd said it to me in a quiet voice. He then said, 'But don't tell anybody.' "

What further stunned Valukas, Pearl, and Randolph was the actual interview between Selcraig and Michael Franzese, done at Terminal Island, where Franzese was serving his ten-year sentence. Michael Franzese told Selcraig that he and Sonny Franzese were lifelong friends of Norby's family, that the two families once vacationed together, and that as a child he knew Walters as "Uncle Norby." Franzese told Selcraig in the article that Walters had asked for his help when Norby was trying unsuccessfully to become the booking agent for the Jacksons' Victory Tour.

Selcraig further reported,

> Justice Department sources told SI that Walters was questioned by a federal prosecutor and acknowledged having discussed with Michael Franzese the Mafia man's possible involvement in the tour. Franzese also told SI that he and Walters discussed using some of Walters's music clients in films he was producing.
>
> Nevertheless, Walters says, "I have nothing to do with the man—zero, zip, zero, zip, zero, zero. Now that's a lot of zeros I just gave you."

George Randolph read the article and didn't know whether to laugh or cry. It was enough fuel to keep his fire burning, but while Randolph had been stonewalled in his efforts to get to Michael Franzese, a reporter had walked in unobstructed and talked with the Mafia captain.

As Selcraig later noted, "There's a lot less red tape for a reporter to talk to a federal prisoner than the FBI." The *Sports Illustrated* article never got the attention it deserved, but it was a catalyst for future events.

It didn't put Michael Franzese in George Randolph's hands right away, though. Even with Valukas's ties to the U. S. Justice Department, somebody or something was blocking access to Franzese. This raised further speculation that Franzese had worked out a deal as an informant with the New York federal agents, but New York officials denied it. The Los Angeles law enforcement officials also denied they had any deal with Franzese.

Strangely, New York and Los Angeles were giving the Chicago prosecution team the exact same line: You're wasting your time with Michael Franzese. That only strengthened George Randolph's resolve.

9

MICHAEL FRANZESE was known as the Mafia Prince or the Yuppie Don. Handsome, cool, and educated, Franzese was ranked eighteenth on *Fortune* magazine's list of "Top 50 Mob Bosses" in early 1986. John Gotti was thirteenth at the time. Franzese, then thirty-five, was by far the youngest Mafia don on the list, already a capo regime in the Colombo crime family.

The government thought that Franzese could be the head of a Mafia empire by the year 2000. That depended, of course, on his ability to stay out of prison and to stay alive.

The Franzese name carried a lot of weight inside La Cosa Nostra. Michael's stepfather, John "Sonny" Franzese, was an absolute force in the mob, particularly during the 1960s. Also a capo regime in the Colombo family, Sonny Franzese had been singled out by family boss Joseph Colombo to eventually take over the enterprise.

Even for a Mafioso, Sonny Franzese had developed a notorious reputation for violence—almost nobody in the Mafia was feared more. The government believed he had psychopathic tendencies. He was suspected of dozens of murders, but the government could never find a witness to step forward.

Getting Sonny Franzese off the streets became a major priority for the government by the mid-1960s. He was finally nailed in 1967 on a bank robbery conspiracy and was given a fifty-year sentence. When his appeal attempts hit a dead end in 1970, he went to prison.

Joseph Colombo was extremely agitated that he had lost his top enforcer and future boss. Colombo organized a group known as the Italian-American Civil Rights League to protest FBI tactics because he believed Sonny Franzese had been framed. Colombo took his protests to the streets of New York, where his speeches gained national attention. Within the mob it was feared that Colombo's public aggression might be bad for business. He was shot in the head at one of his rallies and was permanently disabled until his death seven years later.

Michael Franzese's first run-in with the law occurred after he joined the Italian-American Civil Rights League. While many people his age were protesting the Vietnam War, Michael Franzese picketed the FBI office in New York. He was arrested after confronting FBI agents while carrying a sign that read, I AM A VICTIM OF FBI GESTAPO TACTICS. MY FATHER WAS FRAMED FOR 50 YEARS.

Michael Franzese was born on May 27, 1951. He was a premed student at Hofstra University, where he was studying biology. In 1972, after three years of college, Michael decided he had other ambitions. He wanted to join the Mafia. By 1975 he had become a "made" man, which meant he had taken the secret Mafia oath. Mafia legend dictates that nobody can be inducted without killing someone on behalf of the mob.

During the next ten years Michael Franzese became a star in the mob. He made money for them like almost nobody before him. By the early 1980s he was promoted to capo regime and had forty underlings. Then, from 1981 to 1985, Franzese masterminded a scheme that defrauded the United States government of $1 billion in gasoline excise taxes.

Franzese teamed up with Lawrence Iorizzo, head of Vantage Petroleum, a large chain of gas stations on Long Island and in New Jersey, who had once enlisted the help of Sonny Franzese.

After draining Vantage of most of its assets, Franzese and Iorizzo formed a new company, Galleon Holdings, a gasoline wholesaler, which owned hundreds of stations, storage facilities, and a fleet of tankers. Over the next few years, Galleon sold millions of gallons of gasoline at cut-rate prices. Even name-brand filling stations like Texaco, Shell, and Chevron welcomed Galleon tankers.

Galleon was able to undercut the competition because it wasn't paying any state or federal excise taxes. By using a daisy chain of dummy companies, Franzese and Iorizzo passed along the tax debt until it landed on the doorstep of a company ready to collapse.

Franzese used his influence, power, and muscle to run the operation. On one transaction alone, the government estimated, he made $300 million for the mob. Franzese's personal take on the entire operation was estimated at $50 million.

Michael Franzese also had other ambitions. He wanted to make movies and become a celebrity. During the gasoline scam, Franzese traveled to Florida and formed his own movie production company called Miami Gold. The government had him under intense surveillance at the time and believed he was using the film company to launder his gasoline money. Then, to the government's amazement, Franzese, using the Gambino family's control of trade unions in Miami, managed to produce a series of "B" movies, including *Mausoleum, Savage Streets, Knights of the City,* and *Cry for the City.* The government watched in disbelief as Franzese used one of his "associates," a six-foot-four, 270-pound enforcer named Jerry Zimmerman, as the director of his movies.

Michael Franzese made a big splash in Miami. During the premiere of *Cry for the City,* the mayor presented the Mafia captain with a key to the city. The local Roman Catholic archbishop gave Franzese a Bible blessed by the Pope. When Michael Franzese wasn't being honored by city leaders, he was escorted by his bodyguards. These escorts were steroid-popping bodybuilders, each one with the image of an eagle's claw tattooed on his calf.

Women everywhere were falling for the handsome Mafia prince, even though he was married and had three children. Michael Franzese fell for one of the girls, a young, dazzling brunette named Cammy Garcia, who had been a dancer in *Knights of the City.* He divorced his wife, Maria, married Cammy, and moved to Hollywood to continue his venture into the movie industry.

New York federal organized crime authorities, under the direction of U. S. Attorney Rudolph Giuliani, were not about to let the Mafia boss escape. Franzese remained under intense surveillance in Los Angeles.

Finally the government got a break when it arrested Lawrence Iorizzo, Franzese's partner in the gasoline scam, by chasing him down in Panama. Iorizzo caved in to authorities, entered the Federal Witness Protection Program, and agreed to give information on Franzese. Iorizzo's testimony to a federal grand jury led to a twenty-eight-count indictment against Franzese, ranging from racketeering and loan sharking to extortion, in December 1985.

Franzese's indictment was big news in New York, where his power was well known. Jerry Bernstein, the prosecutor for the Brooklyn Organized Crime Task Force, warned the media about making the Mafia boss a darling. Franzese was capable of traditional mob violence. As part of his prosecution, Bernstein claimed that Franzese had once ordered "the head of a competitor caved in with a ball peen hammer." Rivals always took Franzese's threats seriously.

By March 1986, Franzese's lawyers had worked out a ten-year plea agreement with the government and a landmark restitution order of almost $15 million. Yet Franzese also persuaded the presiding federal judge, Eugene Nickerson, to allow him to go free to earn money in his movie business and legitimately repay the government. Nickerson granted Franzese this unique order, providing Franzese paid for the U. S. Marshals who would have to escort him constantly.

The government thought that if Franzese was free, it might allow them to discover where the millions of dollars had gone from his gasoline scam. But they had clearly disappeared. Franzese actually bounced checks to the U. S. Marshals guarding him, which provoked Judge Nickerson to remand him to his ten-year prison term.

During the summer of 1986, Franzese was moved across the country through the federal prison system until he reached his permanent destination of Terminal Island federal penitentiary in San Pedro, California, in Los Angeles Harbor.

Franzese may have landed in Los Angeles, close to his wife and two young daughters, because he had quietly struck an agreement in November 1986 with the Brooklyn Organized Crime Task Force to provide "deep background" on organized crime activities. Nobody was to know about this agreement. It was one of the FBI's most guarded secrets, and only the highest-ranking bureau officials were privy to the information. There was no way an FBI agent from Chicago named George Randolph was going to find out about this arrangement. The government was going to make certain of that.

Franzese was still conducting some Mafia business out of prison in late 1986, but his wife, Cammy, a born-again Christian, wanted him to quit the mob. The problem, as Franzese explained to his wife, was that there was only one way out of the Mafia, and that was in a coffin. Your sword or the mob's sword.

Franzese's reputation as a Mafia boss became known to prisoners and guards at Terminal Island. He was a "model prisoner" and gained access to the prison's honor section, which meant that he wasn't locked in his cell day or night. Franzese stayed in excellent physical condition and became a star softball player. He was a line-drive-hitting shortstop, and his fellow prisoners affectionately called him Ozzie after St. Louis Cardinals shortstop Ozzie Smith.

By the fall of 1987, Michael Franzese had met secretly with the government on selected organized crime background material. No reports were ever to reveal his name; he was to be identified in reports only as "source."

Franzese by then knew there had been quite a bit of publicity about Norby Walters's venture into the sports business. He had agreed to do an interview with a reporter named Bruce Selcraig of *Sports Illustrated* earlier that summer but didn't think he had told Selcraig anything that revealed the true nature of his relations with Uncle Norby. Besides, Norby was a publicity hound. Franzese didn't mind having his name or picture in the magazine, either. Mob guys love the attention as long as there is no serious damage.

When Franzese was informed by his attorney, Bruce Kelton, that he would be visited by two FBI agents on October 5, 1987, about a matter of minor consequence, the Mafia captain didn't give it a second thought. The same conditions were in force. He was only an unnamed source. The two FBI special agents introduced themselves as John O'Neill and Roger Lehman. As O'Neill recalled, the Mafia captain seemed quite relaxed, and O'Neill himself was casual about this meeting. George Randolph had told him that he really didn't expect much to come of the meeting.

Franzese began by telling the FBI agents about how he had known Norby Walters virtually all his life, just as he had told *Sports Illustrated*. He explained that Norby's father was known as Soldier, or something like that. Soldier Meyer got involved with La Cosa Nostra, and Sonny Franzese in particular, in the 1950s and 1960s. Norby's father ran various nightclubs and paid a percentage of the business to Sonny Franzese and the Colombo family, something he hadn't told *Sports Illustrated*.

Michael Franzese said that eventually Norby Walters assumed his father's business and that Michael began collecting payments on behalf of his father and the Colombo family. Walters also got started in the talent agency business, dealing exclusively with black performers. From time to time Walters called upon Michael Franzese to settle problems with clients and their managers.

Then the FBI agents asked Franzese about the sports agent operation Walters had set up. Franzese told them that he knew about it. He told them he was a partner in the operation. He had invested $50,000 in it.

O'Neill did not understand the impact of what Franzese was telling him. He scribbled down the notes just as casually as Franzese related the information.

Franzese said Norby Walters had a partner in the sports business named Lloyd Bloom, whom he didn't know much about, but he had met him once.

The FBI agents were interrupted by prison officials who said the interview room was needed for another matter. O'Neill asked for ten more minutes. O'Neill then asked Franzese if he knew anything about a sports agent named Kathy Clements getting beat up in Chicago and whether Norby Walters had anything to do with it. Casually, Franzese recalled that there was a time around the first of the year when one of his Mafia associates, Jerry Zimmerman, had visited him at Terminal Island and explained that Norby Walters was having trouble with a rival agent, "some broad" in Chicago, and wanted assistance.

Suddenly O'Neill sat up in his chair and asked what happened after that.

Franzese told O'Neill and Lehman that he instructed Zimmerman to have Norby contact Frankie Campione, another associate of the Colombo family, to handle the matter. But Franzese said he also told Zimmerman to "be careful."

O'Neill asked Franzese to describe Campione, who was also his father's personal driver. Campione was forty-six years old, about five feet seven inches, two hundred pounds, a former sheet metal worker who "was not particularly bright, but he usually gets things done."

O'Neill asked Franzese if he could find out more about the attack on Clements. Franzese said he would try.

"That's all I know," Franzese said.

Prison officials needed the interview room now.

"Anything else?" O'Neill asked while they were getting up.

Franzese threw in that Norby Walters was a well-connected guy in New York. He used the Reverend Al Sharpton to recruit entertainers and athletes, Franzese believed.

Michael Franzese returned to his cell. The meeting didn't strike him as out of the ordinary. He thought he was just living up to his agreement to provide background information on his organized crime associates. He would never be asked to testify before a grand jury, let alone take the witness stand at a trial. Background, that was all. It was in the agreement he had signed back in November 1986.

Michael Franzese hated the word, but he had become an informant. He had hoped his cooperation would help him when he was eligible for parole in 1990. Norby Walters was a longtime friend and business associate, but he was not a made member of the Mafia. Besides, the thirty-minute meeting with the FBI had not been very probing, and it seemed rather harmless.

As Franzese now recalls the FBI's first meeting with him regarding Norby Walters: "I never knew how intense or serious they were or what the angle was. It was in the spirit of cooperation, but I didn't think I was adding anything significant. I told them the truth about my relationship with him [Norby Walters] in the sports agency business. I didn't know if it was going anywhere. . . . I came out of the meeting thinking there wasn't much of a problem."

FBI Special Agent John O'Neill got back to his office and telephoned George Randolph in Chicago. Randolph listened to O'Neill's account of the meeting with Michael Franzese and just about went "bat shit."

Michael Franzese, a Mafia heavyweight, was an actual partner in the sports agent operation? He had invested $50,000? He had given permission to deal with "some broad in Chicago" after Norby Walters had sent a message about trouble he was having with rival agents? Unbelievable.

"Everybody told me this SOB wouldn't say a word," Randolph told O'Neill.

"Well, he did."

"Send me some paper out," Randolph said excitedly.

Randolph needed a teletype, followed by the typewritten report, to begin his own legwork on Norby Walters's connection to Michael Franzese. O'Neill said he'd cut the papers.

Tony Valukas and Howard Pearl were equally stunned by the information from O'Neill. There was a new urgency to the investigation.

Three or four days passed, and there was no paper. O'Neill kept telling Randolph he had "cut it." More days passed and nothing. Finally there was word that O'Neill's paperwork had been killed in Los Angeles.

Randolph started making telephone calls and sending teletypes to the FBI office in Los Angeles, demanding the paperwork. According to federal sources in Los Angeles, the FBI organized crime chief, James Moody, was getting very angry at Randolph, who had threatened to fly to Los Angeles to do his own interview with Franzese. Randolph was ready to cut through FBI protocol. Moody told him to back off.

Bob Walsh, Randolph's boss in Chicago, remembers: "George had some big fights with Moody, who wasn't helping at all. But George has a habit of not backing off from anybody or anything."

Randolph continued to badger the organized crime division in Los Angeles for O'Neill's report. Then one day Randolph got a call from FBI headquarters in Washington. It was from a high-ranking FBI official.

"RANDOLPH!"

Somebody near Randolph could hear the screaming voice through the telephone.

"CAN YOU SPELL?"

Of course.

"F–I–R–E–D!"

Pause.

"DO YOU KNOW WHAT THAT SPELLS?"

Silence.

"YOU BETTER GET YOUR ASS IN HERE!"

Randolph and Walsh traveled together to the meeting with their FBI bosses in Washington. Walsh was going to support his special agent, but he had to remind Randolph occasionally about tact.

"George was never the type of guy to hold anything back," said Walsh. "He's a terrific agent, but he will ruffle some feathers. He'll piss people off, and once in a while it gets him in trouble. We had to make a couple of trips to Washington during this investigation."

George Randolph did not get fired. If anything, he was able to better explain his frustration at having his access to Franzese blocked.

Valukas, Pearl, and Randolph were now quite sure that Franzese had a deal with the government. Everybody in Washington, New York, and Los Angeles denied knowledge of any such deal.

"Fuck this," Randolph finally told Pearl. "Let's just writ him to Chicago."

A writ to testify could bypass some of the other federal authorities and deliver Michael Franzese.

"We'll snatch him," Randolph said. "I don't care if he's Don Corleone, he's my witness now."

Tony Valukas was also tired of waiting to find out how deep the organized crime element cut into the Norby Walters case. Buying Randolph's plan, he gave Howard Pearl the green light to cut a writ that would bring Michael Franzese to Chicago via the U. S. Marshal. They scheduled it for the weekend just prior to Thanksgiving, figuring that their prisoner wouldn't get picked up until around midnight on Friday. They instructed the U. S. Marshal that Franzese had to be in Chicago by Tuesday, which was the day the federal grand jury was sitting. The timing meant there would be virtually no chance for anybody to interfere with the "snatching" of Michael Franzese.

It was 3 A.M. and Franzese was sleeping in his cell at Terminal Island when one of the prison officials woke him up. Franzese says he'll never forget it.

"You're on the list," the official told the Mafia boss. "You're being shipped out."

"Are you kidding me?" Franzese snapped. "This is my designation. I'm here."

"No, Michael, you're on the list," the official replied.

"This has to be a mistake."

"No mistake, you're gone. Pack up."

Franzese couldn't believe what was happening. The most dreaded part of federal prison life was being transported. Handcuffs and leg irons. Processing at every new prison stop until you reach your final destination. Lock down.

"It's a grueling process," Franzese said.

He wondered what he had done to deserve such a rude awakening.

"My immediate reaction was that because I had just done an interview with *Life* magazine, I was being moved someplace," Franzese said.

Then one of the prison guards told him, "You're going to Illinois, and the only place [federal prison] in Illinois is Marion, so that's where you're going."

Franzese thought again. Yeah, maybe it was a security measure because of his interview with *Life*. Or maybe the government was angry at him for talking. He wondered while waiting in the Reception and Delivery room (the R & D, in prison terms). Some three hours passed before he spotted a prison official he thought would shoot straight with him.

"What's going on? What am I going to Marion for?" Franzese asked.

The prison official looked at Franzese's paperwork.

"You're not going to Marion," he said. "This is a writ to testify in Chicago before a grand jury."

Franzese wanted to know what for, but the writ was blank under the case title. Franzese asked if he could call his lawyer, but he knew that normal transport procedure prohibited that. The official affirmed this policy and said that they would have to move quickly because Franzese had to be in Chicago by Tuesday.

"And you gotta go through El Reno," the official told the prisoner.

Franzese hated the words. El Reno, Oklahoma, was a "level four" federal prison. Only a "level five" maximum-security prison harbored worse criminals. Terminal Island was a "level three" prison, and Franzese had a room in the "honor wing." Franzese had been to El Reno before, en route from New York to California, and it was not a pleasant stay.

Before Franzese left, he sent a message to a fellow prisoner to call his wife, Cammy, and tell her he was being transported and to have her call his lawyer to find out what was going on.

Franzese was put in handcuffs and leg irons and driven by bus to an air terminal where he boarded a government plane, a 707 confiscated from drug traffickers, with few of the conveniences of a commercial aircraft. The plane made six or seven stops, dropping off and picking up other prisoners, and took almost eighteen hours to reach El Reno. By the time he got there it was 11:55 P.M. on Saturday, and the first thing he saw was a telephone. It was five minutes before they shut off the phones, but there was a waiting line.

"I knew a few of the guys, so they moved me to the front," Franzese recalls.

Cammy had made contact with his attorney, Bruce Kelton, who had then made a few calls. Now he knew why he was headed to Chicago. It was about Norby Walters. Franzese didn't understand why he was being asked to testify. There was no way he would do that. It wasn't part of his deal with the government. More important, it wasn't part of his deal with the Mafia.

Bruce Kelton, a former prosecutor, told his client to be patient. The lawyer knew a prosecutor in Chicago and would find out more about the writ.

ABOUT THE time Michael Franzese was being woken up at Terminal Island, George Randolph got his own rude awakening. There had been some unrest among Cuban and immigrant prisoners at the Atlanta Federal Penitentiary. Randolph, a member of the FBI SWAT team, had gotten the call.

It reminded him of how he was "recruited" for the SWAT team. He was young and in good physical condition, and had just finished his Marine Reserve Corps duty. He had been assigned to the office in Springfield, Illinois, in 1976 when a superior came looking for "volunteers" for Basic SWAT Training back in Quantico, Virginia.

"Don't look at me," Randolph said.

"You're going."

He was gone.

Randolph was at the Atlanta Federal Penitentiary, and the situation was ugly. Fires were burning inside the prison. At one point he stood on one side of a glass door, aiming his automatic rifle directly between the eyes of one of the Cuban leaders. He was thankful there was no cause to pull the trigger.

Randolph was desperately trying to keep his attention on the crisis at hand, while knowing that "his prisoner"—Mafia captain Michael Franzese—should have been snatched by now. He kept wondering if Franzese had made it to Chicago since the Cuban unrest would keep him locked down until the Atlanta prison was secure.

On Monday, Bruce Kelton and Howard Pearl spoke with each other about Michael Franzese. Kelton explained to Pearl that there was no way Franzese would cooperate in front of a federal grand jury. A series of telephone negotiations ensued, and the result was that Franzese agreed to talk with Pearl and an FBI agent (Randolph), but only back at Terminal Island.

Franzese also requested to be moved immediately, but as Pearl discovered, no prisoners could be transported because of the prison riot in Atlanta. All prison movement was stopped. The Assistant U. S. Attorney asked if a meeting at El Reno was possible. Franzese sent back a swift reply: "No way." He thought he'd be stuck in Oklahoma indefinitely without anybody pushing for his return to California. So Kelton worked out an agreement that when the prison riot was under control, Franzese would get priority attention. Otherwise it could have taken him two or three months to get processed out of El Reno and back to Terminal Island. Pearl made the arrangement with the U. S. Marshals office, but Franzese would have to pick up the tab.

Pearl was wondering how he could get in touch with George Randolph in Atlanta.

George Randolph was wondering how he could get in touch with Howard Pearl. He had already missed Thanksgiving with his family.

Randolph couldn't wait any longer. He worked his way through part of the prison, looking for a telephone. Smoke clouded the air around him. He was trudging through ankle-deep water when he spotted a pay phone. God, he hoped it worked. It did.

"When are you coming back, asshole?" Pearl playfully asked.

Randolph squinted his eyes through the smoke and sloshed his feet. Yeah, like he was on vacation.

Pearl gave him an update on Franzese and explained that a meeting would take place as soon as the prisons were secured.

"Tony wants you back and ready to go out there."

Randolph wanted out. He was prepared to tell the SWAT commander that he had to leave, but it wasn't necessary. The prison unrest was over.

On Saturday morning Randolph caught a flight to Chicago, went home to get some fresh clothes, kissed his wife good-bye again, and met Howard Pearl at O'Hare Airport. They had decided to fly ahead to Los

Angeles to work out a strategy while they waited for Michael Franzese to arrive.

Along the way Pearl handed Randolph some intriguing reading. It was a copy of *Life* magazine with a big article on Michael Franzese.

It was titled, "Quitting the Mafia."

Randolph's gut reaction was, "What the hell is this?"

There was a picture of Michael Franzese looking pensive in a barren interview room at the federal prison in Terminal Island. His hands were folded, and the camera captured his classic Italian good looks.

The caption under the picture quoted Franzese: "Especially after *The Godfather* came out, I had more to deal than I knew what to do with. People came to me and figured they could use my power or my influence."

The authors of the article, Edward Barnes and William Shebar, told a spellbinding story of the thirty-six-year-old Franzese. It began with another quote from Franzese: "I have only one choice. I have to get out and get away. This 'thing' is on its way out. I definitely believe that. The government has made a decision that they are going to bury organized crime. They are going to bury any alleged Mafia guys. I'm finished as far as I'm concerned. I became too high-profile. If they are going to get me, they are going to destroy me."

In the next paragraph the authors began, "There's an old saying that the only way to leave the Mafia is in a coffin. . . . To quit would be to arouse suspicion that you are cooperating with police or federal agents."

That's how Randolph understood it.

Life magazine said that if Franzese held to his word, it "will mark the first time a high-ranking member of the Mafia will publicly walk away from his past."

Randolph devoured the article.

"Michael Franzese has often been compared to Michael Corleone, the fictional character so brilliantly portrayed by Al Pacino in *The Godfather*. However, his character is true; his life is filled with the intrigue, glamour, and suspense that made *The Godfather* such a huge success."

The story brushed on Franzese's background, identifying him not only as a "capo in the Colombo family" but as "heir apparent in the organized crime hierarchy."

The authors wrote that

Michael Franzese once seemed to represent the future of the Mafia in America. His education (three years of college), his financial acumen, his

urbane manner and good looks made him a natural for white-collar crime.
. . . By the age of 33, he was believed to be one of the biggest money earners
in the history of the Mafia, bringing in millions of dollars a week. . . . He
had the dubious distinction of being the youngest capo on *Fortune* magazine's 1986 chart of "The 50 Biggest Mafia Bosses."

His "quitting" the Mafia was viewed dubiously by federal officials, but
New York U. S. Attorney Rudolph Giuliani, whose office was making
headlines on his mob convictions, said, "The Mafia is a thing of the past.
A lot of people within the Mafia don't realize it. Maybe he realized it."

Life magazine reminded Randolph that Franzese's real father's name
was Frank Grillo, but his mother divorced and married Sonny Franzese
when Michael was only two. Sonny Franzese was "the alleged enforcer
of New York's Colombo crime family. Sonny is said by prosecutors to
have committed dozens of murders, though they were only able to jail
him for conspiring to rob banks." Sonny Franzese adopted Michael
Franzese and adored him as one of his own. Michael suspected that he
was in fact Sonny's real boy.

Throughout the story there were little vignettes of Michael's memories
of growing up with a legendary Mafia father, who was treated like
royalty whenever they visited the Copacabana nightclub.

Michael Franzese was quoted as saying, "We always had a ringside
table. He would know most of the acts that were playing, and they would
come and sit with us: Dionne Warwick, Don Rickles, Tom Jones, Bobby
Darin. . . ."

According to *Life,* Michael's parents tried to discourage him from a
career in crime. They wanted him to go to school and be a doctor, so he
enrolled as a premed major at Hofstra University. But Michael told *Life*
he got restless and was angry that his father had received a fifty-year
prison term after being "framed" for the bank robbery conspiracy.
Michael told *Life* that he finally visited his father in prison and asked
permission to align himself with the Mafia. Sonny granted it and, according to Michael, said, "I seen that spirit in you." Sonny arranged for
Michael to meet his friends.

As *Life* wrote, "Sonny's boy was no ordinary soldier." Michael Franzese proceeded to make money for the Mafia virtually in record
amounts.

"Michael's real brilliance was that he was able to attract businessmen
who played on the edge," said Jerry Bernstein, the prosecutor with the
Organized Crime Task Force in Brooklyn.

The article proceeded to tell about the billion-dollar gasoline tax scam that eventually landed Michael Franzese in jail. Franzese told *Life* he was bitter about his former partner, Lawrence Iorizzo, who joined the Federal Witness Protection Program after testifying against him. The article said Franzese was "scornful of informers like Iorizzo; he says the program encourages them to lie in exchange for favors."

Franzese also said, "I am willing to admit certain things, but I'm not interested in pointing fingers."

George Randolph was confused. Something strange was going on here. Michael Franzese was publicly saying he was quitting the mob. Although he suspected otherwise, Randolph had been told that Franzese had made no deal as an informer. He said he despised Iorizzo and the Federal Witness Protection Program. He said he wasn't interested in pointing fingers. And yet Franzese had freely told FBI agents John O'Neill and Roger Lehman about his relationship with Norby Walters.

Things were screwy.

Apparently Franzese was strongly influenced by his wife, Cammy. *Life* quoted prosecutors as saying they had seen the "mob boss turn into a pussycat in her presence."

"He would do anything for me," Cammy told the *Life* authors.

Michael told *Life* that Cammy gave him the final push to turn his back on the Mafia. She corrected him: "No, God gave him that strength."

Randolph knew right then that he would have to deal with Cammy's presence if he was going to get anything done with Franzese.

Life raised the question, Is Michael Franzese still a Mafioso? It answered, yes and no. He defended "the people I share a life-style with." He suggested the Mafia had strong family values and could even be a political force. "Maybe we could be a party of our own, run for the presidency," he said. Franzese also said he still believed in the Mafia code that murder is justified as a "point of honor."

There was further debate about Franzese's intentions. Regardless, *Life* quoted an unidentified former FBI agent who predicted, "He will get whacked."

The story ended with speculation about what will happen when Sonny Franzese is released in 1994 and whether Michael Franzese would return to the Mafia if his father were killed.

"I don't know," he said. "I'd really have to sit down and think about it."

Randolph looked at Pearl. They both had the same reaction.

"Pretty amazing."

Pearl further explained that Franzese had a deal with the Eastern District of New York. That was why access had been blocked. The Chicago prosecution team deemed it insulting that nobody supposedly on the same side of the law had told them of the agreement.

Their plane landed at Los Angeles International Airport. While it had been freezing in Chicago, it was beautiful in Los Angeles. The two men checked into their hotel in Marina del Rey, a long way from the smoke and ugliness of the Atlanta penitentiary.

The next day Randolph drove their rented car on the 405 Santa Monica Freeway south to the 110 Harbor Freeway to San Pedro. They crossed the Vincent Thomas Bridge and drove into the confines of the federal prison at Terminal Island, an ill-named site since it was only a medium-security facility.

George Randolph knew plenty about prisons. His father had been a prison guard and later an official at the Menard Penitentiary, a maximum-security prison that rested between Illinois and Missouri on the Mississippi River. It was known as the Alcatraz of the Midwest because many prisoners had tried and failed to escape on the Mississippi.

Pearl had brought a government proffer signed by Anton Valukas, dated December 4, 1987.

It was addressed to Bruce Kelton, Franzese's attorney, and read in part:

> The government requires a completely truthful statement of your client in this proffer. Anything related to the government by your client during the proffer cannot and will not be used directly against your client, Michael Franzese, in the government's case-in-chief. However, the government is completely free to pursue any and all investigative leads derived in any way from the proffer, which could result in the acquisition of evidence admissible against your client in subsequent proceedings. Likewise, nothing shall prevent the government from using the substance of the proffer for impeachment or in rebuttal testimony should your client subsequently testify contrary to the substance of the proffer.
>
> This letter embodies the entirety of the agreement to make a proffer of your client's testimony. No other promise or agreement exists between your client or this office regarding the proffer.

Bruce Kelton was waiting for Pearl and Randolph at the prison, and it wasn't long before Michael Franzese was escorted into the very same interview room that was pictured in *Life*.

Randolph was sizing up the Mafia don when Kelton and Pearl started to argue quietly about the proffer.

There was a dispute over this sentence: "However, the government is completely free to pursue any and all investigative leads derived in any way from this proffer, which could result in the acquisition of evidence admissible against your client in subsequent proceedings." Kelton insisted that the sentence be deleted and that the agreement with the Eastern District of New York protected Franzese. Pearl demanded that a new agreement be signed because the previous one didn't cover his jurisidiction. They argued, as lawyers do, a little more. Finally Kelton and Pearl decided they needed to hash this out in another room.

George Randolph and Michael Franzese were alone now. One year apart in age but light years apart in life.

"I think there's better communication in my business than yours," Franzese joked to the FBI agent, who shook his head and smiled.

Franzese looked very much like his photo in *Life:* dark hair and deep, piercing brown eyes. Good-looking guy. Intense. He seemed about five feet ten or five feet eleven and was not so much thin as he was wiry, his muscles finely developed.

"Can I get you a Coke?" the FBI agent asked.

"Sure, thanks."

Back from the vending machine, Randolph sat down across from Franzese.

"What's the big deal about Norby Walters?" Franzese asked. "What do you want?"

"We just think you can be helpful on this case," replied Randolph.

Franzese explained that all he would do was provide background on his relationship with Norby Walters, just as he had done with O'Neill.

"Don't expect anything more," Franzese said. "You have to understand, my position doesn't allow me to testify."

Randolph heard the Mafioso in Franzese's words.

"That mob shit doesn't impress me," Randolph said casually.

Franzese snapped his head back. Randolph held up a hand.

"Look, if you're supposed to be Don Corleone, why can't you cut a deal and get out of here?"

Franzese was now looking at George Randolph as some crazed Midwest G-man.

"If you're not Don Corleone, why don't you call him and ask him why you can't clip two New York Jews?"

"You don't understand."

"You don't understand," Randolph replied. "You know that little midnight run you made to Oklahoma? That's nothing."

"You did that?"

"That's right. Now get on the phone and call the Godfather and ask him if you can burn a couple of Jews."

Randolph had a strategy here. He wanted to unnerve the Mafia capo out of Pearl's presence. It wasn't a case of good cop, bad cop. He wanted to see how loyal Franzese was to Norby Walters and whether he'd say anything while he was a little rattled.

"The oath I took, if I testify, they'll kill me," Franzese said.

"What oath is that? I thought you were quitting the mob."

Randolph was trying to keep from laughing. Franzese rolled his eyes.

"Come on," Randolph needled him. "Why don't you get to the Godfather and explain to him, 'I'm a big moneymaker for the mob, Godfather, and I need permission to roll over on Norby Walters. He's only a Jew.' Everybody and their brother is cutting a deal. Maybe you can help yourself out."

Randolph stopped himself. One thing he didn't want to do was start making promises he couldn't keep. Besides, Michael Franzese wasn't changing his tune.

"The one thing I can't do, the one thing I'll never do, is take the stand," said Franzese. "It would be like signing my own death warrant, even for Norby Walters. Besides, he's been a lifelong friend of the family."

"Which family?"

Franzese had had enough of the games. To him, George Randolph was just another hard-ass FBI agent.

"My feelings for the FBI were very, very bad," Franzese recalls. "I hadn't met one [FBI agent] I had any regard for. I wasn't comfortable with George. I wasn't going to say anything until I really knew where he was at. I didn't size him real good in the beginning."

He asked Randolph again about the government's interest in Norby Walters.

Randolph explained that it was about the sports agency operation. Norby Walters and Lloyd Bloom had signed college players at an alarming rate, and they resorted to gangland-type threats to players who tried to back out of the deals. All the cash, so much cash. Smelled of organized crime. And then came Franzese's interview with FBI agents two months earlier.

Howard Pearl and Bruce Kelton returned, having hammered out the proffer agreement. The one sentence was crossed out by Pearl. Franzese read it and understood that his cooperation would do little or nothing to affect his current status as a prisoner.

"Just let my judge and parole board know about it," said Franzese.

Still, Howard Pearl and George Randolph each let Michael Franzese know that he could end up as a defendant, along with Norby Walters and Lloyd Bloom. Only what he said that day could not be used against him.

"There's nothing you can prove that involves me with this case," Franzese said defiantly.

"What if Norby Walters cuts a deal and says you ordered the beating of Kathy Clements?" Randolph asked.

Franzese shrugged. He knew Norby Walters would never, ever risk his life by testifying against him or anybody else in organized crime.

"Don't bullshit me with that," Franzese said. "This will go nowhere with me. Maybe there'll be a little aggravation, but it won't go anywhere. Now let's talk about what we have to talk about."

Franzese verified that Norby Walters had been a friend and business associate of his father's for many years and that the relationship had continued with Michael when his father was sent to prison.

In late 1984 or early 1985, Franzese recalled, Norby Walters had met him at the Polo Lounge in Beverly Hills while the mob boss/movie producer was having lunch with actor Leon Kennedy. Walters told Franzese that he was expanding his agency business from entertainers to sports. He had a new, young partner named Lloyd Bloom who had been a football player.

"He said that, like his entertainment business, he wanted to deal only with black athletes, and he wanted to sign the biggest stars, represent them in their professional contracts as well as their endorsements," Franzese explained.

"I thought it was a good idea. And Norby asked me to participate."

Pearl wanted to know what "participate" meant.

"Like my father and I always had participated with Norby Walters," Franzese replied.

What was Franzese's response?

"I told him I would be interested."

But Franzese also did not want to discuss further business in front of Kennedy. He told Norby they would talk again at a later date.

A few months later, in early 1985, Michael Franzese told Randolph and Pearl, he had another meeting with Norby Walters. This time they met at the agent's Manhattan office. Walters told him that he had officially formed a new company called World Sports and Entertainment. As with the entertainers, they would be using cash to sign the athletes. Franzese said that Walters promised him twenty-five percent of the business if Franzese would put up $50,000 in cash. According to Franzese, Walters told him he'd start getting a return on his money within a year.

Randolph and Pearl were intrigued but tried not to show their excitement.

During the summer of 1985, Franzese was taking his new wife's family for a vacation to Lake George in upstate New York. He sent word to Norby Walters that he would be paying the agent a visit one particular day and that he wanted the "agent to the stars" to meet Fred and Dino Garcia, his new father-in-law and brother-in-law. There would also be a small-time California booking agent named Carlos, a friend of his father-in-law, who was interested in booking acts into the Anaheim Convention Center.

Franzese told Randolph and Pearl that he took $50,000 in cash to Walters that day for a piece of the sports agency business.

"How'd you give it to him?" Randolph asked.

"In a brown paper bag," Franzese said.

That was too good to be true.

"Actually, Dino gave it to him," said Franzese. "I had a habit of having other guys around me carry the money."

Was there anything else about that day?

"Yeah," Franzese said. "I met Lloyd Bloom."

Randolph and Pearl looked at each other. This was what they needed.

"I shook hands with him, and then he left the room," said Franzese. "I think Norby wanted Bloom to make sure I met him. It was the only day I was around Bloom."

Randolph's adrenaline was in high gear again. He couldn't wait to ask about Kathy Clements and the beating that took place on March 16 of that year.

"It's like I told the other [FBI] agent, I didn't know any gal by the name of Kathy Clements," said Franzese. "I did have an associate come to me with a message from Norby that he was having trouble with some other agents and he had mentioned something about a broad in Chicago."

The associate's name was Jerry Zimmerman, a longtime friend of Franzese and Walters, according to the Mafia captain. Zimmerman, who had directed the movies Franzese had produced, had other talents the

Mafia considered handy. He was six feet four inches, weighed 270 pounds, and intimidated people easily. But Zimmerman had his own problems with the law at the time and was simply passing along the message from Norby Walters that there was trouble.

"I told Jerry to have Norby talk to Frankie Campione about it," Franzese told Pearl and Randolph. "Frankie had been my father's chauffeur and bodyguard, and a close associate of mine."

In fact, Franzese said, while he was under indictment he told Walters to "deal with Frankie if he had any problems."

"Did Zimmerman say anything else about the gal in Chicago?" Randolph asked. "Did he get back to you on it? Did anybody get back to you?"

"No," said Franzese. "Jerry didn't give me a whole lot of details. I just told him to have Frankie take care of it but to be careful. I cautioned him."

Nothing else?

"Usually things are taken care of."

Randolph could feel goose bumps on the back of his neck.

What did Franzese's participation mean? What did Norby Walters get in return?

"He gets my influence, my reputation, and my protection," said Franzese. "And I get paid."

Franzese said he hadn't received any money from the sports operation but noted that he'd been in prison virtually the entire time.

"But Norby never had any trouble using my family's name," Franzese said.

Was he aware of threats that had been made to athletes?

"I heard about them, really, through my lawyer," Franzese said. "I haven't sanctioned any threats, with the exception of what I just told you about, with Zimmerman and Campione."

Pearl and Randolph wanted a few more details about Franzese's relationship with Walters and maybe some other ways to verify that relationship. There was nothing in terms of financial records, of course. The mob did its business in cash.

Once, Franzese said, he asked Norby to sponsor him for a membership in the Friars Club. That was about 1984. Norby Walters was hesitant "because Norby said he had his own problems in the club." Norby Walters suggested that Franzese try another Friars member, Julie Rifkind, as a sponsor. Rifkind was associated with the Spring Records label.

Franzese used Walters not as a sponsor but as a reference on his Friars application, which was accepted. That was evidence, if Randolph could find the application.

The meeting came to a close. Pearl and Randolph drove back to their hotel and couldn't quit talking.

Both men believed Franzese was telling the truth. They would want more from him, but he had given them a start. Randolph had some leads. He needed to find Fred and Dino Garcia, Jerry Zimmerman, Frankie Campione, the Friars Club. If he found them, more leads would surely develop. And he was going to work Michael Franzese again.

Back at the hotel, Howard Pearl called Tony Valukas and told them how candid Franzese had been that day.

"Now I knew we had something going," Valukas recalls. "It was the turning point."

10

THERE WAS nothing on Norby Walters's books that showed Uncle Norby had received $50,000 from Michael Franzese, or from anybody else, for that matter. That didn't make it a lie.

The government discovered that the documented deposits, withdrawals, and transfers in Norby Walters's bank accounts didn't remotely add up to the amount of money distributed to the athletes and the entertainers. On the other hand, he had very specific ledgers for each client who received anything of benefit. All that cash was coming from somewhere. In fact, as they discovered, World Sports and Entertainment, Inc., didn't even have a bank account. No bank account, and the fifty-eight athletes had gotten between $600,000 and $800,000 in cash.

Was Norby Walters washing the mob's money? That would be something they would ask Michael Franzese.

"It wasn't my money," Franzese later said.

The Chicago prosecution team accepted that Franzese, whose own personal fortune was still being sought by New York officials, was telling the truth.

Howard Pearl wanted to call in the Internal Revenue Service. No way, George Randolph insisted. He had seen too many cases stalled "for years" when the IRS got involved. They didn't need that headache and, besides, Randolph wanted to see where Franzese's leads took him. They could do their own analysis on Norby's books.

Valukas, Pearl, and Randolph now had a solemn, deep-rooted commitment to this case.

They had a real Mafia boss, hailed as one of the mob's biggest money-makers in the history of organized crime, telling them that he was a silent partner in Norby Walters's sports agent operation. They knew enough about organized crime to know that the mob would love to have a piece of sports action. Norby Walters might have been a witting or unwitting mole for the mob. But, based on the sketch Michael Franzese had just drawn for them, and the evidence that was piling up, the government didn't see Norby Walters as an unwitting party.

Tony Valukas specifically began thinking about the potential of such an operation. "Think about the leverage the mob could have going into a big game," Valukas recalls reasoning at the time. "These players were so vulnerable to blackmail. A week before the Rose Bowl, Norby Walters could go to a star running back and say, 'I'd sure hate to make everybody aware you signed this contract with me. How about dropping the ball a few times when it counts?' "

Asked if he was thinking specifically of Ronnie Harmon, Valukas said, "Ronnie Harmon didn't fix the Rose Bowl, but he was vulnerable, just like everyone else was vulnerable. The mob could have impacted the game simply by seeing that Ronnie Harmon's contract fell into the hands of the NCAA and, boom, the big star running back can't play in the Rose Bowl. That's impact."

Valukas couldn't wait to talk to Michael Franzese about the mob's ultimate intentions in the operation. Neither could George Randolph.

Eerily, in mid-December 1987, another case involving a sports agent did affect a couple of bowl games.

Jim Abernethy, an Atlanta-based sports agent, turned over copies of the contracts he had signed with seven college football and basketball players to the *Atlanta Constitution,* which had been investigating Abernethy for months.

Auburn University All-America defensive back Kevin Porter was declared ineligible to play for the Tigers in the Sugar Bowl against Syracuse. It was a game with national title implications.

Texas A&M offensive tackle Tony Bartley was declared ineligible for the Cotton Bowl.

Two prominent Memphis State basketball players, junior center Marvin Alexander and sophomore forward Sylvester Gray, lost their eligibility early in the 1987 basketball season.

Abernethy's shocking disclosure rattled the state of Alabama, where the assistant attorney general and chief of the criminal division, Donald Valeska, decided he had had enough of sports agents messing with Alabama athletes. He began his own probe.

In late December 1987, Walters and Bloom were dealt a severe legal setback in their effort to prove "contract law" and that NCAA bylaws had nothing to do with them. U. S. District Court Chief Judge Charles Brieant dismissed the $500,000 breach-of-contract lawsuit the sports agents had filed against Brent Fullwood, who had hired a sharp New York attorney named Richard Glickel. Brieant clearly was disgusted with the case.

"We decline to serve as the paymaster of the wages of crime, or referee between thieves," Brieant said in his opinion.

The Chicago prosecution team was elated with the ruling because the federal judge gave them an indication that the "clean" schools were entitled to some protection.

> The agreement reached by the parties here, whether or not unusual, represented not only a betrayal of the high ideals that sustain amateur athletic competition as part of our national educational commitment; it also constituted a calculated fraud on the entire spectator public. Every honest amateur player who took the field with or against Fullwood was cheated by being thrown in with a player who had lost his amateur standing. . . . Both sides of the transaction knew exactly what they were doing, and they knew it was fraudulent and wrong.

In what was an extraordinary and arguably naive decision, Judge Brieant further exalted amateur athletics and the NCAA constitution. He agreed with Glickel's argument that adherence to NCAA rules was in the best interests of public policy.

> Since the advent of intercollegiate sports in the late nineteenth century, American colleges have struggled, with varying degrees of vigor, to protect the integrity of high education from sports-related evils such as gambling, recruitment violations, and the employment of mercenaries whose presence in college athletic programs will tend to preclude the participation of legitimate scholar athletes.

Ridiculous or not, this was a chief federal judge speaking out. It was a big boost for the government at the time.

GEORGE RANDOLPH's new mandate was to pursue the leads provided by Franzese. The next couple of months were critical because the government wanted to put a wrap on the case. More than anything, Randolph wanted to get to the bottom of the Kathy Clements beating. What Franzese had given them was "exciting information," but that's all it was. Michael Franzese had made it abundantly clear that he would never testify.

It was time to do some serious background checks on Sonny Franzese, Norby Walters, and Mafia associates Jerry Zimmerman and Frankie Campione. Randolph wanted to travel to New York, but that required the usual paperwork, approval from the FBI, and some coordination on making files and transcripts available. These things didn't happen overnight.

Randolph wanted to find out how strongly Norby Walters was connected to the mob. He had Franzese's word, but he wanted more evidence to tie Walters to the Mafia and the Franzeses.

Once in New York, Randolph was awed by the volumes of files to study. Sonny Franzese's files were so voluminous, Randolph figured it would take him at least a week to read them. When he was finished, he knew why Sonny Franzese had become a "legendary godfather" and why Sonny was perhaps the most feared Mafia man of his generation. Sonny Franzese was suspected by the FBI of "dozens of murders." Apparently Sonny Franzese never asked anyone to do a job for him. He was a hands-on type of guy.

Randolph learned Sonny Franzese was born in 1919 in Naples, Italy. His father, Carmine, moved his family to New York. Carmine Franzese built his own reputation in the neighborhood. His nickname was Tutty the Lion. People who crossed Carmine Franzese, who ran a bakery, often ended up stuffed in his oven.

Sonny Franzese owned a dry cleaning business in Brooklyn but became the Mafia boss of Long Island. He had an interest in car dealerships, nightclubs, restaurants, topless bars, and quite a few record labels.

That sparked Randolph's interest. Sonny Franzese and Norby Walters now had three things in common: nightclubs, entertainers, and Long Island. Randolph remembered reading that Norby Walters once ran his business out of his home on Long Island.

Sonny Franzese held court in the best Mafia tradition in two nightclubs—the San Su San on Long Island and the Copacabana in Manhattan. Norby Walters's club was next door to the Copa. Plenty of surveillance and informant data showed that entertainers often paid their respect to Sonny Franzese. Dionne Warwick, Sammy Davis, Jr., Bobby Darin, and even Tiny Tim often flocked to his table.

By the mid-1960s, Sonny Franzese was quite powerful in the mob. Randolph even found an article from a New York newspaper which showed that Joe Colombo was "gradually paving the way for Franzese to take over completely." The newspaper also stated, "The Cosa Nostra accepts him as coming king."

Sonny Franzese was respected and feared. One veteran ex-prosecutor in New York said that Sonny Franzese made John Gotti look like a "choir boy." Franzese was fearless. Upon hearing that the Gambino family, the largest of La Costa Nostra, had put a contract on his head, he called a Gambino family associate and screamed that he would be on a specific street corner at a specific hour when everybody was in bed. He assured this associate that he would have no protection other than himself. If the Gambino family wanted him, they knew where to find him. Sonny Franzese was on that street corner at the exact time he promised, alone, pacing up and down like a madman. Nobody else showed.

Sonny Franzese became a top priority for FBI director J. Edgar Hoover. He had been suspected of several murders but had been indicted just once, for the homicide of Ernie "The Hawk" Rapoli, a hit man. Rapoli's body washed ashore on a Long Island beach; he had been shot, stabbed, and tied to cement blocks. Sonny Franzese was indicted but cleared.

He was arrested a number of times, often for theft. That was Sonny. If he saw something, he took it. But any crime of consequence brought acquittals. The government's witnesses often had memory lapses when it concerned Sonny Franzese. Some witnesses just plain disappeared.

Finally Sonny Franzese was indicted and convicted on a bank robbery conspiracy charge, which struck Randolph as odd. Mob guys generally steered away from bank jobs. The risk was too high, and the action was too easy in other scams to take that risk. Sonny Franzese was convicted in 1967 of the conspiracy. His reputation did not escape the judge, who sentenced him to two consecutive twenty-five-year prison terms. After a lengthy three-year appeal process was finally exhausted, Sonny Franzese began serving time in 1970 at Leavenworth.

He was paroled in 1978. His file showed that the FBI had investigated whether Franzese had bribed a member of the parole commission to obtain his release. The FBI did not want Sonny Franzese on the streets, but he made it. It was suspected he was as powerful as ever, but he eventually slipped up by publicly associating with other Mafia members with criminal pasts. His probation officer reported him, and he was sent back to prison in 1982.

Sonny Franzese's second marriage was to Christine "Tina" Capobianco in 1953. He was the father of three children by his first wife. Tina Capobianco had been married to a man named Frank Grillo, and they had a son named Michael, born May 27, 1951. Frank Grillo disappeared when Sonny moved in. Sonny and Tina Franzese had three more children. Whether or not Michael Franzese was Sonny's real boy didn't seem to matter. He clearly was Sonny's favorite.

It also became clear that you didn't mess with the Franzese women. A Colombo family soldier, rumored to be paying too much attention to Tina Franzese while her husband was in prison, was mysteriously executed. The soldier's neck was garroted, his genitals stuffed in his mouth.

There was also the suspicious death of Lawrence Carrozza, a soldier linked to Michael Franzese. "Champagne Larry," as Carrozza was known, may have dishonored one of the Franzese girls. He got whacked in 1983.

Picking through the FBI files, George Randolph found what he was looking for. In wiretaps and other data, the name Norby Walters popped up—not once but several times. It may have been a casual mention or something related to business, but Norby Walters's name was branded. A file showed that Walters was questioned about Michael Franzese's involvement with the agent and a tour by Michael Jackson and his brothers. Norby Walters had told the feds that Michael Franzese, a so-called budding movie producer, had an interest in making some modern musicals involving the Jacksons. This sounded a little fishy.

Norby Walters had been linked to other mobsters besides the Franzeses. In a wiretap and according to other information, he had been associated with New Jersey mobster Thomas "Corky" Vastola. Norby was doing business with these people.

It was enough to convince Randolph that Norby Walters had more than a passing involvement with the mob. He believed Michael Franzese more than ever and couldn't wait to take his notes with him to gather even more information from the Mafia captain.

Jerry Zimmerman and Frankie Campione were household names in the Franzese files. Campione was Sonny Franzese's chauffeur and bodyguard. His reputation was notorious, as well. He was a very nasty man and very loyal to Sonny and Michael Franzese. Randolph figured that if Campione received orders to help Norby Walters with some rival agents, chances were that Campione would take care of it.

Zimmerman had a rather substantial file. He was identified by the FBI as a longtime associate of Sonny and Michael Franzese. And just as Franzese had told them, Zimmerman was an intimidating sight—six feet four inches and 270 pounds.

Jerome Zimmerman, fifty-five, had also been convicted in the gasoline fraud scandal that had nailed Michael Franzese. He had a rap sheet that included a grand theft conviction in Los Angeles. He had been ordering products from companies, selling them, and then failing to pay for them. An old mob trick, only he got caught. He was doing business in New York, Florida, and California for Michael Franzese's film production company.

Zimmerman had been convicted of perjury. Not once, not twice, but three times.

Shit, Randolph thought. Even if Jerry Zimmerman could verify Franzese's story that Norby Walters came to him to deal "with some broad from Chicago," he would easily be impeached as a witness.

Randolph decided to subpoena John Franzese, Jr., Michael's brother. He also was going to track down Frankie Campione.

Meanwhile, the Chicago prosecution team decided to try another strategy. They would try to get at Lloyd Bloom.

Norby Walters had retained Robert Gold, a top-flight New York criminal lawyer. Walters clearly had money to spend on his defense. Gold, a former prosecutor, was gaining a reputation for his defense work in white-collar crime. Gold had made it clear that Norby Walters was not going to submit to the government on this sports agent case. In other words, Walters and Gold had all but dared the government to indict Walters in the case. Gold figured that if the government indicted Walters on the mail fraud charges at this point, it would be a victory for the defense.

If Walters had a weakness, it was Lloyd Bloom. As far as the government could tell, Bloom didn't have enough money to finance a serious legal battle. They knew he had filed for bankruptcy and was at least $200,000 in debt. Maybe Norby Walters would foot Bloom's bill, too, but Uncle Norby had already dug deep into his pockets.

Lloyd Bloom had hired a Los Angeles attorney named Michael L. Trope. Mike Trope had built his reputation as one of the more unscrupulous sports agents in the business. He had quit the sports agent business and had just been sworn in as an attorney in December 1987, after passing the California bar.

Howard Pearl and George Randolph couldn't believe it when Trope called to say he was representing Bloom. They thought it was a godsend. They had just read Trope's book, *Necessary Roughness,* about the sports agent business. They couldn't believe that Bloom was handing them a rookie lawyer. By this time the government felt it had enough evidence to indict Bloom for extortion. He had made most of the threats to the players and had reminded Kathy Clements that "people who don't pay their bills get their hands broken."

Howard Pearl informed Mike Trope that Lloyd Bloom was in a lot of trouble but that the government was willing to talk about a deal, a plea agreement. There was nothing atypical about their offer. If Lloyd Bloom agreed to "flip" on Norby Walters and testify—if he had enough to reveal—the case would be a slam-dunk. It probably would never go to trial. Pearl asked Trope if Bloom would agree to a government proffer. Nothing Bloom told the prosecutors could be used against him unless he took the witness stand and testified contrary to the statement he gave them. Pearl also told Trope that the government might want to make some voice imprints because of the taped threats to Ron Morris.

Trope found the case very curious. He couldn't figure out why the U. S. government was spending so much money to protect the sanctity of college athletics. He was aware of Bloom's threats, but he thought the idea of Lloyd Bloom threatening anybody was laughable.

The appointment was made, and Mike Trope and Lloyd Bloom made their proffer with the government on January 18, 1988, in Chicago. When Trope and Bloom left the meeting with the government, they had a little better understanding of the case.

"It wasn't about schools getting defrauded," said Trope. "It was about the mob. It was about Norby and the mob. They didn't say the name, but they made it clear that they thought Norby was hooked up big-time to the Mafia."

Bloom didn't tell the government very much about Norby Walters and the mob. He acknowledged a lot of other things, though. He confirmed that SMU's Jerry Ball confronted him with a .357 Magnum. He confirmed that he had been angry with players, but he didn't consider his words as "threats," only a hot temper. He did admit, however, that his angry words included the phrase "break your legs" while talking to Ron Morris and Maurice Douglass.

Tony Valukas and Howard Pearl told Trope and Bloom that the government could connect Norby Walters to the Kathy Clements beating. Bloom seemed taken aback, saying he didn't know anything about it. He remained consistent about the Clements affair in subsequent meetings with the government.

But Lloyd Bloom admitted that Walters had once said to him, "Let me worry about Kathy Clements."

Bloom was asked if Norby Walters ever threatened him. He hesitated. Then he told the government about an incident that happened in April 1987. Bloom said that after the rash of publicity, and specifically after the Clements beating and the shooting involving Jeff Atkins's car—which he claimed he knew nothing about, of course—he went to Norby Walters. He had no knowledge of Walters's connection with those incidents, but he wanted to leave New York and move to Los Angeles.

According to Bloom's proffer, Walters warned Bloom about loyalty.

"If I'm in the jackpot, you're in the jackpot," Walters told his young partner.

If Bloom ever thought about crossing Walters, Norby pointed to a black phone on his desk and said that all he had to do was make a call. Then Bloom told the government that Norby Walters had made a gesture with his hand, putting it to his head, like a man pulling the trigger on a gun. Bloom said that Norby made it even clearer: "I'll have you popped."

Tony Valukas and Howard Pearl thought the incident was a nice jewel, and they did their best to sell Lloyd Bloom on making a deal. Once a deal was made, the government might even be able to pull more information out of Bloom. Bloom, however, would have to plead guilty to at least two counts of mail fraud and probably do sixteen months in prison. The government needed the mail fraud conviction to establish jurisdiction and to show a jury that a fraud had been committed.

"Right now," Pearl told Bloom, "you're looking at a considerable portion of your life in prison if you're convicted. It's a hell of a chance."

Bloom wasn't buying it. He said he couldn't do any prison time. No way.

When George Randolph got a moment alone with Lloyd Bloom, he told the young sports agent, "Look, this thing is getting serious. Do yourself a favor. This isn't a joke."

Mike Trope was addicted to negotiations. It had helped him thrive as a sports agent in the late 1970s and early 1980s. He wanted to negotiate further. He was also tempted by the publicity he would receive if the case went to trial. He thought he could beat the government on its mail fraud charges. He also despised the NCAA and what he called the hypocritical state of "shamateurism." Agents buying off college players was common practice, though he had to admit that the $800,000 in cash and expenses Walters and Bloom had spent in two years was mind-boggling.

"I never, ever dropped the kind of money on players that Norby did," said Trope. "I never understood that. It was stupid."

The negotiations were further complicated by the fact that Howard Pearl and Mike Trope didn't like each other.

The government also thought that Trope had a conflict of interest. In one of his last acts as an agent, Trope had given money to TCU's

Kenneth Davis—the same running back who had been suspended for being on the TCU booster payrolls—and then negotiated a split fee with Walters and Bloom. The incident never reached the courtroom, but Pearl eventually tried to use it as leverage on Trope.

THE GOVERNMENT refocused on Michael Franzese. George Randolph decided to send Franzese a message about how seriously they were taking the case.

Sonny Franzese was subpoenaed. John Franzese, Jr., was subpoenaed. Fred and Dino Garcia, Franzese's father-in-law and brother-in-law, were also subpoenaed.

Suddenly Randolph received a call from Bruce Kelton, Michael Franzese's attorney.

"Michael says he wants to talk to you," Kelton said.

George Randolph had a feeling he knew what it was about.

"Time out," Franzese told him.

There was too much exposure here. All of Randolph's inquiries had gotten back to Franzese. People were asking Michael why everyone was getting hassled by authorities in Chicago. Michael played dumb, only acknowledging that he heard something was going on with Norby Walters.

Although the government didn't know it at the time, Franzese had sent a message to Norby Walters. Upset about his relatives being subpoenaed and hassled, the Mafia boss suggested that the agent take a dive for the family.

"I felt obligated to send a message back to Norby to see if he could put a stop to this," Franzese said. "The message was, 'This thing is getting pretty intense. I don't know if you understand what's going on. If you can cop out on this thing, cop out and make it easier on me, my father, and my brother. Get it over with now before it goes any further.' "

According to Franzese, Norby sent a message back saying, "There's nothing to worry about. I'll beat it. . . . Nobody has to worry about anything."

Franzese had the meeting with George Randolph to tell him he needed to cover his leads without exposing Franzese.

After more internal hassles, George Randolph traveled again to Los Angeles. This time he planned to pick up his prisoner and take him to a hotel for a lengthy chat. Only it wasn't that easy. According to an FBI agent in Los Angeles, Randolph again got harassed by James Moody, who wanted to know "what the hell George thought he was doing with a guy like Michael Franzese."

Randolph nevertheless went to Terminal Island at night and took custody of Michael Franzese. He put the Mafia boss in the passenger seat next to him and drove away. It wasn't long before Randolph pulled over, catching Franzese by surprise.

"Look, I'm going to take off the handcuffs," the FBI agent told him. "If you dare fuck with me, it's over. If you break bad on me, you're dead."

Franzese stuck out his hands, and the cuffs came off. Randolph soon pulled into the parking lot of a nice restaurant. Franzese couldn't believe it. He hadn't had a good meal in months, and he couldn't believe the "decency" the FBI agent was showing him. After dinner and some small talk in which the two men felt each other out, Randolph took Franzese to his hotel. They talked about the risk Michael Franzese was taking by cooperating with the government on Norby Walters. Frankly, Norby Walters wasn't worth the risk to Michael Franzese. He told Randolph he needed to be more careful in chasing leads.

"If you talked to the grand jury, it might cut down on a lot of work and exposure," Randolph explained.

Franzese reiterated matter-of-factly that he would never testify before a grand jury. They could put him in front of a grand jury, but he would take five—the Fifth Amendment, which protects citizens from being compelled to incriminate themselves.

Randolph thought about what Franzese said.

"Okay, if you work with me, I'll get a game plan and cover your ass," the FBI agent told Franzese. "If you start fucking with me, I'll fuck with you."

The game plan was that Franzese would lay out everything about his relationship with Norby Walters as well as his father's relationship with Norby Walters. He would provide the FBI with enough details that they could be independently corroborated, and Franzese would never have to testify in front of a grand jury. Franzese agreed.

"But I'm warning you," Randolph explained. "If you fuck with me, we'll step on our dicks out on the street and it's all going to come back to you."

Franzese understood. First, Randolph wanted to know the life story of Norby Walters's relationship to the Franzeses and the Colombo family. They stayed up all night talking as Franzese filled Randolph in.

"My father was originally friendly with Norby's father back to God knows when, before I was born. The two boys, Norby and Walter, were in the agency business. They had the nightclub. They gravitated to my father. He became their man. Let me tell you, and this is the thing people have to understand: Norby, being in the business he was in and being the type of guy he was, he wanted to have a godfather, so to speak.

"The Norby Walters Club, right next to the Copa, was one of the hottest places in town until that shooting happened. My father was a partner. He was there just about every night, and business flooded into the place. To me [Sonny Franzese] was number one. His reputation is what it is. Probably had he not gone to prison that first time, I think without a doubt, he was the guy. In my mind, there was no question. In a lot of people's minds on the street, there was no question. For Norby to say he didn't know who my father was, it was absurd. It was comical, but that's Norby.

"My father was a very likable guy. He was very, very well known, and it was known that if you were with Sonny Franzese, you were with good people. You got some strength, you got some power. And they [Norby and Walter] came to my father. It wasn't a question of him reaching out to them and trying to grab them under. They wanted to be with him, and they wanted to capitalize on that relationship. And they did.

"Especially in the early years when he started out, the word was out: 'Hey, you put Norby Walters's acts in your club because he's got friends. Sonny's his friend. We want his acts in your club.' That's really how Norby became what he became. There wasn't a club he couldn't put an act in.

"I sat down many times with rival agents over their trying to knock his group out of a club. Anytime that happened, Norby would go, 'Hey, I'm with Michael and Sonny, and my act belongs in here, and I want it all.' There was this one rival agent, Ralph Moreno, and we constantly sat down with this guy over territories and clubs and regions Norby was trying to book his acts into. Every time I sat down, it ended up in Norby's favor. He got the club. He got the act. And in his earlier days, this is what really got him off. He was one of the most prolific agents around. That's how it happened. He used this relationship."

In return, Franzese said, Norby Walters paid his father, usually on a weekly basis, and that amount varied, anywhere from a couple hundred dollars to $500 in the early years. When Sonny Franzese was in prison, Norby gave the money to one of his father's close associates, Joe Broncato, Michael Franzese told the FBI. Michael said that Norby once asked him to "please tell your father I am meeting my obligation." Soon Michael started receiving the payments.

When Sonny Franzese was paroled from prison in 1979, he was a bit irritated to hear that Norby Walters had risen as a top booking agent but was not so generous with his purse strings. The money Walters delivered to the family did not seem equivalent to the revenues the agency was generating. Uncle Norby was only coughing up about $2,500 a month, at best, Michael Franzese told the FBI.

Michael Franzese said his father wanted to erase Norby Walters from the books. Despite their lifelong relationship, cement shoes would fit Norby nicely.

But Michael Franzese, as much as he agreed with his father about Norby's stinginess, also had aspirations of getting into the movie business and thought that if Norby didn't cough up the cash, his stable of stars would come in handy. Walters had recently made deals with pop star Michael Jackson and the Jacksons.

Norby Walters was more valuable to them alive than dead, Michael insisted to his father.

Sonny Franzese still wanted to get a message to Norby Walters. Michael Franzese served as the liaison and set up a meeting at the Stage Delicatessen in Manhattan. He explained to Norby that his father was upset about the agent's payments.

Franzese recalled: "My father was quite upset. It wasn't a question of severing relationships with Norby; he wanted to sever something else. Believe me, Norby was white at the end of that meeting because my father told him straight: 'Norby, look, you been using me for thirty-five years. We're friends, and I never thought I'd have to have this conversation with you. But I'm not going to tell you what to do. I'm not going to give you a number. But you do the right thing from this point on.'

"In so many words, Norby knew exactly what was going on. At that time I jumped in. I explained to my father, 'Norby's come to me lately about this thing with Michael Jackson. We got a couple of things going, and the deal we got is fifty-fifty. Norby's using me more personally, so don't worry, the money's gonna come. I talked to him, and Norby's gonna do the right thing, the way he's supposed to do.'

"Norby's impression, he didn't totally recall the meeting he and my father had before my father went to prison. And that meeting was, 'Hey, Norby, I'm setting you up in the agency business. I'm helping you. When I go away, we're fifty-fifty.' And Norby agreed to that."

Randolph asked Franzese how he knew Norby Walters had agreed to a fifty-fifty split with his father.

"Let me tell you one thing about my father. If he said that, then that's what it is. Absolutely. Norby had a different recollection than that. His recollection was, 'I know I'm always obligated to you. I know you're always my partner. But I didn't quite recall fifty-fifty.'

"At the end of the meeting, the matter was resolved that my father and Norby Walters were fifty-fifty partners."

But Michael Franzese admitted that he, too, had gotten frustrated with Norby Walters: "I told my father a number of times . . . 'Look, Dad, I like Norby. I get a kick out of him. It's kind of colorful to have a guy like him close in the industry, celebrities around us, but this guy . . .' Any time he offers us a deal, it's like, what do I have to do to make it happen? He doesn't come to us and say, 'Look, I made a hundred grand, here's fifty for you, here's ten for you.' If we don't know about it, I'll never find out about it. That's the kind of guy he was. And the thing about it is, nobody used us more than Norby Walters."

Randolph wanted to know about specific incidents when Walters used them. On numerous occasions through the years—whether it involved a band, a trumpet player, an agent, or a manager—Franzese used his influence to settle disputes in Norby's favor. Some he could remember specifically, some he could not.

There was the Jacksons incident. Norby Walters had been hired by the group as its booking agent around 1980, and a big tour was planned on the heels of Michael Jackson's hit album *Off the Wall.*

Suddenly the group's manager, Ron Weisner, informed Walters that the Jacksons wanted to end the relationship and had hired a new agent, Howard Rose. According to Franzese, Norby came to him with this problem, and Franzese agreed to meet with Weisner. Franzese said that he told Walters they would handle the problem the way they always did.

Norby would call Weisner and explain to the manager that Michael Franzese was a partner in the operation. If Weisner was worth his salt, he would know Franzese's reputation and the dispute would be settled. If Weisner did not know the Franzese name, Walters would provide the manager with a little background.

If Weisner fought a little more, Norby would set up a meeting in which Franzese and an "associate" would pay the manager a visit. Norby Walters would also attend the meeting, and then Michael would ask

Norby to leave the room while he had a little "heart to heart" with Weisner, with the associate standing by.

"The main thing, I wanted Norby to lay the groundwork before I got there," Franzese told the FBI.

Walters set up a meeting with Weisner, and Michael Franzese took a Colombo family soldier, Larry Carrozza, with him to Hollywood, where the manager's office was located. Randolph knew the incident had to have happened prior to 1983, the year Carrozza was murdered because of his rumored involvement with one of the Franzese girls.

"Carrozza was a real tough kid," Franzese said. "He was pretty intimidating. He had all the moves and all the looks, and if he knew I was going to a meeting for this purpose, he'd get up for it. You gotta understand, Norby was a showman. Anyway, Norby liked Larry and knew he'd be good at this."

According to Franzese, Norby laid the groundwork with the Jacksons' manager by telephone and then made the introduction to Franzese at the meeting in Hollywood. Norby excused himself while Franzese and Carrozza met alone with Weisner.

"Basically, I told him Norby Walters was going to be the agent for the tour or there wasn't going to be a tour," said Franzese. "[Weisner] stated that Howard Rose had been hired as the agent but that he'd see what could be done about it."

Franzese believed the problem would be solved. He had a follow-up telephone conversation with Weisner. He thought the issue was being worked out between the parties, but for some reason he wasn't aware of, Walters backed off.

A year or so later, Franzese told the FBI that he had to make another visit to the same manager about a problem with Dionne Warwick. The manager wanted Norby Walters fired as the singer's booking agent. At the office in Manhattan, Norby asked Franzese for help.

Michael Franzese thought this was kind of funny because Dionne Warwick had been so close to his father, who had virtually owned and operated Buddah Records, one of the singer's early recording labels. Michael Franzese remembers how affectionate Dionne Warwick always was with his father. There were the nights at the Copa, and he remembered she had once attended a party his father threw to celebrate his high school graduation in 1969. He said he'd never forget the first time he met Miss Warwick when he and his father bumped into her on the street.

"They were talking, and she was all affectionate with him and everything. He was kind of embarrassed because I was around. And I see right away . . . Later I said, 'Dad, this woman's got the hots for you.' And he smiled at me.''

Regardless, business was business, and Michael Franzese had a dispute to settle. He knew he wouldn't have to deal directly with Dionne Warwick, he would deal with her manager.

This time Franzese took Jerry Zimmerman along on the flight to Los Angeles. Franzese didn't have to explain much about Zimmerman, the huge mobster. Zimmerman also knew how to act the part. Heck, he wasn't acting. In sunny California that December day, inside the office of Dionne Warwick's manager, Zimmerman never took off his trench coat.

Again, Norby Walters introduced Michael Franzese as his partner. They discussed the disagreement they had about Norby's effectiveness as a booking agent. Finally, Franzese said, he asked Norby to leave the room as Zimmerman lurked behind him in the trench coat.

"I told the guy that I'd appreciate it if he left the act with Norby for at least another six months, through the life of the contract they had signed."

To the best of Franzese's knowledge, Norby Walters stayed on as Dionne Warwick's booking agent for another six months.

Then there was a more recent incident, in 1984 or 1985, a problem with a hot rising group called the New Edition with a talented lead singer named Bobby Brown. They had a platinum record and were arguably the hottest R&B group in the country at the time.

According to Franzese, Norby said he had lent the act $20,000 and was supposed to receive a twenty-five percent share in their business. The New Edition's managers were trying to pull the same trick, dumping Walters. So Norby and Franzese pulled their same trick. This time Franzese didn't take an associate because the managers' offices were in Manhattan. Franzese's reputation was notorious in New York.

There were a couple of managers; Franzese couldn't remember their names. They talked a little about Franzese's new venture in movies and about there being a possible opportunity to get together with the R&B group. One guy kept excusing himself—Franzese thought he seemed extremely nervous, but eventually they got focused on the problem at hand. Michael Franzese told the manager that the $20,000 they had borrowed from Norby was "actually mine." There would be no dumping of Norby Walters.

Norby Walters remained the group's booking agent.

Franzese also remembers a problem with a man named Joe Grant, the manager of Sammy Davis, Jr. In fact, Franzese told the FBI that Norby Walters, along with New Jersey mobster Tommy "Corky" Vastola, asked him to sanction a "hit" on Grant. Randolph recalled that he had noticed Walters's name on a wiretap transcript of Vastola.

"I went into Norby's office one day, and Vastola was there, wanting to meet me, and this was the time that Norby was telling me he was having a problem with Grant, who was now also representing Dionne. Tommy told me, 'Look, this is the guy we had a problem with. . . . This is what we want to do.' My response was, 'If you want to do it, you go do it. Number one, I won't sanction it, and number two, this is not something of that kind of nature that we even have to talk about that.' I said, 'Norby and I will resolve this issue. As far as that, we want no part of it.' But Norby, he was ready to do it. He really was, no question about it."

Joe Grant may have paid homage to Michael Franzese in another way. The FBI was astonished to find out that Sammy Davis, Jr., had appeared in one of Franzese's movies, *Cry for the City.*

Franzese apologized to George Randolph for not being even more specific. Norby Walters was not the central figure in his life as a Mafia captain.

Franzese's stories about Norby Walters were hardly shocking to the entertainment industry. After the initial publicity about Walters's alleged threats to athletes surfaced in March 1987, the Atlanta reporter who worked the story received several telephone calls from people in the music business who wanted to discuss Norby Walters. Two men said they used to play in bands represented by Walters in the 1970s, and another man identified himself as a rival promoter. One of the band members said that "real thugs" actually showed up to beat them up.

Several callers delivered the same message, almost to the word, about the agent to the stars: "Norby Walters's reputation is that he walks with a violin case."

According to Michael Franzese, "Norby was one of the types of guys . . . if he coulda hurt somebody by making an example of somebody, he would want to do it so everybody knew, 'Hey, don't screw with Norby Walters.' Guys like that are dangerous. Another guy I was involved with—only to make a comparison—Larry Iorizzo, who wound up testifying against me. . . . Here's a guy, if I had listened to him, wanted to kill everybody because he was the type of guy who wanted to show his power. Rival guys in the gasoline business, he wanted them dead. That's why I would never respond to *that* type of stuff. I had my own way of handling it. Norby was the type of guy that always said, 'Hey, we gotta show our authority, Michael, in this business, or we're not going to get anywhere. We gotta show that Norby Walters is boss.' He had that head problem without a doubt. Without a doubt."

11

ANTON RONALD Valukas was sworn in as the United States Attorney for the Northern District of Illinois in May 1985, succeeding Daniel K. Webb.

From the day he graduated from Northwestern School of Law in 1968, Anton Valukas embarked on a truly distinguished legal career. His resume was five pages long, and by 1983 he had been identified and listed in the *Best Lawyers in America* publication. Despite all the publicity Rudolph Giuliani received in New York, U. S. Justice Department officials thought of Valukas as their top gun. His office had recorded an unprecedented number of successful white-collar crime and public-corruption prosecutions in Chicago.

Behind his wire-rimmed glasses, Valukas may have looked like a Nazi gestapo officer, but he was really the son of Greek immigrants. He was highly respected in the community and was considered a man of integrity. He had no time for funny business.

Before George Randolph went any further in tracking down the leads provided by Michael Franzese, Tony Valukas wanted to get his own sense of the Mafia boss. He needed to see if the Mafia captain sounded credible. He needed it for his own gut at this stage. George Randolph was just as anxious for Tony Valukas and Howard Pearl to hear first-hand what Michael Franzese had said about Norby Walters. But as much as he wanted them to hear about Walters's dealings in the enter-tainment industry, he thought it was important that they discuss the full implications of the case at hand.

Tony Valukas sat down with Michael Franzese in the spring of 1988. After discussing Norby Walters at some length, George Randolph turned the discussion toward the mob's long-term interest in the operation. If the prosecution team had any doubts about how real a threat Walters's operation was to the game of football, Michael Franzese set them straight.

"There's no question in my mind had Norby been successful, and both my associates and I realized we had somewhat control over a number of major league ballplayers, that at some point in time we'd try and use this to our advantage. Even if it was distasteful to me—and I'm not saying it was totally distasteful—I'm quite sure other family members and superiors in the family would have approached me without a doubt.

"I mean, the mob lives to gamble. The mob is built upon . . . almost everybody is a gambler. It's a major mob enterprise. I saw that as a tremendous possibility. Just establishing a line, throwing the bets the right way, making the bets tilt the right way. That would have been a tremendous advantage.

"I wouldn't say it would be out of the question to speak with an athlete we got close with and, who knows, make it worthwhile to him that if he didn't perform properly in a game . . . say, we wanted to make five million dollars on a game, we could make it worthwhile. . . . Or if he got some inside info on what might happen in a game . . . that we would have taken advantage of.

"I think athletes are vulnerable, and I hate to say it but many of them are unsophisticated. A lot of black athletes, same as a lot of black performers, were unsophisticated. And Norby definitely had a talent for them. He was able to relate to them on their level. I mean, like he was black, just about. He had them eating out of his hand, no question. I think if he had maintained control, he could've spoke to them, 'Let's make some money this way.' There would have been things that if he wanted continued support from the family, which he always got, then he would have been obligated to deal.

"If I remember correctly, the first time we spoke about [going into sports], he laid it out to me. He mentioned Bloom. . . . I thought it was a great deal. Even at that point I considered some of the possibilities of just having athletes, being able to get that close with them, and represent them because I looked at it in a way that if Norby was doing it, it was like me doing it. So I told him, 'Pursue it.'

"There were legitimate things to consider. Take a guy like Michael Jordan. He's making more money off the field than he is on. As his agent we'd get a percentage of all of it. Plus, let's say I had a business I wanted to promote, or a friend of the family had a business they wanted to promote. People would approach me and say, 'I understand you have

Michael Jordan . . .' I could have made some kind of deal for another family member. Or I could have made some kind of deal for someone else.

"It's sorta like a basic practice that if I have this access, then I would have went to the family and said, 'Look, in case you guys ever need anything, Norby's with me, and we represent all these athletes. I'm putting on the table for the family. If there's anything you want, let me know.'

"That's not to say it's free rein for everybody. Things have to be within reason, and it couldn't jeopardize my position, but you had a responsibility to make things available for others."

The government was disappointed that Franzese said he had never discussed the potential of the sports agent operation with Walters. But, as Franzese pointed out many times, it would not have been in Norby's control. He was owned by the mob. He was just a pawn, but Franzese had protected him. Norby Walters owed Michael Franzese his life, not just because of Sonny Franzese's desire to kill Walters back in 1979 but also, he explained to the government, because the Colombo family boss, Carmine Persico, Jr., had it in for Norby, too.

"Carmine Persico used to tell me, 'This guy's a millionaire. What are we getting from this guy? We're only getting peanuts.' And I used to protect him. I'd say, 'Don't worry about it. Things aren't as good as you think, but Norby will come around. We still got influence through him, and we still got what we want through him.' I used to always smooth it out for [Norby].

"There was even one time I said, 'Norby, you're so ripe for the picking. If I ever let the families know I got nothing to do with you, Vastola and a bunch of guys are going to come down on you like a hawk. You're going to be paying a hundred percent. And rightfully so, Norby, because you use us to the hilt.'

"Another time I said, 'Norby, come on, my father's going to reach a point where he's going to get very upset, and there's nothing I can do for you anymore. Come across. Do what you're supposed to do. My father, you been using him for years and years, and you've become one of the biggest agents in the business on his name, so come across.' "

Why then, the government asked, did Norby have the nerve to ask Michael Franzese for $50,000? And why did Franzese deliver it?

"It wasn't for the need of the money that he did it. It was just to bring me in officially. As he built up his agency, he didn't need money, but in the sports business, he wanted me to be his partner. And I had told him,

'Anything you want, anything you need, let me know.' This was the first time he came to me for money. . . . But back when he started in the music business, he asked my father for help. . . . It was more [symbolic]. He just wanted me as a piece of it, he wanted me involved, plus I think he was going to be shelling out a lot of money for these kids. Fifty grand, let me tell you, it would have been more than that. But it just so happened with the timing and I got in trouble. But it would have been more. I understood that it was going to be more than fifty grand. This was really just the start of it. If I would have been home, they would have tapped me for a lot more.

"One thing I figured, that if Norby took money from me, I knew I was going to get my end. There was no way he would not pay me, so it was a solid investment."

They asked Franzese if he had sanctioned the threats Norby Walters and Lloyd Bloom made to the athletes.

"No way. I took that personally offensive. Number one, because I was in prison and my father was in prison. Especially how it related to my father, I took it more personal for him. Guys had used our name so much. This was distasteful. You're not threatening some guy on the street. You're threatening athletes, a representation of America, that normal people really relate to. It's not like threatening a bookmaker or some guy on the street who borrowed shylock money and didn't pay it back. I was personally offended. . . . Lloyd Bloom especially put us at risk. . . . It's bad business. . . . I sent a message to Norby and asked, 'What is this guy doing?' . . . There's a time for everything and a manner in how to do it. . . . Maybe 'cause Lloyd Bloom had met me once, maybe because he knew I was Norby's partner . . . but let me tell you, the guy was stupid."

Franzese told the prosecution team that he didn't believe Norby Walters would have peddled drugs to the athletes to gain further leverage. The government had felt compelled to ask him since several of the athletes had been linked to drug use, though there was no evidence Walters or Bloom ever provided them with drugs.

"You want your performers, your entertainers, at their very best so they can reach their potential. Norby saw a lot of his entertainers ruined by drugs. One time I was in the office and Marvin Gaye was there, begging for five thousand dollars. Norby didn't want to give it to him, but Marvin kept begging. Norby finally had somebody go get him five grand, and he asked Marvin to make sure he didn't blow it on drugs. A couple hours later, we went to lunch and when we came back, there was

Marvin begging Norby for more money. He had went out and bought five thousand dollars' worth of shoes.''

The fact that entertainers and athletes—no matter how much money they make—have a tendency to go broke was not lost on Franzese.

"That makes them that much more vulnerable," said Franzese. "And Norby, he felt even more so with the black performers. Norby liked to act like he was one of them, but Norby didn't respect blacks. Not like he said."

If that were true, then Norby Walters had fooled a lot of people. In its annual celebration of Dr. Martin Luther King, Jr., on January 18, 1988, the Congress of Racial Equality (CORE) honored Norby Walters with an Entertainment Management Award, citing the agent's work with "such greats as Marvin Gaye, Bobby Womack, Dionne Warwick, Rick James, Chaka Khan, Patti LaBelle, Run DMC, Luther Vandross, Kool and the Gang, Ray Parker, and Peabo Bryson."

The CORE program that night specified that "Mr. Walters's 35 years of fighting for racial equality, and his continuing philanthropic efforts in so many areas, make him especially worthy to be honored by the Congress of Racial Equality on this most auspicious evening."

"I suspect this was a time when Norby needed a favor," said Franzese.

Tony Valukas had been rather sure that Norby Walters was a wise guy. But after hearing Michael Franzese's tale, he really wanted George Randolph to tie the case together.

"I wasn't blindly accepting Franzese's word as gospel," said Valukas, now in private practice. "I wasn't naive about that. I knew what a con man he had been. But he was one of the sharpest—maybe the sharpest— organized crime guy I had ever seen. He was no ordinary mob guy. He was extremely bright, very believable. Now, I wanted to see that he was credible, and that was George Randolph's job. I knew I had the right [FBI] agent working the case."

Valukas said, "The scenario about what the mob could do on the eve of a Rose Bowl game was not idle speculation."

On that issue Franzese recalls that somebody on the prosecution team made a "passing remark" about Ronnie Harmon, the Iowa running back whose performance in the 1986 Rose Bowl game raised suspicions.

"We didn't do anything with the kid," Franzese says. "But as an afterthought, it gets you thinking."

Randolph had been thinking about Harmon for some time. In particular, he wanted the forty-minute tape Harmon's attorney, Martin Rauch, claimed to possess. Randolph called FBI agents in Buffalo to grab the tape once and for all.

It was a small microcassette. Rauch and eventually Harmon told the government it was made on the day he signed—March 10, 1985. The government and Rauch struck a deal that Harmon would be admitted to the Pre-Trial Diversion Program for his cooperation.

Harmon and his father, who lived in Brooklyn, had met Walters and Bloom in the agent's office in the spring of 1985. Ronnie Harmon, a streetwise football star who was recovering from a broken leg at the time, had hidden a recorder in a gym bag he carried with him.

Randolph laughed when he first saw the tiny tape. He went crazy looking around the office to find somebody with a microrecorder, but he wanted to be careful with the tape. FBI lab analysts wanted the original piece of equipment before they made a copy. Harmon didn't have the recorder anymore. Randolph called a Radio Shack, and they told him the model had been discontinued. Finally a member of the lab staff found the right recorder.

Unlike the other tapes they had, this was not made over the telephone but in person. Randolph, Valukas, and Pearl were amazed at its excellent quality. They had heard the finest in electronic eavesdropping equipment, but never had they heard the quality of the tape that Ronnie Harmon had made. And it was a critical piece of the puzzle. This was not a threat but rather the sales pitch that all the players had told them about. Now they were about to hear it for themselves.

Rather quickly, Norby Walters found his stride.

WALTERS: Well, you know, I've become the number-one agent in America regarding musical entertainment. As you can see by gold and platinum and some of the posters . . . I mean I represent the cream of America. There's nobody larger than I am, Mr. Harmon.

Norby Walters went on and on, with Harmon's father mostly saying, "Yeah."

WALTERS: Coming from the neighborhood . . . it gives you a hunger, it gives you a strength to really make it happen. So slowly but slowly but slowly and slowly I made it happen. And in the agency business I've moved in to become the number-one representation of entertainment, not only in the country, because it goes beyond that . . . basically, I'm the number-one salesman of entertainment, of black entertainment in the world. . . . You ask anybody you know in the entertainment world, and you say the name of Norby Walters, they'd say he's number one.

Certainly, sports is equal. . . . I won't say it's bigger. . . . Music is
international, sports is only national. . . . The New York Giants, I
mean all you gotta do is cross the border to Mexico, and they say,
"Cómo está usted what?" They don't know shit.

HARMON'S FATHER: Yeah.

WALTERS: You dig? You go anywheres else, and nobody knows about
the New York Giants. Only America. But . . . we decided, let's go into
sports. I feel if I'm the number-one deal maker . . . I make, uh,
multi-multi-mega-million-dollar deals for one of my musical people.
. . . So when I deal with RCA corporation or the CBS corporation or
something like that . . .

Walters then told the Harmons about Lloyd Bloom, who was sitting
in the room, approaching him with the idea of going into sports. Walters
said Bloom was a football fanatic. Then, for effect, Walters whispered,
"He said, 'You know what? It makes a lot of sense.'"

WALTERS: That's where we are today, making our major push into
sports. We've chosen football because of Lloyd's knowledge, being
like an encyclopedia of football.

Valukas, Randolph, and Pearl almost died laughing. They had met
Lloyd Bloom and an "encyclopedia" he was not.

WALTERS: . . . He knows everything about everybody who did everything
and what they did and where they went and why they did it and how
they played and what . . . da, da, da, da, da. . . . So I said, "Great,
there's no sense in going into basketball since we don't know shit.
There's no sense in going into baseball since we don't know shit. So
let's right now make our major push in an area which he knows and
I can sell."

For the next two minutes, in staccatolike fire, Norby Walters started
a rap unlike anything anybody in the room had heard. He talked about
selling products.

WALTERS: So now you make an analysis, well, who do you sell? Who do
you sell? What do you sell? If I'm a businessman and I wanted to be
a salesman, let's see, do I sell telephone equipment? What's a good
product? Do I sell videocassette recorders? Maybe that's a good product. Or do I sell Rolls-Royces? Maybe that's a good product. As a
salesman, what do I sell? Okay, so as a great salesman of entertainment, we honed in on who we should sell. So he's the guy who knows
it all. And he says, "We're gonna sell Ronnie Harmon." Wooo! Right.
Okay. We're gonna sell . . .

There was a popping sound, like Walters slapping his hand on the desk.

WALTERS: Because he understands the marketplace, what people are doing, what's their potential. See, we're not going after established artists. We're not going after established talent. What I learned to do in sports is exactly what I did in entertainment, in the music side of entertainment, is take the young potential star and take them, and turn them into a superstar. Because once they're spoiled out there, they're kinda screwed over. You see, the world of celebrity is a world of screwed-up people. Believe me when I tell ya. I'm dealing with lots of celebrities. It's a lot easier to take a young talent, a young Luther Vandross, who I took six years ago and built him. . . . It's a lot easier to take a young, ah, ah, New Edition, and build these youngsters right now and deal with the family and build these kids than it is to take an older actor. Let me get the young talent and develop them into a star, into a superstar . . . providing they got the talent, providing they can sing, providing they can play, providing they can run and understand their game . . . and therefore have the potential to become a superstar in the world of economics, providing I show them the way. When you've become number one, you've learned to open every single door there is. Why do these people flock to me? They flock to me because I know. . . . They know that I can go into major companies . . . the major football company or record company or television company or motion picture company and make a multimillion-dollar deal . . . that very few people can make a deal like that, with all the built-in bonuses and equities and so on and so forth. Now, in addition to that, the name of the game is to take talent, singing, running, whatever, writing, whatever it is . . . take the talent and open up the doors of the commercial world, such as commercials, such as endorsements, such as partnerships, and so on and so forth. Now, as you know, and as quiet as it's kept, America ain't ready for black, really. They were never ready for black. . . . They still don't want black. They'll take it only reluctantly when it's forced down their throat like good medicine.

Walters railed on about Herschel Walker never capitalizing on endorsements. Same for other black Heisman Trophy winners, such as Archie Griffin and Mike Rozier.

WALTERS: There are two reasons. Number one is that the great white American world ain't into their program. . . . Second is that the football agents of America aren't hip or sophisticated enough or ballsy enough or hungry enough or socially conscious enough to want to do it . . . to rock the boat. . . . Norby Walters is doing it today for Patti LaBelle, Dionne Warwick, the Commodores, the Whispers, Shalamar, Kool and the Gang . . . blah, blah, blah, blah, blah, blah.

Randolph began to laugh. Norby was rolling so fast, he was throwing out "blah, blah, blah." Then he recaptured their attention.

WALTERS: I know how to make the deals with Coca-Cola, Dr. Pepper, Pepsi-Cola. I know who the people are. I know the ones that are willing to take the cash. Can you dig it? Because that's what America is about. You know that, doncha? No matter what level . . any place you want to go . . . to the cop on the beat who takes . . . you slip 'em a few . . . to the guy who fixes a ticket . . . to the governments who give money to situations . . . and to the Lockheed companies and Boeing companies that pay off governments to get deals. Am I right or am I wrong?

To this Ronnie Harmon's father said, "You're right. Everybody's doing it."

WALTERS: I know the guy in Coca-Cola who will give me a deal. . . . If this youngster can be the star I want 'em to be, and if he can get out there and prove himself, I know the guy will give me the deal for half a million dollars. Now that guy knows I'm gonna get my commission, and he says to me . . .

Walters cleared his throat and told the Harmons as an aside, "I've always loved the pressure." Then he went back to putting words in the imaginary Coca-Cola executive's mouth.

WALTERS: He says to me, "He's a good kid. There've been a couple of other people I'm considering. You want to split the commission, I say you got it, bro." . . . I know the captain in every one of those organizations. You can dig that, can't ya?

Huh? They stopped the tape. The reference to "captain" might have been a Freudian slip for Walters. Mafia captain?

WALTERS: I've been shaking those people for years now in that music side of entertainment, now it's time to shake them hard in the sports side of entertainment. So Lloyd, my partner, has picked out . . . bang, okay? Lloyd has picked out three or four great juniors who we believe are gonna be stars, who we believe we can throw our strength, our money, our efforts, our knowledge, and our willingness to develop this handful of young stars into superstars.

Then Lloyd Bloom spoke up.

BLOOM: We're not gonna become an assembly line, like most of the agents that represent a hundred, two hundred ballplayers. We just don't have the time, or we can't give our clients the full attention if we handle fifty, forty ballplayers. A few years from now, we might have a handful, uh, twelve, thirteen ballplayers.

WALTERS: A dozen wouldn't be so bad. . . . Over the next three years we got ourselves a dozen incredible hot stars that we can make a deal—to this one with Dr. Pepper. . . . I can make a deal for this one with Burger King. . . . I can make a deal for this one over here with, ah, ya know, Kentucky Fried Chicken. . . . I can make a deal over here with Pepsi-Cola. . . . Each one of these kids could get anywhere from two hundred and fifty thousand to one million dollars a year for endorsements. When he's become a star, he's gonna have a salesman who's gonna represent him and make deals for him all over. Not a man who's got fifty or one hundred ballplayers so that it's just bullshit, bullshit, bullshit, bullshit assembly line.

To which George Randolph said, "What a bunch of bullshit."

WALTERS: This is my new business. In order for me to be a star, I got to make big deals for him, so that people will say, "Damn, damn, that Norby Walters is in the sports business with a vengeance . . . wow . . . wow."

Uncle Norby was getting ready to pop the real deal on Ronnie Harmon.

WALTERS: Okay, what I want to do is treat Ronnie Harmon as a businessman. The product is Ronnie Harmon. . . . We want to sell the Ronnie Harmon business. Norby Walters and Lloyd Bloom, we want to represent the selling of that product to the market . . . before it comes to market. I say I want to make a deal now. Today. I don't want to wait till January, I want to make a deal now. And I say I'm willing to make the bet. . . . I'm willing to come up with a few thousand dollars, cash American, for Ronnie so that he has it . . . to do as he pleases . . . to give it to the family . . . to take care of some mortgage payments . . . to live his life . . . in addition to that from now, on the first of every month, from now until the day he starts playing ball . . . I will make sure there's a telegram out there in Iowa, or wherever he is. . . . There'll be two hundred and fifty dollars sitting there waiting for him . . . so that Ronnie Harmon can lead a middle-class interesting kind of life without having to have Dad send him one hundred dollars a month, or fifty dollars or seventy-five dollars.

The tape shut off on side A. Amazingly, the government found out that Walters was so wrapped up in his sales pitch, he never noticed that Harmon reached down in his gym bag to flip over the tape. On side B, the start of the tape picked up with Ronnie Harmon's father apparently trying to get Norby Walters to understand that his son would be breaking NCAA rules.

HARMON'S FATHER: I'm not talking about that. I'm just saying that . . . about the ruling.

WALTERS: Sure.

HARMON'S FATHER: A rule is a rule. It's just like that.

WALTERS: Yeah.

HARMON'S FATHER: The same thing with the police.

WALTERS: Yeah, that's—

HARMON'S FATHER: They got rules.

Norby Walters then spun things around on the Harmons. He also unwittingly handed the government a nugget.

WALTERS: Yeah, it's like income tax.

HARMON'S FATHER: Right, they got laws.

WALTERS: Dig it . . . it's just like income tax.

HARMON'S FATHER: Okay, like income tax.

WALTERS: But the name of the game is that we don't give them their money unless we have to . . . that's the name of the game.

Valukas, Pearl, and Randolph looked at one another now. They barely breathed as they listened to Norby Walters. They hung on his words. . . .

WALTERS: As a businessman, unless you're a guy who gets a paycheck from a guy who takes their taxes out . . . if you're in business for yourself . . . you ain't giving it up.

HARMON'S FATHER: You ain't giving it . . .

WALTERS: You're gonna play the game. You all gonna do a razzle-dazzle that the government is gonna have to try to find out what it is that you're doing. . . . And you know what . . . they don't . . . unless you are one of them incredible, insane guys who just flaunt it terribly. . . . But the name of the game is, "I'll report a little bit, and that's that."

As they sat mesmerized, the prosecution team couldn't help but think how powerful this evidence would be to a jury. They were also thinking of Norby Walters's mysterious financial records and all that cash.

WALTERS: If five or seven years down the line you have some kind of audit, and they say you owe 'em another eleven hundred bucks, good,

I'll give it to 'em then. . . . Meanwhile, they don't know about the rest of it.

HARMON'S FATHER: Yeah.

The room went silent for a moment. Then Uncle Norby, in a raspy tone, made it quite clear to the Harmons what he was talking about.

WALTERS: We ain't gonna tell.

HARMON'S FATHER: That I understand.

WALTERS: We are talking about your son's life, and we're talking about business. If we take a piece of the business here right now . . . okay, we're taking care of a piece of business here right now.

BLOOM: (Interrupting) But charity begins at home. I'm an ex-ballplayer. . . . Once Ronnie's season's done this year, they're not even gonna care about him. They'll give you a pat on the back and say, "Hey, man, you did great for the university. . . . Who's the next junior who's taking Ronnie's place?"

WALTERS: But the point is, this thing . . . The schools are taking in millions. Now why shouldn't a youngster who's a star . . . I wouldn't be sitting here talking to you unless I believe we got a star. . . . Solid. The point is if they have a star on their hands who's helping them win games, who is running his ass off out there, who is All-America all over the place, why don't they take care of him? Why don't they give him some money?

HARMON'S FATHER: What I want to know is . . . if you feel that way . . . then why not wait until it's time, instead of taking a chance on getting him in a jam?

WALTERS: Let's put it this way. I hope you accept this. I'm surely as important as your son, in terms of business. If I'm willing to put my business on the line and hope that if he doesn't give me up . . . then I am willing to gamble . . . hey, I can lose that gamble, Mr. Harmon. My feeling is, I'm putting my business on the line, just like he is.

HARMON'S FATHER: Yes, you are. But what I'm saying is this: Even if you put your business up, you still have the power to fight. We don't have any power at all.

WALTERS: You want to know something? I'm gonna give you a good situation. First of all, if we sign a piece of paper and if we do a piece of business . . . I mean, there's four of us here. And then there's Mama. That's the end of that.

HARMON'S FATHER: Yeah.

WALTERS: That's finished business. The fact that he now has a few thousand dollars to take care and help out a little but . . . I mean, that's nobody's business, but right here . . . I mean that's all that is. . . . If we wait until the end of the year, so what have we gained? He's gained nothing. . . . I say why wait now when you have the opportunity to know that you are represented by the man who is number one in the music world? Every person I represent is half an idol of his. . . . Youngsters grow up on rock and roll, so every person I represent is an idol of your son. If he were to go to the Kool and the Gang concert and come backstage with his camera, take pictures and all that, it's a thrill. Okay, I'd say this: If Norby Walters is the agent to the stars . . . why do we have to wait until January? I say, here's a few thousand dollars.

Ronnie Harmon's father had a very good question for the agent to the stars.

HARMON'S FATHER: Why not wait if you got confidence in yourself?

WALTERS: I can wait. . . . What I'm saying is, why wait?

HARMON'S FATHER: See, this is what I'm getting at. . . . It's us that get hurt.

Walters went on a confusing spiel about NCAA rules, involving lawyers and agents. Harmon's father agreed that "the whole thing is fouled up." Walters wouldn't back off.

WALTERS: What we win is that he's got a few thousand dollars in the kicker . . . a few hundred dollars a month at his disposal . . . and come January second, we then send in the paper to the NFL. . . . I am licensed. I'm not gonna walk around and say, "Ronnie Harmon and Norby Walters . . . wooo, I just signed." . . . I'm not crazy. I can't afford to lose my American Federation of Musicians license, which is just like the NFLPA.

HARMON'S FATHER: All right, all right.

WALTERS: If we make a deal with the family, and he signs and I sign, that's the end of that. That piece of paper goes in my vault.

Norby Walters himself talking about that vault.

WALTERS: Come January second, we file the paper, and he has his agent.

Walters and Bloom also talked about the "gamble" they were taking, apparently because Harmon's broken leg was still in a cast that March of 1985. There was more talk about the benefit of getting money now and signing a contract.

WALTERS: . . . A piece of paper goes into your vault at home, and it goes into my vault. That's done. That's the end of that. We're not walking around like chumps or like jerks.

BLOOM: That's not dated today, anyways.

WALTERS: That's right, we're gonna date it January second . . . we're not dating it today. . . . We're dating it January second . . . We're gonna . . . put it away.

Ronnie Harmon finally spoke up. "And how much percentage you take, say six?"

Walters spent the next fifteen minutes talking about percentages, the difference in football and the difference in endorsements.

The tape cut off after about forty minutes.

Howard Pearl asked George Randolph and Tony Valukas, "Do you realize what we have here?"

All of them did. Ronnie Harmon no longer had to worry about being prosecuted. The government needed him desperately now. As far as the sales pitch went, virtually everything the players had told them about Norby Walters was on the tape, in Norby Walters's own words. If a jury didn't understand what the players told them, they could listen for themselves.

12

GEORGE RANDOLPH called his friend, FBI Special Agent John O'Neill, and asked him to track down Ron Weisner. O'Neill had been told that Weisner was the manager of Dionne Warwick, and he was to question Weisner about the day in 1982 when Michael Franzese and Norby Walters paid him a visit.

Weisner explained that he had been threatened by Michael Franzese and Norby Walters, but it was about the Jacksons tour. Dionne Warwick's manager was Joe Grant—he worked out of the same office building on Wilshire Boulevard. Either Randolph or Franzese had been confused. It turned out to be Franzese's mistake, but it was not a major blow.

Weisner had no trouble remembering Michael Franzese or Norby Walters. The manager told O'Neill that the dispute took place from 1980 to 1981 when the Jacksons decided to dismiss Walters as their booking agent. Norby Walters was angry and told Weisner that he would have an associate get in touch with him.

Michael Franzese soon called and introduced himself as that "associate." He wanted to set up a meeting. Weisner agreed to meet him. He told the FBI that he knew the Franzese name from his days in the record business in New York. Ron Weisner had once worked for the same Buddah Records that was controlled by Sonny Franzese.

Walters, Franzese, and "another man" visited him, Weisner told O'Neill. Norby Walters made the introduction and left the room. Franzese explained that he was involved with Walters's agency business and that they wanted to participate in the Jackson tour as partners. They wanted a percentage of the business. Weisner claimed Franzese told him that if Norby wasn't the agent, the tour would have some problems, "or there might not be a tour."

"He was very threatening," said Weisner.

The problem was, Weisner said, the Jacksons did not want to dump Howard Rose as the booking agent and retain Walters. Michael Jackson was particularly adamant about keeping Rose, but his father, Joe Jackson, wanted to stick with Walters, according to Weisner.

Weisner said he decided to reject Franzese and Walters, figuring the Jacksons were too popular for a Mafia captain to expose himself. He informed the group's head of security, Bill Bray, who took only one notable precaution: The Jacksons would not play the Nassau Coliseum on Long Island, where Franzese ruled.

Weisner mentioned that he had been questioned about the incident not too long after it happened. That sent George Randolph on another intelligence check. Sure enough, the organized crime unit of the Los Angeles Police Department had had Franzese under surveillance at that time and had followed up on his visit to Weisner. The FBI had also questioned Weisner a few months later.

The L.A.P.D. believed it had snapped a photo of Franzese that day when he was accompanied by two other men. That would be a real find if one of the men turned out to be Norby Walters. Randolph searched through files and files of photos, but a picture never appeared.

It didn't help when an L.A. detective told him, "I know I saw a picture. I know it."

Nevertheless, Michael Franzese's story had been corroborated.

Next, Randolph went on a wild-goose chase in New York and Los Angeles trying to track down the manager of the New Edition. He discovered there were three—William Dern, Rick Smith, and Steven Machat.

Finally he tracked down Dern, who was very nervous about discussing Norby Walters and a guy named Michael Franzese. Nevertheless, Dern told Randolph that he had borrowed money on the group's behalf from Norby a couple of times. When the New Edition went looking for a new agent, they decided they wanted a multipurpose agency that was also involved in movies. Dern informed Walters his services were no longer needed and began to negotiate with Triad. One day Dern said he was at the Sunset Marquis Hotel in Los Angeles when he received a call from Smith.

"Rick Smith called me and told me he was very upset, and that I should stop talking to Triad," Dern told Randolph. "He said he and Machat decided to keep the group with Norby Walters. He said they had just been visited by Norby and another man, and Rick said the guy was a mob guy. Rick was very upset because I had borrowed the money. He got very excitable. He said he didn't want the mob involved with the group. He sounded very afraid."

Now all Randolph needed was Machat or Smith to tell him about the meeting. They both, however, told the FBI agent they could be of no help.

John O'Neill, at Randolph's request, also met with Joe Grant, the real manager for Dionne Warwick. O'Neill visited him at the same building on Wilshire Boulevard. Grant recalled an incident when he tried to dismiss Norby Walters as the singer's booking agent.

O'Neill's FD 302 revealed that Grant did not recall the name of Michael Franzese, but he remembered that one of the men who visited him was "in his late twenties with black hair." (In December 1982, when the meeting took place, Michael Franzese was thirty-one. His hair was black.)

O'Neill wrote that Grant said the other man with Franzese and Walters was a large man who wore a raincoat and never took it off.

"I thought it was unusual that it did not rain that day," Grant was quoted as saying by O'Neill.

O'Neill's report also said Grant explained that Walters was very agitated and was walking around the office "shouting" and obviously annoyed about Grant's decision to cut him off as the booking agent.

O'Neill's report then said that "the man with the black hair" told Walters to leave the room, and "Walters obeyed."

"The man with the black hair" told Grant he'd appreciate it if Norby Walters remained as the booking agent. O'Neill said Grant was fuzzy about what happened next, but Walters was dismissed the following year.

O'Neill said he went over his notes with Grant and asked "if there was anything you wish to add or correct. . . . He stated 'no.' "

It was more corroboration of Michael Franzese's story about his relationship with Norby Walters.

When Joe Grant was subpoenaed to appear before the grand jury, however, he had a different story. Stumbling on his words over a speakerphone, Grant said that FBI agent John O'Neill must have been confused over the story.

"What?" a stunned Randolph asked on the phone.

Grant said he never had a real problem with Norby Walters, other than a difference on business matters involving Dionne Warwick. There was no incident.

"Why are you lying?" Randolph asked.

Grant stuttered and said he wasn't lying. Howard Pearl looked at Randolph disapprovingly.

The FBI agent leaned toward the speakerphone.

"You're a fucking liar," he told Grant.

Howard Pearl hurriedly pushed the button to disconnect them. He was in a panic over Randolph's words to a potential witness. The prosecutor went straight to Tony Valukas with the problem. Valukas approached Randolph as the two men were walking to their cars late that night.

"Did you just call Dionne Warwick's manager a 'fucking liar'?" the U. S. Attorney asked the FBI agent.

"That's right."

"Why?"

"Because he is a fucking liar," Randolph replied. "And because that's me. That's the way I am, Tony."

Valukas left it alone.

But Randolph was not about to leave it alone. He was going to try to prove that Joe Grant was playing games. John O'Neill was too good an agent, as far as Randolph was concerned, to get jerked around. They could use O'Neill as a witness, but he wanted more.

He remembered from the Ron Weisner/Jacksons incident that the L.A.P.D. and FBI had had Michael Franzese under surveillance. He decided to do another intelligence check. There was nothing about Michael Franzese visiting Joe Grant, but there had been some FBI undercover work with Franzese from 1981 to 1984. Maybe one of the undercover agents heard something.

Phone call after phone call and file after file produced little. Randolph decided to try an FBI agent named Victor Guerrero; he was part of an undercover investigation in 1982, the year Franzese said he met with Joe Grant about Dionne Warwick and Norby Walters. Bingo. Guerrero went undercover in 1981 and met Michael Franzese on March 9, 1982. He had presented himself as a man who had made $15 million in narcotics but needed a place to launder the money.

At the time, the FBI was investigating organized crime's alleged involvement with boxing promoter Don King and civil rights activist Reverend Al Sharpton. This rang a bell with Randolph because Sharpton clearly had been connected to Norby Walters by Franzese, and both Sharpton and King had been signees to the Salute to Norby Walters ad in the *Billboard* magazine supplement. Anyway, Guerrero wanted to launder his money in the sport of boxing. The FBI believed the Colombo family, and particularly the Franzeses, were heavily involved with Don King and Al Sharpton.

Guerrero did his best to infiltrate the operation, but, he told Randolph, Michael Franzese immediately expressed concern that he was an undercover agent. Guerrero proceeded carefully, then in December 1982 he was invited to a social occasion at the Casa Blanca Bar in Huntington, Long Island. The bar was always closed on Monday evenings while Michael Franzese conducted business for friends and associates. Franzese sat in the corner. Much to Guerrero's surprise, Sonny Franzese was there that night. Sonny had been out of prison, and Michael was telling his father that he should retire and enjoy life. John Franzese, Jr., Michael's younger brother, was also there.

John Franzese, Jr., who Guerrero said had a problem with drugs, wanted to align himself with the undercover agent regarding boxing promotions. John Franzese, Jr., tried to impress Guerrero with his "influence in the boxing community." He also claimed to have connections with Al Sharpton, who could steer the best young boxing talent their way. Michael Franzese told Guerrero that night that he would arrange a meeting with Don King on December 14.

Franzese was going to attend the meeting with Guerrero and King but canceled at the last minute.

"Michael told me he couldn't come to the meeting because he had to go to Los Angeles and straighten out a contract problem he was having with Dionne Warwick's manager," Victor Guerrero told Randolph.

George Randolph was exhausted but pleased. He could have kissed Victor Guerrero, and he wanted to call Joe Grant to tell him to kiss his ass. Instead, he bought Guerrero a beer and left Grant alone. He also made a gratifying call to Tony Valukas and Howard Pearl.

Out of curiosity, Randolph asked about Don King. Guerrero said King seemed wise to him.

Michael Franzese later told Randolph, "I told Don King to go ahead and meet with Victor but to conduct business as if he were doing it with the FBI." Franzese had nothing more to say about Don King.

Guerrero also passed along his impression of Michael Franzese: "He was like Michael Corleone. Everything about him. People lined up to see him with their problems. Everything you've seen in the movies, that was Michael Franzese. A very powerful guy. A very sharp guy."

Randolph took a young, eager FBI agent named Pat Buckley to New York with him on a search-and-destroy mission to find other bands Franzese had told them about. Most of the people had disappeared. There was a trumpet player they met under the George Washington Bridge. Some of the people were such lowlifes that Randolph wanted nothing to do with them.

Randolph also asked the New York bureau to deliver a subpoena to the Reverend Al Sharpton. Then he received a telephone call from a fellow agent, asking, "Do you really want to do this?"

Sharpton had been raising cain in the media about police treatment of Tawana Brawley. Sharpton called a press conference at every opportunity. Randolph told the bureau to forget the subpoena.

Two people Randolph did manage to track down were the office girls the athletes had told them about, including Tim McGee. One was an attractive lady, the other was "about three hundred pounds." Randolph begged and pleaded with Richard Tofani, the New York FBI agent who had served the subpoena on Walters when the investigation started, to find the women. Tofani reluctantly ventured into the New York projects where the sewer pipes were busted in the building that housed one of the ladies.

"I had shit and water running over the tops of my shoes," Tofani groused at Randolph. "And the gal wants me to go out and buy her some premium beer before she'll talk. You owe me, you owe me."

Randolph brought both women to Chicago, and then understood exactly what Tofani had experienced. When the FBI agent showed the women a picture of Michael Franzese, they both opened their eyes wide. One of the women said, "That dude, when he comes in, everything gets quiet. Norby gets real nervous, and they always whisper."

The other woman said, "Or they go out on the fire escape and talk."

This was terrific information, positive identification from employees of Norby Walters that Michael Franzese was a regular visitor.

But there was a catch.

"If we testify against the man, we gotta have that witness protection program," one woman said.

That was ridiculous, of course. Their testimony wasn't that compelling, and they weren't the primary witnesses.

The ladies had a counteroffer: "We ain't doing anything until we see Oprah."

Oprah?

"Yeah, you gotta get us into a show."

"And you gotta buy us dinner at her fancy restaurant."

Randolph excused himself and went for the aspirin. He called Tofani.

"You asked for it," Tofani said.

The ladies went to see Oprah Winfrey. They had dinner at the restaurant, Eccentrics. Whether or not they would want to put them on a witness stand was debated privately among the prosecution team.

WORD HAD gotten back to Michael Franzese that some FBI agent was hot on the trail of something concerning Norby Walters, and judging by the feedback, George Randolph had protected Michael Franzese thoroughly.

One of the people who called Michael Franzese at Terminal Island was his mother, Tina. Norby Walters had wanted to know "what was going on." Michael told his mother that nothing was going on. But Tina Franzese told her son something distressing.

"My mom told me that she had took my sister up to Norby's office during this time to get her a job. Norby told her, 'There's no way I can put her to work because I don't have anything for her,' and so on and so forth. And my mother was upset about it because my sister at the time was floundering. She needed work, my father was away, money was a little tight over there. Norby, being a forty-year relationship, I think he could have done that.

"And I think during this time I started thinking: You know, this guy's always been a fringe player. He's used us whenever he could. We never made any big money from him. And I had heard this in the past, that he had told other guys he knew how to use us . . . guys like me, my father, and Tommy Vastola. He knew how to use us in a way that he gives us a little money when he needs us, and we're there. And when he had to jump on the other side of the fence and disavow us, he knew how to do that, too. I had a guy, Julie Rifkind, who worked at Spring Records, who knew Norby for a long time. He knew Norby very, very well. These guys tell me all the time . . . their exact words: 'Norby doesn't go to the bathroom without using your name or your father's. What are you getting from him? Is he really taking care of you?' And the thing with my mother and my sister, it really bothered me."

Again, unknown to the government at the time, Michael Franzese sent a second message to Norby Walters.

"I was really upset with him and told my brother: 'Look, you tell Norby that if he's got a year or so to do on this thing, tell him to do it and end it because I got a wife and kids, and I'm not going to get in a mess over him. This is nonsense.' And if he's not worried about it, then end it for all of us. He didn't adamantly come back and say, 'No, I refuse.' He said, 'Don't worry about it. It'll all blow over. There's nothing serious here. It's not gonna come to that point.' "

As for Jules "Julie" Rifkind, George Randolph finally dug up the Friars Club application that Michael Franzese filled out. The Proposal for Membership was dated January 19, 1984. The "proposer" was Jules Rifkind, and the "seconder" was Bill Spitalsky. Rifkind's handwritten recommendation for Franzese read, "I've known the applicant for many years. Would be an asset to the club. I recommend him for membership."

Franzese's occupation was listed as V. P. Motion Picture Marketing, Inc. The firm's address was in Marina del Rey, California, and his two prior occupations were listed as contractor and leasing system director. His hobbies were "racquetball, yachting."

Where the form asked for the name of an acquaintance other than the proposer and seconder, Norby Walters's name was listed. Michael Franzese's Friars application was accepted on February 7, 1984.

George Randolph wanted and needed to see Michael Franzese again and again. By now a rapport had developed between the FBI agent and the Mafia captain. Franzese was impressed by Randolph's work.

"George proved to me he could nail things down without putting me at risk," Franzese said. "Some of it wasn't easy. But the best thing about George, he didn't bullshit me. He knew how to treat people. Sometimes it was rough, but he knew how to get me to respond."

When Randolph traveled to Los Angeles to take Franzese out of Terminal Island, it was never easy. One FBI agent said, "George was told that Franzese was making a fool out of him."

Franzese had to come up with a variety of excuses to explain to fellow prisoners why he was occasionally being taken from the joint. He had to avoid the appearance of being a snitch. He made up stories about some "shit jails" the government would lock him in to harass him.

On the contrary, Randolph always took Franzese to a nice hotel and got him a good meal. He also developed a rapport with Franzese's wife, Cammy. It didn't come easily, though. Cammy was skeptical of Randolph, suspicious that the FBI agent would expose her husband to harm, even death. Randolph went the extra mile to show he cared. Whenever he could arrange for the family to see each other, he did it. When the lease on Cammy's condominium expired, the FBI agent helped her find a new home.

Randolph knew this kind of treatment stretched the code of security required for a prisoner like Franzese, but he also saw it working. It regularly reminded Franzese of the privileges he had had to give up when he became a federal prisoner.

Randolph told Franzese that the investigation was winding down and the government now had enough evidence to indict Norby Walters and Lloyd Bloom, despite running into a dead end with Kathy Clements.

"It's too bad, Michael, that you helped us out so much, and it probably won't do anything with the judge," Randolph told Franzese. "You shot square with us. Thanks."

Randolph also had hammered into Franzese's head that the Norby Walters case was commanding great publicity. When a case gets publicity, the FBI agent reminded the Mafia boss, judges have a tendency to throw more weight to a government witness's cooperation. He told Michael to think about that.

On April 5, 1988, George Randolph was in the FBI office at the Dirksen Federal Building working on a few other loose ends when he received "an emergency call" from Tony Valukas and Howard Pearl, who were only eleven floors up. Emergency?

"Bruce Kelton just called," Valukas told Randolph. "Michael Franzese wants to testify before the grand jury."

Pearl immediately hammered out an agreement with Kelton for Franzese to accept a subpoena. Valukas made it clear to Kelton that there could be no deal to reduce Franzese's sentence. The deal was struck that Franzese would get immunity for his testimony. He would cooperate fully with the government, and the government in turn would notify Judge Nickerson of his cooperation.

George Randolph went out to California by himself, hurrying before Franzese changed his mind. It was an Easter weekend, which was par for the course, considering Randolph had missed Thanksgiving. He got his prisoner and headed back to Chicago.

Their plane landed between 2 A.M. and 3 A.M. at O'Hare Airport. It was cold, rainy, miserable. Randolph was exhausted, and Franzese was a little cranky, too, because the FBI agent had put the handcuffs back on his prisoner. When the two men got to Randolph's car, the bureau's Oldsmobile, the night got even worse. The car wouldn't start.

So now Randolph, at three in the morning, decided he had better rent a car. Here he was alone in the middle of a dark, wet, freezing parking lot with one of the country's biggest Mafia bosses, and he had no car and no help. He decided he didn't want to hop onto a rental bus with Franzese in handcuffs, so he removed them, but not without one of his "friendly" warnings.

"If you break bad on me, I'll put one in the back of your head," the FBI agent told Franzese, who rolled his eyes.

Franzese had made the commitment to testify before the grand jury, but despite the agreement he signed, he was reluctant. And he was not fully committed to testifying at a trial. Besides, he was counting on the case not going to trial.

Nevertheless, it was a huge step for Michael Franzese.

Franzese said, "Naturally, testifying at a grand jury is easier than testifying at a trial, but this was the first time I was in a grand jury willingly, so to speak. I had been in a grand jury in the past on other matters but always as a defendant. I wasn't comfortable about it. We sat down in Howard's office until I went in. I think I let them understand, right until the minute I walked in there, that I really wasn't happy about walking in there. I said, 'I'm committed, but I don't like this.' They said, 'Hey, you've gone this far.' I don't know if I was ready to back out, but I wasn't really totally committed.

"I wasn't committed because I didn't think it would help me. I never believed it would help me. I was pessimistic all the time. I didn't think it was going to lead to my release. I was more involved in what I was doing, and the implications and the morality of it for me. I said, 'Hey, this is something I've been against all my life. Can I do this?' That's really what I was focusing on."

Franzese said that Randolph had a "calming effect" on him. He had despised FBI agents before, but he trusted Randolph, that he wouldn't betray him. Valukas and Pearl spoke with him, too, before he stepped into the grand jury.

"I have to say it was really important to me, the way I felt about the participants. George, Tony, and Howard . . . it was the way they built my confidence that really made me go in there. They made me feel that they weren't going to screw me and they weren't going to take advantage of me. My faith in George was pretty solid, and it grew."

When Michael Franzese told his story to the grand jury, the prosecution team thought indictment day was just around the corner. That's what they thought.

13

No MATTER how powerful Michael Franzese's testimony may have been, the government still had to face the legal facts of life. Al Capone wasn't nailed for clubbing someone to death with a Louisville Slugger. He was convicted of income tax evasion. Sonny Franzese was not in prison for murder. He was convicted in a shaky case for bank robbery conspiracy.

If the government was going to prosecute the case of the United States of America versus Norby Walters and Lloyd Bloom, they needed to prove there had been an alleged mail fraud violation. In particular, if the Northern District of Illinois was going to prosecute this case, there had to be an alleged mail fraud violation within its jurisdiction. Moreover, if the Northern District of Illinois was going to expose how Walters and Bloom put the world of college and professional sports in jeopardy by allegedly having a big-time Mafia boss as a silent partner, the government had to prove there was a victim of the alleged fraud.

Like it or not, the victims had to be the colleges of the Big Ten Conference. Fortunately, Norby Walters and Lloyd Bloom had ventured deep into Big Ten country, signing up talent from Michigan, Michigan State, Purdue, Illinois, Iowa, and Ohio State.

Even though Tony Valukas was ultimately in charge of the investigation, Howard Pearl had been handling the day-to-day demands of the case for the last fourteen months. Now, after taking every witness before the grand jury, it was his job to draft the 250-page proffer memo analyzing the entire case and to draft the indictment. George Randolph provided the evidence, but Howard Pearl had to make it fit. And there were roadblocks for the government at almost every turn.

As Howard Pearl prepared the indictment, he had the mind-boggling

194

task of getting pre-trial diversion agreements for forty-four of the fifty-eight athletes worked out with their lawyers. The other fourteen would be dismissed for a variety of reasons.

Pearl was also busy trying to find the best way to show a jury that the players were also victims in the case. If any player could reasonably claim to be a victim of this entire affair, it was Ohio State All-American wide receiver Cris Carter, who lost much more than a promising senior season. Unlike Alabama basketball star Derrick McKey, who was declared ineligible in time for the NBA draft, Carter missed the NFL draft and was the target of a severe backlash from college and professional teams. Several NFL clubs decided not to breach the friendly relationship between college and professional football and passed Carter over. The Philadelphia Eagles finally used a fourth-round pick to acquire the wide receiver in the controversial supplemental draft.

Cris Carter lost, conservatively, $1 million when he lost his eligibility. The Eagles signed Carter at a bargain basement price. He had had no other career option. Even better for the government, Ohio State and Carter were Big Ten Conference links to its jurisdiction. Cris Carter had been one of the first players offered a pre-trial diversion agreement, which meant he would avoid prosecution by agreeing to testify truthfully, repaying Ohio State its scholarship money for his junior season and performing 250 hours of community service. He would also draw a one-year probation.

Like all the pre-trial agreements, it was finalized on June 2, 1988. It took the rest of the month to get them all signed and completed. The light was at the end of the tunnel for Howard Pearl and George Randolph. In two weeks the grand jury was prepared to indict Norby Walters and Lloyd Bloom. The government team planned their first vacations in more than a year.

Randolph and Diane Benson, the FBI agent who had so meticulously organized the financial data on every significant party in the case, were double-checking Cris Carter's file when something didn't quite add up. There was a $5,000 deposit in Carter's bank account they had failed to account for during the latter part of 1986, during the middle of his junior season at Ohio State. Something wasn't right because it didn't match up with any of the ledgers they had from Norby Walters.

Randolph was able to ascertain that the money had come from David Lueddeke of Pro-Line Sports in Los Angeles. Neither Randolph nor Pearl remembered Cris Carter telling them about any money coming in from Pro-Line Sports. They hoped it wasn't what it appeared. Every player who had taken money from another agent had eventually been forthright about it. Carter had been questioned not only by the FBI but again in front of the grand jury, and he had never mentioned anything about Pro-Line Sports or an agent named David Lueddeke.

Howard Pearl jumped on the phone and asked Carter point-blank, "Did you sign with another agent named David Lueddeke?"

Carter said no.

Randolph called Lueddeke, and the agent told him the same thing. Nevertheless, Lueddeke was subpoenaed for an appearance before the grand jury on July 12 to clarify the transaction in case it ever was raised at a trial. Lueddeke showed up without an attorney. Pearl and Randolph asked him about his relationship with Cris Carter at Ohio State, and the government stressed to Lueddeke that all they were looking for was the truth. Lueddeke told the government he had met Carter for the first time in Los Angeles on December 8, 1986, and had Carter cosign a promissory note for a "third party" who was not present but needed the money immediately. There was no representation contract signed between the agent and Carter. Lueddeke testified to these facts before the grand jury that same day.

Pearl and Randolph were guardedly relieved. They wanted to believe Lueddeke. Though Carter would be tainted by the transaction, he could be salvaged as a key witness.

Cris Carter appeared in Chicago on a Saturday, July 16, 1988, and met with Pearl and Randolph. By now Randolph had uncovered some evidence that Lueddeke and Carter were involved in a big lie. The cashier's check was dated October 23, 1986.

Incredibly, Carter again denied signing with Lueddeke. He had blown it. Howard Pearl informed him that his pre-trial diversion agreement was being pulled and that he was going to be indicted for mail fraud, perjury, and obstruction of justice.

"Your great football career just went out the window," Pearl told him.

Cris Carter burst into tears.

It was one of the saddest moments of the investigation, but Randolph now had a job to do. He had to formally question Carter about his relationship with David Lueddeke. Carter came clean.

After Ohio State's homecoming game in late October, he met Lueddeke, who had made prior arrangements to visit Columbus. Again, Cris's brother George had been involved. Six Ohio State players had gone across the street from the stadium to the Holiday Inn to party in Lueddeke's room. The players included Carter, Chris Spielman, Tom Tupa, William White, Sonny Gordon, and George Cooper.

Lueddeke said that he wanted to talk to each player individually, and the group moved down to the lobby bar. One by one the players were called to Lueddeke's room for a meeting. Lueddeke had a $5,000 cashier's check in Cris Carter's name. Carter saw a handful of other cashier's checks made out to the other players. Except for George Cooper, he had no idea whether the others accepted the money, but Carter did. And he signed a contractual agreement with Lueddeke on the spot, regardless of his prior arrangement with Walters and Bloom.

Carter also said that Lueddeke had arranged to fly him and Spielman to Los Angeles for the Super Bowl in January 1987. Both players had one season left. They were going to take the trip when Ohio State Coach Earle Bruce learned about the plans and wanted to know how they were going to pay for it. Both players canceled the trip.

George Randolph and Howard Pearl were deeply saddened and disappointed by Cris Carter, a player they had liked and one they had needed for their indictment. They were livid with David Lueddeke. Randolph called Lueddeke on Monday and notified the Los Angeles sports agent that the government had information that he had not been forthright and that he was now the subject of a grand jury investigation. He was to appear again the next day.

Pearl interjected, "You've perjured yourself. Get right out here, now!"

Randolph told Lueddeke to bring all of his records, especially the contracts he signed with Cris Carter and George Cooper. The agent said he thought they were at his home.

"Do not fuck with those records," said Randolph. "Bring them."

David Lueddeke showed up the next day with his records, but what he presented boggled the prosecution team's minds.

Lueddeke had a promissory note that was altered in an attempt to prove that Carter had signed it on December 8, 1986.

There was also a typed "clause" on the note: "Chris [sic] Carter acknowledges that he has violated NCAA rules and jeoporized [sic] college eligibility by previously accepting money from sports agents and hereby releases David Lueddeke of any and all liability and/or damages from said transaction."

He also presented a promissory note with a similar statement, dated November 13, 1986, for George Cooper, who had been kicked off the team.

He had done the same thing with the representation agreements.

It was clear to Randolph and Pearl that the documents were altered.

Cris Carter was brought back in and shown the documents. He denied that he had signed any agreement about his violating NCAA rules. He reiterated truthfully that he had taken the money and signed the contract on October 26, 1986.

Randolph's vacation was ruined. He also had to find George Cooper, who was now in the Miami Dolphins training camp. Dolphins Coach Don Shula was perturbed that the FBI wanted to pull Cooper out of camp. It was a hassle because the Dolphins were preparing to leave for London for an early preseason game.

"Mr. Cooper is having a hard enough time making this football team," Shula told the FBI agent.

Randolph decided he would fly to Miami, which was the last thing he wanted to do. Cooper also shot holes in Lueddeke's testimony. Howard Pearl let David Lueddeke know in no uncertain terms that he was in very deep trouble. He informed Lueddeke that he would be indicted for two counts of perjury and obstruction of justice, and that he was going to put him in front of the grand jury again the following Tuesday, July 25.

This time Lueddeke had an attorney. This time he told the grand jury the truth, testifying that he had indeed doctored the documents with a portable typewriter on the plane ride out to Chicago because he had "panicked."

It didn't really matter that much. If anybody had assured himself of prison time in this bizarre investigation, it was David Lueddeke. Perjury is perjury. It's never forgiven.

It also didn't matter for Cris Carter. He was going to be indicted, too, for mail fraud and obstruction of justice. Because he eventually cooperated and because of his age, the government decided not to charge Carter with the unpardonable crime of perjury. They thought it might keep him out of prison. *Might.*

Ohio State was dropped as a fraud victim. Howard Pearl and George Randolph felt like taking a leap together from the fifteenth floor of the Dirksen Federal Building.

Pearl and Valukas wanted to keep the indictment as streamlined as possible, especially where it concerned the mail fraud. For jurisdictional reasons the Big Ten mail fraud counts could stand alone. But there would also be mail fraud underlying the conspiracy charges and the government's contention that specific worthy schools were defrauded.

Notre Dame was an obvious choice for this approach, especially in that part of the country.

If any college could claim it was a victim of Norby Walters's and Lloyd Bloom's actions, it was the University of Alabama. The NCAA had docked the school $253,447 in basketball tournament money because of the revelation that Derrick McKey and Terry Coner, its two star players, had signed with the sports agents during the 1986–87 season.

Football was another story. The NCAA was not the source of the postseason money that was paid out to colleges. College football bowl games were privately funded, and consequently the NCAA had no jurisdiction in financial penalties. On the other hand, the NCAA basketball revenue came from its own purse.

George Randolph received a call one day from Alabama Assistant Attorney General Donald Valeska and was informed, "We're gonna indict Norby Walters and Lloyd Bloom. . . . Do y'all mind if we borrow your files on Derrick McKey and Terry Coner?"

Randolph said he'd check, but he knew the answer. There was no way the U. S. Attorney could release the players' files during the federal grand jury proceeding. Valeska didn't understand. "Aren't we on the same side?"

Initially the idea of Alabama sticking it to Norby Walters and Lloyd Bloom was welcomed by the Chicago prosecution team. It was even amusing because if nothing ever came of the investigation by the government, a taste of Alabama justice might be just the medicine Norby Walters and Lloyd Bloom deserved.

The government was curious about which state laws Alabama officials would use to indict Walters and Bloom. Alabama, along with seventeen other states, had pushed for criminal legislation against sports agents over the past twelve months, but there had been nothing on the books when Bloom and Terry Bolar, on behalf of Norby Walters, made their deal with McKey and Coner.

When Randolph broke the news to Valeska that their files were untouchable, he asked about the Alabama laws that would be applied to the case. Valeska had dug up three criminal charges he would throw at Walters and Bloom: commercial bribery, unlawful trade practices, and tampering with a sports contest. A state grand jury issued the indictment, but the bill of particulars only ran about a fat paragraph.

Alabama had just been successful in getting a conviction against Atlanta sports agent Jim Abernethy for tampering with a sports contest because of his dealings with Auburn football player Kevin Porter. That law was originally written into the books to cover the state's venture into dog racing, or possibly a bribe to a referee or an athlete to throw a game. But Abernethy was convicted by a Lee County jury for tampering, pending appeal.

The charges were misdemeanors, and each carried a maximum two-year sentence—in the county jail. Abernethy, in fact, was given the maximum sentence in what *Atlanta Constitution* columnist Dave Kindred criticized as "Barney Fife justice."

A trial was set for May 9 in Tuscaloosa County Courthouse, but Mike Trope and Lloyd Bloom tried to play a dangerous game of cat and mouse with Valeska. When Bloom pulled a no-show at his arraignment, Valeska sent a warning that filled the country's sports sections with sensational headlines: ALABAMA WILL "TRACK DOWN" AGENT BLOOM.

Valeska told reporters, "We are going to track down Mr. Bloom, he is going to be arrested, and he will be here. We are going to swear out an arrest warrant in every state in this country. He'll be here. I'll guarantee it. We will track him to all ends of the world."

Valeska even made note of the pending indictment in the federal court by saying, "Mr. Bloom will be in Chicago very soon. If I have to, I'll go to Chicago and bring him back myself."

If Bloom didn't get the message, Alabama Attorney General Don Siegelman put it succinctly, "He will be brought back in handcuffs."

Trope and Bloom—not to mention anybody else paying attention— might have been amused because, after all, these were misdemeanor charges. What were the Alabama lawmen going to do, extradite Lloyd Bloom?

Well, yes. Alabama Governor Guy Hunt signed an extradition order and sent it to California Governor George Deukmejian, asking authorities to arrest Bloom at his home in Los Angeles. Bloom still didn't respond. Then Governor Deukmejian said that he would sign for Bloom's extradition.

Before long, Trope called Valeska and said Bloom would appear "voluntarily" in Tuscaloosa on May 1 for his arraignment. It was a good thing, Valeska informed Trope.

"I may not convict Norby, but I damn sure will convict Lloyd Bloom," Valeska promised Trope.

About this time, Trope told Valeska and the newspapers that Bloom could not afford the plane trip back to Tuscaloosa or an attorney. Valeska offered to pay for the trip and said the state would gladly get

Bloom an attorney. This little matter caught the attention of Howard Pearl and George Randolph in Chicago. Maybe Bloom was now so tapped out of money that he would roll over on Walters.

Then, in a conversation with Mike Trope, Don Valeska said the magic words, "Wanna make a deal?"

Mike Trope couldn't resist. Over a bowl of seafood gumbo, a deal was struck. Lloyd Bloom agreed to plead guilty to one count of unlawful trade practices in Tuscaloosa County. For his sentence he would wash Alabama state trooper cars for one week. But there was a catch. If Norby Walters was found innocent of any of the charges, Bloom would walk free.

It may have struck the country's funny bone, but it sent chills down the spine of Norby Walters. Lloyd Bloom had agreed to testify against him.

Between the few laughs they were able to enjoy, Howard Pearl and George Randolph thought it was terrific news. They would be able to use Bloom's testimony if their case ever went to trial, and they could also subpoena his pre-trial statements to Alabama law authorities, regardless of whether Bloom chose to flip on Walters in Chicago.

Don Valeska defended his deal with Bloom, reminding critics that Norby Walters never set foot in the state of Alabama on the Derrick McKey–Terry Coner transaction.

In response to questions about Lloyd Bloom's sentence of washing state trooper cars, Valeska said, "Hey, if Bloom had pushed it, we probably would have made the deal with no punishment. At least now we get to embarrass him. Without Bloom we can't get the money man."

Valeska had tipped his hand.

On the morning of the trial, Norby Walters sought out Mike Trope during breakfast at the hotel where Bloom had signed McKey and Coner.

"This is the thanks I get for adopting Lloyd Bloom?" Walters snarled at Trope.

"Hey, Norby, you married the guy, I didn't," said Trope with a shrug. "You took him to the altar. I'm just his lawyer. Divorce happens."

Trope then told Walters why he had recommended the deal to Bloom. Prior to the arraignment, Trope was in the chambers of the Tuscaloosa County presiding judge, John M. Karrh. Trope remembers how relaxed Karrh was, all the while listening to Valeska, chatting with a friend in the parking lot through his window, asking "how them catfish biting?"

In the course of conversations about the negotiations between the state and Bloom, Karrh looked at Trope and said, "If I were you, I'd take that deal. Otherwise you're looking at six years in the county jail . . . if convicted, of course."

The story didn't appease Norby Walters, who headed for the courthouse in a sour mood. He knew all about the county jail—Alabama officials took him there to get fingerprinted and photographed at his arraignment.

The case was so big in Alabama that Don Siegelman, the Attorney General, showed up to help try the case. Valeska took one look at Walters, who was wearing expensive threads, not to mention a diamondstudded ring on his pinky, and laughed with his chief trial prosecutor, William Wasden.

"He hasn't got a prayer," Valeska said of Walters just before the prospective jurors were brought into the room.

Trope went over to Walters and whispered, "Take off your pinky ring."

Walters ignored Trope. His own attorneys, Donald Stewart of Anniston, Alabama, and Robert Gold of New York, were huddled in conversation. Gold had his own problems. One of the criminals he had put behind bars as a New York federal prosecutor had just been released from prison, and the FBI had warned him there might be a contract on his life. An armed bodyguard accompanied him, and Valeska offered to secure the courtroom.

The jury proceedings began. Robert Gold and Donald Stewart were prepared to do battle with the state. They were prepared to show that the University of Alabama had graduated just two basketball players in the previous ten years and that both of them were white.

When the jury was struck, Judge Karrh suspiciously called a recess. University officials, including school attorney Robert Potts, hovered around the courtroom. Lloyd Bloom sat in the witness room along with Terry Coner and Derrick McKey, who had been excused by the Seattle SuperSonics in the final stages of their NBA playoff hunt.

Gold and Stewart went into conference with the state prosecutors. Gold looked Don Valeska in the eye and warned him about the public embarrassment due Alabama.

"There will be blood all over the courtroom," Gold told the Assistant Attorney General. "The university will bleed to death if we go to trial."

Valeska chuckled and gave the New York lawyer the facts of life.

"There ain't a judge sitting in Tuscaloosa County who is going to let you destroy the University of Alabama," Valeska told Gold. "We may look stupid, we may talk stupid, but we ain't stupid." Valeska added, "Now, it ain't too late for a deal." Siegelman presented the deal. Gold listened. Then he huddled with Norby Walters and laid down the facts.

The Attorney General of Alabama wanted the agent to pay the university the $253,447 it was docked by the NCAA. Norby Walters thought about the Tuscaloosa County jail. He had seen the jurors who would be hearing his case. He told Gold to start negotiating.

Judge Karrh announced that the trial would be delayed until the following Friday, May 13.

Siegelman and Valeska told Walters that if he paid the money back to Alabama, they would drop the criminal charges.

The negotiations brought some interesting offers. Because Alabama was faulted in part for negligence by the NCAA for improperly pursuing the case, school officials agreed to take $200,000 as a settlement. Walters wanted to pay $50,000 up front and wanted the opportunity to promote concerts in Alabama "with some of my biggest stars," proceeds from which would pay off the balance. University lawyer Robert Potts rejected that idea.

Gold and Stewart countered: The only way Walters would settle was if the University of Alabama filed a civil lawsuit against the agent and a bunch of John Does. That served a couple of purposes. One purpose was to enable Walters to countersue Bloom, McKey, Coner, and perhaps McKey's new agent, Norman Blass of New York.

The university agreed to file the lawsuit, but in doing so on May 12, it did something extraordinary. For the first time ever, a university placed a dollar value on a star athlete. Derrick McKey, the university contended, was worth $500,000 to the school—$250,000 for the championship he helped deliver the season before, and $250,000 for the championship he would be unable to help deliver the next season. It also noted that ticket sales could suffer because of McKey's absence.

Walters also would agree never to again tamper with an Alabama athlete. He signed a consent decree, delivered the $50,000 down payment, and made the arrangements for the balance. It was a done deal.

Judge Karrh reassembled the jurors, declared a mistrial, and dismissed them and the charges.

It also got Lloyd Bloom off the hook from washing state trooper cars. Trope argued successfully that Bloom's guilty plea and sentence were conditional on a conviction for Walters.

Howard Pearl seethed. Alabama had just wiped out the most tangible debt the government had in the Walters-Bloom case. It also had turned a criminal proceeding into a civil settlement. Even worse, Lloyd Bloom did not take the witness stand against his partner, and as Pearl discovered, the state of Alabama had not taken any notes in procuring a pre-trial statement from Bloom. Pearl had Randolph call to make sure.

"Nothing."

This was not funny in Chicago.

Alabama and Carter should have been the showcase to the sports side of the government's unique fraud charges against Walters and Bloom. Instead, they disintegrated as Pearl continued to rework his draft of the indictment.

Of all people, Lloyd Bloom put an end to the government's summer of discontent.

Matthias Lydon, the same former federal prosecutor in Chicago, was representing a half-dozen players in the Walters-Bloom case. He was being advised by an old friend and former prosecutor, Frank Murtha, a suspended lawyer–turned–sports agent. Lyndon was representing Paul Palmer as a criminal lawyer when Murtha thought he noticed something odd about the way Lloyd Bloom had handled Palmer's $450,000 signing bonus from the Kansas City Chiefs in July 1987. Bloom appeared to have comingled the player's funds in a new business the agent had set up, incorporated as Lincolnshire Financial Services in Los Angeles.

Howard Pearl did not find a comingling of funds. He discovered much, much more.

On the same day Palmer received his $450,000 bonus, Bloom took $233,000. After reading through one thousand pages of financial documents, here's what Pearl discovered:

• Bloom purchased a cashier's check for $78,000, payable to Norby Walters Associates, for the commission earned by negotiating Palmer's contract.

• Another cashier's check for $30,000 payable to Norby Walters represented the repayment of the debt Palmer had accumulated since signing with the agent on June 17, 1986.

• A third cashier's check for $125,000 was made payable to Lincolnshire Financial Services, which was listed as a "credit repair" business. Bloom opened a checking account for Lincolnshire on July 27, 1987.

• On the very same day, Bloom wrote a check from the Lincolnshire account for $82,247 for a down payment on the lease of a new Rolls-Royce Corniche convertible, valued at $160,300—which, Pearl found out, was "the most expensive car in the world." On the lease application Bloom wrote that the car was for "personal use."

• The car had to be insured. Bloom covered it with $6,188. He also paid another $200 for detail work on the car.

• Bloom then wrote checks payable to himself for about $27,000. From that he wrote checks to cover personal expenses, such as his American Express bill ($1,577.50), his MasterCard bill ($1,308.51), his Visa bill ($669.88), his accountant ($500), his tailor ($138), his clothier ($6,958.60), and tuition at a karate studio ($150).

• Other checks from the account went to his father, Stuart Bloom, to repay loans ($2,500), to his former wife, Donna Palmiotto, the actress with whom he was still living, for "home, rent, electricity" ($1,200), and for "tableware for home and entertainment" ($792).

By August 8, 1987, nineteen days later, Bloom had spent every penny of the $125,000, including the purchase of a $200,000 life insurance policy for Paul Palmer—with Lloyd Bloom as the beneficiary, to "protect" the company.

One month later Palmer gave Bloom another $20,000 for a percentage in the management of TV actress and model Teri Copley.

When Howard Pearl brought in Paul Palmer to show him exactly what Lloyd Bloom had done to him, Palmer was stunned. Palmer said that Bloom had told him they would be fifty-fifty partners in the investment. Bloom had never invested a penny of his money in the company. A shocked Palmer told the government how Bloom had counseled him about "spending habits" and said "that if I handled myself correctly, I may not have to work after I'm playing football."

When Palmer heard about the Rolls-Royce, he told Pearl an interesting story.

"When I got my signing bonus, I wanted to get my brother and sister each a car," Palmer told the AUSA. "They had never had a car of their own, and I wanted to buy them a Volkswagen Rabbit, something nice but modest. I asked Lloyd what he thought."

Bloom, who had just purchased the world's most expensive car with Paul Palmer's money, had other advice for the player who wanted to treat his brother and sister.

"Look more at a Yugo or Hyundai, something economical," Bloom told Palmer.

Howard Pearl was as disgusted as Paul Palmer.

Then, in January 1987, Mike Trope was paid $25,000 for attorney fees when Trope sold Bloom's Rolls-Royce to Randy Jackson of the Jacksons. It showed Bloom was desperate for money. It also could be used as leverage in an attempt to disqualify Trope as Bloom's lawyer, which would make Bloom even more vulnerable to making a deal with the government.

Lloyd Bloom had just handed the government a gift, a strong fraud case if there ever was one. Pearl couldn't believe that Bloom had pulled these shenanigans five months after it was known publicly that the FBI was investigating the sports agents, and three months after the grand jury was impaneled.

This also turned Palmer, one of the few players who had stuck by the agents, against Walters and Bloom. Palmer was ready to come clean on the agents. He told about the familiar "sales pitch," he told about the orchestrated lies to Temple University and the FBI, and he told about an interesting little exchange he and Lloyd Bloom had had the summer before about rumors that Norby Walters was connected to organized crime.

"We were walking through the airport, discussing the article in *Sports Illustrated,*" Palmer told the government. "Lloyd was getting a big kick out of Norby denying knowing anybody in the Mafia."

Did Bloom say anything else about Norby and the Mafia?

"No," Palmer said, "but he sure thought it was funny that Norby denied it."

The government was dotting its *i*'s and crossing its *t*'s on the indictment when more publicity hit. Matt Lydon admitted to the *Philadelphia Inquirer* that Paul Palmer had taken money prior to his record-breaking senior season at Temple University. Lydon was trying to establish "damage control" by letting the media know the inevitable; Palmer had entered the Pre-Trial Diversion Program as a result of the U. S. Attorney's investigation. But the damage was done. Temple president Peter J. Liacouras immediately announced on July 26, 1988, that he had sent handwritten letters to six opponents from the 1986 season offering to forfeit those victories because Palmer was such a heavy contributor.

"We unwittingly played a player, a star who broke many records at our school, who was actually an ineligible player," Liacouras said. "That's like taking a running back from the NFL and putting him in college. It's just not fair, and if you don't win fairly, you should lose."

Furthermore, Liacouras said, he would declare Palmer's season "null and void" by deleting the Heisman Trophy runner-up's 1986 statistics from the twenty-three school records he had established. That included single-season records of 1,826 rushing yards and 15 touchdowns, including a 349-yard performance against East Carolina.

Not only that, Liacouras said, he would insist that Palmer pay back Temple the scholarship funds he had received for 1986.

The case of Paul Palmer and Temple University seemingly made a nice jewel for the prosecution.

Howard Pearl remembers wanting to construct his indictment like the Golden Gate Bridge with tall, strong supports at each end. In the middle were the smaller supports that nevertheless got people from one end to the other. Michael Franzese was one of the tall supports. The fraud charge involving Paul Palmer was the other. In between were the extortion and the mail fraud charges. Pearl wanted that road to be as short as possible. He knew the mail fraud charge was capable of collapse.

As for the connection between the Mafia and Norby Walters, Tony Valukas and George Randolph wanted to take every step to make sure that Michael Franzese was not pulling one over on them.

According to FBI sources, Randolph had been ridiculed by peers in New York and Los Angeles for even thinking that Franzese would testify before a grand jury. Startled that Franzese had taken that step, various law enforcement officials suggested that everyone could forget this so-called agreement that the Mafia boss would testify at a public trial.

Organized crime officials in New York familiar with Franzese's past thought Valukas and Randolph were living in a dream world if they thought there would ever be a trial. Norby Walters, they speculated, would get whacked before that ever happened. Everyone kept telling Valukas and Randolph that there would never be a trial. Franzese would screw them, or Norby Walters would die. The government sent word to Walters's attorney, Robert Gold, to warn Norby to proceed very cautiously. As it turned out, Gold had already warned the agent.

Valukas and Randolph heard it all again when they traveled to New York. Valukas wanted to see firsthand the government files on Sonny and Michael Franzese. He needed the information "to make a rational judgment" on whether he was about to embarrass the United States Justice Department.

Bruce Kelton, Franzese's lawyer, was pushing for a bigger commitment from the Chicago force to help reduce his client's prison sentence. Valukas arranged with the Justice Department to have every file the FBI and IRS had ever compiled on Michael and Sonny Franzese. When Valukas and Randolph arrived in New York, they had hundreds of files waiting for them.

"I went through every piece of paper," Valukas recalls. "Sonny and Michael Franzese had been involved in one hell of a lot of crime. It underlined in a very dramatic way what the Franzese name meant in New York organized crime."

When Valukas finished, he told Randolph it had become apparent that it was very important that the U. S. Attorney not offer Michael Franzese any significant deal to testify against Norby Walters. Because Franzese's racketeering conviction belonged to another jurisdiction, there was nothing Valukas could do behind the scenes to influence a large reduction in sentence. That didn't bother Valukas. After reading the New York files, he knew Norby Walters was a guppy compared to the Mafia sharks, Sonny and Michael Franzese. But Valukas still believed Walters deserved to be prosecuted for his judicious use and link with such powerful mobsters.

"Norby Walters had placed the national sports scene at risk when he jumped into the business," Valukas said. "We had already established how incredibly vulnerable Norby Walters was, how he had set himself up and his clients for leverage from the mob."

Kelton still wanted some sort of deal for Franzese to testify. Valukas calculated "very carefully" what he was willing to do. Valukas finally decided to recommend to Franzese's judge, Eugene Nickerson, that the mobster's ten-year sentence be reduced by one year. Taking parole into account, that amounted to twenty-eight days.

Nothing more. Take it or leave it. Franzese took it.

"Frankly, I was still skeptical," said Valukas. "I didn't truly believe he would testify."

Without Franzese, Valukas was not certain he wanted to risk trying the sports case.

The indictment already had trimmed twenty-four schools, leaving nine schools worthy of being considered fraud victims. The nine schools were Iowa (Ronnie Harmon and Devon Mitchell), Illinois (Craig Swoope), Purdue (Rod Woodson), Michigan State (Mark Ingram), Michigan (Robert Perryman and Mark Ingram), Notre Dame (Robert Banks and Alvin Miller), Temple (Paul Palmer), Miami of Ohio (George Swarn), and Fort Hays State, Kansas (Frankie Neal).

"I did not want to be in the position of defending college athletics when, in fact, I had been disgusted by what I had seen," says Valukas. "I could have walked away from this case very easily, up to the day I signed the indictment."

As for the threats, they were possibly extortionate as far as Valukas was concerned, but without the fraud allegations, they would have to be dealt out to other U. S. Attorney jurisdictions. It was the same for Bloom's alleged defrauding of Paul Palmer.

Everything was riding on Michael Franzese and the organized crime conspiracy and racketeering counts against Norby Walters.

Randolph had worked his butt off psyching the Mafia boss for his testimony. They had become familiar with each other's family life. One night in the summer of 1988 Randolph treated Franzese to a movie, near the hotel they were staying at in a Chicago suburb. When Randolph took Franzese back to the hotel, there was an urgent message from Cathy Randolph.

Bill Randolph, George's eighteen-year-old son and only child, had been beaned in an American Legion baseball game.

"He might lose sight in an eye, George," Cathy told her husband bitterly. "Where have you been?"

"Why didn't you beep me?" the FBI agent asked his wife.

Randolph called for more FBI security and had to wait before hustling to the hospital. Two days later doctors told George and Cathy Randolph that their son was going to be all right. Franzese showed genuine concern for the situation.

"I think that was one of the incidents along the way that bonded me and George," he recalled. "That really upset him. It was the one time I could console him."

There were other incidents that had some levity, especially after Franzese was transferred to a California federal prison in the desert, Boron, for security reasons.

Once, Franzese was supposed to be dropped off by Boron prison officials at a designated site in a nearby desert city where Randolph would pick him up. The prison officials had gotten the time confused for the exchange and dropped off Franzese one hour before Randolph had scheduled. By then it was okay for the prison officials to remove Franzese's handcuffs, which they did before driving off.

There was Michael Franzese, New York Mafia boss, sitting in the middle of a small California desert town with no money and no ride. After waiting a while, Franzese walked two blocks to a small diner, where he borrowed a quarter. He made a collect call to his wife, Cammy.

"If George calls, tell him I'm at the corner where this little diner is," Franzese told his wife.

Sure enough, Randolph drove to the designated pickup spot about that time, and Franzese wasn't there. He used a car phone to call the prison and panicked when he realized what had happened. He called Cammy Franzese, who told the FBI agent where her husband could be found.

Down the street Randolph drove, still in a panic. There, sitting almost pathetically on the corner next to a phone booth in front of the diner, was the Mafia prince himself.

Another time Valukas told Randolph he wanted one last powwow with Michael Franzese before he would approve the indictment. Randolph and Howard Pearl made the trip west; Valukas was scheduled to arrive later that night. Randolph dropped off Howard Pearl at the Greentree Inn in Victorville, another California desert city. He then picked up his prisoner, Michael Franzese, and drove him to the hotel.

Howard Pearl found out that Franzese was having his wife come out to the hotel because it was "my normal visitation day." Pearl "went nuclear" because Franzese had assured him he would not make that arrangement. He screamed at Franzese about pulling some funny business and called him a "con man."

Franzese's temper also exploded. Suddenly Randolph got a closer look at the Mafia captain, not the government informant.

Franzese yelled in Pearl's face, "Go fuck yourself." Pearl challenged him.

Franzese stepped back and screamed, "Take me back! I'm done. I'm outta here."

George Randolph reached to his backside and grabbed his handcuffs. He ripped them out, then jerked Franzese by the arm and slapped on the cuffs.

"Fuck this," the FBI agent told the Mafia boss. "Come on, I'm taking you back."

Franzese froze, looking at Randolph, whom he had considered something of a close friend by then, searching for support.

"You don't get it, do you?" Randolph lectured Franzese. "You don't fucking get it. We own your ass. You're the criminal. I'm taking you back."

Franzese started to calm down, and Randolph removed the handcuffs. Then Pearl started in again, and before long they were engaged in another verbal war. This time Randolph tried another approach.

"Michael, you're an asshole. You go to bed. Howard, you're an asshole. You go to bed. I'll stay with Michael."

Pearl left the room. Randolph and Franzese had a long talk that night. Franzese admitted he was uptight about the pending indictment, about the step he was taking, about the Mafia oath he had broken. It had been his life, his whole life. Randolph talked to him "like a brother," according to Franzese, who needed reassurance.

Early the next morning Tony Valukas had breakfast with Michael Franzese. Neither man had gotten much rest. Valukas then told Randolph that he wanted to "take a private walk" with the crime boss through the golf course that was adjacent to the Greentree Inn. The U. S. Attorney really wanted "to size him up."

"Okay," Randolph joked, "but if he breaks bad and escapes, it's your ass."

"Wait a minute," Valukas said with a panicked look on his face. "Where are you going to be? Don't leave me hanging with the guy."

"Okay, I'll follow," said Randolph. "If he does break bad, hit the deck. I may have to crank off a few rounds over your head."

Valukas went pale. Randolph smiled. Valukas shook his head.

Tony later put his arm around Franzese and said, "Come on, let's take a stroll."

It was an eerie morning in the desert. Low clouds were hanging, and a mist floated through the golf course from the sprinklers that had been running in the wee hours. Valukas and Franzese walked ahead, and Randolph trailed, stopping when they stopped, keeping his distance, checking out the bushes and the trees. He felt as if he was a secret service man following the President. Randolph wondered how the conversation was going, knowing that all his relentless, hard work was on the line.

Valukas said, "This was a very pivotal moment. I had to get the best feel possible for Michael Franzese. We talked about a lot of things—about his life in the Mafia, about his family, about Norby Walters, about everything that had taken place. And I explained to him the position I was in.

"I did not want to back myself in the corner with a witness such as this. I had been burned once in my life, and I wasn't going to get burned again. I wasn't going to get boxed in unless I was absolutely certain I could trust him. He needed to know where I stood. I wasn't going to get him out of prison for testifying against Norby Walters. He needed to understand that, emphatically. I would do what I promised to, but he had to do what he promised. He couldn't come to us on the eve of the trial and say, 'Tony, I want something more.'

"If Michael Franzese had lied, if he had flipped on us after he committed, it would be devastating and embarrassing, not only to me but to the Department of Justice. I just couldn't have that happen. When Howard and George originally recounted a number of things Franzese had told them, I was really skeptical. People in government thought this was one of the greatest scams ever. I knew what a con man Franzese was, and I knew he was capable of lying, mayhem, and murder. Why would he start telling the truth now?

"But George Randolph had proved to me that Michael Franzese wasn't lying about Norby Walters. He did some great work, and some of that work may never be known publicly. Now, at this moment, I needed to believe that Michael Franzese wasn't lying about his commitment to the government."

On August 24, 1988, Tony Valukas signed the indictment. The United States of America versus Norby Walters and Lloyd Bloom was official. The two sports agents were charged with one count of racketeering, one count of racketeering conspiracy, five counts of mail fraud, and one count of conspiring to commit extortion, mail fraud, and wire fraud.

David Lueddeke was indicted on two counts of perjury and one count of obstruction of justice.

Cris Carter was charged with mail fraud and obstruction of justice.

Forty-four college athletes had entered a Pre-Trial Diversion Program and would have to repay their schools their scholarship money.

It was seventeen months after George Randolph had visited a battered Kathy Clements and began asking questions about Norby Walters. There was nothing in the indictment connecting Uncle Norby to the assault. That bothered Randolph. A lot.

Kathy Clements

FBI Special Agent George Randolph

2

Norby Walters in his Manhattan office.

Lloyd Bloom

4

Lloyd Bloom being escorted by his attorney, Mike Trope, and Alabama Assistant Attorney General Donald Valeska.

5

Assistant U.S. Attorney
Howard Pearl

6

7

U.S. Attorney Anton
"Tony" Valukas

8

Ron Morris

9

Reggie Rogers

Brent Fullwood

Cris Carter

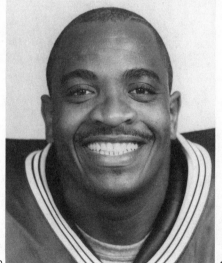

10

11

12
Paul Palmer

13
Ronnie Harmon

Tony Woods

Maurice Douglass

14

15

16

Tony Valukas answers questions from the press following the indictment of Norby Walters and Lloyd Bloom as George Randolph and Howard Pearl look on.

17

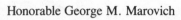
Honorable George M. Marovich

Dan Webb

18

19 Bo Schembechler   20 Father Theodore Hesburgh

FBI photos of John "Sonny" Franzese in 1966.

21

22

Michael Franzese in prison at the federal penitentiary at Terminal Island in 1986.

Lloyd Bloom and Dan Webb leaving court after the trial was delayed when Norby Walters was accidentally knocked to the floor by a file cart.

23

Norby Walters, with defense attorney Robert Gold, prepares to leave the federal court building in Chicago after receiving a guilty verdict.

24

25
George Randolph in 1990.

14

On August 24, 1988, ABC's "World News Tonight" began its broadcast with a story on "the mob and college sports," and the indictment of Norby Walters and Lloyd Bloom. It only touched on the fact that Michael Franzese had been a silent partner and unindicted coconspirator in the case.

It was a significant story in New York; it made the front page of the *New York Times*. The Franzese name was a big one.

Michael Franzese remembers getting a flurry of calls and "messages" from various relatives and Colombo family associates.

"They wanted to know, 'What the hell is going on?' "

Franzese was denying to everyone that he had cooperated with the government. He went so far as to tell the *Atlanta Constitution*—which had obtained prison records showing he had been moved to Chicago twice on a "writ to testify"—that he had used his Fifth Amendment rights before the grand jury.

Asked about the $50,000 he allegedly gave Norby Walters as a start-up investment in the sports agency business, Franzese cutely asked the reporter, "I'm not saying I didn't, I'm not saying I did. But if I did, what's the crime in that?"

The government's discovery of an organized crime link in the case immediately drew a strong reaction from the sports world. Alabama football coach Bill Curry echoed Tony Valukas's fears about how the mob could affect sports. He was quoted as saying, "Then, before the kid plays in a bowl game, the agent goes to the player and says something like, 'I know you haven't fumbled all year, but you're going to fumble the first five times you get the ball in the bowl game, or we'll break your legs. . . . That's

213

where the real money is in this deal. Someone is betting six million dollars on a game. That's the really scary part."

"On the list of priorities," said Colorado sports agent Jack Mills, "a college football player taking money from an agent doesn't really rank right up there. But when you throw in the word 'mob,' it makes it an entirely different kind of case."

The eighty-five-page indictment authored by Howard Pearl painted a lurid picture of Norby Walters and Lloyd Bloom. Pearl had carefully crafted it that way because if the case ever did go to trial, the jury would take the indictment into deliberations. It had to be written clearly, but it had to be sexy.

> It was further part of the conspiracy that defendants NORBY WALTERS and LLOYD BLOOM, together with Michael Franzese, would and did agree to the commission of multiple acts of racketeering on behalf of Norby Walters Associates and World Sports & Entertainment.
>
> It was further part of the conspiracy that defendants NORBY WALTERS and LLOYD BLOOM would and did use their association with Michael Franzese to obtain and retain clients of Norby Walters Associates and World Sports & Entertainment by extortionate means. . . . NORBY WALTERS and LLOYD BLOOM would and did use their association with Michael Franzese and his reputation in the community as a member of an organized crime family to convey directly and indirectly threats of economic and physical harm to actual and potential clients of Norby Walters Associates and World Sports & Entertainment.
>
> It was further part of the conspiracy that in or about late 1984 and early 1985, defendant NORBY WALTERS discussed with Michael Franzese expanding the business of Norby Walters Associates to include the representation of college athletes in their professional careers and in marketing their abilities. Defendant NORBY WALTERS asked Franzese for $50,000 to help fund that expansion, which money Franzese provided to defendant NORBY WALTERS in cash . . . would continue to use Michael Franzese and his reputation as a member of organized crime to obtain and retain clients. . . .

The racketeering conspiracy, which covered seven years, from 1981 to 1987, specifically named the Jacksons tour as the beginning. It also alleged other extortionate activity to "obtain, retain, and settle disputes with entertainment clients of Norby Walters Associates."

Under the racketeering conspiracies it charged the "extortion of student athletes."

Ron Morris, Maurice Douglass, Everett Gay, and Tony Woods were the alleged targets of these specific extortions.

Of the extortion allegations involving Morris, the indictment charged Bloom had told Morris that Walters and Bloom "would have someone break his legs and that Morris would never play football again. Defendant LLOYD BLOOM reminded Morris that the money given to Morris came not from defendant NORBY WALTERS but rather from 'bigger backers' from Los Angeles who 'don't care about what they do,' including blowing up the house of Morris's new agent."

There was no way the government was going to bring Auburn's Brent Fullwood into the mix, despite his allegation that Bloom threatened to "bump off" his new agent.

The "fraud upon Paul Palmer" was charged, detailing Lloyd Bloom's spending flurry with the player's money.

But what eventually steered media attention away from the organized crime element were the "novel" mail fraud and wire fraud charges—that Norby Walters and Lloyd Bloom had orchestrated a scheme to defraud Big Ten universities by signing the student-athletes and concealing that arrangement through elaborate means. The fraudulent certifications on eligibility and financial aid documents allowed the student-athletes to remain eligible when in fact they were not, and furthermore allowed them to collect scholarship benefits of room, board, books, and tuition. The concealment of the arrangement caused the universities, the Big Ten, and the NCAA to use the U. S. Postal Service to certify the players as eligible to receive those benefits.

Notre Dame, Miami of Ohio, and Temple University—non–Big Ten schools—were covered under the conspiracy charges.

At the press conference in Chicago to announce the indictment, Tony Valukas was in control of the microphone as Howard Pearl, George Randolph, and his boss, FBI Special Agent in Charge Bob Walsh, stood by. Valukas was guarded in his remarks and refused to discuss whether Michael Franzese had cooperated.

The subject of Kathy Clements surfaced.

"The investigation is ongoing," Valukas replied.

George Randolph was very frustrated. It had been seventeen months since the Clements beating, and the information that Franzese had supplied renewed his suspicions, but there were so many roadblocks. If it had been the only charge he was investigating, maybe he could have gotten to the bottom of it. Maybe he could have spent more time in the streets to shake something loose.

But there had been so much to this investigation. It seemed as if there was always a new curve around the next corner. It could have gone on another year, but they had to bring it to a conclusion. Tony Valukas was planning to leave office, as was Howard Pearl.

Yet Randolph also felt that the indictment gave him an opening to pursue the two critical links to solving the Clements beating. He decided to hunt down Jerry Zimmerman and Frankie Campione, the two Colombo family associates that Franzese had named as liaisons between the Mafia boss and Norby Walters. Now that Franzese's name was out in public—as well as the mob boss's denial that he had cooperated with the government—Randolph thought he could question the organized crime associates without risk to Franzese. He began to plot out how he would track down Zimmerman and Campione.

About this time, arrest warrants were issued for Norby Walters and Lloyd Bloom. Both men arranged to turn themselves in and sent their passports as an act of good faith.

Walters and Bloom entered innocent pleas to the charges. They were released on $250,000 bonds. The trial date was set for February 27, 1989.

"It will be a war," promised Robert Gold, Walters's attorney.

Besides the fact that it met almost everyone's schedule, the timing of the indictment had a specific purpose. It was August, just prior to college football season, and the prosecution team meant to send out a warning to college players getting ready to sign their eligibility forms. The stakes had just gone up.

The trial date would allow the players named in the indictment to finish their National Football League seasons without interference.

After a brief break, the government team planned to reassemble and begin preparing for its pre-trial hearing and arguments. Norby Walters was all set with his reputable New York attorney, Gold, and local counsel Robert Stephenson. Lloyd Bloom was still being represented by Mike Trope.

As far as the government could tell, Bloom's resources seemed to be tapped out. There still seemed to be a pretty good chance they could reach a plea agreement with Bloom, which could keep the case from going to trial because the deck would be so heavily stacked against Walters.

But, the government soon learned, no matter how much disdain they may have had for him, they should never have underestimated Mike Trope. The closer Trope examined the case, the more he realized that Lloyd Bloom's citizenry was in real jeopardy. He did some homework and discovered just how powerful and nasty the Franzese name was in organized crime. He further deduced that Norby Walters had indeed had a lengthy association with Sonny and Michael Franzese, and other organized crime members.

Trope decided it was time to get on the telephone with Bloom's parents, Stuart and Myrna Bloom, who, unbeknownst to the government, were very wealthy. Trope knew that Lloyd had aggravated his parents over the years—Lloyd aggravated almost everybody—but Trope thought of Bloom as a wild puppy dog, a rascal that you might want to kick once in a while but hug and kiss just the same. Certainly his parents had to feel that way, and they had shown genuine concern when their son had his run-in with Alabama authorities.

"Mr. and Mrs. Bloom, do you love your son?" Trope asked them.

They were taken aback. Of course they loved Lloyd.

"Your son is in very serious trouble," Trope then explained.

It was going to cost money, a lot of money, to front the legal battle that could possibly keep their son out of federal prison.

"How much money?" Stuart Bloom asked.

"An estimate—and it's just an estimate—but I'd say"—Trope took a deep breath—"a quarter of a million dollars."

The Blooms were shocked.

"If it goes to trial, it could be more."

Mike Trope had a proposal for the parents. It was the old advance trick. Lloyd Bloom would borrow against his future, quite literally. Stuart and Myrna Bloom would advance Lloyd the money and deduct it from his inheritance, Trope proposed.

"Your son needs a good lawyer," Trope told them earnestly. "He needs to hire the best available, and I want to help him find that person."

Tearfully, Stuart Bloom gritted his teeth, pursed his lips, nodded his head, and said, "Okay."

Trope began his search in Chicago, putting out the word that he was searching for the best lawyer in the city.

Two of the candidates were Patrick Tuite and Dan Webb.

Trope interviewed both men on behalf of Bloom. Each lawyer wanted the case, which was not only extremely high-profile but interesting and winnable. Trope made a decision and a recommendation to Lloyd Bloom.

"Hire Dan Webb."

Webb was rated among the nation's top ten trial lawyers and had been the U. S. Attorney in Chicago prior to Tony Valukas. Trope had seen a viciousness in Howard Pearl, and Webb had been Pearl's boss. There was no way that Pearl could intimidate Webb. And, Trope reasoned, Webb should be able to go toe to toe with Valukas.

When it came time to notify the government that Dan Webb was now representing Lloyd Bloom, it was a stunner. Pearl was speechless.

"Oh, no," George Randolph said.

The government knew all about Webb. He was as sharp as he was tenacious, and as a trial lawyer, he was brilliant. He was also highly regarded by the Justice Department. As the Northern District's lead prosecutor, he was feared.

Randolph remembered getting a call from Webb in early 1987.

"What would you think if I were your boss?"

"Huh?" Randolph answered.

U. S. Attorney General Edwin Meese III had offered Webb the job of FBI director. Webb turned it down.

Many Illinois Republicans saw Webb as top political timber, perhaps because he was the former protégé of Illinois Governor James Thompson, but Webb postponed any political aspirations, partly on the advice of Thompson.

"I told him he was at a stage when he should devote more time to private practice to get his family settled financially," the governor explained.

Webb, then forty-two, was doing just that, racking up more than $2 million worth of business a year for Chicago's Winston & Strawn law firm. His personal draw was $600,000 a year and rising. Big-time commercial companies were lining up to have Webb represent them because, as one CEO noted, the mere mention of Dan Webb on your side generally kept the client from drawn-out litigation.

But money was not the only thing that motivated Webb. When the government needed a special prosecutor in the Iran-Contra mess, he couldn't resist and stepped out of private practice to personally prosecute John Poindexter, who was convicted on all five counts against him. Those who had seen Webb in a courtroom were almost always dazzled by his brilliance. His opponents usually felt down two strikes walking in. Even when Dan Webb was not brilliant, something about his boyish "Beaver Cleaver" looks always played well to a jury.

"He's got a boyish, almost 'oh gosh' demeanor, but he's the smartest kid on the block," said Scott Turow, the best-selling novelist who worked for Webb as a prosecutor.

During his seventeen-year career, Webb had lost just one trial. He personally tried eight cases as U. S. Attorney, sweeping all eight. One trial that drew a lot of attention to him was the Marquette 10 prosecution in 1982, in which ten Chicago police officers were accused of taking payoffs and extorting money from heroin dealers. The prosecution team felt that after three months of trial and testimony from sixty drug dealers, only five of the ten police officers would be convicted. Webb's closing rebuttal argument lasted five hours without notes, and observers trumpeted it as sensational. All ten defendants were found guilty.

Webb also went after the entire Cook County judicial system in the landmark Operation Greylord, which resulted in thirteen judges and sixty-three lawyers, court officers, and police officers being convicted on charges ranging from extortion to case-fixing to bribe-taking.

Webb also prosecuted James Lewis, the only person convicted after eight people died from ingesting cyanide-laced Tylenol in 1983.

"Dan has a unique faculty of relating to the jury and knowing what a jury thinks is important. He's very shrewd and crafty that way," said Max Wildman, a prominent Chicago attorney who once lost a $47 million judgment to one of Webb's clients after Webb tore apart his primary witness in cross-examination.

The Chicago media loved Dan Webb. He was an easy guy to love. The *Chicago Tribune* dubbed him Dan Skywalker as a U. S. Attorney. The newspaper also had a daily gossip column called "The Webb Net," featuring rumors and tidbits about who Webb was going after next.

Randolph said the FBI loved Webb as U. S. Attorney because "there's never been a prosecutor who had a bigger set of balls." Randolph often would sit in Webb's office listening to one side of the dealmaking.

"We had one case we thought was shaky as hell, and Webb was telling the attorney, 'Ten years, or we're going to trial.' And he'd hang up the phone. I'd sit there and tell him he was crazy. Ten minutes later, the lawyer would call back and take the deal . . . graciously."

The *American Lawyer* quoted a client about Webb's capacity for work: "I was in his office one day for a conference, and he's got about twelve pink slips in front of him. He's looking at my brief and discussing it with me and talking on the phone with someone at the same time. Another lawyer pops in, and Webb discusses something with him. Then he notices the shoeshine guy in the hallway, so he brings him in to shine his shoes, orders some lunch, and still discusses my case with me, all at the same time."

His partners at Winston & Strawn had been urging him to become more of a senior statesman, even at his young age. But Webb thrived on action.

"I want to be in the trenches trying cases," he told everyone.

Now he was going to be in the trenches with Norby Walters and Lloyd Bloom.

If Pearl and Randolph were shocked by this development, Tony Valukas claims he was "delighted." Webb was one of his closest friends from the days when they worked together as young prosecutors under Thompson. They had also had some tremendous courtroom battles when Valukas was in private practice and Webb was in office.

The Chicago media would hype this new case as "The Battle of Heavyweights."

Webb put two younger associates, Steve Molo and George Lombardi, to work immediately on the case. Because of Webb's immense worklog, Molo and Lombardi would be significant contributors.

U. S. District Court Judge George M. Marovich, who had been appointed to the federal bench the previous year, drew Case No. 88 CR 709, the United States of America versus Norby Walters and Lloyd Bloom.

With the lines drawn, a series of pre-trial battles got underway. All of the defense work by Dan Webb and Robert Gold, and their associates, was aimed at getting Marovich to dismiss the charges. The pre-trial motions also provided a view of how Marovich would preside if the case ever went to trial.

By November, Gold was seeking dismissal of the indictment on the grounds that Norby Walters had acted on "advice of counsel" and therefore could not have had criminal intent when he pursued the college athletes. Walters claimed he had been told by his lawyers at Shea & Gould that he was doing nothing illegal by going after these players. Consequently, Gold pointed out to the court, it was Walters who brought attention to himself by filing the six lawsuits against the players who had reneged on their contracts.

Norby Walters, the agent to the stars, spoke his mind in a full-page ad he placed in *Billboard* magazine in early November 1988.

In the ad, headlined AN OPEN LETTER TO THE INDUSTRY FROM NORBY WALTERS, the agent boldly lambasted the government, claiming the "Department of Justice has decided to act as the champion of the NCAA and the sports establishment and has filed an indictment against me."

Walters defended paying college athletes in the ad:

As you know it is not unusual in the entertainment industry that record companies, managers, and booking agencies are frequently called upon to make loans to clients against their future earnings. We had frequently done that for our music clients, and we offered similar accommodations to our new sports clients. We entered into agreements with, and made loans to, many college athletes. In doing so, we believed completely that our conduct did not violate any state or federal law. And when some of those athletes refused to honor their obligations to our firm, our attorneys filed lawsuits against those athletes to protect our contractual rights, which we and our attorneys believed to be lawful, binding and enforceable.

The government had already known back in January that this would be Gold's strategy. It had a chance to be effective, but the government could show that the filing of lawsuits meant nothing because Walters was using them to follow up on his threats to expose the players publicly as well as to prove to the players he still had under contract that he meant business.

Besides, Tony Valukas wanted this case indicted not because Walters allegedly defrauded colleges, but because this was a case about an agent who had used organized crime and had spread that element in the sports world.

On face value the advice-of-counsel defense looked powerful as it related to the alleged criminality of Norby Walters and the signing of college football and basketball players.

A person goes to his lawyer and asks, "Am I breaking any laws?"

The lawyer responds, "No, you're messing with NCAA rules, but you are not breaking any laws."

But Dan Webb was not as certain about joining this defense. He would be forced to waive Lloyd Bloom's lawyer-client privileges from his days as a client of Shea & Gould, which meant that Bloom's lawyers at the time would be subject to questioning by the prosecution about their dealing with the defendant.

Webb traveled to New York to meet with Walters's sports lawyers and studied the files. He never explained it, but if there was something that discouraged him from joining the advice-of-counsel defense, it may have been the same correspondence the government eventually got its hands on during discovery in the weeks leading up to the trial.

A prominent New York sports law firm, Weil and Gotshal, which had also been retained by Walters for advice, strongly condemned Walters and Bloom for their disregard of protocol in pursuit of college football and basketball players. The relationship with the agents was severed by the law firm.

James Quinn, a highly reputable sports attorney, sent a letter to Lon Trost, Walters's cousin and lawyer at Shea & Gould. It said in part,

> We also advised WSE and its principals on several occasions that agreements entered into with college players prior to the expiration of that player's eligibility contravened both NCAA regulations and the then-proposed and now operative rules of the National Basketball Association regarding the conduct of player agents. . . .
> This firm has developed a reputation in the field of sports law. . . . We have no intention of allowing the reputation of this firm to be sullied by the conduct of your clients.

Howard Pearl was ecstatic at this find. Perhaps it did not cut to the heart of whether laws were being violated, but it did prove very early that Walters had gotten legal advice that disapproved of his conduct.

Webb must have also wondered what sort of exhaustive research the Shea & Gould law firm did before telling Walters he would not be breaking any laws. In the boxes of files from Shea & Gould there was no memorandum or notes from the meeting or meetings in which Walters asked whether he was breaking any laws.

Not only that, but the federal judges in New York, the Honorable Charles Brieant and the Honorable Myriam Altman, who had dismissed the sports agents' lawsuits against Brent Fullwood and Ronnie Harmon, had lashed out at Norby Walters and Lloyd Bloom for their "pernicious" and "fraudulent" activity in signing the players while they still had college eligibility.

Webb eventually decided to drive a wedge between Walters and Bloom as codefendants. Webb also attempted to have the indictment dismissed. The most obvious and anticipated motion was to dismiss the mail fraud charges because, Webb argued, the universities were not defrauded of anything and therefore did not meet the test of the McNally ruling by the U. S. Supreme Court in June 1987, which struck down "intangible rights."

Webb also argued that the NCAA was in violation of antitrust laws and that the NCAA and NFL were engaged in illegal price-fixing practices—all sound arguments. But they would have to wait for Judge Marovich to make a ruling.

The greatest pre-trial battles occurred when Gold and Webb subpoenaed the NCAA and Big Ten schools for virtually every piece of data that related to any student-athlete investigation since 1978.

One subpoena requested

> records and files, or other written or recorded materials, relating to investigations conducted by or on behalf of the NCAA, at or of its member institutions, into questions of eligibility of student-athletes attending its member institutions, including, but not limited to, reports of investigation, printouts, surveillances, tape recordings, reports of interviews, summaries, results, evaluations, and actions taken or recommended by member institutions and/or NCAA ... reports, affidavits, filings, statements, submissions, investigations, allegations (whether substantiated or not), reports of interviews, reports of actions recommended or actions taken ...

Marovich told the defense lawyers to stick to the schools named in the indictment.

Thus, the attorneys also requested from the Big Ten schools the

> academic records, including but not limited to those consisting of transcripts taken, grades received, classroom attendance, academic, social, or disciplinary probation, scholarships and counseling received by or provided to the student ... disciplinary records, including but not limited to those consisting of references to disciplinary proceedings, allegations of violation of university rules, files of the office of the Dean of Men, Dean of Students, or the equivalent office, records of any disciplinary actions taken, including probation, censure, warnings, curfews, suspension of privileges, and other sanctions ... records of investigations [of the players named in the indictment].

One theory Webb was working on was that a player did not necessarily lose his scholarship after being declared ineligible. He was right—the most recent example came when Georgia Tech stripped a football and baseball star, Riccardo Ingram, of his eligibility but not his scholarship when his dealings with Atlanta agent Jim Abernethy were exposed in November 1987. But Georgia Tech and Riccardo Ingram were not in the indictment.

The government, along with NCAA and Big Ten attorneys, fought the broad scope of Webb's subpoenas as a "fishing expedition." The NCAA also cited the Buckley amendment, which prohibited disclosure of a student's grade transcripts.

Marovich granted the defense team the transcripts that related to the specific players named in the indictment but issued a protective order.

Webb's presence also motivated the government to drop Craig Swoope and the University of Illinois from the indictment around this time. There had been enough rumblings that the Fighting Illini's program was dirty, and Webb had recently represented their athletic director, Neal Stoner. Pearl figured that Stoner knew where all the Illinois skeletons were and would obligingly turn them over to Webb now that the athletic director had been fired.

Judge Marovich gave the government its biggest pre-trial boost in a ruling that upheld its application of the mail fraud statute as it related to the Walters-Bloom case. Webb had argued for Bloom, joined by Walters, that the mailings of the documents to the Big Ten did not further the alleged fraud scheme, and therefore there was no venue for this case to be heard in the Northern District of Illinois. The mail fraud statute specifically provides that the mailings must be "for the purpose of executing the scheme."

Marovich sided with the government and ruled,

> The court finds that a jury could reasonably conclude that the mailings in this case are an essential part of the scheme because they facilitated concealment of the scheme. If the universities or the Big Ten Conference had been given truthful information on the forms, the universities could have terminated the student-athletes' football scholarships and prevented the athletes from playing with the team. Such an occurrence could seriously affect a particular athlete's value to defendants.
>
> The documents mailed in this case were essential to the perpetration and concealment of the alleged fraud. The success of the scheme depended in part on the student-athletes' receipt of scholarship monies. The mailings postponed the day of reckoning. . . . We therefore conclude that the government could produce evidence at trial showing that the mailings were for the purpose of executing the scheme.

Marovich also wrote,

> In the court's view, this indictment does not run aground on McNally.
>
> The indictment alleges a very basic fraud scheme: particular student-athletes obtained tangible property from their universities based on fraudulent misrepresentations. . . . Walters submits that the universities got exactly what they paid for: football players.
>
> Contrary to Walters's assertions, the universities did not get what they paid for. . . . Based on the fraudulent representations, the universities anticipated receiving eligible football players who would not be subject to the risk of disqualification. If the student-athletes' ineligibility were discov-

ered during the football season, the universities' football program could be disrupted and universities could suffer damage to their reputations. Instead of receiving eligible players, the defendants caused the universities to receive ineligible athletes with all the attendant risks.

As for the right of the universities to allocate their property rights, Marovich agreed with the government:

The right to control the property is as much property as the property itself. Defendants interfered with the property right by feeding the universities false information.

As for Walters's motion that he could never have considered his action criminal because of this first and novel application, Marovich ruled:

While the court agrees that the precise factual situation here is a case of first impression, the court finds that the fraudulent nature of the transactions with the student-athletes is sufficiently clear to have afforded Walters notice.

An essential component of the scheme was ensuring that the athletes retained their football scholarships and continued to play football up to the time they would be eligible for the professional football draft where defendants would represent them. The student-athletes' submission of false statements to universities in order to receive scholarship money was a necessary component to the scheme. The illegality of a scheme to deprive an entity of money through the use of fraudulent misstatements is consistent with the common understanding of fraud.

Most significant to the court are the allegations that Walters attempted to conceal his activities. Actions such as postdating the agency contracts, paying wire transfers of cash to third parties, and instructing athletes not to tell the universities about the contracts are strong evidence that Walters himself knew his actions were wrong.

There was no doubt now that the case was going to trial. The prosecution and defense considered Marovich's ruling on mail fraud to be most critical—and favorable to the government.

DURING THE pre-trial fights by the attorneys, Randolph made it his mission to keep Franzese in willing spirits, and to try every last angle possible to solve the beating of Kathy Clements. But now that the indictment had been brought, removing Franzese from prison was not as simple. Whereas before Franzese could be released on a "writ," every move after the indictment required a court order. And, seemingly, Randolph's every move meant some offer of ridicule from jealous peers or superiors.

Franzese's visitor list showed that Jerry Zimmerman had visited Michael Franzese in late 1986 and early 1987, the very time frame Randolph was trying to pin down in the Clements case. Randolph needed Jerry Zimmerman and discovered he had reported to the probation office that he had found a place in Los Angeles. Randolph filed more paperwork to begin travel, waited for it to get approved, and received permission to take along a young, eager, street-tough FBI agent named Pat Buckley. Not without a hassle, of course.

One Los Angeles agent said, "[Los Angeles FBI boss] James Moody kept telling Randolph that Franzese was going to make a fool out of him. He thought George was a country bumpkin. Moody never had a grasp of George's work in organized crime, and he'd make fun of George, as if George didn't understand that New York and Los Angeles were big cities. That used to piss George off; I mean, Chicago's no farm town, and its history in organized crime was a little deeper than L.A.'s."

Although Randolph knew he would never be able to use Zimmerman as a witness, he hoped he might provide a significant lead. He also, for his own mind and instincts, needed to corroborate Franzese's story. He began by trying to find Zimmerman. That wasn't easy.

During a three-day trip to Los Angeles, Randolph and Buckley found themselves getting the runaround. They showed up at places where they were told to look for Zimmerman and always found out that they had "just missed him."

Finally they went to the rental agency in Woodland Hills that had signed an agreement with Zimmerman, figuring they could get information about where they could find the gangster's girlfriend. The rental agency was reluctant to show the FBI agents the application. A little persuasion worked, though, and soon they were talking to the girlfriend. She told them about a textile company across town where Zimmerman could be found. They drove across town. No Zimmerman. Back to the other side of town. It went on for about twelve hours before they gave up for the night. Randolph and Buckley had a few beers, went to bed, and arose the next morning.

"We're not leaving without finding this jag-off," Randolph told Buckley.

Randolph called Zimmerman's attorney and threatened to report the suspicious conduct to Zimmerman's probation officer. The attorney suggested they try the Woodland Hills residence in the afternoon. Randolph and Buckley drove there, parked, and waited. And waited. Finally a car pulled up in front, and out of the passenger side emerged a very large man. Randolph hardly hesitated before he recognized Zimmerman.

"Come on," he told Buckley, and they bolted out of the car.

Randolph and Buckley each took out their badges and identified themselves as FBI agents. Zimmerman froze in his steps. He froze in the middle of the street with two cars headed toward him.

"Get out of the road before you get killed," Randolph said.

Zimmerman had known there were FBI agents after him, but he didn't know why. He stammered, he waved his hands, he talked so much gibberish that Randolph could barely get in a word. Zimmerman cried that he'd been clean. Randolph thought the guy was going to have a heart attack.

"Calm down!" he finally yelled.

Zimmerman wanted to call his attorney. Randolph said okay. The attorney arranged for all of them to meet at his office.

Randolph knew how he wanted to approach Zimmerman. He decided to exaggerate the circumstances to get his attention. Randolph explained that an investigation had been ongoing for two years. Other bureaus had compiled information and data about Norby Walters and Michael Franzese. They had surveillance that showed Zimmerman was a go-between, and the surveillance showed that Zimmerman had brought a message to Michael Franzese from Norby Walters about "dealing with some broad in Chicago."

But Randolph didn't want to put too many words in Zimmerman's mouth.

"I've seen your file, I know your record, and if you lie to me, one way or the other, I'm gonna report you," Randolph said. "If you shoot straight with me, I think we'll be okay. I've done a lot of work here, so I can tell if you're lying."

The six-foot-four, 270-pound Zimmerman was still nervous but said, "I wanna help." Zimmerman admitted he knew Norby Walters and had for a long time. Zimmerman said that he and Norby used to work on some movie and music deals together. They were always "bullshitting" about the business. Norby was one of the most colorful guys he knew. They were good buddies.

Randolph wanted to know about Norby asking for help with Michael Franzese. Zimmerman stumbled and wouldn't even say the name Franzese. Randolph figured he feared the consequences, so he explained that they had proof such a conversation had taken place.

"I told you, shoot straight," Randolph reminded him.

Finally Zimmerman said that Norby Walters had asked for help with the sports agent business. Norby claimed he was having some of the same types of problems in sports that he used to have in the music business. There was trouble with some agents stealing his clients, and there was trouble with some gal, and Norby wanted help. The message was delivered to Michael Franzese. That's all Zimmerman knew.

"Does the name Kathy Clements mean anything?" Randolph asked.

"No," Zimmerman replied. "Not at all."

How about a gal in Chicago? Zimmerman wasn't sure. He only thought it rang a bell.

How about Frankie Campione? Wasn't there a return message? Wasn't that whom Zimmerman contacted, as Franzese instructed?

Zimmerman didn't remember, claiming the incident escaped him because it was not a matter of great significance as far as he was concerned.

Maybe it was John Franzese, Jr., Michael's brother, who had delivered the message. Zimmerman couldn't quite get his memory fixed, but he would not connect Campione.

And Zimmerman said he had no knowledge that any woman actually got beat up.

The meeting ended. Randolph was exhausted but upbeat because he believed Zimmerman was being square with him about Norby Walters, but he was frustrated that Zimmerman wouldn't give up Frankie Campione.

Campione, the thug who allegedly would have dealt with the problem, would not cooperate when Randolph traveled across the country to New York.

"All I could tell you about Norby Walters is on my fingertip," Campione groused.

The five-foot-seven, two-hundred-pound fireplug was a nasty man with a reputation for violence. FBI surveillance routinely caught Sonny Franzese's former driver and bodyguard in acts of intimidation. If he ever went to a restaurant to dine and the waiter dared bring him a check, Campione would go berserk.

Randolph had explored whether Walters used other associates in organized crime and whether the job was delegated to motorcycle gang members who did this sort of work. Motorcycle gangs have a national syndicate not unlike the Mafia. Randolph worked that angle, remembering the masked intruder who beat Kathy Clements had a "greasy" odor about him. It was another dead end.

Although Randolph had run out of leads, he pleaded with Valukas and Pearl not to dismiss Clements. He never stopped believing there was a connection to Walters. He just couldn't forget Walters's venomous response to Clements's recruiting of Doug Dubose. In the days leading up to the beating he had called her a "gutter whore" in a series of nasty calls. He had told Bloom to leave Clements alone because he would handle her. There was also Walters's mysterious overnight trip to Chicago right after the beating. There was Michael Franzese's story of how Walters had reached out to him through Zimmerman about the trouble he was having with a rival female sports agent and how Franzese had delegated the matter to New York.

There was the beating itself. A masked man finds her office in a maze of buildings and beats her up. No sexual assault. No robbery.

Valukas and Pearl thought there might be a way to introduce the Clements beating at the trial, perhaps even superseding the indictment by amending the conspiracy charges to include information on the threat to Clements and her subsequent beating.

The prosecutors called Robert Gold, Walters's attorney, a month before the trial to notify him that the government would, in fact, supersede the indictment to include Kathy Clements. Gold was shocked and argued vehemently that unless the government charged Walters with the actual beating, he would vigorously pursue a dismissal of the charges as well as a mistrial once the trial got underway.

About this time Randolph again left for California to pick up the government's star witness and prisoner, Michael Franzese. The trial was scheduled to begin on February 27, 1989, just a few weeks away. When he returned, the FBI agent was bitterly disappointed to learn that Valukas had decided not to supersede the indictment with the Clements information.

Randolph had to focus now on securing his prisoner. They would not lock down Franzese in the Metropolitan Correctional Center, which caused intense dispute internally. Randolph felt that the FBI could protect Franzese better on its own, and he also wanted Franzese in a good frame of mind before the tense days when he would take the witness stand.

Franzese was secured in a downtown hotel site with armed FBI agents around the clock. According to a government source, Randolph was unaware at the time that his FBI peers had circulated a "petition" to superiors, asking that Franzese get locked down in prison because they feared the duty was "too hazardous." Randolph's bosses ignored the petition.

Franzese was being moved to the Dirksen Federal Building almost daily to meet with Valukas. He was brought through the basement and ushered around in secrecy. Franzese never left the hotel without putting on a bulletproof vest. The Mafia captain seemed to be enjoying this top-security attention, until Randolph cracked, "You know, Mike, a vest won't do anything for a head shot."

Valukas wanted to be absolutely certain about Franzese. If he thought for a moment that the Mafia boss was wavering on anything, he wanted a cushion to offer the defense an easy out. The most sensitive and critical moment came when Valukas "pre-tried" Franzese in his office with Randolph standing by. This was the first rehearsal.

Valukas took Franzese through some routine matters before he decided to ask Franzese about "prior bad acts." Valukas asked the mob boss whether he was directly involved in any murders.

"Yes, I was," Franzese responded.

Valukas froze. He started to ask another question, then shot out of the room like a bullet.

Randolph thought Tony was "just getting to the good stuff."

Franzese looked at Randolph and asked, "George, what's the matter?"

Randolph didn't know. Soon Valukas came back to his office and coldly instructed Randolph to "get him out of here," referring to Franzese.

Randolph may not have been a genius, but he knew something was terribly wrong. When Randolph returned to Valukas's office, the U. S. Attorney was on the telephone with high-ranking Justice Department officials in Washington.

"Franzese could be going back," Valukas told the FBI agent. "I am not going to trade Norby Walters for some Mafia boss who openly admits to an act of murder. The entire department will be embarrassed."

Howard Pearl freaked out. He thought their case was dead but quickly began to organize trial strategy without Michael Franzese. It was as if somebody had delivered a sledgehammer to the back of Randolph's head.

Franzese said, "The next morning George came to me and said that I might be going back. I wanted to know what happened because all I could think was that Tony had asked me if I were involved in homicide and I said to him, yeah. But my thinking was that we had already discussed this, already gone over this. I had already been questioned about this. I was thinking from the standpoint that, hey, I was a captain, and I had knowledge. There were discussions and I had knowledge. But nobody was telling me anything. George would not tell me and said he wasn't at liberty to share anything."

The problem was that Tony Valukas felt they might just have received a confession from Franzese, and it had to be reported to the Justice Department.

"Michael's plea agreement with New York did not exempt him from prosecution for crimes of violence," Valukas says. "It had been my understanding that he had not participated in homicide. I was not going to be put in the position of where he walks into that courtroom where acts of murder were brought out in detail for the first time."

George Randolph decided he needed to have a heart to heart with the U. S. Attorney. He had never felt so humbled.

"Tony, I've got to talk to you," the FBI agent said. "Maybe I screwed this thing up. I thought we covered all these areas, but maybe it's my fault. Maybe I missed something, but I need another chance."

Randolph proposed that he and another veteran FBI agent, Scott Jennings, conduct another in-depth formal interrogation of Michael Franzese, specifically dealing with his knowledge of any and all homicides. Jennings had accompanied Randolph earlier on a few of the meetings with the players; he had also successfully worked with Randolph on other difficult cases.

"This is of the highest sensitivity," Valukas warned Randolph.

They called Jennings on the telephone and asked him to come up to Valukas's office. Jennings was busy and wanted to know why.

"I can't tell you until you get here," Randolph said.

"Forget it. Get somebody else," Jennings replied.

Randolph earnestly pleaded with Jennings to come upstairs. "Trust me."

"It better be good," Jennings finally said.

Jennings could see by the looks on their faces that Valukas and Randolph considered it something serious indeed.

Valukas told him, "What I'm about to tell you stays in this room."

Randolph and Jennings later sat down with Michael Franzese and grilled him on his years as a Mafia captain. Franzese explained that as a capo regime in the Colombo family he attended numerous meetings where homicides were discussed. He routinely sat in on meetings with the heads of the five New York crime families.

Their interrogation was of some length. Afterward, Randolph and Jennings went over their notes and went to see Valukas.

"What's the recommendation?" Valukas asked.

"If we don't use Michael Franzese on this case, we're crazy," Randolph said. The FBI agent explained that he felt comfortable with Franzese's explanation and forthrightness about the workings of the Mafia. Franzese was adamant that he never personally ordered a "hit" on anybody or committed the act himself.

But Franzese was a "made man" in 1975 when he swore the Mafia oath. Every organized crime expert knew you could not be "made" unless you murdered. Franzese had explained to them that he did not have to commit the act because he was Sonny Franzese's son and because the Mafia books were opened after being closed for so long. The mob was desperate for new blood, and Franzese insisted he didn't have to spill any to get inducted.

Valukas looked at Jennings and asked, "What do you think?"

Jennings was impressed with Franzese and believed the crime boss was being truthful. He told enough just by acknowledging the various acts that would have seemed so protective. He agreed strongly with Randolph.

"There's no way you can't use this guy," said Jennings.

Valukas looked as if a five-hundred-pound boulder had just been removed from his back. His face lit up. The U. S. Attorney smiled for the first time in days.

"Get Franzese back over here," Valukas told Randolph. "We're going to use him."

THE GOVERNMENT continued to get ready for the case. Pearl and Randolph worked hard to get the athletes into town to prepare them for their testimony. The government had some seventy-five potential witnesses, and the list would open some eyes.

The actual date of the trial was moved from February 27 to March 1. A potential thirty-day delay had arisen because Valukas contemplated adding new charges of perjury and obstruction of justice against Walters related to his grand jury testimony prior to the indictment. He didn't file the new charges because Gold told the judge that it would require the lawyer to testify and cause him to withdraw from the case, thereby causing a lengthy delay.

Marovich warned the prosecutors and defense attorneys to get ready to enter the ring.

"I don't mean to be wishy-washy, but somebody is going to trial Wednesday," he told the lawyers. "It is time to put a tourniquet on this baby and stop the bleeding."

By this time Dan Webb was convinced that Lloyd Bloom had every legal right to demand a severance from Walters and consequently a separate trial because he had not waived his attorney-client privilege as Walters had done. Therefore, the two sides were in direct conflict, and Webb argued vehemently that Bloom would be dragged down by this strategy.

Marovich denied this more than once, ruling that the government was prosecuting the two men as business partners and that the attorney advice they sought was for the corporation of WSE, and Walters, as president of the corporation, had the power to waive that right.

Dan Webb believed that Marovich had erred so critically that Lloyd Bloom would have an easy victory in an appeal.

Webb was also having trouble convincing Marovich to let him broaden the scope of his potential cross-examination of the athletes regarding their academic transcripts. Marovich was opposed. Webb argued repeatedly.

"There may be many ills that beset intercollegiate athletics, but they are not going to be remedied in a federal courthouse," Marovich said. "We're going to have a trial here. We are not going to have a morality play. Do we understand?"

Dan Webb was getting ready for Act One.

15

BETWEEN THE indictment and the trial, Howard Pearl and Tony Valukas had cleared out a twelve-by-sixteen space on the fifteenth floor of the
Dirksen Federal Building. The office was established as a command post
for the Walters-Bloom case, and it was where George Randolph and
fellow FBI agent Diane Benson moved their work.

Two separate telephone lines were installed in the office, which was
way too small for the boxes of files that were stacked up to the ceiling.
There was barely enough space for a small metal desk, and the room's
claustrophobic effect was relieved only by the presence of a window.

Nevertheless, the command center allowed Pearl quick access to files
as he and Valukas polished their trial strategy. Most of it had already
been done in drafting the eighty-five-page indictment, which had been
drawn from Pearl's 250-page proffer memo that analyzed the entire case.
The analysis had been based on the information and evidence that Randolph had supplied.

"We could have had a six-month trial if we wanted," Pearl said.

Randolph was all for it. He would have loved for the government to
sling one big mud ball against the courtroom walls. Every dirty little deal
would show just how ugly the Walters-Bloom operation had been, he
reasoned. It would also have shown his nonstop work over the twenty-
three-plus months. It might even justify missing two summers of sailing
and watching the best baseball seasons of his son Bill's life.

But even Randolph understood that trials were about winning and
losing. Prosecutors kept score, and considering Valukas himself was
involved, the FBI agent knew it was going to be a conservative game
plan. There were not going to be a whole lot of surprises. First and
foremost, the government's primary objective was to convince a jury that

there was a fraud and that the colleges were justifiable victims of the Walters-Bloom operation. The government had to get at least one mail fraud conviction or else all the other charges would be dismissed for lack of jurisdiction.

They would attempt to establish the mail fraud violations by presenting the Big Ten Conference players to the jury right from the beginning.

Ronnie Harmon would be the leadoff witness, that much was established. The government weighed this as a calculated risk because the Iowa running back had many flaws. His streetwise nature could occasionally make him look like a smart ass. He had also been allowed by a labor arbitrator to keep almost $50,000 without repayment to Norby Walters.

There was also the question of his grade transcripts. FBI agent Diane Benson had scrutinized the transcripts and warned Howard Pearl they presented potential problems. Pearl didn't seem concerned because Marovich had expressed his desire again and again not to conduct a "morality play." And Big Ten attorney Byron Gregory, who was in constant communication with the government during the subpoena battles with the NCAA and Big Ten schools, assured the government that Harmon remained eligible under NCAA rules.

Ronnie Harmon, however, was an ideal leadoff witness in the government's plan because of the forty-minute tape recording in which Norby Walters made his sales pitch. Right off, the jury would get to hear from the defendant's mouth how the agents did a little "razzle-dazzle" and how, in America, almost anything goes. The jury would be able to connect the testimony from the other players to the sensational tape, the government figured.

Harmon would also lead a procession of the other Big Ten players: teammate Devon Mitchell of Iowa, Rod Woodson of Purdue, Mark Ingram of Michigan State, and Robert Perryman and Garland Rivers of Michigan. Pearl would direct the players through very tight testimony in order to simplify the case as much as possible for the jury and leave Dan Webb as few openings as possible on cross-examination.

The players would explain that they entered into a plea agreement with the government in which they would pay back their universities the money they had stolen when they lied on their scholarship forms. They would be performing 100 to 250 hours of community service, they would be on probation one year, and they agreed to testify truthfully. In return, the players would tell the jury, their satisfactory adherence to the pretrial agreement meant they would not be indicted for mail fraud.

Pearl would make certain that each player explained the process of certifying each year. In order to receive tuition, room, and board, the players had to fill out several forms and sign affidavits. They would tell the jury how, when they had taken money from Walters and Bloom, they lied on the forms to get their tuition, room, and board and remain eligible to play football. They would also tell the jury of the sexy, driving sales pitch that Walters and Bloom had made and the deception that had been designed to cover their illicit arrangement with the sports agents.

That would be it for Pearl's direct of the Big Ten players. He would do the same with the players from three other schools because of their connection to the conspiracy act: Robert Banks and Alvin Miller of Notre Dame, Paul Palmer of Temple, and George Swarn of Miami (Ohio), another school with a strong academic reputation. Swarn also had an interesting story to tell because he had turned down Walters and Bloom three times until their persistence paid off.

Michigan and Notre Dame would be the jewels in the fraud presentations. The government would have a chance to use two legends from the schools—Michigan Coach Bo Schembechler and Notre Dame's Father Theodore Hesburgh.

There was also Walters's furtherance of the conspiracy when he withheld the contracts of six underclassmen from the grand jury. Because Walters had elected to waive his attorney-client privilege, Michael Feldberg himself would be called as a government witness against the agent.

The government would need guilty verdicts on at least two separate criminal acts to establish a racketeering conviction. Thus, the heart of the conspiracy also would contain the extortionate threats that Walters and Bloom allegedly made to SMU's Ron Morris, Texas's Everett Gay, Pittsburgh's Tony Woods, and the Chicago Bears' Maurice Douglass.

To make these threats feel as real as possible, Michael Franzese would step forward as a Mafia captain and tell the jury that he was a silent partner of Norby Walters in both the entertainment and sports operations. Franzese would tell the jury of the extortionate services he rendered personally for Walters. Witnesses such as Ron Weisner, manager of the Jacksons, would step forward to corroborate Franzese's testimony. Corroboration was vital because there was no question the defense would attempt to show that Franzese was a liar.

Then, as a finale, the government would attempt to show how Lloyd Bloom ripped off Paul Palmer. It was an act that could explain to the jury why so many players decided to renege on their contractual agreements with Walters and Bloom.

It would be a tight, neat prosecution. The government was joined by Assistant U. S. Attorney Helene Greenwald, who would take notes, offer suggestions, and help with a witness or two. They knew there would be bumps because the defense team of lawyers, led by Dan Webb and Robert Gold, were too skilled not to stage a vigorous battle.

But overall the government was highly confident that it was going to win this case. Marovich's mail fraud rulings had provided the necessary lift. Franzese had survived the intense pre-trial grilling of the tough Irish prosecutor, Joe Duffy. Walters and Bloom had buried themselves on the rest. The government also didn't believe the New York lawyers arguing on Walters's behalf would play well to a Chicago jury.

It was time. It was March 2, 1989.

Almost two years from the day Kathy Clements was beaten, U. S. District Judge George M. Marovich took his seat on the bench on the seventeenth floor to preside over the trial of Norby Walters and Lloyd Bloom.

Marovich was a personable judge with less than two years' experience on the federal bench. He was short, about five feet eight inches, and somewhat rotund, but his black robe helped disguise his belly. His thick, dark-brown hair was always slicked down as if he might still be using Vitalis.

Marovich had shown a knack for enjoying good theater, and he wanted a proper environment. Because he was a newcomer to the federal bench, his working courtroom at the end of the seventeenth floor had been sawed off to about two-thirds the size of a normal U. S. District Court. On the morning of March 2, he took one look at the mess of media representatives and courtroom artists jockeying for position in the gallery and announced, "We're moving to a larger courtroom down the hall on Monday to accommodate the media and spectators."

Whether it was for appearance or not, Norby Walters and Lloyd Bloom were chatting around the defense table as if nothing had come between the two men. If ever there was a time that Norby Walters needed a friend, this was it.

Walters was dapper in a gray suit, and he looked refreshed, confident, almost upbeat. He played with the courtroom artists and reporters.

Bloom seemed more aloof than upbeat. One didn't get the sense that he felt he was in any trouble at all. Bloom was pointing at an Associated Press picture of himself in the *Chicago Sun-Times*. "That's one of the better shots, don't you think?" he asked a reporter.

Bloom was not very photogenic at the moment. After walking to the courthouse in the freezing Chicago wind, he had a purple and puffy face, and his shirt collar seemed to be choking him.

"My feet are frozen," Bloom told everyone.

Bloom also told spectators jubilantly that his "wife" (now actually his live-in ex)—Donna Denton by her stage name—had landed the role of Althea on the soap opera "General Hospital." She was a villainess, naturally.

Bloom's black-and-silver tweed suit did nothing to alter his villainous reputation.

The herd of attorneys was called to the judge's chambers. Walters was represented by Robert Gold and a New York associate, Ethan Levin-Epstein, as well as local Chicago attorney Matthew Kennelly. Bloom's team consisted of Dan Webb, Steve Molo, and George Lombardi. Without question Walters's team looked very New Yorkish, Bloom's team very Chicagoish.

Much to Pearl's objection, the defense team had a seventh member—Mike Trope. That made for a very crowded defense table, with Walters and Gold at the end nearest the spectator gallery, and Webb and Bloom in the center facing the jury box across the room.

The prosecution table was directly in front of the jury box. The prosecution team, from right to left, was Tony Valukas, Howard Pearl, Helene Greenwald, and George Randolph.

The lawyers were called back to Judge Marovich's chambers for a conference. That left Randolph alone at the prosecution table, reading a newspaper. The attorneys returned ten minutes later, and Walters put his arm around Gold, his diminutive lawyer, who had the look of a youthful Roy Scheider with jet-black hair.

"All rise," the clerk ordered the court. "The Honorable George M. Marovich presiding. Court is now in session."

The judge instantly told the lawyers he wanted no theatrics.

"No pacing," he said. "No funny looks at the jurors."

Marovich nevertheless had his own fun and games with the prospective jurors. Because the trial promised to be somewhat lengthy, Marovich anticipated that many of the sixty citizens who were ushered into the courtroom would beg off duty. He therefore tried to sell the prospective jurors: "Most trials are boring. . . . I think that in your lifetime if there was ever one trial that you would like to sit in on, this is it."

Roy Scott was the first prospective juror questioned. Unemployed, he was a Bears and Cubs fan. Almost everyone was a Bears fan. In fact, the first ten jurors described themselves as Bears fans, then a man stood up and confessed he was a St. Louis Cardinals fan, football and baseball.

Marovich said, "So there's still some of you left, huh?"

"I'm a rabid Bears fan," bragged Steve Meyer, an English high school teacher and coach. "I coach freshman soccer, basketball, and baseball."

"So you're very much a sports fan?" Marovich asked.

"It's my religion," the juror cracked, and the courtroom erupted in laughter.

Walters and Bloom relaxed in their chairs. This wasn't so bad.

An elderly man, Noah Wright, described himself as "divorced and a grandfather." He stated the latter fact with unblushing pride.

Marovich perked up. "I know what you mean about being a grandfather," the judge told the man. "Want to see some pictures?" He started to take out his wallet, then he put it back. "Want to see them again?" the judge asked, smiling. Again, drawing laughter.

Wright was asked about his sports knowledge. He said he knew former Bears great Bill George.

"Do you still see him on a regular basis?" asked the judge.

"No. . . . He's dead now," the juror replied. The place was rolling.

The first female juror described herself as "a sports fan by default."

The jurors were occasionally asked about their TV viewing preferences. One liked "gangster movies." Another preferred "Star Trek."

"I watch sports, ESPN, and Morton Downey, Jr.," one juror proclaimed.

There were twenty jurors before one was reached who said she wasn't a sports fan. The rest of them let out a mock gasp.

"I prefer to go shopping," she said.

"So would my wife," the judge cracked, working the room again.

Another woman said she was a "reformed sports fanatic." "It used to run my life," she explained. "Now I can take it or leave it."

"Which teams did you follow?" asked Marovich.

"Oh, used to be the Bears, the Bulls, and the White Sox," she said.

"All of whom have given you cause for a broken heart—is that why you are reformed?" the judge asked warmly.

"It certainly is," she said.

The next woman left the courtroom in a more sober mood. She was elderly and retired. She said she was a sports widow and didn't sound all that happy about it. She had a daughter who had been raped at sixteen. She would be one of the jurors selected.

One man went out of his way to eliminate himself when he stated, "In all honesty, judge, I must say I have great admiration for all law enforcement agencies."

Gold and Webb instantly crossed him off the list.

Though some jurors admitted they had heard vaguely about Walters and Bloom, one Notre Dame season-ticket holder explicitly pointed out that he had read the *Sports Illustrated* article the previous summer. At that point Gold asked for a conference in the judge's chambers. He wanted the juror dismissed by the judge so he did not have to waste a challenge, which is how opposing lawyers eliminated candidates.

When they returned to the courtroom, Marovich told the man, "Sir, you are excused."

By the end of two days, both sides surprised each other by a near-unanimous agreement on the fourteen jurors, which included two who would not be told until the end of the trial that they were alternates. This would assure everyone's attention. There were ten women and four men—an all-white jury with the exception of one black man.

The judge told the jury that to make the lengthy trial less intruding on their personal lives, he was going to give them every Friday off, which he would use to hear the inevitable motions by the government and prosecution that would pop up. The jurors went home for the weekend and would return on Monday, March 6, for the trial's start.

Ronnie Harmon was brought to Chicago on Sunday for the sixth time since he reached his pre-trial agreement. His lawyer now was Samuel Skinner, the former Secretary of Transportation.

By now Pearl and Randolph had grown to enjoy Harmon. Perhaps it was his guts to tape Walters right under the agent's nose, or perhaps it was the clever instincts he used to successfully fight Walters on the $50,000 he had received. A con man had conned a con man.

Harmon was usually low-keyed but occasionally opened up to share some of his secrets with the prosecution team. As a black kid from the streets of New York, he never believed he fit in at Iowa. His career had ended bitterly when his teammates, led by quarterback Chuck Long, pointed fingers at his indifferent attitude after losing four fumbles and dropping a touchdown pass in the Rose Bowl three years earlier. That incident only further fanned the flames of suspicion among Iowans after Harmon's relationship with Walters was revealed publicly.

Pearl had told Harmon he felt the press had acted irresponsibly in trying to link the government's investigations to his Rose Bowl performance. Iowa lawmakers were ready to probe Harmon's performance before Valukas used his Justice Department connections to cut them off.

A fix didn't make sense to Pearl: "The kid had more money to make in the NFL draft with a great performance. It was his last college game before the greatest audience."

The government also sensed that Harmon was not a happy camper in Buffalo after two National Football League seasons. Finally Harmon confided that he despised Bills quarterback Jim Kelly because Kelly "played favorites." Obviously Harmon wasn't one of the favorites.

If Harmon was bitter about being the government's pawn, he didn't show it that weekend. He gave every indication that he was ready for the witness stand. He wouldn't fumble this one, they thought.

Like players before a big game, the prosecution and defense teams had trouble sleeping. A lot was riding on this matchup. "The Clash of the Titans," the *Chicago Sun-Times* dubbed it.

On Monday, March 6, the courtroom was filling fast between 9:30 A.M. and 10 A.M. A variety of media people were on hand, including the regular local courtroom reporters: Big John Gorman of the *Chicago Tribune,* Adrienne Drell of the *Chicago Sun-Times,* and Dan Weir of the City News Bureau. The *New York Times* had decided to pay local correspondent Steve Fiffer to cover the trial daily. The artists jockeyed again for prime position and began sketching the participants. The buzz around the courtroom made the trial feel like a heavyweight boxing match.

As promised, the new courtroom was more spacious. The walls were paneled with a rich maple wood, and a large silver shield—UNITED STATES DISTRICT COURT, NORTHERN DISTRICT OF ILLINOIS—hung high above the judge's bench. To the right of the judge was the jury box. The prosecution table again was situated directly in front of the box, and the defense table was on the opposite side.

Before proceedings began, Dan Webb wanted another meeting in the judge's chambers to engage Marovich in further arguments.

"Dan's gonna find out how close to the edge we can get," a member of the defense team whispered to the front row of reporters.

Webb pushed hard about the scope of his cross-examination of the student-athletes. Marovich did not want him dissecting the academic transcripts. Webb refused to take no for an answer. He told the judge that he could prove that many of the student-athletes were ineligible, and therefore the college officials themselves had falsely certified the players to receive their scholarships. That struck a chord.

"If you can show that the players were ineligible— Mmm, that would be interesting," Marovich thought aloud.

Valukas and Pearl went on the offensive. Webb countered. Okay, Marovich ruled, Webb could question the players about their academic standing, but the judge promised to cut Webb off "as soon as you take it too far."

"I do not want a morality play in my courtroom," Marovich sternly warned again.

Valukas and Pearl were disappointed. They returned to the courtroom grim-faced. Randolph and Greenwald could tell there was something wrong. Webb led the defense team back into the courtroom, his head cocked, his eyes racing with his mind.

"All rise."

Marovich entered the courtroom and took his seat at the bench. He seemed in high spirits and glanced up at the clock to his left, beyond the defense table. It was time for opening statements by the lawyers. He instructed the white-haired, pinkish-faced U. S. Marshal to bring in the jury.

Through the door to Marovich's right, the jurors walked reverently and orderly to the two rows of black-leather chairs in the jury box, which was elevated about two feet. The attorneys on both sides never took their eyes off the ten women and four men. The two alternates didn't know it, but they were seated in the last two chairs in the second row.

The jurors received a little pep talk from Marovich: "I will be the judge of the law, you will be judge of the facts."

Tony Valukas was no longer wearing wire-rimmed glasses as he rose to address the jury with his opening argument. His glasses were more conventional, but he still had the look of a Nazi gestapo officer. He stepped to the podium that had been turned to face the jury eight feet away and placed his notes in front of him. He smiled and introduced the jury to the government's case.

There was nothing emotional about Valukas's presentation. He simply accounted the facts of the indictment, but he made certain to tell the jury right away that Norby Walters's and Lloyd Bloom's quest to sign the nation's elite "student-athletes" was backed by a silent partner named Michael Franzese, a captain in the Colombo crime family. Valukas pronounced the Mafia boss's name as Fran-zeese instead of the traditional Fran-zee-see, apparently at Franzese's request.

Valukas tried to make it as simple as he could for the jury to understand the mail fraud scheme, stating that it was not the government's position that the student-athletes did something illegal when they took money from Walters and Bloom. Rather, through the extensive concealment by Walters and Bloom, the student-athletes committed this fraud when they signed false certifications to obtain their scholarships.

Valukas briefed the jury on the government's witnesses and charges. The jury would hear firsthand from Franzese about the services he performed for Norby Walters and how the Mafia boss met Lloyd Bloom on the day that he passed $50,000 in cash to "Uncle Norby."

Valukas finished his statement in forty-seven minutes.

"Mr. Webb," Judge Marovich said.

Dan Webb grabbed his notes and made his way to the podium. His light-brown hair, parted on the left, was already a little mussed. He put his hand in his left pocket and at a high volume introduced himself to the jury: "Hi, I'm Dan Webb. . . . We've never met before, but I represent Lloyd Bloom, one of the defendants in the case."

They may never have met before, but Webb proceeded to talk to the jury like a friend confiding a secret to another friend.

"I could have fallen off my chair when Valukas told us that Michael Fran-cheezi, who apparently is going to tell us that he's a member of an organized crime family, could identify my client. When he gets on the witness stand, I'm going to ask Bloom to stand up, and I'm going to walk him right up to the witness stand and say, 'Look at me and tell me if it's true, if you've ever seen Lloyd Bloom before.' If he tells the truth, he will tell you that he doesn't know who Lloyd Bloom is, that he's never met my client."

Webb stepped back from the podium. Marovich kept an eye on him, no doubt remembering his warning about "theatrics." Webb opened his arms and then gently broke the news to the jury.

"But that's not what this case is about, ladies and gentleman. . . . You are going to hear a very sordid tale of scandal that has overtaken the world of college football."

Valukas jumped to his feet and objected. "That's not what we're here for, your honor," Valukas said.

Marovich said, "I'll allow him to make the argument. Ladies and gentlemen of the jury, I'll remind you that opening statements are not evidence. . . . Proceed, Mr. Webb."

"If a college can put together a great football team, they make millions of dollars. . . . We're going to prove to you that the universities are not victims. They weren't defrauded of anything."

Webb hammered home his points and berated the government for bringing a case to court in which there had been only a "violation of rules of a private club known as the NCAA. . . . These rules are not laws."

During the sixty-minute argument, Webb constantly pushed the envelope to the edge as Tony Valukas jumped to his feet seven times to voice objections when Webb told the jurors they would learn that the student-athletes "often fell behind in their studies only to have the schools cover up and allow the student-athletes to take soft courses so they can get their grades up . . . to make millions of dollars for the school."

Webb cited George Swarn, the running back from Miami of Ohio, as an example.

"He was on academic probation, he was kicked off the football team, and then in his third year he takes a summer course called Trees and Shrubs—honest, that's the name of the course—and he got his grades up so he could play football."

Webb did take chances with Bloom when he addressed some of the extortion charges, admitting that "Lloyd Bloom did say nasty things, like, 'I'm going to break your legs,' but you have to understand the crime of extortion. . . . Several of these athletes decided to walk away from Walters and Bloom. No question Bloom became frustrated and angry. The only way for them to make money was to represent these athletes that had made contractual agreements with them. . . . These athletes knew Lloyd Bloom as somebody with a big mouth. They swatted these away like a fly on a nose."

When Webb finished, Robert Gold took the podium, at 3:40 P.M., to make his opening statement. He explained that he represented Norby Walters and somberly told the jury, "You can be sure this is the most frightening day of his life." Gold explained Walters's defense, specifically telling how the agent went to the prestigious New York law firm of Shea & Gould—Walter A. Shea, he explained, is whom Shea Stadium was named after—and asked about his legal rights in pursuing college athletes. Again, Walters was advised he was not breaking any laws.

Gold then moved into the racketeering charges and said, "Norby Walters for twenty years was the leading agent of black musical talent. Mr. Walters had very powerful friends . . . and very powerful enemies."

He mentioned specifically the name of pop star Michael Jackson, and the jury perked up. He talked about Ron Weisner, the manager who claimed to be threatened by Walters and Michael Franzese.

"Mr. Weisner was desperate. . . . He was afraid he would lose Jackson as a client, and we will learn why. Weisner was not liked by Michael Jackson's father, who fired Ron Weisner and hired Norby Walters."

Gold then turned his attention more specifically to Michael Franzese. He told the jury of Franzese's trouble with the government and how

Franzese hated prison and, consequently, became an informer in order to obtain a quicker release from prison.

"Michael Franzese, we will show you, is a slick, conniving, lying con man. . . . He is not to be believed."

Gold was finished after a polished performance, one mixed with sincerity and anger.

Marovich looked up at the clock. It was 4:30. He told the jury it would begin hearing testimony at ten o'clock the next morning. It was dismissed but not without a warning: "Avoid reading the newspapers, don't watch the TV, don't listen to the radio. . . . I don't want to sequester you."

16

GEORGE RANDOLPH arrived early on Tuesday morning, March 7, to set up the electronic recording equipment and speakers. He made certain he had a box of black headsets, which he put under the prosecution table. He tested the equipment, which was working fine. He wired the speakers for the audience to listen, all standard procedures.

Judge George Marovich welcomed the jurors and then instructed the government: "Bring in your first witness."

Shortly, through the rear doorway of the courtroom, a stocky, well-dressed young man walked toward the witness stand next to the judge. The witness was sworn in, and Howard Pearl, standing behind the far end of the prosecution table and nearest the government's cart of files, opened deliberately in the same manner that would be used with every witness: "State your name."

Ronnie Keith Harmon, now employed by the Buffalo Bills, was taken through a meticulous process of telling the jury about the University of Iowa's rules concerning signing prematurely with an agent. The curly-haired Pearl asked Harmon what would happen if the school found out about such an arrangement.

"You would not be able to play football, and you would lose your scholarship," Harmon said matter-of-factly.

Pearl advanced Harmon to the spring of 1985, in early March.

"I was in my dorm room when Lloyd Bloom called and told me that this was my lucky day," Harmon testified. A few smiles spread through the courtroom. "He told me they represented big-time stars and asked me to fly to New York. They said they would arrange to pick me up in a limo and take me to their office."

If anything, it meant Harmon would get a free trip home. An airline ticket arrived by Federal Express the next day, March 9. They met for about thirty minutes, and Norby Walters, the agent to the stars, asked Harmon to bring his father the following day. The limousine dropped Harmon off at his parents' apartment in Queens. It did not go unnoticed in the neighborhood.

Jessie Harmon, the player's father, accompanied his son. Ronnie Harmon told how he brought along a tape recorder and taped much of the conversation that day. Pearl didn't ask him why. It was now time to listen to that tape, and Randolph, along with assistant prosecutor Helene Greenwald, distributed the wireless headphones to each member of the jury.

As it had with the prosecution team, the tape mesmerized the courtroom and the jurors, who nevertheless remained expressionless as they listened intently. The rapid-fire sales pitch was punctuated with finger snaps and hand slaps on the desk. Norby Walters may or may not have been the agent to the stars, but he sure sounded like America's top salesman. No actor could have played the role better. About forty minutes later, when the tape had run out, the prosecution team studied the jurors, who removed the headsets. A few jurors then studied the codefendant, Norby Walters, across the room.

Pearl let Harmon finish telling the story, how Walters spread $2,500 on the table and left the room. Harmon decided to take the money and sign, but the agents did not ask his father to cosign, despite the fact that the player was only twenty years old at the time.

Harmon testified that Bloom offered him $1,500 to set up a meeting with Iowa teammate Devon Mitchell, a defensive back, three months later. The meeting was set up, Mitchell signed, and Harmon was paid his finder's fee in $500 installments.

Harmon also testified that once early that season he looked up and saw Bloom inside the locker room. The player moved the agent outside. Bloom cutely showed him a letterhead from a New York hospital claiming to sponsor an All-American team—that's how the agent got access to the Iowa locker room, Harmon testified.

Pearl then introduced all the paperwork that Harmon falsely signed and certified in order to play football that season and receive his scholarship. These exhibits, neatly placed in thick black binders divided by the alphabet, were examined by the jury, along with the promissory note and representation contract that Harmon had signed with Walters and Bloom. A copy of the taped transcript was also at the end of Harmon's exhibit file.

After almost two and a half hours on the stand, Harmon was finished with Howard Pearl's direct. Marovich called a lunch break and resumed at two o'clock. During the break, there was another conference among the lawyers in the judge's chambers. These conferences were generally used to establish ground rules, to argue the depth and breadth of direct testimony and cross-examination.

The jury was brought in again, as was Ronnie Harmon. Dan Webb stepped to the podium in the middle of the courtroom with a notepad and some other papers.

Webb started politely, "Good afternoon, Mr. Harmon. My name is Dan Webb, and I represent Lloyd Bloom."

Webb began by getting Harmon to admit that he signed of his own free will. Then Webb started asking about Harmon's taking some $54,000 over fifteen months, and Harmon seemed agitated.

"They offered, I didn't ask for it," Harmon replied. Suddenly he didn't seem shy. He was a football player with a chip on his shoulder.

Webb also dropped his nice-guy act. They started talking about Lloyd Bloom's negotiations with the Buffalo Bills and about how Harmon eventually signed a contract for $1.4 million.

"One-point-three million," Harmon corrected the defense lawyer.

"Oh, I'm sorry. You only got one-point-three million dollars," Webb responded with a touch of sarcasm.

Webb's intensity level seemed to jump. The jury also sat more erect, their eyes moving back and forth from Webb to Harmon, as if they were watching a tennis match. Webb asked Harmon about switching agents after Bloom had already begun negotiations. Webb's voice bounced off the walls.

"You didn't have the decency to call him yourself."

Webb got back to the $54,000. He started breaking down the payments—$2,500 here, $3,000 there, $5,000 here, $32,500 for a Mercedes. Suddenly Webb looked up at Harmon and raised his voice.

"You took the famous Norby Walters to the cleaners, didn't you?" Webb asked incredulously.

"How can I take him to the cleaners?" Harmon shot back defiantly.

The prosecution table looked nervous.

"You made a profit of forty-nine thousand dollars, didn't you?" Webb asked, pointing out that Harmon didn't pay back the agent.

"He said he was gambling on me," Harmon said.

"He was gambling on you to be fair and not stiff him at the last minute," Webb countered.

"What do you mean stiff?"

"Didn't you end up with forty-nine thousand dollars?"

Harmon went quiet. Webb asked him about the tape and wanted to know if the player had set up Norby Walters. No, replied Harmon. Webb stared at him. Beaver Cleaver had left the courtroom.

Suddenly Webb shifted his tone, speaking softly again. He asked Harmon about his signing a letter of intent on February 10, 1985, and asked the player what he received. Room, board, tuition, and books were his only compensation, right? Right.

Webb asked Harmon about the hours a week it took to play football.

"You feel you earned your scholarship, didn't you?" Webb asked.

"Yes."

"You were second-leading rusher in the nation before breaking your leg as a junior. . . . As a senior you took your teammates to the Rose Bowl, didn't you?" Webb asked.

"No, I didn't take them to the Rose Bowl."

Webb paused.

"Because of your success at Iowa, because of your team's success, you were aware that the university made millions of dollars, weren't you?"

Webb proceeded to get into Big Ten rules and whether a school would actually cancel a scholarship for a player who dealt early with an agent. Webb asked Harmon if he knew that the school would cancel his eligibility but not necessarily his scholarship. Valukas objected. There was a conference in the judge's chambers.

Webb next asked Harmon some questions about "loans" and "compensation," contending that Norby Walters has simply made a loan to Harmon and that loans were legal under NCAA rules. The contract he signed with WSE didn't kick in until January 2, right? Then Webb asked Harmon if he had ever discussed the eligibility forms he had to fill out with Norby Walters or Lloyd Bloom.

"No."

"When you signed that statement, it makes a point about bona fide loans. . . . When you got the loan from Norby Walters and Lloyd Bloom, that was a legal loan you were obligated to pay back, wasn't it?"

"Yes."

Webb paused for effect.

"Was it your plan to cheat or defraud the university out of a scholarship?" Webb asked the witness.

Harmon squirmed, and so did the prosecution team.

"No," Harmon said softly.

"What is it the university lost when you signed an agreement with Norby Walters?" Webb asked.

Valukas jumped to his feet. "Objection!"

"I don't know what they lost," Harmon said.

Valukas and Pearl got even more uncomfortable when Webb mentioned the magic word, "education." Webb wanted to talk about Harmon's fourth year in school, about meetings with the academic adviser, about a discussion when Ronnie Harmon was informed that he was "not working toward a degree."

Harmon said, "They never told me that."

Webb nodded his head. He almost smiled.

"Okay," the defense lawyer said with a hitch of his pants, "let me refresh your memory."

Webb had in his hands Ronnie Harmon's academic file, and the lawyer read the notation from the Iowa academic adviser, "Still not working toward degree—no one-hundred level this semester. He dropped all . . . encouraged him to take one-hundred level next semester. This semester is a disaster."

"Remember that?" Webb asked.

Harmon's memory was refreshed, sort of.

"I guess so."

Judge George Marovich raised his eyebrows.

"How close did you come to getting a degree?" Webb soon asked.

"Not close."

"And when you took your team to the Rose Bowl, you were aware of the millions of dollars in profit that the school made."

"Objection!"

"Sustained."

"Okay," Webb went on, "besides NCAA rules that state that a student-athlete should be working toward a degree, he also is required to be in good academic standing, right?"

Harmon squirmed again. Webb shuffled some papers in front of him.

"Let's take a look at your academic transcript. . . . Let's see, at the end of your first year, you had a one-point-six-two grade point average. . . . I see you were allowed to take a number of interesting courses . . . billiards . . . coaching basketball . . . bowling . . . soccer . . . coaching football . . ."

Webb noted that Harmon entered Iowa as a communications major.

"I wanted to take all my physical education courses," Harmon said.

"Get them out my way so I could start working toward an education."

"A one-point-six-one GPA is not very good."

"It's okay for me . . . maybe not by your standards."

Marovich raised his eyebrows again. George Randolph was staring down at the table in front of him.

Webb noted that Harmon had to take a summer school course to become eligible for football in 1982. He took Fundamentals of Military Organization. Harmon got an A in the course, which the player conceded that the school recommended. Webb noted that the class was full of football players and that a teammate, Devon Mitchell, got a B and four hours of credit.

Webb then noted that Harmon also got an A and one hour of credit every semester for "special conditioning in football."

Webb started rattling off Harmon's various grade point averages: 1.86, 1.80, 1.69, 1.82.

"Do you agree that NCAA rules state that you are no longer eligible when a student-athlete is not in good academic standing?"

"Yes."

"You weren't in good academic standing in May 1985, right?"

"Right."

"And that summer you needed to get eligible. . . . Let's see, you registered for an elementary Spanish course for four hours. . . . Ah, but you withdrew. . . . And you took watercolor painting for three hours."

Harmon continued to squirm as the prosecution table fought back red faces.

The best was yet to come.

"And you got a D for watercolor painting," Webb stated. "And you were still not in good academic standing."

The courtroom stirred. Marovich raised those eyebrows again.

"You played every football game of that 1985 season, is that correct?" Webb asked the witness.

"Yes."

"Were you aware that university officials and the Big Ten Conference certified you to be eligible and to play football and to play in the Rose Bowl?"

Of course Harmon was aware of that. Then Dan Webb asked Harmon about what happened after he played in the Rose Bowl.

"You registered for classes, but you withdrew from all but one— Social Work and Racism—didn't you?"

"Yes."

"Do you remember how many credit hours you had toward your major when you finished your career at Iowa?"

"I don't remember."

Webb was almost done. He asked Harmon about Iowa's investigation in March 1987 after the *Atlanta Constitution* article exposed his dealings with Walters and Bloom. Harmon acknowledged meeting with school officials.

"Did anyone tell you that you had cheated the university out of a scholarship?" Webb asked.

"No."

"When was the first time somebody told you the University of Iowa was the victim of a crime?"

Naturally it was when Harmon met with Howard Pearl, the bespectacled and clearly flustered Assistant U. S. Attorney.

Robert Gold, Walters's attorney, took a crack at Harmon, but the buzz at the end of the day was on Webb's damaging cross-examination.

Big Ten Conference attorney Byron Gregory, sitting in the courtroom, tried to huddle the media around to claim that Webb had viciously misrepresented Harmon's transcripts. Nobody was buying it. Nobody asked any questions about the tape of Norby Walters pitching how to cheat on taxes, how to "razzle-dazzle" the government, how to keep the big lie.

Down on the fifteenth floor, Tony Valukas huddled with a seething Howard Pearl and George Randolph. Nearby was Diane Benson, the FBI agent who had warned the prosecutors about Harmon's grades. She also had foreseen other problems with upcoming witnesses.

Randolph felt whipped. "Shit, there goes our case," he said, feeling a migraine coming on.

Gregory raced downstairs and protested to Pearl that the prosecutor had let Webb run all over Harmon. They discussed the transcripts.

The next morning, headlines in the Chicago newspapers read, HARMON WAS INELIGIBLE AT IOWA.

The government put Ronnie Harmon on the stand for a redirect. Pearl, more intense than the day before, got Harmon to testify about tutors and study halls and how serious Iowa was about his attending class and how the academic counselor once telephoned his parents. Harmon testified about how wrong he was to sign with agents. It just didn't carry much weight, however.

Webb got back up and again asked Harmon pointedly, "Did you

intend to cheat and defraud the University of Iowa out of a scholarship?"

"I don't think so."

Webb then went into Ronnie Harmon's pre-trial diversion agreement, which stated that he had "participated in a scheme to defraud" Iowa.

"You were told you would not be indicted if you signed this agreement, right?" Webb asked Harmon.

"It was my option to choose," the player answered.

"Well, either you lied to the jury about whether you cheated the university, or you lied when you signed this form," Webb snapped.

Marovich intervened. He clearly thought that Webb already had destroyed the witness. He was ready to stop the bout. TKO, Dan Webb. Somebody help Mr. Harmon from the witness stand, please.

Valukas, Pearl, and Randolph huddled over the damage that had been done. They had not planned on calling an Iowa school official at this stage, but the government felt compelled to put Iowa assistant athletic director Fred Mims on the stand to tell the jury that Harmon's real grade point average of 1.91 made him eligible for the 1985 season. But Webb easily shot holes in that contention, recalling NCAA rules that state the student-athlete must be "a degree-seeking student" at all times.

"Were you aware the athletic department was kind of bending the rules by keeping players eligible so they could play on Saturday afternoon?" Webb coyly asked Mims.

Mims replied, "Not at any time!"

Webb picked apart Harmon's transcript again, playing with that watercolor painting summer course. Mims kept fighting the lawyer, so Webb painstakingly took him through various steps and finally asked, "When the president of the university and the athletic director certified Ronnie Harmon as being eligible, were there people on the staff who stated that he was not working toward a degree?"

Mims replied softly, reluctantly, "Yes."

Webb had something else in store for Mims. It concerned the government's next witness, Iowa defensive back Devon Mitchell. Webb showed the jury that, believe it or not, Mitchell's grade transcripts were even more embarrassing than Harmon's.

Mitchell, a five-year player, was still 105 hours short of earning a degree by the end of his fourth year, Webb noted. The lawyer picked the transcript apart, and Mims left the witness stand battered and embarrassed.

Nevertheless, the government asked for more punishment by putting Devon Mitchell on the stand.

A Brooklyn native, Mitchell did tell the jury how Walters referred to himself as "the agent to the stars." This time, Walters and Bloom came to his house and in front of his family and a close family friend, Norby gave the big sales pitch again and then spread $2,000 on the living room table.

James Harris, the family friend, asked, "Isn't this illegal?" Mitchell testified.

"But Norby said, 'Yeah, it is, but we'll just postdate the contract and put it in a safe.'"

Mitchell's cross-examination would come on Thursday, March 9, but not before Dan Webb renewed his motion for severance of Bloom from Walters, specifically referring to the letter that New York sports attorney James Quinn penned about the agents "sullying" their firm by pursuing college-eligible athletes. Webb argued that the letter was damaging and that Bloom had not waived his attorney-client privilege. Marovich denied the motion again.

Devon Mitchell took the stand, and Dan Webb took to his feet. Webb started gently with Mitchell, who told the jury how he was married with one child prior to his senior season at Iowa. He testified that he needed the money "very much so."

"Your only compensation at Iowa was a scholarship. . . . It's pretty hard to support a family under those terms."

"Objection!" Valukas jumped to his feet. Sustained.

Webb asked Mitchell about his academic courses, but he was much more compassionate with this Iowa player than Harmon. Mitchell spoke with a sincerity in his voice when he told the jury, "My priority was playing football. . . . In order to play football, I have to go to class and remain eligible. Ever since I was a little boy I wanted to play football. But you have to go to college. You can't go to the pros out of high school. . . . It's the only way."

Webb also scored points when he asked Mitchell if the FBI had told him on May 17, 1987, that he was being charged with a crime.

"No."

Webb explored the government's threat to prosecute the player and the subsequent pre-trial diversion agreement.

"Did you want to plead guilty to mail fraud?"

"In my opinion, I didn't think I was guilty."

"When you entered into the agreement with Walters and Bloom, were you planning to cheat the university out of a scholarship?" Webb asked.

"Objection!"

"Judge," Webb said, "I have to establish whether there was criminal intent."

Overruled.

"Like I said," said Mitchell, "I didn't feel like I was cheating. . . . In my opinion, I was just borrowing against my future."

At the defense table Norby Walters nodded approvingly.

"You put that money to good use for your family, didn't you?" Webb asked.

"Yes."

Soon Webb got Mitchell to admit he had borrowed a car from an Iowa booster during his sophomore and junior seasons. This struck a nerve with Mitchell, who asked Webb, "You got a problem with that?"

"I thought NCAA rules say you can't accept gifts."

"I didn't take a gift," said Mitchell. "I borrowed a car."

Mitchell left the stand, and he was followed by Rod Woodson, the former Purdue star defensive back and number-one pick of the Pittsburgh Steelers. Valukas took the direct with Woodson, and the two told the familiar story of Norby Walters and Lloyd Bloom doing their thing.

"Norby had four thousand dollars in hundred-dollar bills in an envelope. . . . He laid it on a coffee table and said that if I signed, I could have it now," Woodson told the jury.

Woodson signed, continued to receive payments, and got a car in which the title was in his grandmother's name. He said that Purdue coach Leon Burtnett asked him about the car, and Woodson said he told him that his grandmother got it for him for his senior year.

"Was that a lie?"

"Yes," Woodson said.

Valukas also asked Woodson about whether he lied to FBI agents in April 1987 when he was questioned.

"No, I did not lie, but at the time I had no idea what was going on. I told them partly what happened, but not everything."

Valukas was almost finished when he had Woodson admit that he had been arrested once for shoplifting and again for charging telephone calls to another number. He did forty hours of community service and paid the phone bill of about $600.

Valukas sat down. Webb had his tall, lanky associate, Steve Molo, continue to flush out Woodson's past, which included a conviction for petty theft. Molo's style was not unlike Webb's—he was polite in the beginning, he spoke in a relatively loud volume, and he casually set up his witness for the kill after mentioning three run-ins with the law that Woodson had, including stealing the money from a bartender's tip jar.

"And what was your major at Purdue?" Molo asked.

"Criminal Justice."

Marovich stared at the gallery, where snickers could be heard among the spectators.

Molo started to review Woodson's transcripts, but Valukas cut him off and objected, saying, "He's misreading the transcript."

Marovich was irritated. He said, "I am not getting off this bench for one more sidebar to explore areas we have covered."

Molo was asking Woodson to review his own transcript, and the player inadvertently said, "I don't even know how to read this thing, to be honest."

After running through it, Molo stopped and asked Woodson, "Rod, you played your heart out for your school, didn't you?"

Woodson made a face that indicated how stupid he thought the question was and looked at Molo. In an unmistakably sarcastic tone he said, "Yeaahh."

Molo asked Woodson if Howard Pearl wanted him to plead guilty to mail fraud.

"Yes."

"Did you think you were guilty?"

"We didn't understand what was going on, how they got mail fraud out of it."

The members of the prosecution table tried to look cool, but they were burning.

The government needed help. As Valukas would later say, "I knew Webb had scored some very big points and had turned the table on us out of the box."

Former Michigan running back Robert Perryman, then with the New England Patriots, would salvage part of the opening week when he took the stand. Howard Pearl scored when he asked Perryman about the day he signed with Walters and Bloom, and whether they discussed Michigan coach Bob Schembechler. The player was very articulate and cocksure.

"Lloyd knew what kind of coach Bo was," Perryman testified.

"Tell us what would have happened if Coach Schembechler had found out," Pearl asked.

"I told Lloyd that if Bo ever found out, I'd lose my scholarship," Perryman replied.

This was big and in direct conflict with Webb's contention that players would not necessarily lose their scholarships. Perryman's next response was bigger.

"[Bloom] knew we had to fill out forms," Perryman said.

"Why did he know?" Pearl asked.

"Because I told him."

"What did he say?"

"He said there'd be no problem."

If the government had established nothing else this week, they established that Lloyd Bloom knew that the players had to sign certification forms. It was in direct conflict with the defense's pre-trial motions and defense strategy that the agents had had no knowledge of the complex eligibility forms. Perryman's testimony had just raised the agents' culpability.

Pearl also asked Perryman about what had happened in March 1987 when the player received a message to see Schembechler, who was responding to an inquiry by an Atlanta reporter. Perryman told the jurors he decided to call Lloyd Bloom before he called the coach.

"I asked Lloyd, 'What should I do?' Lloyd told me to stick with our story. . . . I didn't have any more ties to Bo, so I didn't have to tell him the truth."

When Schembechler confronted Perryman, the player told the jurors he denied signing with Walters and Bloom.

Perryman was also around the athletic office when Schembechler confronted teammate Garland Rivers, "yelling at the top of his voice."

Bloom tried calling Schembechler directly to clear the players, Perryman testified. Bo declined to talk to him. But soon Perryman had a problem with the agents when he refused to sign a new contract.

"Then Bloom pointed out that I had just played in the 1987 Rose Bowl and that he would incriminate my name with the Big Ten."

Many jurors looked across the room at Lloyd Bloom, whose reddish face still looked as if it was ready to burst.

Webb let his youngest associate, George Lombardi, take a crack at Perryman. Lombardi, fair-haired with eyeglasses, had many of Webb's mannerisms, but he sounded exactly like Jimmy Stewart.

When Lombardi tried to bring Perryman down for reneging on his contract with the agents, Perryman got feisty. "This is America. You can fire anybody you want. . . . I've never known a lifetime contract in America."

Then suddenly Perryman was asking Lombardi a question, "Okay, answer this—"

Marovich jumped in, "Hold the phone. We're getting our roles confused."

Lombardi asked succinctly, "Have you paid back the money you borrowed from Norby Walters and Lloyd Bloom?"

"No, I haven't paid them back."

Lombardi then moved to the FBI's interview with him in June 1987.

"Did you answer them honestly?" Lombardi asked.

"I didn't have to," Perryman said.

If looks could kill, George Randolph would have had to answer for the homicide of Robert Perryman on the spot.

Lombardi also tried to get Perryman to talk about how football was a "first priority" and how it was a dream come true when he was drafted by the New England Patriots.

"Actually," Perryman answered, "I didn't want to play in New England, to tell you the truth."

Lombardi sat down, but Robert Gold's associate, Ethan Levin-Epstein, wanted to ask Perryman a few more questions. Levin-Epstein wanted to explore the government's scheme to make criminals out of the players for breaking NCAA rules. The attorney asked Perryman about George Randolph and conversations he might have had about his criminality.

"I remember George Randolph, but I talked to him so many times, I can't remember."

Perryman finally said, "I don't know if I committed a crime at all. . . . You talk about crimes as if I sold drugs. But as far as I know, I broke NCAA rules, until Mr. Pearl told me I had committed a crime. To tell you the truth, I wasn't scared because I didn't know it was a serious crime."

Robert Perryman left the witness stand, and the prosecution team didn't know whether to hug him or slug him.

At this stage Howard Pearl and George Randolph were barely talking to each other. Pearl occasionally would turn and whisper to Randolph to "look confident, sit up straight, get rid of the hangdog look." The prosecutor did not want the jury to see the government's battered face.

"I felt as if we had almost lost George during the trial," Pearl said. "He had been so pumped up, and then the Iowa shit hit the fan. I knew the wonders of Webb . . . it can demoralize you. And there was no question that we went through a period of demoralization."

Randolph finally told Pearl, "We're blowing the fucking case."

Valukas got the government team together. It was time to call an audible.

"We have to get Franzese on the stand now," the U. S. Attorney said. The weekend couldn't have come at a better time.

17

THAT WEEKEND, after the blows delivered by Dan Webb, the tension was almost unbearable for the government.

Tony Valukas was a nail biter, and he was down to the nubs on his fingertips. The U. S. Attorney still thought that Michael Franzese could pull a fast one and bail out. Or Franzese could get stage fright; he could come unglued and unravel on the witness stand.

If Franzese did unravel, there was always the chance he would start mixing the truth on Norby Walters with lies about organized crime associates that he wanted to protect. If the defense could prove he was lying out of one side of his mouth, it could raise a reasonable doubt about whether he was lying out of the other side.

"We were going against some of the best lawyers in the world," Valukas recalls.

The U. S. Attorney wanted Franzese thoroughly prepared for the week ahead of him. It would be a grueling experience. During a scheduling session, Robert Gold told the court he expected to have Franzese on the stand "for at least three days." He had spent most of the previous two months, using his resources as a former federal prosecutor in New York, to prepare for Franzese.

Gold already had announced his intentions to the jury—he would show that Michael Franzese was a "slick, cunning, lying con man."

Valukas assigned his number-one assistant, Joe Duffy, to cross-examine Michael Franzese in rehearsals. Duffy not only excelled as a trial lawyer, he was a big, intimidating Irishman.

Valukas felt confident that if Franzese could stand up to Duffy, he could stand up to anyone. Duffy was given the entire Franzese file and spent two weeks preparing for this dress rehearsal. Valukas wanted to see if Duffy could unnerve the Mafia boss.

Duffy said, "I probably spoke to Michael Franzese like he had never been spoken to, and treated like he had never been treated. Tony put no restrictions on me. I went as aggressively after this guy as I could. I was as insulting as I could be. Quite frankly, I used a few tactics that never would have been admissible in court, so he had to be prepared for the worst.

"Michael had no advance notice of how I was going to treat him. I think at first he was arrogant. He was taken aback. The first day he just wasn't ready for me. I made him sit at the conference table, and I said, 'You're going to act like you're in a courtroom.' It was just the two of us alone in the room. I pointed my finger in his face. I screamed at him. The first few times, you could see him squeezing his hands, like he wanted to jump up himself and respond to me verbally.

"The next day he was much better. Then he impressed me; he asked me if I could fit a third day into my schedule. On the third day he was excellent. I crossed him on everything, about his organized crime past, his associates, his finances, his families, his own family relations, adultery—areas that were quite sensitive. It was not only humiliating, it was brutal. I used every tool I knew to get under his skin."

"It was very, very tough," said Franzese. "It hurt so bad. The word *informer* was very distasteful to me. It was so difficult. He asked me straight out if I was a government informant, and honestly, I had never considered myself that. It was the first time I had to come to grips with what was happening."

Duffy ridiculed Franzese. He grilled him about the initial confusion on whether Ron Weisner or Joe Grant represented the Jacksons. Duffy crossed Franzese to exhaustion.

"When we were done, I was impressed with him. I was impressed with his intelligence and his quick study. I'm not sure I've ever seen a mob guy as sharp. After we were done, we talked about his facial appearance, his demeanor, how to dress, how to respond. I told Tony he was going to be a great witness. I didn't get to see him testify, but when he was done, he came down to thank me. A very interesting guy. Very bright."

CAMMY FRANZESE, along with their two daughters, joined her husband to give him moral support. Cammy was a born-again Christian and was slowly converting Michael.

On Sunday, March 11, Michael Franzese asked his FBI guards to take him to church, where he could pray before taking this huge step in his life. George Randolph wasn't around; he was meeting with Ron Weisner and Notre Dame players Alvin Miller and Robert Banks at the U. S. Attorney's office. The FBI agents obliged Michael Franzese and drove the family to the church.

During the service Franzese's two young daughters got the spirit. They started singing. They jumped into the aisles and danced. When the pastor took the pulpit, he clearly had noticed the disruption where the Franzeses were sitting near the front.

"Sometimes," the pastor tried to say as nicely as he could, "it's difficult to compete with the young ones."

The sermon began, but before too long the Franzese girls were at it again. They were happy to be around their daddy again, but the church members were not happy. An usher finally came forward and told Franzese that if he could not control his children, then it might be best to leave. The FBI agents sitting behind the Mafia don got nervous. One tapped him on the shoulder.

"Come on, let's get out of here," the agent told Franzese.

It was a sight. The family got up to leave in the middle of the sermon, and two men in dark, conservative suits followed them out. The unknowing congregation kept their eyes on the strange scene. Franzese had some final words with the usher who had suggested they head for the exit, and pretty soon the words became heated. The FBI agents grabbed the Mafia captain and escorted him to the car.

"You did what?"

George Randolph was back at the hotel Sunday night, hearing the story from the FBI agents. He couldn't believe they had let Franzese talk them into taking him to a public church on the eve of his testimony.

"Don't you know the word *NO?*" Randolph asked his partners. "Tell him he can get religion after the trial."

Then the FBI agent turned his attention to Franzese.

"You asshole, you're really pushing it," Randolph told him. "Don't be pulling this shit anymore."

ON MONDAY, March 14, one of the jurors reported to the court that she had sprained an ankle over the weekend, but as Marovich told spectators, "she has agreed to play hurt."

Norby Walters had gotten a haircut and was looking dapper. Lloyd

Bloom was looking better. The media reports of the first week's trial had lifted their spirits. The public focus had been shifted to the disgraceful revelations about Ronnie Harmon and Devon Mitchell, and the government was on the defensive.

Norby Walters turned around to the front row of media people and said, "Isn't Dan Webb something?"

The jury was brought into the courtroom in an orderly fashion, the last member the young lady with the sprained ankle. She had it heavily wrapped, so they positioned her on the front end, near the witness box, and allowed her to prop up the foot.

Court was in session, and Ron Weisner, entertainment manager, walked to the witness stand. He was sharply dressed in a gray suit. He had long black hair combed straight back. Howard Pearl handled the direct.

Weisner told the jury that he had been in the music business for twenty years. He currently managed such stars as Paul McCartney, Steve Winwood, Rick Springfield, and Robbie Nevil. Past clients included Madonna, the Jacksons, and Michael Jackson.

Pearl went deeper into Weisner's background as the manager told the jury he was employed fifteen to twenty years ago by Buddah Records in New York in promotions, marketing, and sales.

"Did you know a man by the name of Sonny Franzese?" Pearl asked.

"Objection!" This time Gold was on his feet. Marovich overruled the objection and allowed the question.

"I knew the name," Weisner said. "I heard his name through various means. I'd see him around the office a few times."

Pearl asked about Michael Franzese. Weisner said he also had seen Michael Franzese a few times.

The prosecutor then asked the witness, "Did you become aware of Michael Franzese's reputation?"

Gold objected, and both sides left the courtroom for a sidebar with Marovich. Back in court, Pearl was allowed to explore the area, but this time asked first about Sonny Franzese and then Michael Franzese.

"I knew they were involved in organized crime," Weisner said.

Of course Weisner was there to testify about the threats that Michael Franzese had made on behalf of Norby Walters relating to the Jacksons, so Pearl advanced him several years. Pearl had Weisner clarify that he and partner Fred DeMann managed "the day-to-day operations" of the Jacksons while Joe Jackson, the group's father, also served as a manager.

Weisner testified how Walters had been the booking agent for the group, which was trying to revive its popularity. It was the fall of 1980, and Walters wanted to start booking dates. Weisner testified that the group decided not only that it wasn't ready for a tour—maybe 1981 would be better—but that the Jacksons "didn't want to be involved with Norby."

Weisner testified that in early 1981 Walters called and set up a meeting in Los Angeles, expressing interest again in doing the tour. But the group had hired another booking agent, Howard Rose, and Weisner informed Walters again that the group wasn't interested in him.

Weisner proceeded to tell the jury about the day he was paid a visit by Norby Walters and an "associate" who was Michael Franzese, along with another man he did not know.

"Norby introduced Michael Franzese . . . and asked if I remembered him from New York. . . . I knew the name. . . . He was involved in organized crime. . . . Norby Walters left, and Michael Franzese and the other man stayed."

Weisner told the jury that Franzese had a "very serious" talk with Weisner about using Walters as the booking agent on the tour or there "might not be a tour."

"It was threatening. . . . The point came across," Weisner testified. "In one respect I was scared, but in another I didn't want to give in to them."

Weisner said that Franzese followed up with several telephone calls, as did Walters. Weisner simply asked the group if it wanted to reconsider but testified that "they didn't want to pursue" an arrangement with Norby Walters.

Weisner testified that he notified Bill Bray, head of the group's security, about the threat. The tour went on but avoided Long Island's Nassau Coliseum.

Gold cross-examined Weisner and got the manager to admit that he and Joe Jackson did not get along very well. Weisner conceded that Joe Jackson was in favor of Walters promoting the tour and in fact hired Walters as a "consultant" in May 1980. Gold submitted correspondence as exhibits, including a letter Weisner had written to Joe Jackson, claiming, "This is what we are paid for."

Gold then asked, "Two weeks later, on June 9, 1980, isn't it true that Michael Jackson approved Norby Walters as a consultant and as the booking agent?"

"No," Weisner responded.

There was further dispute over that fact, then Gold shifted to another alleged meeting that year in which there was a discussion about Michael Franzese producing a musical based on the Dead End Kids movies, with the Jacksons in starring roles.

"No," Weisner answered, disputing that that had been the subject discussed at that meeting.

The cross-examination soon ended, but not before Gold tried to make a point that Weisner was hardly intimidated by Franzese because there were no extraordinary security measures taken for the subsequent tour.

But Howard Pearl was then able to ask Weisner on redirect about the apparent surveillance that led to Los Angeles police officials and the FBI questioning him about Franzese's meeting.

Dan Webb was brief in a comical stint with Weisner. He asked if the manager knew Lloyd Bloom.

"Who?"

Webb then pointed to Bloom and said, "This man right here."

"Never seen him before," Weisner said.

Webb then asked if "Mr. Fran-cuuzee" ever mentioned Lloyd Bloom. "No."

Weisner was a solid witness for the government and at the very least established a connection between Walters and Franzese.

There was still time left on Monday—it had been anticipated that Weisner might take up the entire day—so the government decided to call in succession two Notre Dame players, Alvin Miller and Robert Banks.

Miller gave the jury the same basic story the other players had about meeting the "agent to the stars." But there was a different twist because Miller testified that immediately after he signed at the Marriott in South Bend on February 11, 1986, he called Norby Walters and asked him "to please take back the money and the contract." Walters refused. Miller told his mother what happened, and she threatened "to tell Coach Holtz what happened." Miller again called Walters to try to back out of the deal, but the hotel informed the Notre Dame receiver that the agent had checked out.

Dan Webb established that Alvin Miller had once been the nation's hottest high school star but that his college career had been hampered by injuries. He was one of eleven children. When his father passed away, Miller admitted asking Walters for extra money, and Walters sent it. Miller also said he wanted to help one of his sisters financially.

Webb then asked about the time Notre Dame coach Lou Holtz had inquired about rumors. This was a mistake because Miller told the jury, "Coach Holtz more or less asked, 'Are you involved with gamblers?' "

Eventually Holtz learned the truth, and Miller was able to gracefully end his career, citing his knee injury as the cause.

Webb then started probing in the area of the certification forms and the scholarship benefits.

"Did anybody come to you and say, 'Because you have violated NCAA rules, we are terminating your scholarship and pay?' " Webb asked Miller.

"No."

The next several questions raised several objections as Pearl fought to keep Webb from gaining momentum in this area.

"Time out," Marovich finally called. "Do we need a referee with a whistle?"

Miller also admitted, "I never planned on cheating or hurting anyone." He was most remorseful. The cross-examination ended.

Miller walked out of the courtroom. In the hall, he bumped into the next witness, Father Theodore Hesburgh, unquestionably the most revered authority at Notre Dame. Miller tried to say something to him but broke down sobbing. Hesburgh consoled him before being escorted into the hushed courtroom as the next witness. Father Hesburgh, wearing the collar, was a picture of glory. His angelic white hair only enhanced his aura.

The clerk of the court swore in Father Hesburgh and spoke the words, "So help you God?"

A spectator whispered, "That is God."

Tony Valukas accepted the honor of directing Hesburgh, who apologized for having the flu. He looked around the courtroom and said, "So everybody stay away."

Valukas established Hesburgh's credentials, as if it were necessary. He was now president emeritus and chair of the five Notre Dame institutes. He had been the active university president for thirty-five years, from 1952 to 1987. He held 115 honorary degrees.

Hesburgh told the jury that the school received eighty-five thousand to one hundred thousand applications per year and that only eighteen hundred were accepted. Valukas very simply wanted to know from Hesburgh what would have happened if the university had found out that two players had signed with an agent. Naturally, the school would have revoked their scholarships, Hesburgh said.

Valukas left it at that. The Man had spoken.

Dan Webb very politely and reverently started inquiring of Hesburgh about NCAA rules and whether the rules required that scholarships be revoked in such a case. Hesburgh didn't really care about the NCAA rules. The scholarships would be revoked.

"That action would be taken based on our own rules at the university, which are more important and which I happened to have written. . . . I can't even remember a case like this," Hesburgh said.

The smiles at the prosecution table were evident.

Webb pushed on and was able to show that Hesburgh was unfamiliar with specific actions regarding NCAA rules. Then Webb asked about Notre Dame players taking all-expense-paid trips to Miami for the *Playboy* magazine All-America teams. (These trips had been approved by the NCAA.)

"I don't know. . . . I don't even read *Playboy* magazine," Hesburgh said.

The courtroom and jury laughed. Webb smiled and nodded his head. He started to press on, but Hesburgh interrupted.

"Let me say one thing flat out: I never in all my years ever had a scintilla of doubt that if the university knew that rules were being broken, then we would take action immediately."

Hesburgh finished shortly. It didn't matter whether he was confused about NCAA rules. His message got across: Right is right, wrong is wrong.

But then something happened that almost made the prosecution fall out of their chairs.

The juror with the sprained ankle leaned over and asked Father Hesburgh for a "blessing."

"That's all we need . . . a mistrial," Randolph said later.

The afternoon was getting late, but there was time for one final witness that Monday. It was Robert Banks, the other Notre Dame player who signed for $5,000 in cash prior to his senior season in 1986.

Matthew Kennelly had a brief, effective cross-examination of Banks from the standpoint of giving the jury another picture of what it was like to be a college football player. Banks explained how, between his junior and senior seasons, he was asked to switch from linebacker to defensive tackle and therefore had to "put on more weight." His clothes didn't fit anymore.

"I didn't have enough money to buy new clothes," Banks testified.

The day ended with the attorneys arguing in the judge's chambers, which by now had become routine and somewhat in line with most courtroom procedures during a trial as combative as this one.

Specifically, Robert Gold wanted more material from the government on Franzese's bad acts. They talked about Franzese's "use immunity" and his previous deals with New York prosecutors. Gold wanted information on any homicides Franzese may have been involved in. It was also pointed out that "six or seven" lawyers from the New York crime families were expected to be present when Franzese took the stand.

Marovich finally warned the lawyers, "We are not having a murder trial in this courtroom for Michael Franzese."

It was the eve of the big day. Both sides were anxious, and both sides knew the repercussions of the next witness. The case could be won or lost with Michael Franzese.

It was a sleepless night for Franzese. What he was about to do was break the Mafia oath. More than that, he would become the highest-ranking member of the New York crime families to ever testify as a government witness at a federal trial.

Tony Valukas asked Franzese again if he wanted to enter the Federal Witness Protection Program. Franzese refused. It puzzled the prosecutors, and it continues to puzzle New York federal enforcement authorities.

Franzese explained why he turned down Valukas: "I would never do it. . . . I could never do this and go into the program. Number one, I'm trying to straighten out my life, and the program never straightened anything out, from what I know of the program. I'm not giving up my life. Second of all, if I go into the program—to me, that's like an admission that I'm doing something wrong and going into hiding. Quite honestly, without being a hero or a martyr, I'd rather take my chances on the street. If something happens, it happens. At least I know inside that I felt okay about it. You do this and you go into the program, the guilt never goes away."

Michael Franzese arose early that morning, showered, shaved, and dressed in a conservative blue suit. Randolph had had FBI agents take Franzese shopping for a new suit the week before. Pat Buckley, an agent who was fascinated with the organized crime figure, had wanted Franzese to looked the part of a gangster. He talked about one of those pinstriped suits. Franzese wanted a double-breasted outfit.

"Don't screw around," Randolph instructed. "Nice, conservative, not too expensive."

Franzese met with Tony Valukas that morning at the Dirksen Federal Building. Security was very high. Randolph wanted Franzese to continue to wear his bulletproof vest. The FBI agent figured that if defense lawyers tried to show that Michael Franzese wasn't such a big deal and questioned security, then the Mafia boss could always whip off his shirt and show the vest. Franzese insisted that he not wear it that day. He wanted to be comfortable.

Franzese was led into a special witness holding area, connected directly to the courtroom on the opposite side of the jury box. FBI agents covered every door to the courtroom. They were wired with tiny earphones, not unlike the Secret Service. Nobody smiled. There was a special table set up where Justice Department officials would sit. The metal detectors were at the highest sensitivity downstairs at the courthouse entrance.

If nothing else, the security measures would leave the jury members feeling that this was no ordinary day in court.

A crowd of spectators arrived earlier than normal, still buzzing about Father Hesburgh's appearance the day before. There would be a line to get into the courtroom. There were new faces in the crowd. Men in gray suits—lawyers rumored to represent the five crime families of New York. The New York *Daily News* sent its star organized crime reporter, Jerry Capeci.

Irene Walters, Norby's wife, arrived for this day. She was nervous and shaken.

"I can't believe Michael is going to do this," she told a couple of reporters. "We've known him since he was this high." Petite in size, she put her hand at the level of her knees. Perhaps she did not understand that she was telling the reporters they had had a lifelong relationship with Franzese.

U. S. District Judge George M. Marovich entered the packed courthouse, and everyone rose.

There was a discussion between Tony Valukas and Dan Webb, who the day before had renewed his motion for severance, this time in light of the fact that the racketeering conspiracy charges began in 1981, three years before Bloom joined Walters. Nevertheless, Marovich cited precedent that Bloom was accountable for joining the conspiracy.

But Valukas, Webb, and Marovich then discussed whether there should be a "limiting instruction" to the jury regarding Franzese's testimony on his relationship with Norby Walters prior to 1981.

Moments later, at 10:17 A.M., Marovich said, "Let's have the jury."

"Bring out Mr. Franzese," Valukas said.

The door to the side of the courtroom swung open, and Michael Franzese, conservatively attired and wearing glasses, was led to the witness stand. The jury was then brought in. The courtroom had never

been so quiet. Some of the jurors glanced around the courtroom. It was
different. Everything about it felt different. The defense table also had a
new look. Whereas Lloyd Bloom had always sat in the middle, facing the
jury, he was now at the far end of the table, his back to the judge and
witness stand. His chair and body were tightly pressed against the table,
as if he were trying to disappear under it.

"Please be seated. Good morning. . . . Mr. Witness, will you be
sworn," Marovich said.

Franzese raised his right arm and was sworn.

George Randolph looked around the courtroom. He had been told
this day would never come.

Marovich then spoke to the jury. ". . . You are about to hear testimony
from Mr. Franzese, and that testimony concerning the nature and scope
of the relationship between Mr. Walters and Mr. Franzese prior to 1981
is offered against Mr. Walters only and should not be considered by you
for any purpose against Mr. Bloom."

Marovich turned over the court to Tony Valukas. The U. S. Attorney
had already decided he was going to have a precise direct. He would not
steer away from the allegations in the indictment. He also would not ask
Franzese about the potential of the gambling and point-shaving operation because Franzese had not had specific discussions with Norby Walters about it. In Valukas's mind, to raise it on direct could cause a
mistrial.

Tony Valukas was not going to get into that aspect of the mob and
college sports; he would wait for the defense to give him the opening.
Franzese could be on the witness stand for the rest of the week, which
would give the prosecution and the witness plenty of time to raise it. One
slip by the defense, and Franzese likely would jump on it himself.

Valukas methodically took Franzese through his biographical data:
thirty-seven years old, married, five children, three by a first marriage.
His father's name was John Franzese.

"Does he have a nickname?" Valukas asked.

"Yes."

"What is that?"

"Sonny."

The jury learned that Franzese went to Holy Cross High School in
Flushing, New York. He graduated in 1969 and attended Hofstra Uni-
versity as a biology major, premed student. He left school in 1972.
Franzese appeared relaxed, confident, but had been asked to speak

directly into the microphone after Gold complained that he "can barely hear."

Valukas asked, "Mr. Franzese, from the period of time 1973 through 1986, were you associated with any organized crime family?"

"Yes."

"And which family was that?"

"Colombo family in New York."

"And did there come a time when you held a supervisory position within that organized crime family?"

"Yes."

"And what was that position that you held?"

Some of the men in gray suits were taking notes in the audience.

"I was a captain in the family," Franzese said.

"Mr. Franzese," Valukas asked, "are you familiar with your father's public reputation for association with organized crime?"

"Yes, I am."

It was established that Sonny Franzese also was a captain in the Colombo crime family.

Then Valukas asked, "Do you know a person by the name of Norby Walters?"

"Yes, I do."

"And do you see that person in the courtroom?"

Before Franzese could point, Robert Gold stood up and said, "We will stipulate to the identification."

Valukas asked Franzese how long he had known Norby Walters.

"Just about all my life."

The relationship from 1972 to 1986?

"I had both a social and a business relationship with him."

Did his father have a relationship with Norby Walters?

"He also had a social as well as a business relationship with him."

Valukas took Franzese through his indictment and conviction on racketeering and fraud, his plea agreement, his ten-year prison sentence, and his fine and restitution amounting to $14,783,000.

Then Valukas, speaking of the agreement with the New York office, got the jury's attention when he said, "In connection with this agreement, was it further your understanding that if a matter was then under investigation by any of these agencies with the exception of murder, that you could not and would not be prosecuted for that matter?"

"That's correct."

"And did they also state that they had no evidence that you in fact were involved in murder?"

"That's correct."

Valukas went through the second agreement made with the Brooklyn Strike Force in November 1986, and Valukas established that nothing in the previous agreements had to do with the U. S. Attorney's office in Chicago.

Valukas covered other crimes Franzese admitted he was involved in: loan-sharking, labor racketeering, theft of securities, and mail fraud.

Valukas moved on to the proffer Franzese first signed with his office on December 4, 1987. Valukas established that other than obtaining truthful testimony there "were no other agreements."

Then Valukas referred to the agreement and immunity order he had signed on April 5, 1988. He further established that any recommendation for reduction in Franzese's sentence had to be made by the Brooklyn Task Force chief Ed McDonald and that the recommendation by Mc-Donald for his cooperation in this case was a reduction of one year, or twenty-eight days on the basis of parole.

Valukas then asked Franzese about the agreement that had brought him to the stand that day against Norby Walters.

"It's my understanding," said Franzese, "that my testimony cannot be used against me in any subsequent proceedings. However, again, anything from independent sources can be used against me in subsequent proceedings."

"Meaning you could be prosecuted for the crime to which you are testifying . . . its leads could be used against you?" Valukas asked.

Gold said, "I object. . . . It's a leading question."

"It's like getting the toothpaste back into the tube, isn't it?" Judge Marovich asked.

"I couldn't agree with you more," Gold said.

Valukas established that the one crime regarding Franzese's testimony that could be used against him was perjury.

Valukas then showed the ladies and the gentlemen of the jury that Franzese in fact had committed perjury at a detention hearing before a federal judge when he denied he was involved in loan-sharking.

"And when you lied about other organized crime associates, would you tell the ladies and gentlemen of the jury what we are talking about?" Valukas asked.

"There were other associates of mine in the family that I didn't feel I was at liberty to talk about, and I denied knowing them."

Randolph felt good about what was happening in the courtroom. Proud, too. He had prepared Valukas well.

Back to the business of Norby Walters, Franzese talked about the social relationship he and his father had with Norby Walters.

"We often ate together, we vacationed together," Franzese testified.

There was testimony about Sonny Franzese and Buddah Records.

"Was [his name] on any of the records?" Valukas asked.

"I don't believe so, no."

There were some smiles in the courtroom.

Franzese then testified how his father was sentenced to prison for fifty years and how Walters kept meeting his obligation by paying Joe Broncato, and eventually Michael Franzese himself. The payments continued on a weekly or monthly basis, Franzese testified. The money was usually delivered at meetings at Norby's offices or at the Stage Deli in Manhattan.

Then Franzese told the jury how, from 1975 to 1979, he performed services for Norby Walters: "Norby was the agent for many groups, rock groups on Long Island, Manhattan, and New Jersey. Quite often he would have problems with various clubs and various club owners whereby they would not want to accept his act or they wouldn't want him as the agent for the club. Oftentimes these other club owners were associated with other organized crime members, and oftentimes I would sit down and resolve disputes with him and other members of the family when they arose."

Valukas asked Michael Franzese about the time his father was paroled in 1979. He talked about the dispute over the revenue split and how "at the end of the meeting it was resolved and decided they were fifty-fifty partners."

Valukas let that sit with the jury for a few seconds, which seemed longer. Michael Franzese told the story just as Randolph had heard it. It sounded exactly like something out of *The Godfather*. And if Sonny Franzese was the godfather, then Michael Franzese very much looked and sounded like Michael Corleone.

They had other discussions that day, Franzese testified, about "various ways that money could be generated through the agency."

Franzese proceeded to move away from that meeting and mesmerized the courtroom with explicit testimony about his threats on behalf of Norby Walters to the managers of the Jacksons, Dionne Warwick, and the New Edition.

The jury listened intently to each and every alleged incident. They studied Franzese, who was precise, without hesitation, so believable. Norby Walters was busy whispering to Robert Gold during much of the testimony.

Valukas moved on to late 1984, and Franzese told the jury that Walters approached him about the sports agency business. They had a subsequent meeting.

"Norby . . . explained to me at that time he would be using cash to sign a lot of these athletes, and he asked me at that time to participate on a cash basis."

"What did he ask for?" Valukas asked.

"Fifty thousand dollars."

"And what, if anything, were you to receive in return for the fifty thousand dollars?

"Twenty-five percent of the business," said Franzese.

"Were you to perform any services in connection with this?" Valukas asked.

"I would continue to perform the service I had always performed for him, yes," Franzese explained.

Valukas advanced the conversation to the summer of 1985 and the time Franzese and his in-laws, Fred and Dino Garcia, paid Norby a visit. This was the day Franzese gave Norby his $50,000 cash, Franzese testified. He described who was at Norby's office that day. He named Lloyd Bloom. It was a first meeting. Franzese said that after the introduction, Bloom left the meeting. It seemed to surprise Dan Webb.

"Can you identify the Lloyd Bloom you met that day in the courtroom today?" Valukas asked.

Franzese looked over to the defense table. Walters was at one end, nearest the first row of spectators. Bloom was at the other end, his back to the judge and only an angle of him facing the witness. Bloom was stiff, like a mannequin. Franzese studied the defense table of eight men, including the six lawyers. Finally he pointed at Bloom and said, "I believe he's sitting with his back to me at the end of the table." Bloom's purple face turned sheet white.

"We will stipulate if he says he recognizes him," Webb said.

"Yes," Franzese said.

"That's fine," Webb said.

After Valukas got through this phase of his testimony, he turned to Marovich and said, "Your Honor, with the Court's permission, this might be an appropriate time to break."

Both sides apparently knew what this was about. The team of lawyers headed for the door to the judge's left, and Marovich held court in the hallway. Spectators in the court, as well as the jury, never heard what was being discussed.

It was about Kathy Clements.

Valukas told the judge that because the government had presented Jerry Zimmerman as an associate of Franzese, he wanted to expand on that relationship.

Valukas said, "After Mr. Franzese was incarcerated in March 1986, Mr. Zimmerman comes out to Mr. Franzese and tells him Norby Walters is having trouble with the agent who is signing his players away in connection with the agency business, and he wants some help. And Franzese tells Zimmerman to see Frank Campione, who is a person associated with the Colombo family and a person who Walters knows and who in fact is Franzese's bodyguard and chauffeur.

"Kathy Clements, who is a subsequent witness, in fact will testify that in early 1987 she and Steve Zucker, who were agents together, were having problems with Mr. Walters, that they had a dispute about signing certain individuals, including Tim McGee and Doug Dubose, two football players. Thereafter, Walters and Bloom, speaking with Doug Dubose, were mad and agitated about the situation.

"Subsequent to that event, Kathy Clements was one day sitting in her office. . . . An individual came in with a ski mask and beat her for no apparent reason."

Webb raised concern about testimony by Clements. Valukas said that he merely wanted to show that Walters was "reaching out to Franzese in connection with the sports agency business" and that "Zimmerman would be an individual who would carry a message back."

Gold interrupted, pointing out that Zimmerman was an "essential link."

"This is very prejudicial," Webb said.

Valukas argued that the Warwick incident had established that Franzese, Walters, and Zimmerman had a continuing relationship and added, "I think we can expand on that."

Marovich suggested that a limiting instruction be made to the jury, explaining that the testimony would be admissible to establish only that such a conversation took place.

Gold tried to speak to Marovich. "Judge, I have a terrible problem . . ."

Marovich, Valukas, and Webb did not hear Gold. The discussion continued as Valukas said, "The government is not at this point saying we are going to prove the beating."

Marovich ruled that he was going to allow the questioning of Franzese on the conversation he had with Zimmerman. Gold spoke up:

"I never said this to you before. This is the single, by far the single most troublesome ruling in the case, and I want Your Honor to know that Mr. Valukas called us a couple of weeks ago and told us he was thinking of superseding the indictment to add these charges and he apparently, for reasons he considered best, decided not to proceed. I firmly believe, and I think Mr. Webb shares my belief, that if there were any solid evidence linking the defendant to the beating, we'd be looking at something other than a conspiracy case . . . and probably charges in another court."

Gold pointed out that Zimmerman was not a scheduled witness and that "a conversation occurred between Mr. Zimmerman and Mr. Franzese, a conversation I will never be able to cross-examine."

Marovich had a look of surprise on his face.

Surrounded by the lawyers in the hall, away from the jury, the judge said, "I may have been confused here, and if I am, I want to have the opportunity to have my mind clarified. Are you saying that I am maybe mistaken, that as we speak there is nothing in the indictment that has to do with the beating of Kathy Clements? Is that what you are saying?"

"Yes, sir," Gold responded.

"Yes," Webb chimed in.

"Vehemently," Gold added.

"I may have been under a misapprehension," Marovich said. "In that case, if for no other reason, I'm going to keep it out because I don't see the relevance of tying it to charges in this indictment. And let me thank you for clearing my mind out. I was under the wrong impression. Let's go."

It was that close. The government almost introduced the Clements beating at this point.

Valukas later explained that he was not crushed by this ruling. "I knew it would be next to impossible to get it in. We just could not prove the beating. But I wanted their side to think about it, to be somewhat consumed by it, to create doubt in their mind about the potential testimony of Michael Franzese."

Back in court, Franzese was still on the witness stand, and Valukas resumed his direct. He was able to establish another fact, just in case.

Valukas asked, "Prior to your [incarceration] in March 1986, did you have occasion to have a conversation with Mr. Walters about a person by the name of Frank Campione?"

"Yes," Franzese answered.

"Who is he?"

"He was a close friend and an associate of mine and my father's."

"Was he also associated with the Colombo family?" Valukas asked.

"Yes."

"Where did this conversation occur?"

"I believe it was someplace in Manhattan," Franzese said. "I believe it was in Norby's office."

"To the best of your recollection, was anybody else present besides you and Mr. Walters?"

"No, not that I recall," Franzese answered.

"At the time you had this conversation, did you know that you were going to be indicted?" Valukas asked.

"Yes."

"And to the best of your recollection, what did you say to Mr. Walters and what did Mr. Walters say to you?"

"I told Norby that if he had any problems in the future to be in touch with Frankie," Franzese said.

Robert Gold got to his feet and protested to Marovich that the direct from Valukas was leading to "the same place" that everyone had discussed outside the presence of the jury. Valukas told the court he was not going to ask those questions. Marovich let him go on. Valukas took Franzese to March 1986, when he was in a halfway house in Los Angeles.

"Did you have occasion at that time while you were in a halfway house to have a conversation with Norby Walters?" Valukas asked.

"Yes."

"During that time, did you ever have a conversation which related to the sports agency business?"

"Only insofar as that the business was going well," Franzese said. "We never got into any details about it."

Valukas ended his direct. The prosecution figured it would save any further damaging testimony from Franzese for its redirect. But it would have to wait to see what doors the defense would open first.

ROBERT GOLD rose to his feet. Before the court was in session, he told a few acquaintances that he was "pumped." Gold cut right to the core of his cross-examination. He showed that Michael Franzese had lied before in court but had not been convicted of perjury.

Then Gold asked, "Mr. Franzese, when did you start wearing glasses?"

"About seven or eight years ago."

"Are they for reading or distance?"

"They're for distance."

Gold then took Franzese down a long, winding road of his twenty-eight-count federal indictment and the potential that Franzese could spend the rest of his life in prison.

"And that was not in your game plan, was it?" Gold asked.

"I did not want to spend the rest of my life in jail, no."

Gold went through the various counts of his indictment, which included mail fraud, counterfeiting, extortion, kickback, embezzlement, credit card fraud, wire fraud, conspiracy, racketeering—it all added up to a maximum of 113 years in prison and fines of $3,250,000.

Franzese agreed with everything Gold was saying.

Gold then took Franzese on his trek through the prison system and his plea agreements, including the deal in which he would serve ten years in federal prison and pay almost $15 million in fines and restitution. Gold further established that Franzese still owed the government at least $10 million.

Gold got Franzese to admit that he had made "several million dollars," but when Gold suggested the figure reached "more than three hundred million dollars," Franzese said, "No, not more than three hundred million."

Gold pressed him about making $300 million in one transaction alone, then he asked him about the amount of money he had in foreign banks. The members of the Justice Department were paying keen attention at this point.

"None," replied Franzese.

"You have no money in any bank account in Mexico—is that your testimony?"

"Absolutely not."

"You had no money in any bank account in Austria?"

"I had no money in any foreign bank account anywhere."

Gold picked at some of the earlier agreements with the government, and then there was a break for lunch.

Nothing Robert Gold did could unnerve Michael Franzese, who remained cool and answered the attorney with clarity and certainty.

There were two key, critical areas that Gold explored. One involved the $50,000 Franzese testified that he had passed to Norby Walters in a "brown paper bag" for his partnership in the sports agency business. Gold established that Franzese was obligated to tell federal officials whether he was "due any fees, commissions, or bonuses, or anything of value in return for services rendered by any corporation or individuals."

Gold established that on April 30, 1986, Franzese failed to tell federal officials about his partnership with Norby Walters.

"At the time my membership in an organized crime family would not allow me to speak about any of my associates, and therefore I was not able to talk about that, I felt," Franzese said.

"Are you telling us today as you sit here right now that you have committed another perjury you never told these gentlemen about before right now?" Gold asked.

Everyone waited for the answer. Franzese still looked calm.

"That's correct, yes."

Gold seem taken aback at Franzese's admission, but not as stunned as when he asked Franzese about his other criminal acts in organized crime. Gold gave Franzese a big test about whether he was really prepared to tell the truth as a Mafia captain. He went through some key acts in the Justice Department files and asked Franzese after each alleged act, "Do you deny committing that crime?"

Some crimes Franzese denied, some he did not. Finally Gold asked for a brief moment because, in his mind, he was about to get to the stuff that would either make or break Franzese as a witness.

"The Justice Department files also reflect that sometime in early 1985 you participated in discussions with the ruling commission of organized crime in New York city in connection with taking certain retaliatory action against law enforcement officials," Gold said. "Do you deny having committed that crime?"

"I agree that I was a party to a discussion," Franzese said, "that I've heard discussions about it, yes. I didn't participate, but I heard about it, yes."

"And what is the ruling commission in connection with which you remember having this discussion?"

"It was a leadership body, comprised of all five families in New York."

The defense team could not believe Franzese was talking about this.

"And do you know the names of the persons with whom you spoke at that time?"

"Yes, I do," Franzese said.

The defense team looked tense now. Gold was nervous. The lawyers in gray suits sitting in the gallery looked anxious.

But Valukas jumped to his feet and said, "Objection as to relevance, Your Honor."

"Sustained."

Gold asked for "one second." He looked again at his paperwork. This was it. He was going to find out if Franzese would cut into the heart of the Colombo family.

"Those files reflect, Mr. Franzese, that in March 1986 you participated in a conspiratorial discussion in which a man by the name of Carmine Persico (the acting boss of the Colombo family) and others discussed the possibility of taking retaliatory action against law enforcement officials who were prosecuting Mr. Persico." Gold took a deep breath. "Do you deny having participated in that conspiratorial discussion?"

Franzese did not hesitate. "No."

The defense team was devastated.

Gold ended his cross-examination seconds later. Three days of cross-examination had turned into three hours. It was only 2:45 P.M.

When the afternoon ended, Robert Gold privately told George Randolph, among others, "If Michael Franzese was willing to give up the head of the five New York crime families, the boss of his own crime family, then what was going to keep him from giving up Norby Walters?"

There was yet another matter for Michael Franzese. Dan Webb had to take a crack on behalf of his client, Lloyd Bloom.

"As you might imagine, I don't have very many questions to ask of you," Webb opened. "As I have listened to you testify here for the past several hours and read over the material the government has given me, would it be fair to say that during most of your adult life you have been involved in organized criminal activity?"

There were several smiles that broke throughout the courtroom.

"Yes, it is."

Before too long Dan Webb turned around to the defense table and said, "Mr. Bloom, I want you to please come up here."

Bloom walked toward Webb, who grabbed his client by the arm and escorted him to the front of the witness stand. Bloom crossed his hands in front of him.

"Sir, I want you to take a look at my client. I noticed this morning you seemed to have trouble picking him out in the courtroom. Is that because you indicated you only think you met him on one occasion?"

Valukas jumped to his feet and objected to the characterization. Not only that, he pointed out that Webb himself had stipulated to the fact.

Webb grabbed Bloom by the arm again and asked Franzese, "Is this someone who you ever, ever in your life were associated with in criminal activity?"

"No."

"You were not trying to leave the impression with the jury this morning that you were ever associated with the man, with this man, in performing any type of racketeering activity? Is that a fair statement?"

"I was never associated with him personally, no."

Webb and Valukas then went on a heated volley as Webb tried to ask Franzese further about his knowledge of Bloom's criminal activity. Webb lost and moved on to the meeting in which Franzese said he met Bloom briefly on the day he passed $50,000 to Norby Walters.

"Sir," Webb said, "the fact is, as you lived your life and you are introduced to people, you don't go around bragging about the fact that you're a member of the New York mob family, the Colombo family, do you?"

"No, I do not."

Webb tried to ask Franzese whether Bloom would not recognize him as a criminal. Objection. Sustained.

Finally Webb asked, "At that time, did you have any discussion with Mr. Bloom at all about your background?"

"No."

Time passed before Webb also asked, "And in fact it's fair to say that because you didn't know Bloom or anything about him, you didn't want him around, did you?"

"That's correct, yes."

"Because a man who's in the business that you are in, you do try to operate in some type of concealed, secret fashion, is that a fair statement?"

"Yes, it is."

"In fact, if Mr. Bloom had even been present, you would have felt extremely uncomfortable, wouldn't you?"

"Yes."

Webb further established that Franzese would have been uncomfortable talking business around Lloyd Bloom. He explored the sports agency business more.

"I mean, you didn't get stock issued to you or anything?"

"No," Franzese said. "I don't believe Mr. Walters wanted to have stock issued."

There were some snickers in the audience. Webb soon got himself in a little trouble with the Mafia witness and almost opened the door to the Kathy Clements beating.

"Did you ever go to any meetings or meet anybody or promote their company or do anything like that?"

Valukas took to his feet and and made a very chilling point. "Your Honor, I'm going to make note that if that question is answered, that other issue we were talking about, we are going into it on redirect."

The government actually didn't want to put Kathy Clements in a position where she would have to take the witness stand. Through conversations with Clements's attorney, they knew that Clements's personal life had been subjected to intense scrutiny from Webb and Molo. They believed Clements had been "chilled" by Webb before the trial. One member of the government team felt Clements was "being treated like a rape victim."

Tony Valukas later admitted, "If I did anything in the Clements area, it was primarily to keep the defense guessing. I never saw it as a realistic opportunity."

Webb restructured his question and then got to other matters relating to Franzese and Bloom.

"And at no time did Mr. Bloom directly or indirectly ever ask you if he could use your name or try to use your reputation to threaten people, did he?" Webb asked.

"Directly, no," Franzese answered.

"Indirectly, did Mr. Bloom ever do anything to indicate that he was going to use your name to threaten people?"

"No, but if he was Norby's partner, he had the same ability to use my name as Norby did."

That was a gift from Michael Franzese to the government and a payback to Lloyd Bloom for "being so stupid."

Webb soon finished his cross-examination, and Valukas had a few questions on redirect to establish that Franzese had moved his residence to Los Angeles in 1984.

When he was done, Valukas announced, "I have no questions."

Gold had none. Webb had none. It was 3:20 P.M. of the same day that Michael Franzese took the witness stand, and he was done.

George Randolph looked around the room, and he seemed to be on the verge of smiling. He fought it back. It was only halftime.

But Michael Franzese did what everybody had told him would never happen. He testified, and as New York law enforcement officials later conceded, Franzese became "the most significant organized crime member ever to cooperate with the government."

18

A MODEL of icy cool—like Michael Corleone—on the witness stand, Michael Franzese was disconsolate when he returned to his "safe house" the night after his testimony against Norby Walters. FBI agents thought he was borderline suicidal. George Randolph sat him down to talk about it.

"I can't believe I did this," Franzese said, on the verge of tears. "It's against everything I stood for."

Franzese sobbed. Randolph consoled him.

"George and I talked about it," Franzese said. "He came to me and asked me how I felt. I told him, 'I feel like shit.' It really hurt. I told him, 'George, no matter what, it might be the right thing morally, but inside I don't feel right about it. Again, it wasn't so much that it was Norby, it was just the idea. It was the day I broke my oath.'"

"Fuck the oath," Randolph told him. "Everything's going to be okay."

It's not what the government necessarily believed. FBI and Justice Department officials agreed that if Franzese refused to enter the Federal Witness Protection Program he would get whacked, it was just a matter of time. And it was something Franzese discussed with his wife that night.

"I told Cammy, 'Look, Cam, I lived this way all my life, and I seen guys get killed around me my whole life. It's not something different than what I had before. There's always been the possibility it could happen to me.'"

Franzese would have to remain in Chicago for the duration of the trial in case he was recalled as a witness.

Randolph was able to spend some extra time with the now-former

Mafia boss because there were no witnesses waiting when Michael Franzese finished his testimony. The government scrambled to get their lineup in order, and Marovich gave them until 2 P.M. the next Wednesday, March 15.

Now that the jury had heard the chilling testimony of Michael Franzese, the government wanted them to hear about some of the threats the players received.

On Wednesday, when the government was ready to proceed, Randolph happened to peek into the witness room and almost fainted.

Maurice "Mo" Douglass, the Chicago Bears defensive back, was dressed in a flamboyant, baggy, gold-threaded suit with gold suede cowboy boots—and an earring, of course.

It shouldn't have been a shock since in his meetings with the government, Douglass was always attired in some "getup." Valukas had specifically asked Randolph to make sure that Douglass wore a conservative suit the day he testified.

Randolph did have a "heart to heart" with the player. "Maurice, do you own a nice suit and a tie? Can you wear that when you testify?" he asked.

"Yeah, yeah, yeah, no problem," Douglass said.

This was a problem. Randolph was in a panic, thinking to himself, "How do I get court recessed?" Howard Pearl saw Douglass and panicked, too. He also thought about a delay and sending somebody down the street to buy Douglass a new suit.

All of a sudden Tony Valukas stuck his head out the courtroom door and yelled, "Get him in here!" Randolph nodded to another FBI agent to escort Douglass to the courtroom. He went and sat down at the prosecution table.

Then the door swung open and in came Maurice Douglass. Little Richard could not have made a more gala entrance. Tony Valukas glanced over his shoulder and froze. Valukas's eyes shot daggers at George Randolph, whose ears were turning red. The gold suede boots made a clip-clop sound on the floor as Douglass marched to the witness stand.

Howard Pearl had the dubious task of handling the direct on Douglass. As it turned out, looks were deceiving. It didn't take long to see that Douglass was thoughtful, articulate, and credible. The Chicago Bears safety told the jury what happened when he tried to fire Lloyd Bloom and Norby Walters as his agents.

"Bloom called at my mom's home in Cincinnati two or three times. He told me if I didn't return the money I borrowed, he'd have somebody rough me up. He told me I might not make it to the draft. He said he may have somebody break my legs."

Members of the jury looked across the room at Lloyd Bloom, who had his head down. Pearl asked Douglass how he responded to that threat.

"I was worried. I wasn't worried personally. I figured I could handle my own if he came after me. But they had so many clients, and he had a lot of money, and I started thinking that he could probably have somebody do something. At the time I was really, really scared."

"What did you do then?" Pearl asked.

"I told my mom that if anything happened to me, notify the police that it was Lloyd Bloom who threatened me."

Douglass testified that he reconsidered firing the agent because "I thought that if I have to go through this, it's not worth it." Then he said he thought again and decided to stick to his original decision to leave Walters and Bloom.

"I decided that if they were going to threaten me with bodily harm, then I'm not going to have those kind of people handle my money."

Douglass told the jury he decided to pay the money back. He gave them half the $9,000, and a check for $4,356.26 was submitted to the jury as evidence. He explained to Bloom that he planned to pay back the rest in the near future. When time lagged during the 1986 football season, his phone rang again.

"Bloom said, 'If you don't send the rest now, then I'll send somebody down there to rough you up.' I told him we didn't have the money right then but that I would pay him later, which we did," Douglass testified.

Howard Pearl introduced another check for $4,356.26.

Flamboyant or not, Douglass was convincing.

Dan Webb tried to show that the Bears player was "double-dealing" agents over a pair of $100 payments. This struck a nerve with Douglass, who started arguing with Webb over the fact.

Marovich intervened: "Whoa, Maurice, time out!"

Douglass kept arguing.

"The whistle was blown, Maurice," Marovich said.

That got the player's attention. Marovich smiled and looked at Webb. "Now . . . time in."

Webb also established that other than his mother, Douglass told nobody about the threat.

"Did you call police?"

"No."

"Did you change your telephone number?"

"No."

"Did you tell your coaches?"

"No."

Another defensive back, ex–Michigan star Garland Rivers, was brought to the witness stand. He received that old familiar call from Lloyd Bloom back in February 1986, just after his junior season.

"He [Bloom] told me they were the agents of the stars and that I was a star. He said that if I wasn't a star, he wouldn't be talking to me."

Rivers signed a contract, took the cash, and received another $1,000 bonus for turning over teammate Robert Perryman. Then he became disillusioned in February 1987 and tried to fire the agent. He testified that Walters and Bloom threatened to expose him.

"They said that if I didn't go back, they'd call Coach Bo and the NCAA and turn me in," Rivers told the jury.

Rivers told the agents he would keep them.

Soon after, in March 1987, he was called to Coach Bo Schembechler's office, where he discovered two FBI agents waiting for him. After the meeting Rivers called Bloom and told him he had told the FBI the truth. "Bloom said that was okay, that they can't prove it. They had the documents, and they were not going to turn them over. He said he would straighten everything out."

Rivers testified that when Schembechler found out, he exploded and "my scholarship got snatched away. . . . He took away my Big Ten championship ring."

It would have been ideal if Schembechler could have followed Rivers to the witness stand, but his schedule wouldn't allow it. Instead, momentum shifted again when former Michigan State wide receiver Mark Ingram testified.

Ingram, speaking in almost inaudible tones, testified that Michigan State was "strict" about rule adherence.

Steve Molo, Webb's associate, had prepared Webb well for Ingram, the number-one draft pick of the New York Giants in 1987. Ingram had received $7,500 from Walters and Bloom for signing prior to his senior season at Michigan State, and a total of $25,000 over four months.

Ingram had been arrested three times during his career at Michigan State for theft. He served one-third of a ninety-day sentence in January 1986 after a felony theft conviction in which, as Webb so aptly pointed out to the jury, Ingram was caught stealing money from school dorm rooms.

Webb pointed out a variety of Michigan State rules that the school could use to revoke a scholarship. Ingram signed a document in which one rule dealt with "undesirable behavior on and off the field" and another with "serious misconduct warranting substantial penalty." Nevertheless, Ingram always remained eligible to play football at Michigan State.

"Is it still your testimony that the school followed strictly by the rules?" Webb asked sharply.

During Webb's cross-examination there was an interesting note scribbled by Lloyd Bloom and passed around the table.

"This guy's not too brite. . . ."

Michigan State's faculty representative, Gwendolyn Norrell, was an annoying witness. She was an elderly lady, and her labored breathing went directly into the microphone. Molo led her through some embarrassing testimony in which she said, "I believe the rules [concerning behavior] are discretionary. The rule involving sports agents is not."

Monday, March 20, was one of the strangest days of the trial. George Randolph was sitting at the defense table at about 9:40 A.M., twenty minutes before the trial was scheduled to resume, when he heard people yelling, "Get a doctor, get a doctor!"

Somebody stuck his head into the courtroom and yelled, "It's Norby Walters!"

Randolph went sprinting out of the courtroom and down toward the commotion near the bank of elevators.

Walters was spread over some lounge chairs, one leg hanging off, and he was grabbing his right arm, agonized by the pain.

"I thought he'd been shot," Randolph said.

Walters had been rammed in the elevator by an unidentified clerk with a metal cart full of files. The agent was pinned in the elevator, then fell, according to Robert Gold, who was trying to comfort his client.

A nurse in the building finally came to the agent's aid.

"I think his arm is broken," Gold said.

The nurse examined Walters and downplayed the injury, but he was taken to Northwestern University Hospital and treated. Marovich sent the jury home.

This gave both sides time to argue more motions. The government needed to retrieve the lead and was ready to put former SMU star wide receiver Ron Morris on the stand to testify about the illicit threats from Lloyd Bloom and Norby Walters and to play the six taped phone conversations. But Webb had filed a motion seeking to inquire about Morris's lurid history as an SMU recruit and student, noting that Morris had testified before the grand jury that he was offered $400 a month and a car from SMU as a high school player.

Tony Valukas argued that the government did not allege SMU as a "fraud" victim, and Morris was there strictly as an extortion victim. The pre-trial agreement that Morris signed was specifically tailored to preclude any claim that the player participated in a scheme to "defraud" SMU. Instead, the agreement said that Morris and the agents participated in a scheme to "conceal" the arrangement and remain eligible.

"I have probably said, ad nauseam," said Marovich, "there are many ills that trouble college sports, and I am totally aware SMU received the death penalty from the NCAA for recruiting violations. But I am at a loss as to what bearing it had on Ron Morris."

Webb said he felt "very strongly about this" and argued vehemently that Morris's credibility was at issue because he had filed "false statements" with SMU. Not only that, but the government was requiring Morris to make restitution to SMU.

Marovich changed directions and ruled he would let Webb probe only the specific offer Morris received from SMU.

The judge warned Webb: "If you want to put SMU on trial before this jury, I'm not going to accommodate you. . . . I think you want to tell the jury more than they need to know."

Webb innocently said, "No, Judge, just the four hundred dollars monthly and the car. . . . I think it's important."

Tony Valukas turned around to Howard Pearl and George Randolph. He didn't look pleased. Randolph knew what that meant. If the government gave Dan Webb an opening to SMU—no matter what Marovich would do to combat it—the truly sordid tale of college football could contaminate the entire case. Of all the witnesses Morris most concerned Pearl because of his attitude about breaking NCAA rules.

"If anything," Pearl said, "Morris thought he was underpaid in college. There wasn't a player who had a greater sense of entitlement. He may have been the greediest, on those terms."

Ron Morris and the tapes never made it to the courtroom.

They also argued about what kind of testimony could be elicited from Texas running back Edwin Simmons, who was there to testify about the extortion of ex-teammate Everett Gay. Webb wanted to be able to question Simmons about the time he was found naked in the backyard of a booster's home—the booster was out of town—on September 29, 1986. The police report stated that Simmons had admitted smoking marijuana, but he couldn't remember who he was or where he was, only that he was a football player.

"And he knew his jersey number," Webb told the judge.

Webb said he wanted to see if Simmons's drug usage was such that he had a right "to examine defects in his memory."

Marovich told Webb to forget it. The next day Norby Walters was in court with his arm in a sling. It was not broken.

The next player to testify was former University of Pittsburgh All-America linebacker Tony Woods. The hour-long tape was played in which Bloom and Walters threatened to expose Woods and his brother to the NCAA and Walters told Woods, "This is my life on the line. Now it is your life. . . . Everything's going to be tainted and tainted bad."

There was laughter in the courtroom when Norby Walters told Woods on the tape, "That's a big set of New York balls, right?" But the jurors did not laugh.

Woods also told the jury how the agents played their hand with the entertainers. Walters took him to a party for actor/comedian Eddie Murphy. He played around with singer Rick James. He was impressed.

Webb tried to establish that Woods was another "double-dealer" when it came to Walters and Bloom and his new agent, Bruce Allen. He got Woods to admit that a local Pittsburgh insurance agent, Eric Metz, had recruited the player during his senior season for Allen. Webb also got Woods to admit that Walters had helped his parents out of a bind with their janitorial service.

As for the threats, Webb tried to establish for the jury that the tape was actually made after Walters had already filed his lawsuit against the player in a New York court. Thus, he argued, wasn't Walters just pointing out the realities of life?

Howard Pearl was shaking his head at the prosecution table, as if to say, "No, no, no. The threat was made before the lawsuit."

Pearl would get a shot on redirect after a lunch break, but this had been a rough day for the prosecutor. A marathon runner, he routinely got dressed in his office after a jog. This day Pearl had mistakenly mismatched his suit; he was wearing the wrong coat with the wrong pants.

"Everybody noticed, but nobody, not even my own team, told me," he said, laughing.

Regardless of his apparel, Pearl appeared to reestablish that the tape was made before the lawsuit was filed. Another point was made by Woods as to why he left the agents.

"I had heard that Norby was involved with the Mafia and drugs," Woods testified. "At first I didn't want to believe it. I thought it was jealousy."

Webb wanted another shot at Woods. The lawyer was agitated.

"I must have asked you twelve times about the tape, and you knew it took place after the lawsuit was filed," Webb told Woods. "Now, we had a lunch hour. What happened during the lunch hour?"

"What do you mean?"

"What happened to make you change your mind about the time frame?"

"Nothing. I'm just not real good with dates."

"But what happened at lunch?"

Woods paused. He gave it some thought. Everybody waited for the answer.

"I was eating—at Popeye's Chicken."

Laughter erupted in the courtroom. Webb shook his head.

Woods was finished, and there was a break at 2:30 P.M. He headed for the men's room. Randolph was standing in front of the urinal next to him. Webb started laughing. Randolph started laughing.

"You know, Dan," Randolph said, "that Popeye's chicken can do wonders for your memory."

Edwin Simmons and Everett Gay testified next about Bloom's threat to Gay.

"He said that's why they had partners in California, to make sure they don't get messed over," Gay told the jurors.

Later Tony Valukas asked, "Do you know who those partners were in California?"

"Somebody bigger than him," Gay said.

The battle in court continued to go back and forth. Tipped by Webb's opening statement to the jury about George Swarn getting eligible with the Trees and Shrubs class at Miami of Ohio, the government dropped Swarn and the college from the mail fraud allegations under the conspiracy charge. They should have done the same with Paul Palmer and Temple University.

Palmer's academic records made Ronnie Harmon look like an honor student. He flunked remedial writing four times. One semester his classes consisted of bowling, racquetball, recreation and leisure, human sexuality, and writing again, from which he withdrew.

Then Webb produced a letter that academic adviser Ron Jenkins wrote to the athletic department about Paul Palmer, star football player.

Jenkins specifically referred to the four failures in remedial writing and said the player's academic showing "must affect his eligibility."

Most damaging, Jenkins had written, "If Paul Palmer wins the Heisman Trophy, he will be an embarrassment to the university because of the academic record."

Palmer's performance in the classroom never improved, but he always played football. The "embarrassment" was spared because Palmer finished as the Heisman Trophy runner-up to Vinny Testaverde one year later. Temple faculty representative Joseph Marshall had trouble explaining how Palmer had just seventy-three hours when he left Temple.

Webb interrupted him and, disgusted, raised his voice. "Sir, that was an absolute sham, wasn't it?" he asked.

There was no redirect from the prosecution.

That night Michigan coach Bo Schembechler came into Chicago for his testimony the next day. He arrived a little after 7 P.M., and they had dinner delivered as Pearl pre-tried the legendary coach. Pearl spent most of his time cross-examining the coach in Valukas's spacious office. The prosecutor could see that Schembechler was fired up for the testimony, but he also worried that the coach could explode on the witness stand. Just the mention of "sports agents" seemed to set Bo off. It delighted Randolph. It bothered Pearl.

"I could see how volatile Bo could be," Pearl said. "He had a chance to be a great witness, but I also thought he was a walking time bomb. And Michigan was already our cleanest school. They couldn't even touch Perryman's transcripts."

When they were finished pre-trying Schembechler, it was 11:45 P.M. They were all ready to go home when Bo asked Pearl to "show me your office."

They took a walk alone down the hall. When they reached Pearl's office, Schembechler asked how the trial was going.

"I don't know," said Pearl. "We suffered some real damage with Iowa."

Coach Bo put his arm around the downcast thirty-five-year-old prosecutor.

"Let me tell you something, son. . . . This is a great thing you're doing. Win or lose, you're making a difference."

Pearl was sky high when he left the office after midnight, but he was still concerned about Schembechler's temper.

Randolph told Pearl to stop worrying. "Just let him come out firing with his six guns."

That's what happened.

The next morning the Michigan football coach and athletic director walked deliberately into the courtroom, which was packed for the occasion. Schembechler stared at the defense table, trying to figure out which one was Norby Walters and which one was Lloyd Bloom. He was sworn in: "Glenn Edward Schembechler."

Howard Pearl led Schembechler through NCAA rules, Michigan rules, and Bo rules. Schembechler didn't need the microphone. There was no mistaking how he felt about rules.

But much to Pearl's delight, Schembechler was very calm and in control as he told the jury how he cautioned Garland Rivers about "being careful" prior to his senior year not to do anything to "jeopardize your eligibility. . . . I wanted to help him keep his nose clean . . . but the fourth year, he was disappointing. He didn't do well academically, he did not play as well as a football player, and he wasn't the same kind of young man I had for the previous three years."

Schembechler also told how Rivers's teammate Robert Perryman denied to his face in March 1987 that he had signed with an agent prior to the 1986 season, when Michigan won the Big Ten and went to the Rose Bowl. Schembechler said, "A fellow by the name of Lloyd Bloom called to try and verify his story. . . . I didn't want to talk to him."

Garland Rivers also denied his involvement until the day the FBI arrived. Schembechler forcefully told the jury what happened that day.

"I told him he could have cost us the Big Ten title and the Rose Bowl," the coach groused. "I told him that at that time he was a disgrace to Michigan. I suspended his grant-in-aid, I took away his Big Ten ring, I closed off his locker, and I had his picture taken off the wall."

There was silence in the courtroom, almost an echo to Schembechler's angry recollection.

Pearl had no more questions. Marovich called a short recess. The defense team huddled off to the side.

When Marovich called the court to order ten minutes later, Webb and Gold told the judge, "We have no questions."

Schembechler looked startled and disappointed. Outside the courtroom he said, "I am disappointed. I was hoping they would have some questions for me. I was ready."

Outside of Michael Franzese's testimony, it was the single greatest day of the trial for the government. Bo Schembechler had given the prosecution a slam-dunk for at least one mail fraud conviction in their venue. They hoped.

Next came Paul Palmer, not to talk about his academics but to talk about how Lloyd Bloom ripped him off. Palmer also told the jury how Bloom had laughed that "Norby denied knowing" any Mafia members after the *Sports Illustrated* article. The facts about Bloom's conduct were so overwhelming, they appeared indefensible.

Dan Webb tried, of course, when Los Angeles accountant Joel Levy was put on the stand. Levy, who was given immunity to testify, had been hired by Palmer and Bloom to handle the player's investment in Lincolnshire, the credit repair company Bloom had established. Levy said he confronted Bloom a couple of times, but Webb showed that the accountant never alerted Palmer.

The cross-examination also got comical as Webb totally shifted the blame to Levy. Webb actually got Levy to admit that, in essence, he was really Palmer's "agent." Nothing mattered, though. As much as Webb shredded Levy, Bloom had burned Palmer's money and leased the Rolls-Royce Corniche, while advising Palmer to get a Yugo or Hyundai for the player's brother and sister.

There was also the matter of Walters's obstruction of justice charges under the conspiracy count. In a unique twist the government was able to call Michael Feldberg, the agent's attorney when the investigation started, to the stand because Walters already had waived his attorney-client privilege.

Feldberg admitted he was surprised when Pearl called him back in April 1987 to complain that the government believed Walters had withheld contracts of certain underclassmen as subpoenaed. Feldberg told the jury he met with Walters.

"I told him I had a disturbing telephone call from Mr. Pearl, and I told Mr. Walters he had an obligation to produce all the contracts," Feldberg testified. "Mr. Walters had not understood he was required to produce the contracts of students with remaining eligibility. He felt by doing so it could be very harmful to the students and destroy their careers. He said, 'Do I really have to produce these contracts?' I said, 'You really have to produce those contracts.'"

It was Thursday, March 24. The government rested its case. It was time for Norby Walters and Lloyd Bloom to put up their defense.

Once again Dan Webb made his motion for severance, knowing that Walters was about to send the attorneys for Shea & Gould to the witness stand. Once again Marovich shot him down, but throughout the trial Webb had his highly respected paralegal, Mary Kenny, taking critical notes in preparation for an appeal. This was Bloom's ticket, Webb believed all along.

That weekend Walters and Gold traveled to Los Angeles. They had a meeting with Joe and Katherine Jackson, parents of the group the Jacksons. Michael Jackson, according to Walters, threw his arms around the agent and called him "Uncle Norby."

Uncle Norby asked Joe and Katherine Jackson if they would allow Michael to testify on his behalf.

The answer was no.

Only Joe Jackson, who had disliked Ron Weisner as the group's manager, volunteered to testify.

Marovich wouldn't let him, citing the fact that Walters was already able to introduce evidence that Joe Jackson wanted him as the booking agent.

Webb also wanted to have an "expert" witness testify about the practices of sports agents to establish the "state of mind" Walters and Bloom developed when they entered the field in 1985. Mike Trope would testify that many sports agents from 1973 to 1985, including himself, traditionally signed college athletes in violation of NCAA rules and that he was unaware athletes were required to sign NCAA affidavits.

"Ignorance of the law is no excuse," the judge ruled. "Criminal law, as opposed to the civil side, is a moral code made by society. If we allow somebody to say, 'I did not know about that' or, 'My mommy said it's okay,' it allows the individual to separate their morality from society's morality."

Joe Grant, the manager for Dionne Warwick, was the first witness called by the defense. Nervous, he disputed Michael Franzese's testimony that he was threatened to keep Norby Walters as the singer's booking agent.

"No, no. Threatened? Ha, ha, ha," Grant said.

He admitted meeting once with Norby and "two other gentlemen." One was wearing a ragged raincoat, but it "was a very nice meeting."

Grant appeared excitable. He had never heard of or seen somebody named Michael Franzese.

Tony Valukas had a terrific cross-examination of Grant. He showed how Grant wanted to fire Walters but how, after that meeting, Walters did indeed stay on as the agent for six more months.

Valukas then asked Grant about his interview with FBI agent John O'Neill in which Grant said that Walters had been accompanied by a man with "dark hair" and another in a trench coat. Grant denied telling the FBI agent that Walters was "agitated" and that he left the room so that the other two men could talk to him. Grant denied just about everything in O'Neill's report.

Valukas mentioned that O'Neill offered Grant the opportunity to review his notes. Grant had refused.

"Perhaps I was naive," Grant said.

Then Valukas asked about the man in the raincoat.

"Was it raining that day?" Valukas asked.

"No," said Grant. "I do believe I said it was strange that he had kept it on."

Valukas then asked Grant how many times Miss Warwick played Las Vegas and Atlantic City. It was often. Valukas asked Grant if he had ever heard of Sonny Franzese, and Grant nervously answered, "Yes."

Valukas asked Grant if he knew about Franzese's reputation and position with the Colombo family and whether he knew the Franzeses controlled the guard unions in Atlantic City.

"I've heard the name, but I don't know if it's true," Grant said.

Grant testified that the only reason Walters stayed on was because his contract was still in force.

Valukas told Grant not to leave town until his subpoenaed records arrived.

The defense's next witness was Dionne Warwick.

For some reason Marovich allowed her to testify, perhaps to sign the autograph he requested for himself and his wife after her testimony.

Warwick's presence caused a stir. She was sworn and apologized for her hoarseness—"I just finished Las Vegas."

Marovich could not resist saying, "Sing into the microphone."

Warwick testified that she had known Walters for twenty years. She said she had chosen Walters as a booking agent and said it was her decision to "let him go" because she did not feel he was meeting his obligation. She said that now when she bumped into Walters occasionally, "we always hug and kiss."

Norby Walters was grinning from ear to ear in the courtroom.

Ethan Levin-Epstein asked Warwick if she had ever been threatened by Walters.

"Never."

Howard Pearl's cross-examination was brief and gentle. As Dionne Warwick left the witness stand, she stopped to hold hands with Norby Walters.

Outside the courtroom Norby Walters cutely told the media, "That's what friends are for."

The next day Joe Grant's records did show up. A stipulation of evidence was read to the jury. New contracts between Norby Walters and Dionne Warwick had been signed after the meeting in December 1982, after Michael Franzese visited Joe Grant.

Valukas, Pearl, and Randolph did not think Warwick's testimony was damaging, and they thought the jury responded well to FBI agent Victor Guerrero as a rebuttal witness.

Guerrero told the jury about being an undercover agent in 1982 when he was involved in surveillance on, among others, Michael Franzese. He testified that in December 1982, Franzese canceled a meeting because "he had to go straighten out a contract problem with Dionne Warwick's manager." Guerrero also painted a convincing picture for the jury that Michael Franzese was indeed a powerful organized crime figure.

The guts of Norby Walters's defense was his contention that—in relation to the mail fraud charges—there was no criminal intent because he had been told by his lawyers he was not breaking any laws.

Feldberg, Lon Trost, and Morris Shelton testified on the agent's behalf. Trost was Walters's first cousin, which didn't necessarily help Walters's case.

Feldberg testified, "Mr. Walters asked me if I thought he had broken any laws, and I told him he had not. I told him his conduct was in violation of NCAA rules, but the rules of the NCAA are not law."

Feldberg also testified that he advised Walters against filing a lawsuit against Ronnie Harmon: "I told Norby . . . it's a bad idea. I told him the lawsuit would get a lot of bad publicity, it would hurt him in his business, and he would likely be a pariah or an outcast. But Norby said, 'I can't live this way. I have to find out if I can function in this business.' "

In response the government asked Marovich to instruct the jury that

the government agrees that it is not unlawful to sign representative contracts with and pay money to undergraduate athletes. This activity is not alleged to be criminal. It is, however, a crime to file false certification with a university and to obtain scholarship money on the basis of that false certification. Defendant Walters has done nothing to demonstrate or even suggest that he received any legal advice whatsoever with respect to the allegedly false statements and certifications to the universities. . . . Defendant Walters is not charged with entering illegal contracts with athletes, he is charged with defrauding the university of money and property.

Trost testified that his cousin Norby found out that other agents signed players prematurely. Walters asked him if it was possible to write a contract around NCAA rules. Trost said he told Walters, "No ... [but] that's what life is all about in big-time college sports."

Trost testified: "We had two separate discussions, one on the basis of a civil lawsuit and the ramifications, and another when Norby asked if he had done anything illegal. We told him specifically that he had not, that he was not a member of the NCAA, that these were NCAA violations, but that it had never raised above the violation of the law.

"We advised against the lawsuits because of the serious ramifications. We told Norby that universities might institute civil lawsuits for damages, that he would be subject to bad publicity, that he might be subject to congressional examination and state legislations. ... We did not think there would be [criminal prosecution]."

There was no denying that the advice-of-counsel defense was very effective, but while Feldberg was on the witness stand, the government argued (out of the jury's presence) that the results of the lawsuits, particularly the rulings in the cases of Brent Fullwood and Ronnie Harmon, should be submitted as evidence. Valukas argued, "There has been an impression left that this was good advice. ... One judge said it was a contract between thieves and referred to it as a fraudulent contract."

Naturally the defense protested, and Marovich needled sarcastically, "You just don't want the jury to know that the grade-A advice turned out to be advice, and he [Walters] lost all the lawsuits. Great advice."

Nevertheless, the judge ruled in favor of the defense, keeping the lawsuits and their results away from the jury.

Another argument during this time was raised by the defense, which claimed the investigation was spurred by the NCAA and publicity, which it argued was the direct result of Walters's lawsuits.

"I will show it [the investigation] was generated by the beating of Kathy Clements," Valukas argued.

Valukas was limited to the following question when he resumed his terse cross-examination of Feldberg: "Are you aware of the fact that this investigation was not started by the lawsuits, the NCAA, publicity, or any other information such as that?"

"I am aware that you have said that," said Feldberg, "and that Mr. Pearl told me in April 1987."

"Did you understand they advised students to lie?"

"They did not say that."

"Did you advise them about the filing of false certifications?" Valukas asked.

"No, there was never any discussion concerning certifications."

"Did you ever advise your clients to tell students to lie to the university?"

"No, we did not," Feldberg answered.

"Did you ever advise Walters and Bloom to threaten physical harm to the student-athletes if they did not adhere to their contracts?"

"Of course not."

Valukas also asked Feldberg and Trost if there were any notes or memoranda taken from these meetings with Walters. There were not. Valukas was prepared to have the lawyers search through more than twenty boxes of files that had been subpoenaed from Shea & Gould.

Feldberg was finished, and so was the advice-of-counsel defense. Valukas's cross-examination was sensational, but it still raised doubt about Walters's criminality relating to mail fraud.

Privately Dan Webb also thought the testimony from Shea & Gould was more effective than he had anticipated. Nevertheless, for the court record and the subsequent appeal, he renewed his motion for a mistrial on behalf of Bloom, who had not waived his attorney-client privilege.

"I do believe the testimony from Shea and Gould was very harmful to Mr. Bloom," Webb told Marovich. "New York lawyers to a Chicago jury goes over like a lead balloon."

"It could have been worse if I had allowed the results of the lawsuits into evidence," Marovich responded.

Marovich denied Webb's motion, again citing the fact that Walters as president of WSE had the right to waive the attorney-client privilege on behalf of the corporation. Valukas pointed out that Trost testified the advice given to Walters and Bloom was billed to WSE.

Other witnesses resumed taking the stand. FBI agent John O'Neill was called and rebutted testimony by Joe Grant, the manager for Dionne Warwick.

Two managers of the New Edition—Steven Machat for the defense, and William Dern for the prosecution—gave conflicting testimony about Franzese's visit and threat, but it was Dern who admitted borrowing money from Walters and supported the government's evidence. Dern told the jury that Machat and Rick Smith, the group's other manager, called him and were very upset because they had just been visited by Norby Walters and a "mobster."

Some sixty stipulations were read to the jury as evidence, and therefore no testimony was needed.

The most interesting stipulation concerned Norby Walters's bank account: "Norby Walters Associates and World Sports and Entertainment have no records reflecting the generation of cash that was used to pay so-called loans, nor are there any records of any cash received or generated by or through, or for the benefit of the business."

It would be left at that because Norby Walters and Lloyd Bloom were not going to testify. The government knew Bloom would never take the stand because he had revealed so much in his proffer in January 1988.

The only witness Webb produced was a linguistics professor, Dr. Timothy Austin, from Loyola of Chicago. Webb wanted Austin to explain the technical definitions and differences between "loan" and "compensation."

Howard Pearl got up for a swift, humorous cross-examination.

"Are you being paid by the defense for your appearance here today?" he asked.

"Yes."

"And that, it is safe to say, is compensation, correct?"

"Correct."

The prosecution team also figured Walters would never take the stand because Randolph had compiled a substantial file of various alleged organized-crime activities that were never charged in the indictment. The government figured it could keep Walters on the witness stand "for a good week, without question."

19

By THE end of March 1989 there was no mistaking the impact of the Walters-Bloom trial. Dan Webb had shown the public the ugly side of college football. And the government had put a powerful Mafia boss on the witness stand to tell the country that he was a silent partner in a sports agent operation that had corralled fifty-eight players in a little more than two years.

As the trial was nearing its end, the University of Illinois was playing in the NCAA Final Four basketball tournament. Dan Webb pointed out to the judge that pro-NCAA advertising time had been purchased, and the ads would show several former college athletes who have done well in the business world. This seemed to be a direct response to the publicity generated from the trial about the downside of college sports.

Marovich, an Illinois alumnus who professed his fanaticism for the basketball team, decided he would not sequester the jury. Instead he advised them, if they were going to watch Illinois in the Final Four, to avoid watching the NCAA commercials. "Go get a beer or something. . . . Ignore it or do not watch. Are we square on that?"

Tony Valukas had his own countermove. He wanted the jury to avoid reading that week's cover story in *Time* magazine entitled "The College Trap." The story dealt with the failure of colleges to properly educate athletes and alluded to testimony given at the Walters-Bloom trial about the academic failures of big-name football players.

Marovich asked the jurors if any of them had seen *Time* that week, and all the jurors answered they had not.

"Good. Don't go looking for it, either," the judge instructed.

The trial appeared to be "dead even" after four weeks. Dan Webb had been very effective in attacking the colleges as well as the majority of players, who he contended were "deadbeats" and "greedy." Webb's strategy had been clear from the beginning. He wanted to show the jury that college football was so dirty that the entire case should be thrown out. He wanted them to feel, much like the federal judge in the Brent Fullwood case, that they deserved each other. They were all dirty—the players, the colleges, the agents, Franzese.

The government clearly understood that it did not have a victory sewn up, but despite the points Webb had scored, the government had delivered some killing blows with Michael Franzese, Bo Schembechler, and Paul Palmer.

The Honorable George Marovich gave both sides three days to prepare for their closing arguments. During this time the judge also discussed with both sides the instructions he would give the jury.

Both sides knew the closing arguments and jury instructions could make the difference between acquittal and conviction. For Tony Valukas and Howard Pearl it was one of the most gut-wrenching weekends of the trial. Pearl would deliver a lengthy closing argument, and Valukas would offer the rebuttal to Dan Webb and Robert Gold. The arguments would take two days, then the jury would be left to deliberate.

At this stage Webb clearly frightened the government. He had won too many cases with his closing argument to even think about relaxing. Closing arguments were when Dan Webb was at his best.

Howard Pearl literally got sick that weekend, still feeling the aftereffects of a bout with double pneumonia two months earlier. George Randolph just felt helpless. Pearl felt as if he had lost ten pounds during the trial, and Randolph felt as if he had lost even more hair. Nobody slept very well.

On Monday, April 4, the courtroom was packed shoulder-to-shoulder as many in the Chicago legal community took the day off to listen to the closing arguments by some of the top trial lawyers in America. The podium was again positioned to face the jury. Marovich entered the courtroom shortly after 10 A.M. and listened to the lawyers make some last requests about instructions. Marovich also announced that one of the jurors, Dawn Stark, had become ill and would have to be excused. The first alternate, a lady named Doris Schloeman, would replace Stark, an unremarkable switch because the jurors had not been told whether they were alternates. The jurors were brought into the room, and Marovich broke the news to them that they had lost one to illness.

"With that understanding, Mr. Pearl, you may address the ladies and gentlemen of the jury."

The Harvard prosecutor was nervous, his mouth dry, and an unsightly white substance developed around his lips as he began to speak. He grabbed a glass of water, took a gulp, and told the jury, "Good morning. When we began . . . it may have appeared that the case was somewhat complex or somewhat confusing, but at the end of this case, ladies and gentlemen, you will see that it is neither. That, in fact, this case is quite straightforward and quite simple."

Pearl took another drink of water. He was using his hands but also reading material in front of him, flipping the pages as he went along. His emotions were in check.

"What this case is about, ladies and gentlemen, is the illegal activities of Norby Walters and Lloyd Bloom, two hustlers from New York who traveled the country in pursuit of a mission . . . a mission to become agents to the stars.

"Lloyd Bloom and Norby Walters desperately wanted to rise to the top of the world of sports and entertainment, and in order to do so were prepared to, and did, whatever they felt was necessary, legal or illegal, to attain that goal, including doing business in partnership with organized crime, using threats and extortion to obtain business, to obtain clients and retain clients . . . using fraud and deceit to sign college athletes early, to keep them in school until the day they were ready for the National Football League, to sign contracts, from which contracts Lloyd Bloom and Norby Walters would also attain their fame and their fortune.

"Now, in pursuit of that mission to become agents to the stars, Lloyd Bloom and Norby Walters were completely unchecked by any concern whatsoever for the illegality of their actions. These defendants steamrolled over the interests and rights of anyone, any institution, that they perceived as standing in their way. And they did that through fraud, they did that through deceit, and they did that through extortion.

"The reason this mission was unchecked by any genuine concern for illegality was that this mission operated on the basis of the fundamentally corrupt and perverse notion of what this country is about.

"You recall, we began this case listening to the tape that Ronald Harmon made of Norby Walters and Lloyd Bloom. Mr. Walters explained in great detail his vision of what this country is about. Mr. Walters talked about how people pay cash bribes to corporate executives. . . . Mr. Walters talked about the cop on the beat who people pay cash bribes to get what they want. . . . Mr. Walters talked about cheating on taxes.

"And what does Norby Walters say about this vision of America, about these corrupt activities? That's what America is about. Those are Norby Walters's words, 'That's what America is about.' And Norby Walters's vision of America is one that he shared with Lloyd Bloom. It's a vision that brought them together, and it's a vision that they pursued for the next several years in the form of their illegal enterprise. Corruption, greed, illegal activity—for them, that is what America is about."

Pearl continued to flip the pages. His voice carried throughout the courtroom in an even presentation. Tony Valukas, sitting nearby at the prosecution table, watched the jurors intently. George Randolph did, too. Pearl tried to bring home the facts and went over the various counts of the indictment.

When he touched on the extortion charges, Pearl said, "Now, you heard a lot of cross-examination in this case about whether the person who was threatened in fact called the police or reported that to anyone. . . . Judge Marovich will instruct you that it is not necessary for the government to prove that the victim actually felt any fear but only that the defendant intended to instill that fear in the victim."

Pearl then moved on to Michael Franzese. "You can and should regard his testimony with caution and with great care. . . . The other evidence in this case completely corroborates Michael Franzese's testimony on those important points. . . . It wasn't just the government's evidence that Norby Walters and Michael Franzese were partners . . . Steve Machat, the manager for the New Edition, who testified for the defendant Walters, said that Norby Walters had brought Michael Franzese to a meeting and introduced him as his partner. So it's the defendant's own evidence that Michael Franzese was telling you the truth that he and Norby Walters were partners."

Pearl went over the threats Franzese and Walters made to Ron Weisner, the Jacksons' manager.

Next, Pearl attacked the testimony of Joe Grant, the manager for Dionne Warwick. Recounting conflicting testimony and the earlier FBI report, Pearl said forcefully, "Ladies and gentlemen, Joe Grant is a liar." He repeated himself. George Randolph could barely keep from smiling, remembering how angry Pearl had been when he had called Grant a liar months earlier over the speakerphone.

Pearl went on: "Joe Grant at some point had a change of heart and a change of testimony. And Joe Grant, who books acts in Las Vegas, who books acts in Atlantic City, wasn't going to come in here and tell you he had a conversation with someone who was a member of organized crime in connection with an act that he represents."

Pearl then lashed out at Machat, the New Edition manager who tried to dismiss the alleged threats by Franzese and Walters.

"Whether out of friendship or fear, Steven Machat came in here, and he also lied to you. You heard testimony yesterday that one of the other managers of the New Edition, Mr. Dern . . . who told you what really happened. After that meeting, Machat and his partner, Rick Smith, called Dern in California. And what did they say? They said, 'We have just been visited by Norby Walters and a mobster. . . . We have decided we better stay with Norby Walters because we don't want any problems.' How do you know Dern was telling the truth? You'll recall Mr. Levin-Epstein, no stranger to lengthy cross-examinations, had absolutely no questions to ask of Dern."

Pearl then reminded the jury how, in 1984, Walter and Bloom joined together "in their mission to become agents to the stars and rise, not just to the top of the entertainment world, but sports as well.

"Again, Norby Walters is a pattern player. . . . He consistently used his connection to organized crime . . . so it's natural that when he was expanding his business from entertainment into sports, he turned to the same player that he had been partners with for years, Michael Franzese."

If the attention of the jury had slipped at all, it was recaptured at the mention of Michael Franzese.

Pearl wanted to deliver a message to the jury, something they hadn't heard because of the short, ineffective cross-examination of Michael Franzese.

"Michael Franzese's job was to make money for an organized crime family, and he was good at it. When Norby Walters talked to him about getting into the business with Lloyd Bloom and him . . . this sports business, Michael Franzese recognized it as a good opportunity."

Pearl stepped to the side of the podium, opened his arms, and held out his hands.

"Of course, it was a good opportunity. Here you had a member of the Colombo family involved in things like gambling and loan-sharking. And now they have the opportunity to have premier college athletes, who are certain to turn professional, literally on their payroll and in their debt."

Pearl paused. He wanted the jury to think about that for a moment. He wanted to bring the point home as he turned his head slowly to look into the eyes of every attentive juror.

"You can imagine, ladies and gentlemen, had Michael Franzese not been incarcerated by the government at the very beginning of the

scheme . . . had the government not gotten involved in this investigation
. . . just what the possibilities were."

George Randolph was now looking at the jury. He wanted Howard
Pearl to repeat those words. But there was more to come.

"Franzese, recognizing this as a good opportunity, agreed to provide
fifty thousand dollars in cash."

Pearl reminded the jury that Franzese met Lloyd Bloom on that day,
and he reminded the jury of Dan Webb's promise in his opening statement.

"Webb boldly and confidently came out and said, 'I'm telling you that
if Michael Franzese identifies Lloyd Bloom, I will fall out of my chair.'
Lloyd Bloom, apparently less confident than Mr. Webb, for the only day
in the entire trial of this case, sat here, right here with his back to the
witness, instead of as he is now and always was, facing the court and the
witness.

"And you will recall that after looking around, Mr. Franzese said, 'It
is the individual over there sitting with his back to me.' Mr. Webb didn't
fall out of his chair; instead, he rose out of his chair and stipulated to that
identification. Ladies and gentlemen, Michael Franzese met Lloyd
Bloom that day."

The jury seemed to be hanging on every word now, and Pearl used the
time to make another important point that had almost gone unnoticed
during the trial.

"Now, the evidence shows that Michael Franzese was, in fact, one of
the sources of the cash that went through this business. His testimony on
that is supported by the evidence . . . every one of the players who
testified in this case told you that their signing bonus, the amounts they
received when they signed, were paid in cash." (Pearl paused.) "So the
question is: Where did all the cash come from?"

He paused again. Then he reminded the jury of the day that more than
sixty stipulations were read into the record as evidence.

"Stipulations are generally a good thing. They help. They save everyone time and effort of not having to provide testimony that's agreed
upon. The problem with stipulations, as you can recall and feel, is that
they're more difficult to comprehend as they're read, and they don't leave
the same impression that live testimony does. So I need to remind you
of one of the stipulations." (Pearl glanced down at his notes.) "It was
stipulated in this case that Norby Walters Associates and World Sports
and Entertainment have no records reflecting the generation of cash that
was used to pay these so-called loans. Nor are there any records whatso-

ever of any cash received or generated by or through or for the benefit of that business.

"Ladies and gentlemen, this is a company that when it comes to its expenses, keeps great records. You can look at the records in this case and see what day Paul Palmer was given twenty-five dollars in musical cassettes. You can see, and you heard in the testimony, that the defense was able to show you what day Lloyd Bloom was reimbursed for purchasing a sweatsuit for Everett Gay.

"But there are no records, no records whatsoever, of all this cash that Norby Walters and Lloyd Bloom went across the country passing out to student-athletes. That shouldn't surprise you. When you take the mob's money, there are no records. You don't issue stock certificates, and you don't give—and you don't get—receipts."

George Randolph wanted to kiss Howard Pearl. But the prosecutor wasn't even halfway through his closing argument.

"Did Lloyd Bloom know Michael Franzese was a partner in the business? Of course he knew. Does it make any sense whatsoever that Norby Walters would tell Ron Weisner that he was partners with Michael Franzese, that he would say to Steven Machat that he was partners with Michael Franzese, but that somehow he would hide or conceal that from his other partner, Lloyd Bloom?"

For the first time Dan Webb jumped to his feet to address the court: "Judge, I object to that argument because of the evidence presented. The evidence was that nothing was ever said to Lloyd Bloom. I object to that argument."

Marovich turned to the jury and said, "The jury has heard the evidence, and I will instruct you from time to time. If the arguments of counsel are contrary to your collective memories as to what the evidence is, just ignore the arguments."

Pearl thanked Marovich and then reminded the jury, "Lloyd Bloom knew that Norby Walters and Michael Franzese were partners, and that's why the day in the airport he had told Paul Palmer that he thought it was pretty funny that Norby Walters in *Sports Illustrated* had denied even knowing Michael Franzese.

"How else do you know that Lloyd Bloom knew Michael Franzese? When Lloyd Bloom called Everett Gay in November 1986, a transaction I'll talk about later, he says to Gay, 'That's why we have partners in California, so no one messes around with us.' Now, at that point, Michael Franzese had been in California for two years. Lloyd Bloom's statement that 'we have partners in California and that they make sure no one messes around with us' is either an incredible piece of luck or a very accurate understanding of who his partners were and what their function was."

Pearl proceeded to move into the deception of the Walters-Bloom operation. He also got to the heart of what was ailing the government's case.

"I want to be blunt. The student-athletes that we called to testify are not heroes. They were here as coschemers, as coconspirators with Norby Walters and Lloyd Bloom. We are not asking you to give them your cheers, your applause, or your admiration. These are individuals who participated in a scheme with these defendants to defraud their universities, to file false certifications, sometimes even under oath, in order to obtain their scholarships.

"Some of them testified that they didn't know it was a crime, but I suggest to you, ladies and gentlemen, that long before you came to this courthouse you knew that lying in order to obtain money from someone was a crime."

Pearl ran through the various players and universities. He also attacked Walters's advice-of-counsel strategy. Pearl used the fact that Walters had withheld the contracts of the six underclassmen at the start of the investigation as evidence for the jury to contemplate.

"Mr. Walters had said on the Harmon tape, 'It's just like cheating on your income tax. If you get caught, you give them a little, and you never disclose what you are doing.' That, ladies and gentlemen, is living representation of what he meant. What Michael Feldberg didn't know is that they had concealed from him the fact that there were other contracts out there for underclassmen, guys in the class of 1988 and beyond. . . . What does it show you? It shows you that Norby Walters and Lloyd Bloom concealed critical evidence from their very own attorneys."

Pearl tried to defend some of the players, such as Michigan State's Mark Ingram, who had remained eligible despite his criminal convictions: "Hopefully he learned some from that punishment, from his thirty days in jail. Mark Ingram was allowed to return to the university. He played football, played well, and got his degree. He started with a career in the NFL, and he has got his degree. . . . That's better than becoming a college dropout and ending up back in jail."

Pearl tried to patch every other hole the defense had made. He also wanted to stress the testimony of Notre Dame's Alvin Miller.

"Alvin Miller, ladies and gentlemen, is memorable because he was the one who, after signing one night in a hotel a contract with Norby Walters and Lloyd Bloom, he couldn't sleep. He felt horrible about what he had done to himself and Notre Dame. He called his family on the phone, and early the next morning he called Mr. Walters and said, 'I'm going to come and give you your money back.' Alvin Miller found out that when a loan shark like Norby Walters or Lloyd Bloom had their money into you, you are stuck. They own you. Norby Walters told him, 'Don't worry about it. No one will find out.' He refused to take the money back. He refused to rip up the contract.''

George Randolph again studied the jury, as if to ask, "Did you hear that?"

Pearl went over the extortion charges. About Maurice Douglass, he said, "I suggest to you, ladies and gentlemen, that when someone goes to his mother and says, 'If anything happens to me, tell the police that Norby Walters and Lloyd Bloom were the ones who did it,' then that is an individual who is truly scared."

Pearl pointed out that almost every player testified that Walters and Bloom threatened to turn them in to the NCAA and expose their violation of the rules. The threat to expose Tony Woods's younger brother was bothersome, Pearl said, "because that was a threat that Tony Woods clearly cared about."

Howard Pearl was winding down his argument and then said, "At that point you must have wondered what would have happened had these athletes, in fact, stayed with Norby Walters and Lloyd Bloom and allowed them to serve as their agents. Paul Palmer, ladies and gentlemen, provides to you exactly the answer to that question. Paul Palmer decided to stay with Norby Walters and Lloyd Bloom even though, as you heard on the Tony Woods tape, there were rumors that Norby Walters had been involved with the Mafia."

Pearl proceeded to verbally slap Lloyd Bloom all over the courtroom for ripping off Paul Palmer. Then he brought his two-hour-plus argument to a conclusion.

"The vision of America that Norby Walters sets forth on the Ronnie Harmon tape, the same pitch he used traveling across the country . . . is a vision of America where illegal activities are rampant. . . . It's this perverse, corrupt vision of America that Norby Walters and Lloyd Bloom believed would take them to the top, would make them agents to the stars and would make them reach the pinnacle of the world of sports and entertainment.

"Norby Walters talks on that tape about how his business practices involve what he calls a razzle-dazzle, a razzle-dazzle designed to make sure that the government doesn't find out what about. . . . I suggest to you, ladies and gentlemen, that what happened in this case is that the government did find out what Norby Walters was about, what Mr. Bloom was about.

"You are now beyond the razzle-dazzle. . . . It is time to remind ourselves as a community that what this country is about is people like Father Hesburgh, people like Coach Schembechler, people who believe that as a society we live and play by the rules. That's what America is about . . . not the corrupt activities of Lloyd Bloom and Norby Walters."

Howard Pearl finished moments later. It was 12:30 P.M. There was silence in the courtroom after his argument. If Howard Pearl had shown signs of cracking during the previous two years, he had just performed brilliantly when it counted most.

Judge Marovich recessed the courtroom for lunch. Tony Valukas, Helene Greenwald, and George Randolph jumped up to shake Pearl's hand.

No matter how terrifically Dan Webb would perform, Howard Pearl had delivered a powerful closing argument. Yet, there was still a queasy feeling in the pits of their stomachs. Dan Webb would be on center stage in ninety minutes.

20

THE COURTROOM buzzed as two o'clock approached. Norby Walters turned around in his chair nearest the first row in the gallery, shielded his mouth with his hand, and told a reporter, "This . . . is where we're going to win."

Walters took one look at Dan Webb, who was seated in the middle of the defense table; the lawyer's head was cocked, and he was scribbling away on a legal notepad.

"I have never seen anybody like this guy," Walters said admiringly. "I love Bob Gold, but I wish, I really wish, I woulda hired Dan Webb. Can you believe the luck of that schmuck over there?"

The schmuck was Lloyd Bloom, who still looked casual, aloof, and overconfident, despite a most convincing closing argument by Howard Pearl.

Without notice, Judge Marovich entered the courtroom. Everyone rose except Webb, who was still scribbling away.

"Are you at the top of your game, Mr. Webb?" Marovich asked.

Webb jumped to his feet. "I didn't hear you, Judge."

"Are you at the top of your game?" Marovich asked again with a smile.

"I don't know, but I'm ready to go anyway, Judge."

Soon the jury was brought into its box. Marovich gave Webb the go-ahead, and the six-foot-one lawyer rose from the defense table and approached the jury with his hands in his pockets. He looked like a kid, like Beaver Cleaver. He leaned on the podium near the jury and began speaking.

"Racketeer. Racketeer. . . . It's kind of a harsh, kind of an evil-sounding word."

He stepped to the side of the podium so the jury could see him better. He wasn't looking at his notes. He simply tuned in to the nine women and four men sitting in front of him. His voice was loud, but it sounded warm, sincere, trusting.

"I think the first time I ever heard that word, ever in my life, was when I was a small kid. I grew up in a small rural community in downstate Illinois, and this little one-horse town had a movie house. But they ran movies only on Saturday afternoon. And they ran all these B-grade movies—Westerns . . . crime movies."

Tony Valukas raised his eyebrows at the jury, hoping to catch their attention. Valukas had heard this story before. He knew this was going to be an argument of passion—Webb's passion.

Webb continued, "And I remember watching a movie when I was ten, twelve years old, called *Racketeer*. Ironically, it was a movie about Chicago. It was a movie about Al Capone. It showed during the Capone era . . . murder and mayhem and violence, and it was called *Racketeer*. And that's where I first heard that word."

Webb's strategy was clear. You take Al Capone, and you look at Lloyd Bloom.

"Little did I know that thirty-some years later I would be standing in a Chicago courtroom with the government contending that this man became a racketeer because, according to this indictment, because he became associated with a man by the name of Michael Franzese, apparently a New York mobster, and that because my client became associated with Michael Franzese . . . that he is guilty of racketeering. That's the heart of the government's charge. I'll read it to you from the indictment . . . but in a court of law, words are empty.

"During the course of this trial I promised you in my opening that when that man Franzese got on the witness stand, I was going to bring him, Lloyd Bloom, out of the witness chair, I was going to put him right in front of Franzese, and I was going to ask him these questions. And I did. I did that very thing. I said, 'Mr. Franzese, did you ever have anything to do with Mr. Bloom?' He said no. I think he said, 'I met him once and shook his hand.' Three seconds . . . five seconds? How is Lloyd Bloom supposed to remember that he shook the man's hand five years ago? That, ladies and gentlemen, that handshake is what the government says makes Lloyd Bloom a racketeer."

Webb then spoke of the government's burden of proof. He began to talk about Judge Marovich's forthcoming instructions about that burden, and Valukas rose to his feet, knowing that Webb would continue to push the envelope to the edge in his closing argument.

"Your honor, I object."

"About defining the—" Marovich began.

"That's correct."

"I'm not defining it, Judge," Webb said.

"Don't," Marovich ordered.

"I don't intend to," Webb said.

"Good."

Webb proceeded, "Let me start with the fraud on the universities, the allegation that when Lloyd Bloom acted as a sports agent, he defrauded these universities. Now, Mr. Pearl told you this morning, 'Look, this isn't very complicated; it's very simple. You just kind of find that Lloyd Bloom is a bad guy, just go convict him.'

"This so-called fraud on the universities clearly appears to be a very, very important part of the government's charges against my client, Lloyd Bloom. . . . As I understand the government's theory, the government's theory is that when Bloom and Walters operated as sports agents, that they signed players, student-athletes, to contracts, to representation agreements, early, before their eligibility expired, made loans to them, and that this violated these rules called the NCAA that you have heard so much about.

"Mr. Pearl forgot to tell you this morning something that Judge Marovich is going to tell you: Violation of NCAA rules is not a crime because they are not law. The NCAA is a private club, no different than the Lions Club or a community group you belong to. They can pass any rules they want, but they are not laws at all. And, therefore, at this point when Walters and Bloom signed these players, no crime has occurred.

"But the government says you have to look at what happened afterward. These players did not tell their schools that they violated NCAA rules." (Webb threw out his hands.) "Not hard to understand. Of course they didn't tell them. Of course they didn't. There is absolutely no question that the students did not tell the universities that they had violated NCAA rules. There is no question that Bloom knew that. No question about it."

Webb cocked his head again and opened his hands to the jury.

"But that's not a crime, either. Just so you understand, you're going to be instructed by the judge that merely intending to deceive someone is not a crime. The crime here is you have to intend to deceive and also intend to actually defraud someone of property.

"The crime of mail fraud occurs, under the law . . . when a defendant actually devises and intends to devise—that means to plan out—a scheme that is specifically intended to cheat someone out of their property—like the scholarship, which is the property charged here. And after that, the United States mails are used by that person, or that person causes the United States mails to be used, to carry out the fraud scheme.

"The simplest example: If I were trying to cheat someone and I sent letters in the mail saying, 'I've got this hair cream I'll sell you that will grow hair on your head,' and it's just a fraud—it's actually vinegar and oil—but I send out these letters in the mail, and I say, 'Buy my cream for fifty dollars, and you'll grow hair on your head,' and I send that through the mail, and someone sends me back fifty dollars, and I send them out their cream, and I've cheated them out of fifty dollars—in that case, I had planned a scheme, specifically intended to cheat somebody out of their property, and then I used the United States mails."

Valukas got to his feet again. "Your Honor," he said. "I'm going to object to the argument as to how the law ought to be interpreted. That's not correct, insofar as it's leaving out elements—"

"Well, you will have your turn," Marovich said. "I will allow the argument."

Webb nodded and continued.

"I believe when you hear the instructions from Judge Marovich, that's exactly what the crime of mail fraud is. What is charged here and why it's important—I want to talk about it—is that Lloyd Bloom, in order to find him guilty beyond a reasonable doubt, the government has to prove that he actually sat down and planned and devised a scheme to defraud the universities out of their scholarship money."

Valukas objected again. "Your Honor, this is not what we are required to prove."

"You know the instructions that we worked on so diligently, Mr. Webb," Marovich warned Webb.

"What is required is that he participate in the scheme," Valukas said. "He doesn't have to devise it himself."

Marovich told Webb to proceed. Webb talked about how the nine athletes were also the bad guys, under the government's charges, and conspired with Bloom to cheat the universities.

Webb told the jury, "Then I took a chance. I asked every one of them the ultimate question in this case. I said to them, 'Sir, when you and

Walters and Bloom sat down, were you planning or intending to cheat the universities out of the scholarship?' Nine of them said no. Now, is that proof beyond reasonable doubt?

"Judge Marovich is going to instruct you that there is a concept in the law known as good faith. . . . If you find that Bloom acted in good faith, that is complete defense to those allegations, and you must find the defendant not guilty. That's the law. The question is: Was Lloyd Bloom, as he was out there carrying out his duties as a sports agent, was he acting in good faith?"

Webb then told the jury that there were two different series of events that "establish without question that Lloyd Bloom was acting in good faith." Every member of the prosecution table looked at the jurors and raised their eyebrows.

Incredibly, Webb adopted Walters's defense by pointing out that Bloom discovered that sports agents traditionally signed players before their eligibility ran out and then he went to Walters's attorney, Lon Trost, who said, "That happens all the time."

"Norby Walters, who was financing the operation, took this young man, who was twenty-four years old, to one of the biggest and most prestigious law firms in America, in New York, called Shea and Gould. . . . What did the law firm tell them? You are doing nothing illegal. What else could he do? He went in and consulted with the law firm, and that's what they told him."

After hammering that some more, Webb then pointed out something that hadn't been revealed to the jury. "From about January of 1985 until March of 1987, during that time period, they signed a total of fifty-eight student-athletes from a total of thirty-two different universities in the United States of America. Now, think about that. As far as what you have heard here, the government presented out of fifty-eight athletes . . . nine. And out of thirty-two schools, they presented six universities that they say were victimized. They left out twenty-six schools and forty-nine student-athletes.

"Now I'm asking you: How can it be that with twenty-six schools there is no fraud, but with these nine schools there is some type of fraud that occurred here?"

Valukas leaped to his feet: "I object, Your Honor, because there is no suggestion there wasn't fraud at the other schools. We merely chose not to charge them."

Webb shook his head.

"Oh, Judge, I—"

"You can argue your inferences," Marovich said.

Webb began again.

"And I'm asking you to look at it from that standpoint. How is he supposed to distinguish, when he's dealing with thirty-two different schools, that someday the government is going to pick six of those schools and parade them into a courtroom and say, 'Aha, I'm a fraud victim'? What about the others, the other twenty-six schools? They weren't fraud victims, but these six were?"

The incredulous tone in Webb's voice ricocheted off the courtroom's maple-brown walls. Webb raised his voice several more decibels. He only occasionally glanced at his notes.

"I do want to talk about the university witnesses. You want to know why? Because I think there was a sham that was pulled off in this courtroom. I think there was testimony presented in this courtroom that was fudged by these universities. And I don't attribute any ill motive to them. The government returned an indictment in this case which named them as fraud victims, and they did their very best to pretend to be a fraud victim. . . .

"And, as testimony revealed, the universities make in many cases millions of dollars off their football program. And it's very important that if you are going to have a football team, the better the team, the more money you make. Because if you go to the Rose Bowl or the Orange Bowl or all those bowl games, you make a lot of money. But you've got to have an awful good team to do that."

Webb argued that Big Ten schools were not allowed to cancel the athletes' scholarships. He also got into the question of whether the student-athletes broke the rules when they took money from Walters and Bloom. Loans were okay by the rules, but not compensation. The sports agents had made loans to the players, right?

"I'm dealing with this twilight zone . . . of what would have happened.

"It was a full-time job for those kids. They earned those scholarships. And those schools . . . they're coming into this courtroom, and they're testifying, 'I'm a poor beleaguered fraud victim because I made millions of dollars off these kids. They worked their tails off to play football, but we got cheated out of the scholarship.' " (Webb paused for effect.) "I find that hard to believe. I really do. I find that real hard to accept."

Webb proceeded to renew his attack on the athletes' academics, all the while pointing out that the colleges required the student-athletes to work "thirty to forty hours a week" on football.

"It's not a hobby . . . but under NCAA rules, because they have this facade that it's supposed to be only to get an education, their very own rules say right on the face that if a student is not in good academic standing, if he's not satisfactorily progressing toward a degree, then the school is supposed to decertify him as a football player. Of course that's not what happened."

The defense attorney tore through Ronnie Harmon's transcripts again, and he ripped the university's explanation.

"That's a disgrace to your intelligence as jurors," Webb said.

Athlete by athlete, Webb started to break down their testimony. He referred to the crimes committed by Rod Woodson and Mark Ingram.

"There's something wrong if a student-athlete commits crimes and continues to play football and receive his scholarship, but if the student-athlete signs with an agent, they have to revoke the scholarship. . . . I don't believe that."

As for Bloom's threats, Webb ridiculed them, pointing out that ten of the thirteen players who testified "ripped off" Walters and Bloom.

"I don't feel sorry for Walters, and I don't feel sorry for Bloom. But I tell you, putting that into perspective . . . you can imagine the frustration and anger Lloyd Bloom might feel. I don't think there is any question, and I don't doubt for a moment that when Bloom had conversations with Maurice Douglass, Everett Gay, and Edwin Simmons, there were some harsh words spoken in phone conversations. . . . All those players made a deal with the government that they would not be prosecuted for anything they had done if they would testify against Bloom and Walters. Do you think those players might lie on the witness stand?"

"I object, Your Honor," Valukas said. "Maurice Douglass received no deal."

Webb went on, "And talk about a sham. . . . In those pre-trial diversion agreements, they said, 'Well, we will make restitution and pay the school back the scholarship.' They didn't do it. They all testified, except for Harmon, 'We have never paid the school a dime.' "

Webb got back to Bloom's threat to Douglass. "All of a sudden an angry phone call has been blown into a federal criminal charge of extortion.

"The next government witness was even more laughable. Tony Woods. Woods changed his testimony four times.

"After lunch, Mr. Woods changed his testimony back. I got up and I was angry. And I asked him, 'Mr. Woods, what in the devil happened over the lunch hour that caused you to change your testimony?' Do you remember what he said? He said that it popped out of a chicken. That's what he said. I didn't even go any further. I was angry about that. I'm sorry. It's a crime, what he's on trial for, and it popped up out of a chicken."

Valukas, Pearl, and Randolph almost jumped out of their seats. Webb had just turned "I ate at Popeye's Chicken" into something else.

Webb started to wind down, somehow trying to argue that Bloom didn't rip off Paul Palmer. "You can say he shouldn't have done it. I agree. He shouldn't have done it. I can't quarrel with that. It was a stupid thing to do, but he wasn't intending to defraud Paul Palmer. . . . He went to Palmer's accountant, Joel Levy, and the accountant recorded on the books as loans . . ."

Then, trying to justify the Rolls-Royce that Bloom bought, Webb said, "The evidence has established that Bloom, in running this entertainment business to go out and try to sign up Hollywood stars, was successful on one occasion. I don't live in Southern California. I don't know why a Rolls-Royce is necessary to go out and impress movie stars. But I have been out there a few times, and I've seen the cars those people drive out there. At least I understand what the thinking was."

The clock ticked past four. Webb knew he had to finish, passionately, gloriously, sincerely.

"I have talked on long enough. I started out by telling you that to say Lloyd Bloom is a racketeer is so unfair, but that's the charge. That he and Franzese committed all these crimes by associating with Franzese just isn't fair.

"What really happened in this case is that a course of conduct that maybe shouldn't have happened—I mean violating NCAA rules, I'm not going to give anyone a medal of honor for that. But everyone agreed that it didn't violate any laws. And the government has taken that course and tried to explode it into this courtroom, suggesting they have proven beyond a reasonable doubt that Lloyd Bloom became a racketeer.

"I told you at the outset of the case, and I will tell you again, I don't suggest to you that Lloyd Bloom is a saint. I believe that the evidence has established there were times that he made mistakes in judgment. He lost his temper. But we don't convict someone of being a racketeer beyond reasonable doubt, and all the consequences that follow from that, based on the fact that the government wants it to be that way. They have got to prove it.

"But there really are no saints in this case, are there? Look at the participants, the thirteen student-athletes who ripped off Walters and Bloom. I'm glad they didn't get prosecuted. I'd rather watch them. They are playing football now, God bless them. Okay? Every one of them was promised by the government they won't be prosecuted. They got off scot-free.

"Did they make money off this deal? A lot. They all made money. Bloom and Walters—it was his money—the kids realized what a soft touch it ended up being, and they ripped him off. Did they make money? Absolutely.

"What about the universities? There's no saints there. This facade of amateurism, in which these universities pretend that academics is what's important and that playing football is a hobby, is a charade. It is an absolute charade. And that's got to be changed someday, but you are not going to change it in this trial. But did they make money? Millions of dollars.

"You know the one group of people that made no money? Walters and Bloom. They made nothing. The evidence is Walters, in financing it, lost it all. The kids ripped him off. Then he couldn't negotiate their contracts, so he made no profits.

"It's not fair to make Walters and Bloom the scapegoat out of this whole sordid development of events, which we have all now seen in the courtroom, where football players are being used by the universities to make money. The football players then use the agents.

"Maybe all of this ought to change, but that's not something you are going to be able to do or that I'm going to be able to do because we are involved in a criminal trial here with very serious criminal charges filed against Bloom and Walters. And I suggest to you that to make Bloom and Walters the scapegoats for what's wrong in college football today is simply not fair.

"And I worry about that a bit. The government called these very prominent, some very famous, witnesses to the stand, obviously with the hope that you would rush to judgment. Rush to judgment.

"I want to tell you something. I have spent my life, my adult life, trying cases before juries. And I have watched you during this trial. I have never seen a jury more attentive. I don't believe that because two or three prominent witnesses testified for the government that you are going to rush to judgment and find this man guilty beyond reasonable doubt . . . I believe very sincerely that you are going to follow the law. I believe you are going to make a fair and impartial judgment.

"Yes, Lloyd Bloom's fate is in your hands, but I want to tell you something. I say it on behalf of him and on behalf of me. I trust you. Whatever your verdict is, I accept. But I'm confident that this evidence, after you have listened to it, now that you have heard it all, once you are instructed by the judge, that you will find that the government has not proven their case beyond a reasonable doubt."

Then Webb made a push for a hung jury.

"And if you do, please don't abandon this man. Judge Marovich is going to further tell you, never surrender your honest beliefs about the weight and the effect of the evidence simply for the purpose of reaching a unanimous verdict. If you believe that the government has failed to sustain its burden of proof, don't walk away. Stick by your guns. . . . Thank you for being so attentive."

Norby Walters had tears in his eyes when Dan Webb finished. Lloyd Bloom looked up at Dan Webb like a big brother who had just stood up for him. And he had, of course. The sting of Howard Pearl's splendid argument had been softened. It was 4:35 P.M. on April 4. The jury would go home and come back the next morning to listen to Robert Gold and then to Tony Valukas's rebuttal argument.

Somebody asked George Randolph what he thought.

"Fuckin' Webb," he grumbled out of the courtroom.

21

ON APRIL 5 everyone was in place when Robert Gold, the affable, diminutive attorney, took to his feet to deliver his closing argument on behalf of Norby Walters. The jury understood that it would in all likelihood get the case that afternoon or the next morning.

Gold knew that his basic job was to shred Michael Franzese's credibility because Franzese had been a potent witness on the stand. Like Webb, Gold shifted between anger and sincerity. He attacked Michael Franzese constantly as a "liar . . . a professional liar."

"Michael Franzese was the poison, not the evidence. He tried to convince you that Norby Walters was a gangster. Michael Franzese, by spilling poison over the courtroom, was here to distract you and prevent you from doing your job."

Gold did take the courageous but necessary step of acknowledging that there was a relationship between Norby Walters and Michael Franzese.

"There's no doubt that Norby Walters knew a man by the name of Michael Franzese. There's no issue on that point. There's also no doubt that Norby Walters has been in the entertainment business for thirty years, and the one thing Michael Franzese has been in his life is a movie producer. Norby Walters went to Michael Franzese, the movie producer, for opportunity. That may have been ill-conceived and stupid, to say the least, but it does not make Norby Walters a racketeer."

As for the $50,000 seed money for the sports business, Gold argued: "Fifty thousand dollars makes no sense. It doesn't start to put a dent in the amount of money Mr. Walters advanced to these players."

Gold hammered on Walters's "state of mind" when he sought legal advice.

"It was no storefront law firm—it was the best he could find."

322 Chris Mortensen

His argument, like the one to follow, was brief as decided by Judge Marovich.

"For Norby Walters, his life will be in your hands. For a long time he's had to live under the cloud of this investigation. He's already suffered the anguish . . . the embarrassment. . . . Send him home to his family by returning a verdict of not guilty."

It was all left to the forty-five minutes allotted to Tony Valukas. The U. S. Attorney had thought about what he would say and how he would say it.

He later explained, "I was not going to be emotional, certainly not on behalf of college athletics. I had to make the jury believe this was a very simple case of fraud. Without the fraud, everything else would be thrown out."

Valukas followed his game plan. Calmly and in control he said, "These are matters my children could understand. If you lie to someone in order to obtain money, it is fraud."

Valukas said that Robert Perryman was "the single most important witness in the case because he established that he had discussed the certification papers and the documents with Norby Walters and Lloyd Bloom, and they told him to lie on those documents and submit them to Michigan. A scholarship is money, Michigan's money, and the university is entitled not to have that money taken away by fraud."

Valukas tried to get the jury to "understand that Mr. Webb is an extremely talented lawyer. . . . There was no cross-examination of Bo Schembechler. There were no what-ifs with Bo Schembechler."

Valukas ridiculed Walters's advice-of-counsel defense by referring to Trost as Cousin Lon. "Not even Cousin Lon testified that he advised Walters and Bloom to have the student-athletes lie to the schools. . . . There also is not a single document that shows research on the legality or illegality in the conduct the agents engaged in. . . . The law firm was unable to give good faith advice because good faith requires that you do not lie or conceal information."

Valukas pointed out that "the lawsuits gave Norby Walters a lever."

Then he told the jury how a former attorney general of Illinois filed a divorce action against his wife that revealed income tax cheating. From the lawsuit the attorney general was prosecuted and convicted of tax fraud.

"The lawsuits by Norby Walters were a calculated risk by a very savvy businessman," Valukas told the jury.

The U. S. Attorney made a point to call Walters "Uncle Norby."

Valukas had let Howard Pearl make the pertinent points about Michael Franzese's involvement with Norby Walters, and he added, "I wouldn't ask you to believe Michael Franzese unless he was corroborated."

Valukas then wheeled and pointed at Norby Walters. "We didn't bring Michael Franzese into the courtroom. His partner did."

The remark struck Dan Webb as funny. It was a standard line by prosecutors, and it was the line he had used seven years earlier in the Marquette 10 case when he defended the government's use of drug dealers to testify against Chicago police officers.

Tony Valukas was finished. So was the trial. Now the case was going to the jury.

The next day, U. S. District Court Judge George M. Marovich provided the eight-woman, four-man jury with ninety-nine jury instructions on the law. They had been argued by the lawyers in the past week. Marovich had them typewritten. Both sides knew that one of the most critical instructions involved the judge's interpretation of the mail fraud statute and college scholarship benefits. A handful of instructions stuck out.

• "The government must prove that an act in furtherance of the conspiracy occurred within the Northern District of Illinois. You are instructed that the Northern District of Illinois includes Chicago, Lake Forest, and Schaumburg, Illinois."

• "To sustain the charge of mail fraud, the government must prove the following propositions as to a particular defendant:

"First, that the defendant knowingly participated in the scheme to defraud to obtain money or property by means of false and fraudulent pretenses, representations as described in the indictment;

"Second, that for the purpose of carrying out the scheme or attempting to do so, the defendant used the United States mails or caused the United States mails to be used in the manner charged in the particular count or racketeering act; and,

"Third, that the defendant did so knowingly and with the intent to defraud."

• "Use of the mails need not be contemplated by the scheme, and the defendant need not do any actual mailing."

• "I instruct you that the term 'property' includes tuition, room, board, fees, financial assistance, and the right to control the allocation of athletic scholarships to student-athletes."

• "I hereby instruct you that the defendants Norby Walters and Lloyd

Bloom cannot be found guilty of any charges in the indictment simply because you find that he was involved in the violation of the rules of the NCAA, the Big Ten Conference, or any university. These rules do not have the status of law."

• "If you find that defendants Walters and Bloom acted in good faith when engaging in the conduct as sports agents . . . then you must find defendant Bloom not guilty to these criminal acts of mail fraud and wire fraud."

• "Attempted extortion through 'fear of economic harm' or 'fear of physical harm' may be established by showing that the defendant attempted to instill in the alleged victim a fear of economic or physical harm if the victim did not cooperate with the defendant's alleged request. Attempted extortion . . . does not require proof of defendant demonstrating force or threat. It is unnecessary for the government to prove that the defendant actually created fear in the minds of the victims."

• "You have heard evidence that government witness Michael Franzese has received benefits from the government in connection with his testimony. You may give his testimony such weight as you feel it deserves, keeping in mind that it must be considered with caution and great care."

The ninety-nine instructions took an hour to read, and they were given to the jury before it started deliberating.

The deliberations began. The government thought it had a fair chance for victory if it could get one mail fraud conviction. The defense thought it had a solid chance because of Webb's attack on the colleges.

Three days passed, and there was no verdict. Then four days. The jury was being allowed to go home each day around six o'clock. Marovich preferred not to sequester them but said he would consider doing so after a week. Randolph was agitated, hanging out with fellow FBI agents downstairs. Howard Pearl actually felt relieved now that the case was out of his hands. He watched television in his office and had to put up with Tony Valukas's occasional frowns. Valukas wanted everyone to bite their nails with him.

"What could be wrong?" he asked Pearl.

By the fifth day somebody had an idea. Why not have both sides get together for drinks at Binyons, the restaurant-bar down the street from the federal building? Government, defense, the media—in Chicago, they all made strange bedfellows.

That night, on the second floor at Binyons, a party of fifteen shared drinks and laughs. Then something extraordinary happened. Lloyd

Bloom showed up. Before anyone knew it, Bloom and Pearl were sitting next to each other at the bar, talking about the case.

"Lloyd still did not understand what was going on," said Pearl.

Then Norby Walters walked in and froze. He thought this was a get-together for his lawyers and the media. When he saw Webb joking with Valukas, and Pearl talking with Bloom, he turned away bitterly.

From Binyons the party hopped to Harry Caray's and The Lodge on Rush Street. Randolph went home early, exhausted.

The edge had been cut from everyone's anxieties except Norby Walters's. Except for Michael Franzese's.

Even if it only meant "one year or twenty-eight days" for his cooperation in the Norby Walters case, it was still time off that was coming to Michael Franzese. A conviction would strengthen the recommendation. He wished the defense team had tried to keep him on for three days so he could explain to the jury that the "mob's biggest enterprise was gambling."

Franzese said, "I kept thinking it was going to come up, but it's not exactly the great secret that the mob is heavily involved in gambling. Any jury probably would understand the possibilities. I was ready to tell them about it. Nobody asked. I think the government really thought there would be an opening. But this was something I wouldn't have had to discuss with Norby. Nobody knew about the mob more than Norby.

"The bill was going to come due, especially with Norby. . . . He tried to be too much of a wise guy. If I hadn't been in prison, if I hadn't made this decision to walk away . . . Norby had his day coming, and he knew it. We would have jumped all over the sports operation. Norby had to pay, but then all that stuff happened, and it fell apart . . . and Norby had to pay in another respect.

"I really want to make this point about Norby. You can only do things so long before it catches up to you. He had a long run. Let's put it this way: He had a long run, and it caught up with him. I never thought that I'd be the player, but you never know. I learned that myself. You can only go so far. It catches up with you."

Franzese was asked what his father, Sonny Franzese, would think of his son for turning in a "lifelong friend."

"My father and I were on the same wavelength as far as our feelings about the life, and we shared the same feelings about Norby Walters.

"However, we had a different philosophy. My father's philosophy was, 'Hey, I'm sixty-something years old. This is how I lived my whole life, this is how I'm going to die.' My philosophy was, I'm thirty-something years old. I got a wife and five children. I got my whole life ahead of me. My family has been destroyed. I'm not going to put my wife and kids through this, not for something I don't believe in or that I've lost touch with.

"Basically that's what my decision came down to: Am I going to stand on ceremony because, number one, I'm afraid to come forward, or am I just going to keep my mouth shut the rest of my life, go along, even though I don't want to be part of it anymore? Or was it going to be: I got a wife and kids, and that's where my priority's going to be. That's where it's at, and that's what I got to worry about.

"To me it didn't make sense living that way anymore. I had another year or so to do in jail. I would have been drawn back into the life, and it's not something I wanted. It just didn't make sense. I wanted out, and I wanted to send a message that I was out. When I took the witness stand against Norby Walters, that was it. I think right now [the mob] pretty much got the message. Actually, it was a message I sent through the government, by taking the witness stand, by cooperating, by saying, 'Hey, that's it. That's the end of it.' I wasn't trying to be cute. I just told the truth."

Michael Franzese was still in Chicago under FBI guard. Federal law enforcement authorities in New York wanted to strike while the iron was hot to make a deal. Franzese didn't want to deal with the New Yorkers, but he said Randolph had another "heart to heart" with him.

"Mike, you already took the witness stand, and you broke your oath," Randolph told Franzese. "If you're a dead man, you're a dead man. But you ought to try doing something for yourself while you're alive."

"Without George being there," Franzese said, "prodding me, challenging me, showing me I could trust somebody in government, I never would have taken the step. It may sound very strange to some, but I consider George Randolph a friend, a brother. He may not be able to accept that. I did a lot of crying on his shoulder, I agonized about every step, and he showed me there's such a thing as trust. Hey, that's even if he did give me a hard time."

On the sixth day of deliberations, Tony Valukas and George Randolph were nervous wrecks. Howard Pearl was curious but still cool, watching TV in his office. Something had to be wrong. The jury wasn't buying the mail fraud, they thought.

Then came word. A verdict had been reached. It was Thursday, April 14.

The jury was ushered into the courtroom. Bob Gold knew something was wrong because none of the jurors looked at the defense table. Norby Walters and Lloyd Bloom had their heads bowed, perhaps saying a prayer.

The clerk was handed the verdict. He gave it to the judge, who gave it back to the clerk.

"We the jury find the defendant Norby Walters . . . Count one: guilty . . . Count two: guilty."

A sensational feeling was growing inside George Randolph. Those were the racketeering and conspiracy counts.

"Count three: Not guilty."

Oh, no, that was Iowa.

"Count four: "Not guilty."

That was Michigan State.

"Count five: guilty. Count six: guilty."

George Randolph's head dropped in a prayer of thanks. The jury had found Walters guilty of defrauding Michigan and Purdue. Everything else was gravy now.

Walters was also found guilty on counts seven and eight—the conspiracy acts, including extortion.

Lloyd Bloom was guilty of the same acts.

There was a hush in the courtroom. The jury was polled. The defense lawyers made motions for acquittal, and, of course, the appeal was on the way. Dan Webb and Robert Gold were certain there was a reversible error or two.

The crowd left the courtroom as the sports agents stayed behind with their lawyers. When they headed for the exit, Walters was grim-faced and teary-eyed but composed. "We'll take 'em in the next round," he promised.

Lloyd Bloom, who had seemed so aloof, was sobbing, comforted by Dan Webb and his father, who also cried. Lloyd Bloom was unable to speak.

The jury foreman, Marjorie Benson, said, "We did want to send a message to the schools that they need to look at themselves, just as Norby Walters and Lloyd Bloom needed to do."

Why did it take six days?

"We had a seventy-eight-page indictment and one hundred pages of exhibits, and all that testimony."

What did they think of Michael Franzese?

"We thought he was a very scary man but very intelligent. Everybody believed him. It changed the trial. There were too many other things that supported what he was saying."

"I knew Michael Franzese was going to be devastating," said Tony Valukas. "I just didn't realize how devastating until he took the stand and showed he was willing to tell the truth about anybody and everybody, whether it was Norby Walters or people much greater than Norby Walters in the organized crime scheme of things."

Valukas, Pearl, and Randolph went downstairs to the fifteenth floor. Everybody in the U. S. Attorney's office understood the rocky road the trio had traveled. Champagne was on ice. There were toasts and hugs and kisses.

Then Tony Valukas wanted a moment alone with George Randolph.

Valukas said, "This case was controversial as hell. I never believed we were on a mission to defend college athletics. This was a mission to expose the tentacles of organized crime. You know, George could never tell me what was going on all the time within the bureau, but you hear things. There were those who thought Michael Franzese was going to make a fool out of George. But George just worked through that stuff. There was so much pressure on him. I told him, 'Enjoy this, savor it. Be proud of what you did.' College sports, the National Football League, even the NBA . . . they owe George, but they'll never know how much."

Both men, along with Howard Pearl, soon went downstairs to meet the press. Mobs of newsmen gathered around Valukas and Pearl, who soon left to be with his sick father.

George Randolph was watching the scene, and he no longer was suppressing his emotions. He had to be thinking about two long years. About Kathy Clements. About Norby Walters and Lloyd Bloom. About Sonny and Michael Franzese. About Jerry Zimmerman and Frankie Campione. About sixty athletes. Or was it one hundred? About Ronnie Harmon, Paul Palmer, Mark Ingram, Rod Woodson, Ron Morris, Maurice Douglass, Reggie Rogers, Brent Fullwood.

What little was left of George Randolph's innocence had vanished.

"I'll never be able to watch another game the same," he said.

Somebody slapped him on the back. It was another fellow FBI agent who hugged his neck.

"Binyons?"

Two long years since he had really tied one on. George Randolph grinned and smacked the back of his wallet.

"Come on," he said. "I'm buying."

Epilogue

On September 4, 1990, shortly after the football season had begun, George Randolph received the news. The U. S. District Seventh Circuit Court of Appeals overturned the conviction of Norby Walters and Lloyd Bloom. He remembers that it hit him like a ton of bricks. Howard Pearl went into shock. He took a long walk that night and just kept on walking. Tony Valukas's stomach churned. The court cited two errors by presiding judge George M. Marovich:

• Marovich should have granted Lloyd Bloom a separate trial, just as Dan Webb had argued.

• Marovich should have provided the jury with a critical additional instruction before it began deliberating: that if the jury believed Walters and Bloom had acted in good faith on the advice of their lawyers, then it should acquit the agents.

Norby Walters broke down and cried, saying, "God bless the judges."

It wasn't over.

The appellate court touched on no other issue, such as the mail fraud charges, and instructed the government to proceed, if desired, with two new separate trials of Norby Walters and Lloyd Bloom.

Marovich was said by federal sources to have been very puzzled by the appellate court's ruling. Marovich thought he was correct, that the advice Walters and Bloom sought from the Shea & Gould law firm was as a corporation, not personal in nature, and therefore Walters as the president of the corporation had the power to waive the attorney-client privilege. Therefore, he reasoned, Bloom had to be tried together with Walters.

As for the failure to instruct the jury properly, Marovich thought he was covered when he told the jury, "If a defendant acts in good faith, that establishes that he did no act with specific intent to defraud. Thus, if you find that a defendant acted in good faith when engaging in the conduct as a sports agent set forth in the mail and wire fraud charges, then that defendant's good faith is a complete defense to those allegations of mail fraud or wire fraud. If you find that [Walters and Bloom] acted in good faith, then you must find the defendants not guilty as to these criminal acts of mail fraud and wire fraud."

Marovich's error was omitting "the advice of counsel" in his good-faith instruction, the appellate court said.

Would it have mattered?

Marjorie Benson, the jury foreman, was specifically asked after the verdict about the "advice-of-counsel" defense.

"It was clear to us that Walters and Bloom didn't reveal everything to their lawyers," said Benson. "We didn't see any good faith. How could their lawyers have given proper advice?"

Almost forgotten in the blitz were the cases of Los Angeles sports agent David Lueddeke and Ohio State wide receiver Cris Carter. Carter sobbed when he begged the court for mercy at sentencing. Mercy, he got. He was placed on five years probation, fined $15,000, and had to perform fifteen hundred hours of community service for his guilty plea to mail fraud and obstruction of justice.

Lueddeke also cried and pleaded for mercy at sentencing. Mercy, he did not get. Under the more restricted federal sentencing guidelines, he received a twenty-six-month prison term for two counts of perjury and one count of obstruction of justice. He entered the federal penitentiary in Lompoc, California, on May 11, 1989, and was released from a halfway house on July 31, 1991.

Through the summer of 1991, David Lueddeke was the only person in the Walters-Bloom case to do jail time.

Walters and Bloom had their sentencing hearing on June 19, 1989. Walters was sentenced to five years in jail and forfeiture of his assets collected under this enterprise, which by then were down to $200,000. Bloom was sentenced to three years in jail and ordered to make restitution of $145,000 to Paul Palmer.

Marovich used the sentencing hearing to make a statement about the hypocrisy and corruption of college athletics:

"If Walters and Bloom are guilty of mail fraud, racketeering, and conspiracy, so too may be alumni and other boosters who pass money or cars under the table and conspire with the athlete to lie about it, so too may be the coach or administrator who acts in a like fashion."

Nevertheless, Marovich clearly believed that organized crime brought the case into the courtroom. And he told Norby Walters why he was getting the more severe prison term:

"I concur with the jury in deciding that Mr. Michael Franzese is a big presence in this picture, and you will pay the price for Mr. Franzese being in this picture. . . . That's a big part of this price."

Norby Walters spoke to the court that day, fighting back tears, choking, and telling Marovich, "I'd really like to say that I am really sorry for all the problems that I caused. If I had known what I know now, I never would have gotten involved in the sports agent business. . . . I lost it all."

Walters took a chance and called Michael Franzese a "liar" and a "bum."

Franzese heard about those epithets, laughed, and responded, "That's Norby, doing the act he needs to do. I didn't mind. He was trying to save his butt. We all understand that. But, trust me, Norby would never walk into this room here, look me in the eyes, and call me a bum or a liar. Trust me. The only thing Norby could ever do is to ask—respectfully, I might add—'Michael, why'd you do it?' Because if it were down to just me and him, he knows I told the truth. And he knows there was a lot more to tell."

Norby Walters had plenty of friends to support him, just as his enemies tore him down. There is no denying the charm of the man, often described as a "character out of a Damon Runyon story." Norby Walters can hold an audience captive for hours.

"That was the thing about Norby . . . he was probably the most fun guy in New York to hang around with, and it's probably what kept him alive," said Franzese.

Howard Pearl and George Randolph each saw the allure of Norby Walters.

"Oh, there's no doubt that he was a fascinating character," said Pearl.

Marovich allowed Walters and Bloom to remain free pending their appeal because they were not a "flight risk."

And despite their convictions being overturned, Norby Walters and Lloyd Bloom discovered their celebrations were in fact to be put on hold. The government announced it would proceed with separate trials for both men.

Norby Walters then began negotiations with the government, pending a ruling from a judge other than Marovich on the use of the mail fraud charges in the case. If the judge rules that the federal mail fraud statute should not have been applied in the case, Walters probably will walk free.

Lloyd Bloom was awaiting the ruling, too, before he negotiated a deal. His new trial was scheduled for December 1991.

Tony Valukas and Howard Pearl had left office by the time the appellate ruling was handed down. That meant new prosecutors had to be assigned to study and defend the bulky, complex issues left hanging with the appellate decision.

One irony is that Howard Pearl went to work for Dan Webb after Webb asked the Assistant U. S. Attorney to assist him as the special prosecutor in the Iran-Contra case of the United States of America versus former Navy Rear Admiral John Poindexter.

John Gorman of the *Chicago Tribune* also wrote a story in 1990 which revealed that fewer than half of the forty-four athletes in the Pre-Trial Diversion Program had lived up to their obligations to repay their scholarships and do community service.

Valukas defended the U. S. Attorney's office on this matter, saying that under government procedure the United States Probation Office had sole responsibility to see that the players met their obligation. The probation office renewed its supervision of the case.

George Randolph is still an agent with the FBI. When asked about Randolph, Howard Pearl said lovingly, "George is a great agent, but George is crazy."

Bloom himself remains a fascinating character. He returned to Hollywood to be with his ex-wife, actress Donna Denton. He started managing Hollywood stars and soon was doing business with the likes of Kirstie Alley, Linda Evans, and Ken Wahl.

It wasn't long after the trial that Bloom, eating in a Hollywood restaurant, spotted Michael Franzese at another table. Bloom went over, incredibly, to shake Franzese's hand. They chatted.

"No hard feelings," said Franzese.

"I understand," said Bloom, respectfully.

Nevertheless, it sent Dan Webb storming back to Judge Marovich to argue that the government lied to the jury when it said that the reduction of Franzese's sentence for his cooperation in the Norby Walters case would amount to no more than twenty-eight days in terms of parole. Bloom had bumped into Franzese a little more than a month after the trial. What was he doing free?

"[Franzese] is the linchpin of the testimony that convicted both these individuals," Webb argued, saying it was clear to him that the government had a better deal on the table all along.

Howard Pearl argued that there were no secret deals with the Chicago prosecutors: "The presumption is not just outrageous and baseless, it is flat-out wrong, Judge."

"Your Honor," Webb argued, "then [we are to believe that the government proposed] that because he's a bad man, because he was a member of the Mafia, because he murdered people, because he killed and maimed people, we only want him released by one year . . . and then on his own, Judge Nickerson decided that Franzese was such a marvelous human being that he ought to be released immediately. I can't believe that happened."

Pearl argued to the court that Franzese's records were sealed.

Marovich decided he would review the government's deal with the Mafia captain, reasoning, "I think the verdict is implicit that the jury did believe him."

Shortly thereafter Marovich informed Webb that the government did not lie to the jury.

"I am satisfied that no undisclosed promises were made to Michael Franzese at the time he testified, and his subsequent release in no way affects the credibility of his testimony in this case," the judge ruled.

Instead, just as George Randolph had urged as the trial wound down, Michael Franzese struck a new deal with Ed McDonald, chief of the Brooklyn Organized Crime Task Force. Franzese agreed to cooperate and testify against other organized crime associates if he would be set free immediately.

To McDonald it was a worthwhile deal because, as he said, "Franzese was the most significant organized crime member to ever cooperate with the government."

But even in this deal Franzese cleverly negotiated terms that bothered other government authorities. He would cooperate and testify in New York, but all of the cases involving his testimony had to be filed within one year of that date in May 1990.

By May 1991, other than in the Walters case, Franzese testified publicly just once, and the result was a conviction involving a bribe. But his cooperation, according to McDonald, also resulted in the imprisonment of Frank Campione on a matter unrelated to the Kathy Clements beating.

Franzese remained in Hollywood, living in a $3 million home and driving two expensive cars. The major networks all rushed to do pieces on the Mafia Prince living this life of luxury while he still owed the government more than $10 million.

Two major questions were raised: How is Franzese living this life-style and getting away with it? Why is he still alive?

The government renewed its surveillance to determine how Franzese was able to live so high on the hog.

As for his staying alive, McDonald believed it was only a matter of time before Franzese was murdered by the mob.

But McDonald did theorize that it was possible Franzese had made his own secret deal with the Mafia and that much of the $50 million–plus he personally made in the gasoline scam was handed over to La Cosa Nostra to pay for his life. Franzese still claims he has quit the mob.

James Moody, the Los Angeles organized crime chief who had mocked Randolph for believing Franzese would ever truly testify, has since been promoted to chief of organized crime in the Justice Department.

Earlier this year Moody acknowledged that gambling was still a multibillion-dollar industry controlled by organized crime. Yet Moody said he doesn't believe it's very likely that a professional athlete could be bribed into a fix because of the high salaries players command in this era.

The problem with that theory is that high-salaried athletes go broke every day, their money drained by bad investments, a blind trust in their advisers, and lavish life-styles. As Michael Franzese said, athletes today remain "vulnerable."

Ronnie Harmon's performance in the Rose Bowl on January 1, 1986, may have been innocent, but it did raise suspicions. Iowa fans thought something was fishy; so did his teammates. It hardened him.

It's also naive to believe that players don't realize how much power they have. In the fall of 1988, Paul Palmer got into the doghouse with the Kansas City Chiefs when, on a team bus ride, the running back was overheard grumbling about his coaches. Palmer suggested that he held the coaches' security in his hands. All he had to do, he told a teammate, with a coach within earshot, was "to put the ball on the ground."

It creates doubt when mob money has wittingly or unwittingly been passed into a player's hand.

Every time George Randolph and Howard Pearl pick up a newspaper or turn on a football game, something lingers from the case that devoured their lives for more than two years.

One Saturday afternoon in January 1990 the Buffalo Bills were driving for the apparent winning touchdown in the final seconds of an AFC playoff game against the Browns. Bills quarterback Jim Kelly dropped back and saw his man break open as he aimed a tightly thrown spiral to the corner of the end zone. The ball bounced off the hands of the receiver. The receiver was Ronnie Harmon. The Browns won, 35–31. Bookmakers had favored Cleveland by three and a half points.

Randolph watched the play, scratched his head, and wondered. Naah, he thought. He hoped.

Three weeks later Ronnie Harmon, a number-one draft pick four years earlier, was "not protected" by Buffalo on their Plan B free-agent list. They let Harmon sign with the San Diego Chargers.

One year later, in January 1991, like millions of people around the world, Howard Pearl watched the Super Bowl, the New York Giants playing the Bills. The Giants were trailing in the fourth quarter when wide receiver Mark Ingram made a third-down pass reception and proceeded to break tackles, spinning and clawing his way to a first down that set up the team's winning touchdown in the closest Super Bowl ever played.

Pearl remembered all the days he had spent with Mark Ingram inside the U. S. Attorney's office and later inside a federal courtroom. Now Ingram was racing across his television screen with the biggest catch in the biggest game.

"I wondered how much money that catch meant," he said.

He also remembered what he had told the jury on April 4, 1989:

"Here you had a member in the Colombo family involved in things like gambling and loan-sharking, and now they have the opportunity to have premier college athletes, who are certain to turn professional, literally on their payroll and in their debt. You can imagine, ladies and gentlemen, had Michael Franzese not been incarcerated by the government at the very beginning of the scheme, had the government not gotten involved in this investigation, just what the possibilities were."

Acknowledgments

Michael Franzese and I spoke by telephone four or five times over the course of three years. Telephones are nice tools, but there is nothing more constructive for a reporter than to sit down face-to-face with somebody who has a story to tell.

I had been consumed by the story of Norby Walters and Lloyd Bloom since January 1987, and I already knew it was a colorful story. Then Michael Franzese showed me just how colorful it really was. He gave his time generously, and for this I am grateful. He did not do it for me, he said. He did it because of George Randolph, the FBI special agent who worked the government's case against Norby Walters and Lloyd Bloom. I needed to know more about the FBI agent's experiences in getting the Mafia boss into a federal courtroom. Franzese told me more, and then some. He told me things he had passed to Randolph and the government behind closed doors. He told me more about Norby Walters and Lloyd Bloom—especially Norby Walters.

So, Michael, the deepest thanks for your generosity of time and mind. Thanks to Cammy, too.

Next, George Randolph, a humble man when it comes to talking about himself. I got to know this FBI agent during the trial and post-trial phase of the Norby Walters and Lloyd Bloom case. It is easy to appreciate Randolph. His work is not unlike that of a reporter. It does not take a genius to crack a case or a story. It takes some intelligence, but that is useless without persistence, guts, heart, a little insanity, and more than anything, instincts. Without instincts—which are part gift and part experience—an investigator is worthless.

I found nothing very sophisticated about George. Refreshingly, there is no false facade about him.

337

"I am what I am," I heard him tell his wife, Cathy, after a rather blunt remark.

But painting an accurate picture of George is very difficult because he guards many of his most private thoughts.

This book attempted to retrace his footsteps. That wasn't easy, either, because they went in so many different directions. But I also want to thank some of those who helped me trace those footsteps:

Cathy and Bill Randolph.

Howard M. Pearl, former U. S. Attorney, who probably will never get the full recognition he deserves for this intense period in his life.

Anton "Tony" Valukas, former U. S. Attorney, Northern District of Illinois.

Joe Duffy, former First Assistant U. S. Attorney.

Bob Walsh, Victor Guerrero, Pat Buckley, Diane Benson, George Spinelli, John O'Neill, Scott Jennings, Joe Masterson, Dan O'Sullivan—some of the FBI's finest.

Dan Webb, Steve Molo, and George Lombardi—a terrific trio of lawyers.

Robert Gold, one of the nicest men I have ever met, and his trial associates, Ethan Levin-Epstein and Matthew Kennelly. Also, Lon Trost and Michael Feldberg.

Wayne Duke and Byron Gregory.

Mike Trope, the one and only, and I mean that. You're weird, Mike, but brilliant.

U. S. District Court Judge George M. Marovich.

Donald Valeska, the Assistant Attorney General of Alabama, and Bill Wasden.

Kathy Clements, Steve Zucker, Jami Zimberoff, George Kickliter, Matthias Lydon, Frank Murtha, Cris Carter, George Carter, and Terry Bolar.

Special thanks to Ralph Cindrich and Peter Johnson.

Bruce Selcraig, whose work and integrity I will always admire.

Gary Defauw for a spellbinding tale.

Strangely, I have to say thanks to Norby Walters and Lloyd Bloom. For the most part they never stopped talking. Norby Walters is without a doubt one of the most interesting characters I have ever met. In black and white, it is easy to distinguish good and evil. Norby Walters, however, is a man of many colors. He is what he is.

Mel Falk, for his friendship and support.

John Gorman, Adrienne Drell, Dan Weir, and Katherine Schweit—the Chicago beat reporters who shared their expertise, their work space, and their warmth.

Steve Fiffer for the inspiration. We had fun.

The mess of lawyers and players I bugged over the years. You know who you are.

Apologies and thanks to David Black, who first approached me about the idea of this book, but at a time when I had trouble focusing on it. Angela Miller for helping me fulfill this dream.

Gratitude must be expressed to my editors, Jeff Neuman and Stuart Gottesman. They believed in this book and consequently believed in me, and showed it with their patience. More important, they got me to focus on what this book was all about. As I told them over and over, the material is better than the writer so . . . help!

I cannot forget my editors and associates at the *Atlanta Journal and Constitution.* I wrote more than two hundred stories about this adventure, and they held my hand all the way: Van McKenzie, Tim Tucker, Mike Tierney, Bud Shaw, Tom Stinson, Ron Martz, and Glenn Hannigan. There was tremendous moral support from a mix of people who sometimes clashed but must be recognized: *Atlanta Journal and Constitution* publisher Jay Smith, and former editors Bill Kovach, Wendell "Sonny" Rawls, Jr., and Glenn McCutchen.

An endearing thanks to Dave Kindred, the best journalist in the world.

I can't forget Frank Deford, a truly wonderful human being, or Vince Doria for giving me some space.

My old sports editor at the *Daily Breeze,* Mike Waldner, and all the gang there in my hometown of Torrance, California. I miss you all.

Jim O'Brien and Ed Maldonado, the two best friends a man could want, who picked me up when I was down.

In memory of Guy Old, Jr., my journalism teacher. Oh, how I wish you were here to share this.

Bruce Springsteen, whose inspiration reached deep into my gut one day and pulled me out from the wreck.

A note to my brother Joe: I hope one day to be the man you are—full of faith, humility, consideration, and love. Those are the riches of life.

My entire family, too many to name but never too big to love.

Mother, what can I say? Words cannot express my admiration and appreciation for your patience and guidance.

Shannon, my dear daughter, you are always in my heart and thoughts. Beware of the world. Forgive me for not measuring up.

Alexander, my energetic young son, thanks for the daily inspiration.

Finally, I must thank my loving wife, Micki, who knows my imperfections and yet hangs on. I promise to clean up my office . . . tomorrow.

Index

341

350 Index